Book of Daniel

Daniel

God

King James Bible, Douay Rheims, American
Standard Bible, BBE, Webster Bible

Matthew Henry

"Blessed be the name of God for ever and ever: for wisdom and might are his: And he changeth the times and the seasons: he removeth kings, and setteth up kings: he giveth wisdom unto the wise, and knowledge to them that know understanding: He revealeth the deep and secret things: he knoweth what is in the darkness, and the light dwelleth with him."

-    Daniel 2: 20-21

CONTENTS

DANIEL

THE BOOK OF DANIEL

KING JAMES BIBLE

1

1:1 In the third year of the reign of Jehoiakim king of Judah came Nebuchadnezzar king of Babylon unto Jerusalem, and besieged it.

1:2 And the Lord gave Jehoiakim king of Judah into his hand, with part of the vessels of the house of God: which he carried into the land of Shinar to the house of his god; and he brought the vessels into the treasure house of his god.

1:3 And the king spake unto Ashpenaz the master of his eunuchs, that he should bring certain of the children of Israel, and of the king's seed, and of the princes; 1:4 Children in whom was no blemish, but well favoured, and skilful in all wisdom, and cunning in knowledge, and understanding science, and such as had ability in them to stand in the king's palace, and whom they might teach the learning and the tongue of the Chaldeans.

1:5 And the king appointed them a daily provision of the king's meat, and of the wine which he drank: so nourishing them three years, that at the end thereof they might stand before the king.

1:6 Now among these were of the children of Judah, Daniel, Hananiah, Mishael, and Azariah: 1:7 Unto whom the prince of the eunuchs gave names: for he gave unto Daniel the name of Belteshazzar; and to Hananiah, of Shadrach; and to Mishael, of Meshach; and to Azariah, of Abednego.

1:8 But Daniel purposed in his heart that he would not defile himself with the portion of the king's meat, nor with the wine which he drank: therefore he requested of the prince of the eunuchs that he might not defile himself.

1:9 Now God had brought Daniel into favour and tender love with the prince of the eunuchs.

1:10 And the prince of the eunuchs said unto Daniel, I fear my lord the king, who hath appointed your meat and your drink: for why should he see your faces worse liking than the children which are of your sort? then shall ye make me endanger my head to the king.

1:11 Then said Daniel to Melzar, whom the prince of the eunuchs had set over Daniel, Hananiah, Mishael, and Azariah, 1:12 Prove thy servants, I beseech thee, ten days; and let them give us pulse to eat, and water to drink.

1:13 Then let our countenances be looked upon before thee, and the countenance of the children that eat of the portion of the king's meat: and as thou seest, deal with thy servants.

1:14 So he consented to them in this matter, and proved them ten days.

1:15 And at the end of ten days their countenances appeared fairer and fatter in flesh than all the children which did eat the portion of the king's meat.

1:16 Thus Melzar took away the portion of their meat, and the wine that they should drink; and gave them pulse.

1:17 As for these four children, God gave them knowledge and skill in all learning and wisdom: and Daniel had understanding in all visions and dreams.

1:18 Now at the end of the days that the king had said he should bring them in, then the prince of the eunuchs brought them in before Nebuchadnezzar.

1:19 And the king communed with them; and among them all was found none like Daniel, Hananiah, Mishael, and Azariah: therefore stood they before the king.

1:20 And in all matters of wisdom and understanding, that the king enquired of them, he found them ten times better than all the magicians and astrologers that were in all his realm.

1:21 And Daniel continued even unto the first year of king Cyrus.

2

2:1 And in the second year of the reign of Nebuchadnezzar Nebuchadnezzar dreamed dreams, wherewith his spirit was troubled, and his sleep brake from him.

2:2 Then the king commanded to call the magicians, and the astrologers, and the sorcerers, and the Chaldeans, for to shew the king his dreams. So they came and stood before the king.

2:3 And the king said unto them, I have dreamed a dream, and my spirit was troubled to know the dream.

2:4 Then spake the Chaldeans to the king in Syriack, O king, live for ever: tell thy servants the dream, and we will shew the interpretation.

2:5 The king answered and said to the Chaldeans, The thing is gone from me: if ye will not make known unto me the dream, with the interpretation thereof, ye shall be cut in pieces, and your houses shall be made a dunghill.

2:6 But if ye shew the dream, and the interpretation thereof, ye shall receive of me gifts and rewards and great honour: therefore shew me the dream, and the interpretation thereof.

2:7 They answered again and said, Let the king tell his servants the dream, and we will shew the interpretation of it.

2:8 The king answered and said, I know of certainty that ye would gain the time, because ye see the thing is gone from me.

2:9 But if ye will not make known unto me the dream, there is but one decree for you: for ye have prepared lying and corrupt words to speak before me, till the time be changed: therefore tell me the dream, and I shall know that ye can shew me the interpretation thereof.

2:10 The Chaldeans answered before the king, and said, There is not a man upon the earth that can shew the king's matter: therefore there is no king, lord, nor ruler, that asked such things at any magician, or astrologer, or Chaldean.

2:11 And it is a rare thing that the king requireth, and there is none other that can shew it before the king, except the gods, whose dwelling is not with flesh.

2:12 For this cause the king was angry and very furious, and commanded to destroy all the wise men of Babylon.

2:13 And the decree went forth that the wise men should be slain; and they sought Daniel and his fellows to be slain.

2:14 Then Daniel answered with counsel and wisdom to Arioch the captain of the king's guard, which was gone forth to slay the wise men of Babylon: 2:15 He answered and said to Arioch the king's captain, Why is the decree so hasty from the king? Then Arioch made the thing known to Daniel.

2:16 Then Daniel went in, and desired of the king that he would give him time, and that he would shew the king the interpretation.

2:17 Then Daniel went to his house, and made the thing known to Hananiah, Mishael, and Azariah, his companions: 2:18 That they would desire mercies of the God of heaven concerning this secret; that Daniel and his fellows should not perish with the rest of the wise men of Babylon.

2:19 Then was the secret revealed unto Daniel in a night vision. Then Daniel blessed the God of heaven.

2:20 Daniel answered and said, Blessed be the name of God for ever and ever: for wisdom and might are his: 2:21 And he changeth the times and the seasons: he removeth kings, and setteth up kings: he giveth wisdom unto the wise, and knowledge to them that know understanding: 2:22 He revealeth the deep and secret things: he knoweth what is in the darkness, and the light dwelleth with him.

2:23 I thank thee, and praise thee, O thou God of my fathers, who hast given me wisdom and might, and hast made known unto me now what we desired of thee: for thou hast now made known unto us the king's matter.

2:24 Therefore Daniel went in unto Arioch, whom the king had ordained to destroy the wise men of Babylon: he went and said thus unto him; Destroy not the wise men of Babylon: bring me in before the king, and I will shew unto the king the interpretation.

2:25 Then Arioch brought in Daniel before the king in haste, and said thus unto him, I have found a man of the captives of Judah, that will make known unto the king the interpretation.

2:26 The king answered and said to Daniel, whose name was Belteshazzar, Art thou able to make known unto me the dream which I have seen, and the interpretation thereof? 2:27 Daniel answered in the presence of the king, and said, The secret which the king hath demanded cannot the wise men, the astrologers, the magicians, the soothsayers, shew unto the king; 2:28 But there is a God in heaven that revealeth secrets, and maketh known to the king Nebuchadnezzar what shall be in the latter days. Thy dream, and the visions of thy head upon thy bed, are these; 2:29 As for thee, O king, thy thoughts came into thy mind upon thy bed, what should come to pass hereafter: and he that revealeth secrets maketh known to thee what shall come to pass.

2:30 But as for me, this secret is not revealed to me for any wisdom that I have more than any living, but for their sakes that shall make known the interpretation to the king, and that thou mightest know the thoughts of thy heart.

2:31 Thou, O king, sawest, and behold a great image. This great image, whose brightness was excellent, stood before thee; and the form thereof was terrible.

2:32 This image's head was of fine gold, his breast and his arms of silver, his belly and his thighs of brass, 2:33 His legs of iron, his feet part of iron and part of clay.

2:34 Thou sawest till that a stone was cut out without hands, which smote the image upon his feet that were of iron and clay, and brake them to pieces.

2:35 Then was the iron, the clay, the brass, the silver, and the gold, broken to pieces together, and became like the chaff of the summer threshingfloors; and the wind carried them away, that no place was found for them: and the stone that smote the image became a great mountain, and filled the whole earth.

2:36 This is the dream; and we will tell the interpretation thereof before the king.

2:37 Thou, O king, art a king of kings: for the God of heaven hath given thee a kingdom, power, and strength, and glory.

2:38 And wheresoever the children of men dwell, the beasts of the field and the fowls of the heaven hath he given into thine hand, and hath made thee ruler over them all. Thou art this head of gold.

2:39 And after thee shall arise another kingdom inferior to thee, and another third kingdom of brass, which shall bear rule over all the earth.

2:40 And the fourth kingdom shall be strong as iron: forasmuch as iron breaketh in pieces and subdueth all things: and as iron that breaketh all these, shall it break in pieces and bruise.

2:41 And whereas thou sawest the feet and toes, part of potters' clay, and part of iron, the kingdom shall be divided; but there shall be in it of the strength of the iron, forasmuch as thou sawest the iron mixed with miry clay.

2:42 And as the toes of the feet were part of iron, and part of clay, so the kingdom shall be partly strong, and partly broken.

2:43 And whereas thou sawest iron mixed with miry clay, they shall mingle themselves with the seed of men: but they shall not cleave one to another, even as iron is not mixed with clay.

2:44 And in the days of these kings shall the God of heaven set up a kingdom, which shall never be destroyed: and the kingdom shall not be left to other people, but it shall break in pieces and consume all these kingdoms, and it shall stand for ever.

2:45 Forasmuch as thou sawest that the stone was cut out of the mountain without hands, and that it brake in pieces the iron, the brass, the clay, the silver, and the gold; the great God hath made known to the king what shall come to pass hereafter: and the dream is certain, and the interpretation thereof sure.

2:46 Then the king Nebuchadnezzar fell upon his face, and worshipped Daniel, and commanded that they should offer an oblation and sweet odours unto him.

2:47 The king answered unto Daniel, and said, Of a truth it is, that your God is a God of gods, and a Lord of kings, and a revealer of secrets, seeing thou couldest reveal this secret.

2:48 Then the king made Daniel a great man, and gave him many great gifts, and made him ruler over the whole province of Babylon, and chief of the governors over all the wise men of Babylon.

2:49 Then Daniel requested of the king, and he set Shadrach, Meshach, and Abednego, over the affairs of the province of Babylon: but Daniel sat in the gate of the king.

3

3:1 Nebuchadnezzar the king made an image of gold, whose height was threescore cubits, and the breadth thereof six cubits: he set it up in the plain of Dura, in the province of Babylon.

3:2 Then Nebuchadnezzar the king sent to gather together the princes, the governors, and the captains, the judges, the treasurers, the counsellors, the sheriffs, and all the rulers of the provinces, to come to the dedication of the image which Nebuchadnezzar the king had set up.

3:3 Then the princes, the governors, and captains, the judges, the treasurers, the counsellors, the sheriffs, and all the rulers of the provinces, were gathered together unto the dedication of the image that Nebuchadnezzar the king had set up; and they stood before the image that Nebuchadnezzar had set up.

3:4 Then an herald cried aloud, To you it is commanded, O people, nations, and languages,

3:5 That at what time ye hear the sound of the cornet, flute, harp, sackbut, psaltery, dulcimer, and all kinds of musick, ye fall down and worship the golden image that Nebuchadnezzar the king hath set up: 3:6 And whoso falleth not down and worshippeth shall the same hour be cast into the midst of a burning fiery furnace.

3:7 Therefore at that time, when all the people heard the sound of the cornet, flute, harp, sackbut, psaltery, and all kinds of musick, all the people, the nations, and the languages, fell down and worshipped the golden image that Nebuchadnezzar the king had set up.

3:8 Wherefore at that time certain Chaldeans came near, and accused the Jews.

3:9 They spake and said to the king Nebuchadnezzar, O king, live for ever.

3:10 Thou, O king, hast made a decree, that every man that shall hear the sound of the cornet, flute, harp, sackbut, psaltery, and dulcimer, and all kinds of musick, shall fall down and worship the golden image: 3:11 And whoso falleth not down and worshippeth, that he should be cast into the midst of a burning fiery furnace.

3:12 There are certain Jews whom thou hast set over the affairs of the province of Babylon, Shadrach, Meshach, and Abednego; these men, O king, have not regarded thee: they serve not thy gods, nor worship the golden image which thou hast set up.

3:13 Then Nebuchadnezzar in his rage and fury commanded to bring Shadrach, Meshach, and Abednego. Then they brought these men before the king.

3:14 Nebuchadnezzar spake and said unto them, Is it true, O Shadrach, Meshach, and Abednego, do not ye serve my gods, nor worship the golden image which I have set up? 3:15 Now if ye be ready that at what time ye hear the sound of the cornet, flute, harp, sackbut, psaltery, and dulcimer, and all kinds of musick, ye fall down and worship the image which I have made; well: but if ye worship not, ye shall be cast the same hour into the midst of a burning fiery furnace; and who is that God that shall deliver you out of my hands? 3:16 Shadrach, Meshach, and Abednego, answered and said to the king, O Nebuchadnezzar, we are not careful to answer thee in this matter.

3:17 If it be so, our God whom we serve is able to deliver us from the burning fiery furnace, and he will deliver us out of thine hand, O king.

3:18 But if not, be it known unto thee, O king, that we will not serve thy gods, nor worship the golden image which thou hast set up.

3:19 Then was Nebuchadnezzar full of fury, and the form of his visage was changed against Shadrach, Meshach, and Abednego: therefore he spake, and commanded that they should heat the furnace one seven times more than it was wont to be heated.

3:20 And he commanded the most mighty men that were in his army to bind Shadrach, Meshach, and Abednego, and to cast them into the burning fiery furnace.

3:21 Then these men were bound in their coats, their hosen, and their hats, and their other garments, and were cast into the midst of the burning fiery furnace.

3:22 Therefore because the king's commandment was urgent, and the furnace exceeding hot, the flames of the fire slew those men that took up Shadrach, Meshach, and Abednego.

3:23 And these three men, Shadrach, Meshach, and Abednego, fell down bound into the midst of the burning fiery furnace.

3:24 Then Nebuchadnezzar the king was astonished, and rose up in haste, and spake, and said unto his counsellors, Did not we cast three men bound into the midst of the fire? They answered and said unto the king, True, O king.

3:25 He answered and said, Lo, I see four men loose, walking in the midst of the fire, and they have no hurt; and the form of the fourth is like the Son of God.

3:26 Then Nebuchadnezzar came near to the mouth of the burning fiery furnace, and spake, and said, Shadrach, Meshach, and Abednego, ye servants of the most high God, come forth, and come hither. Then Shadrach, Meshach, and Abednego, came forth of the midst of the fire.

3:27 And the princes, governors, and captains, and the king's counsellors, being gathered together, saw these men, upon whose bodies the fire had no power, nor was an hair of their head singed, neither were their coats changed, nor the smell of fire had passed on them.

3:28 Then Nebuchadnezzar spake, and said, Blessed be the God of Shadrach, Meshach, and Abednego, who hath sent his angel, and delivered his servants that trusted in him, and have changed the king's word, and yielded their bodies, that they might not serve nor worship any god, except their own God.

3:29 Therefore I make a decree, That every people, nation, and language, which speak any thing amiss against the God of Shadrach, Meshach, and Abednego, shall be cut in pieces, and their houses shall be made a dunghill: because there is no other God that can deliver after this sort.

3:30 Then the king promoted Shadrach, Meshach, and Abednego, in the province of Babylon.

4

4:1 Nebuchadnezzar the king, unto all people, nations, and languages, that dwell in all the earth; Peace be multiplied unto you.

4:2 I thought it good to shew the signs and wonders that the high God hath wrought toward me.

4:3 How great are his signs! and how mighty are his wonders! his kingdom is an everlasting kingdom, and his dominion is from generation to generation.

4:4 I Nebuchadnezzar was at rest in mine house, and flourishing in my palace: 4:5 I saw a dream which made me afraid, and the thoughts upon my bed and the visions of my head troubled me.

4:6 Therefore made I a decree to bring in all the wise men of Babylon before me, that they might make known unto me the interpretation of the dream.

4:7 Then came in the magicians, the astrologers, the Chaldeans, and the soothsayers: and I told the dream before them; but they did not make known unto me the interpretation thereof.

4:8 But at the last Daniel came in before me, whose name was Belteshazzar, according to the name of my God, and in whom is the spirit of the holy gods: and before him I told the dream, saying, 4:9 O Belteshazzar, master of the magicians, because I know that the spirit of the holy gods is in thee, and no secret troubleth thee, tell me the visions of my dream that I have seen, and the interpretation thereof.

4:10 Thus were the visions of mine head in my bed; I saw, and behold a tree in the midst of the earth, and the height thereof was great.

4:11 The tree grew, and was strong, and the height thereof reached unto heaven, and the sight thereof to the end of all the earth: 4:12 The leaves thereof were fair, and the fruit thereof much, and in it was meat for all: the beasts of the field had shadow under it, and the fowls of the heaven dwelt in the boughs thereof, and all flesh was fed of it.

4:13 I saw in the visions of my head upon my bed, and, behold, a watcher and an holy one came down from heaven; 4:14 He cried aloud, and said thus, Hew down the tree, and cut off his branches, shake off his leaves, and scatter his fruit: let the beasts get away from under it, and the fowls from his branches: 4:15 Nevertheless leave the stump of his roots in the earth, even with a band of iron and brass, in the tender grass of the field; and let it be wet with the dew of heaven, and let his portion be with the beasts in the grass of the earth: 4:16 Let his heart be changed from man's, and let a beast's heart be given unto him; and let seven times pass over him.

4:17 This matter is by the decree of the watchers, and the demand by the word of the holy ones: to the intent that the living may know that the most High ruleth in the kingdom of men, and giveth it to whomsoever he will, and setteth up over it the basest of men.

4:18 This dream I king Nebuchadnezzar have seen. Now thou, O Belteshazzar, declare the interpretation thereof, forasmuch as all the wise men of my kingdom are not able to make known unto me the interpretation: but thou art able; for the spirit of the holy gods is in thee.

4:19 Then Daniel, whose name was Belteshazzar, was astonished for one hour, and his thoughts troubled him. The king spake, and said, Belteshazzar, let not the dream, or the interpretation thereof, trouble thee. Belteshazzar answered and said, My lord, the dream be to them that hate thee, and the interpretation thereof to thine enemies.

4:20 The tree that thou sawest, which grew, and was strong, whose height reached unto the heaven, and the sight thereof to all the earth; 4:21 Whose leaves were fair, and the fruit thereof much, and in it was meat for all; under which the beasts of the field dwelt, and upon whose branches the fowls of the heaven had their habitation: 4:22 It is thou, O king, that art grown and become strong: for thy greatness is grown, and reacheth unto heaven, and thy dominion to the end of the earth.

4:23 And whereas the king saw a watcher and an holy one coming down from heaven, and saying, Hew the tree down, and destroy it; yet leave the stump of the roots thereof in the earth, even with a band of iron and brass, in the tender grass of the field; and let it be wet with the dew of heaven, and let his portion be with the beasts of the field, till seven times pass over him; 4:24 This is the interpretation, O king, and this is the decree of the most High, which is come upon my lord the king: 4:25 That they shall drive thee from men, and thy dwelling shall be with the beasts of the field, and they shall make thee to eat grass as oxen, and they shall wet thee with the dew of heaven, and seven times shall pass over thee, till thou know that the most High ruleth in the kingdom of men, and giveth it to whomsoever he will.

4:26 And whereas they commanded to leave the stump of the tree roots; thy kingdom shall be sure unto thee, after that thou shalt have known that the heavens do rule.

4:27 Wherefore, O king, let my counsel be acceptable unto thee, and break off thy sins by righteousness, and thine iniquities by shewing mercy to the poor; if it may be a lengthening of thy tranquillity.

4:28 All this came upon the king Nebuchadnezzar.

4:29 At the end of twelve months he walked in the palace of the kingdom of Babylon.

4:30 The king spake, and said, Is not this great Babylon, that I have built for the house of the kingdom by the might of my power, and for the honour of my majesty? 4:31 While the word was in the king's mouth, there fell a voice from heaven, saying, O king Nebuchadnezzar, to thee it is spoken; The kingdom is departed from thee.

4:32 And they shall drive thee from men, and thy dwelling shall be with the beasts of the field: they shall make thee to eat grass as oxen, and seven times shall pass over thee, until thou know that the most High ruleth in the kingdom of men, and giveth it to whomsoever he will.

4:33 The same hour was the thing fulfilled upon Nebuchadnezzar: and he was driven from men, and did eat grass as oxen, and his body was wet with the dew of heaven, till his hairs were grown like eagles' feathers, and his nails like birds' claws.

4:34 And at the end of the days I Nebuchadnezzar lifted up mine eyes unto heaven, and mine understanding returned unto me, and I blessed the most High, and I praised and honoured him that liveth for ever, whose dominion is an everlasting dominion, and his kingdom is from generation to generation: 4:35 And all the inhabitants of the earth are reputed as nothing: and he doeth according to his will in the army of heaven, and among the inhabitants of the earth: and none can stay his hand, or say unto him, What doest thou? 4:36 At the same time my reason returned unto me; and for the glory of my kingdom, mine honour and brightness returned unto me; and my counsellors and my lords sought unto me; and I was established in my kingdom, and excellent majesty was added unto me.

4:37 Now I Nebuchadnezzar praise and extol and honour the King of heaven, all whose works are truth, and his ways judgment: and those that walk in pride he is able to abase.

5

5:1 Belshazzar the king made a great feast to a thousand of his lords, and drank wine before the thousand.

5:2 Belshazzar, whiles he tasted the wine, commanded to bring the golden and silver vessels which his father Nebuchadnezzar had taken out of the temple which was in Jerusalem; that the king, and his princes, his wives, and his concubines, might drink therein.

5:3 Then they brought the golden vessels that were taken out of the temple of the house of God which was at Jerusalem; and the king, and his princes, his wives, and his concubines, drank in them.

5:4 They drank wine, and praised the gods of gold, and of silver, of brass, of iron, of wood, and of stone.

5:5 In the same hour came forth fingers of a man's hand, and wrote over against the candlestick upon the plaster of the wall of the king's palace: and the king saw the part of the hand that wrote.

5:6 Then the king's countenance was changed, and his thoughts troubled him, so that the joints of his loins were loosed, and his knees smote one against another.

5:7 The king cried aloud to bring in the astrologers, the Chaldeans, and the soothsayers. And the king spake, and said to the wise men of Babylon, Whosoever shall read this writing, and shew me the interpretation thereof, shall be clothed with scarlet, and have a chain of gold about his neck, and shall be the third ruler in the kingdom.

5:8 Then came in all the king's wise men: but they could not read the writing, nor make known to the king the interpretation thereof.

5:9 Then was king Belshazzar greatly troubled, and his countenance was changed in him, and his lords were astonished.

5:10 Now the queen by reason of the words of the king and his lords came into the banquet house: and the queen spake and said, O king, live for ever: let not thy thoughts trouble thee, nor let thy countenance be changed: 5:11 There is a man in thy kingdom, in whom is the spirit of the holy gods; and in the days of thy father light and understanding and wisdom, like the wisdom of the gods, was found in him; whom the king Nebuchadnezzar thy father, the king, I say, thy father, made master of the magicians, astrologers, Chaldeans, and soothsayers; 5:12 Forasmuch as an excellent spirit, and knowledge, and understanding, interpreting of dreams, and shewing of hard sentences, and dissolving of doubts, were found in the same Daniel, whom the king named Belteshazzar: now let Daniel be called, and he will shew the interpretation.

5:13 Then was Daniel brought in before the king. And the king spake and said unto Daniel, Art thou that Daniel, which art of the children of the captivity of Judah, whom the king my father brought out of Jewry? 5:14 I have even heard of thee, that the spirit of the gods is in thee, and that light and understanding and excellent wisdom is found in thee.

5:15 And now the wise men, the astrologers, have been brought in before me, that they should read this writing, and make known unto me the interpretation thereof: but they could not shew the interpretation of the thing: 5:16 And I have heard of thee, that thou canst make interpretations, and dissolve doubts: now if thou canst read the writing, and make known to me the interpretation thereof, thou shalt be clothed with scarlet, and have a chain of gold about thy neck, and shalt be the third ruler in the kingdom.

5:17 Then Daniel answered and said before the king, Let thy gifts be to thyself, and give thy rewards to another; yet I will read the writing unto the king, and make known to him the interpretation.

5:18 O thou king, the most high God gave Nebuchadnezzar thy father a kingdom, and majesty, and glory, and honour: 5:19 And for the majesty that he gave him, all people, nations, and languages, trembled and feared before him: whom he would he slew; and whom he would he kept alive; and whom he would he set up; and whom he would he put down.

5:20 But when his heart was lifted up, and his mind hardened in pride, he was deposed from his kingly throne, and they took his glory from him: 5:21 And he was driven from the sons of men; and his heart was made like the beasts, and his dwelling was with the wild asses: they fed him with grass like oxen, and his body was wet with the dew of heaven; till he knew that the most high God ruled in the kingdom of men, and that he appointeth over it whomsoever he will.

5:22 And thou his son, O Belshazzar, hast not humbled thine heart, though thou knewest all this; 5:23 But hast lifted up thyself against the Lord of heaven; and they have brought the vessels of his house before thee, and thou, and thy lords, thy wives, and thy concubines, have drunk wine in them; and thou hast praised the gods of silver, and gold, of brass, iron, wood, and stone, which see not, nor hear, nor know: and the God in whose hand thy breath is, and whose are all thy ways, hast thou not glorified: 5:24 Then was the part of the hand sent from him; and this writing was written.

5:25 And this is the writing that was written, MENE, MENE, TEKEL, UPHARSIN.

5:26 This is the interpretation of the thing: MENE; God hath numbered thy kingdom, and finished it.

5:27 TEKEL; Thou art weighed in the balances, and art found wanting.

5:28 PERES; Thy kingdom is divided, and given to the Medes and Persians.

5:29 Then commanded Belshazzar, and they clothed Daniel with scarlet, and put a chain of gold about his neck, and made a proclamation concerning him, that he should be the third ruler in the kingdom.

5:30 In that night was Belshazzar the king of the Chaldeans slain.

5:31 And Darius the Median took the kingdom, being about threescore and two years old.

6

6:1 It pleased Darius to set over the kingdom an hundred and twenty princes, which should be over the whole kingdom; 6:2 And over these three presidents; of whom Daniel was first: that the princes might give accounts unto them, and the king should have no damage.

6:3 Then this Daniel was preferred above the presidents and princes, because an excellent spirit was in him; and the king thought to set him over the whole realm.

6:4 Then the presidents and princes sought to find occasion against Daniel concerning the kingdom; but they could find none occasion nor fault; forasmuch as he was faithful, neither was there any error or fault found in him.

6:5 Then said these men, We shall not find any occasion against this Daniel, except we find it against him concerning the law of his God.

6:6 Then these presidents and princes assembled together to the king, and said thus unto him, King Darius, live for ever.

6:7 All the presidents of the kingdom, the governors, and the princes, the counsellors, and the captains, have consulted together to establish a royal statute, and to make a firm decree, that whosoever shall ask a petition of any God or man for thirty days, save of thee, O king, he shall be cast into the den of lions.

6:8 Now, O king, establish the decree, and sign the writing, that it be not changed, according to the law of the Medes and Persians, which altereth not.

6:9 Wherefore king Darius signed the writing and the decree.

6:10 Now when Daniel knew that the writing was signed, he went into his house; and his windows being open in his chamber toward Jerusalem, he kneeled upon his knees three times a day, and prayed, and gave thanks before his God, as he did aforetime.

6:11 Then these men assembled, and found Daniel praying and making supplication before his God.

6:12 Then they came near, and spake before the king concerning the king's decree; Hast thou not signed a decree, that every man that shall ask a petition of any God or man within thirty days, save of thee, O king, shall be cast into the den of lions? The king answered and said, The thing is true, according to the law of the Medes and Persians, which altereth not.

6:13 Then answered they and said before the king, That Daniel, which is of the children of the captivity of Judah, regardeth not thee, O king, nor the decree that thou hast signed, but maketh his petition three times a day.

6:14 Then the king, when he heard these words, was sore displeased with himself, and set his heart on Daniel to deliver him: and he laboured till the going down of the sun to deliver him.

6:15 Then these men assembled unto the king, and said unto the king, Know, O king, that the law of the Medes and Persians is, That no decree nor statute which the king establisheth may be changed.

6:16 Then the king commanded, and they brought Daniel, and cast him into the den of lions. Now the king spake and said unto Daniel, Thy God whom thou servest continually, he will deliver thee.

6:17 And a stone was brought, and laid upon the mouth of the den; and the king sealed it with his own signet, and with the signet of his lords; that the purpose might not be changed concerning Daniel.

6:18 Then the king went to his palace, and passed the night fasting: neither were instruments of musick brought before him: and his sleep went from him.

6:19 Then the king arose very early in the morning, and went in haste unto the den of lions.

6:20 And when he came to the den, he cried with a lamentable voice unto Daniel: and the king spake and said to Daniel, O Daniel, servant of the living God, is thy God, whom thou servest continually, able to deliver thee from the lions? 6:21 Then said Daniel unto the king, O king, live for ever.

6:22 My God hath sent his angel, and hath shut the lions' mouths, that they have not hurt me: forasmuch as before him innocency was found in me; and also before thee, O king, have I done no hurt.

6:23 Then was the king exceedingly glad for him, and commanded that they should take Daniel up out of the den. So Daniel was taken up out of the den, and no manner of hurt was found upon him, because he believed in his God.

6:24 And the king commanded, and they brought those men which had accused Daniel, and they cast them into the den of lions, them, their children, and their wives; and the lions had the mastery of them, and brake all their bones in pieces or ever they came at the bottom of the den.

6:25 Then king Darius wrote unto all people, nations, and languages, that dwell in all the earth; Peace be multiplied unto you.

6:26 I make a decree, That in every dominion of my kingdom men tremble and fear before the God of Daniel: for he is the living God, and stedfast for ever, and his kingdom that which shall not be destroyed, and his dominion shall be even unto the end.

6:27 He delivereth and rescueth, and he worketh signs and wonders in heaven and in earth, who hath delivered Daniel from the power of the lions.

6:28 So this Daniel prospered in the reign of Darius, and in the reign of Cyrus the Persian.

7

7:1 In the first year of Belshazzar king of Babylon Daniel had a dream and visions of his head upon his bed: then he wrote the dream, and told the sum of the matters.

7:2 Daniel spake and said, I saw in my vision by night, and, behold, the four winds of the heaven strove upon the great sea.

7:3 And four great beasts came up from the sea, diverse one from another.

7:4 The first was like a lion, and had eagle's wings: I beheld till the wings thereof were plucked, and it was lifted up from the earth, and made stand upon the feet as a man, and a man's heart was given to it.

7:5 And behold another beast, a second, like to a bear, and it raised up itself on one side, and it had three ribs in the mouth of it between the teeth of it: and they said thus unto it, Arise, devour much flesh.

7:6 After this I beheld, and lo another, like a leopard, which had upon the back of it four wings of a fowl; the beast had also four heads; and dominion was given to it.

7:7 After this I saw in the night visions, and behold a fourth beast, dreadful and terrible, and strong exceedingly; and it had great iron teeth: it devoured and brake in pieces, and stamped the residue with the feet of it: and it was diverse from all the beasts that were before it; and it had ten horns.

7:8 I considered the horns, and, behold, there came up among them another little horn, before whom there were three of the first horns plucked up by the roots: and, behold, in this horn were eyes like the eyes of man, and a mouth speaking great things.

7:9 I beheld till the thrones were cast down, and the Ancient of days did sit, whose garment was white as snow, and the hair of his head like the pure wool: his throne was like the fiery flame, and his wheels as burning fire.

7:10 A fiery stream issued and came forth from before him: thousand thousands ministered unto him, and ten thousand times ten thousand stood before him: the judgment was set, and the books were opened.

7:11 I beheld then because of the voice of the great words which the horn spake: I beheld even till the beast was slain, and his body destroyed, and given to the burning flame.

7:12 As concerning the rest of the beasts, they had their dominion taken away: yet their lives were prolonged for a season and time.

7:13 I saw in the night visions, and, behold, one like the Son of man came with the clouds of heaven, and came to the Ancient of days, and they brought him near before him.

7:14 And there was given him dominion, and glory, and a kingdom, that all people, nations, and languages, should serve him: his dominion is an everlasting dominion, which shall not pass away, and his kingdom that which shall not be destroyed.

7:15 I Daniel was grieved in my spirit in the midst of my body, and the visions of my head troubled me.

7:16 I came near unto one of them that stood by, and asked him the truth of all this. So he told me, and made me know the interpretation of the things.

7:17 These great beasts, which are four, are four kings, which shall arise out of the earth.

7:18 But the saints of the most High shall take the kingdom, and possess the kingdom for ever, even for ever and ever.

7:19 Then I would know the truth of the fourth beast, which was diverse from all the others, exceeding dreadful, whose teeth were of iron, and his nails of brass; which devoured, brake in pieces, and stamped the residue with his feet; 7:20 And of the ten horns that were in his head, and of the other which came up, and before whom three fell; even of that horn that had eyes, and a mouth that spake very great things, whose look was more stout than his fellows.

7:21 I beheld, and the same horn made war with the saints, and prevailed against them; 7:22 Until the Ancient of days came, and judgment was given to the saints of the most High; and the time came that the saints possessed the kingdom.

7:23 Thus he said, The fourth beast shall be the fourth kingdom upon earth, which shall be diverse from all kingdoms, and shall devour the whole earth, and shall tread it down, and break it in pieces.

7:24 And the ten horns out of this kingdom are ten kings that shall arise: and another shall rise after them; and he shall be diverse from the first, and he shall subdue three kings.

7:25 And he shall speak great words against the most High, and shall wear out the saints of the most High, and think to change times and laws: and they shall be given into his hand until a time and times and the dividing of time.

7:26 But the judgment shall sit, and they shall take away his dominion, to consume and to destroy it unto the end.

7:27 And the kingdom and dominion, and the greatness of the kingdom under the whole heaven, shall be given to the people of the saints of the most High, whose kingdom is an everlasting kingdom, and all dominions shall serve and obey him.

7:28 Hitherto is the end of the matter. As for me Daniel, my cogitations much troubled me, and my countenance changed in me: but I kept the matter in my heart.

8

8:1 In the third year of the reign of king Belshazzar a vision appeared unto me, even unto me Daniel, after that which appeared unto me at the first.

8:2 And I saw in a vision; and it came to pass, when I saw, that I was at Shushan in the palace, which is in the province of Elam; and I saw in a vision, and I was by the river of Ulai.

8:3 Then I lifted up mine eyes, and saw, and, behold, there stood before the river a ram which had two horns: and the two horns were high; but one was higher than the other, and the higher came up last.

8:4 I saw the ram pushing westward, and northward, and southward; so that no beasts might stand before him, neither was there any that could deliver out of his hand; but he did according to his will, and became great.

8:5 And as I was considering, behold, an he goat came from the west on the face of the whole earth, and touched not the ground: and the goat had a notable horn between his eyes.

8:6 And he came to the ram that had two horns, which I had seen standing before the river, and ran unto him in the fury of his power.

8:7 And I saw him come close unto the ram, and he was moved with choler against him, and smote the ram, and brake his two horns: and there was no power in the ram to stand before him, but he cast him down to the ground, and stamped upon him: and there was none that could deliver the ram out of his hand.

8:8 Therefore the he goat waxed very great: and when he was strong, the great horn was broken; and for it came up four notable ones toward the four winds of heaven.

8:9 And out of one of them came forth a little horn, which waxed exceeding great, toward the south, and toward the east, and toward the pleasant land.

8:10 And it waxed great, even to the host of heaven; and it cast down some of the host and of the stars to the ground, and stamped upon them.

8:11 Yea, he magnified himself even to the prince of the host, and by him the daily sacrifice was taken away, and the place of the sanctuary was cast down.

8:12 And an host was given him against the daily sacrifice by reason of transgression, and it cast down the truth to the ground; and it practised, and prospered.

8:13 Then I heard one saint speaking, and another saint said unto that certain saint which spake, How long shall be the vision concerning the daily sacrifice, and the transgression of desolation, to give both the sanctuary and the host to be trodden under foot? 8:14 And he said unto me, Unto two thousand and three hundred days; then shall the sanctuary be cleansed.

8:15 And it came to pass, when I, even I Daniel, had seen the vision, and sought for the meaning, then, behold, there stood before me as the appearance of a man.

8:16 And I heard a man's voice between the banks of Ulai, which called, and said, Gabriel, make this man to understand the vision.

8:17 So he came near where I stood: and when he came, I was afraid, and fell upon my face: but he said unto me, Understand, O son of man: for at the time of the end shall be the vision.

8:18 Now as he was speaking with me, I was in a deep sleep on my face toward the ground: but he touched me, and set me upright.

8:19 And he said, Behold, I will make thee know what shall be in the last end of the indignation: for at the time appointed the end shall be.

8:20 The ram which thou sawest having two horns are the kings of Media and Persia.

8:21 And the rough goat is the king of Grecia: and the great horn that is between his eyes is the first king.

8:22 Now that being broken, whereas four stood up for it, four kingdoms shall stand up out of the nation, but not in his power.

8:23 And in the latter time of their kingdom, when the transgressors are come to the full, a king of fierce countenance, and understanding dark sentences, shall stand up.

8:24 And his power shall be mighty, but not by his own power: and he shall destroy wonderfully, and shall prosper, and practise, and shall destroy the mighty and the holy people.

8:25 And through his policy also he shall cause craft to prosper in his hand; and he shall magnify himself in his heart, and by peace shall destroy many: he shall also stand up against the Prince of princes; but he shall be broken without hand.

8:26 And the vision of the evening and the morning which was told is true: wherefore shut thou up the vision; for it shall be for many days.

8:27 And I Daniel fainted, and was sick certain days; afterward I rose up, and did the king's business; and I was astonished at the vision, but none understood it.

9

9:1 In the first year of Darius the son of Ahasuerus, of the seed of the Medes, which was made king over the realm of the Chaldeans; 9:2 In the first year of his reign I Daniel understood by books the number of the years, whereof the word of the LORD came to

Jeremiah the prophet, that he would accomplish seventy years in the desolations of Jerusalem.

9:3 And I set my face unto the Lord God, to seek by prayer and supplications, with fasting, and sackcloth, and ashes: 9:4 And I prayed unto the LORD my God, and made my confession, and said, O Lord, the great and dreadful God, keeping the covenant and mercy to them that love him, and to them that keep his commandments; 9:5 We have sinned, and have committed iniquity, and have done wickedly, and have rebelled, even by departing from thy precepts and from thy judgments: 9:6 Neither have we hearkened unto thy servants the prophets, which spake in thy name to our kings, our princes, and our fathers, and to all the people of the land.

9:7 O LORD, righteousness belongeth unto thee, but unto us confusion of faces, as at this day; to the men of Judah, and to the inhabitants of Jerusalem, and unto all Israel, that are near, and that are far off, through all the countries whither thou hast driven them, because of their trespass that they have trespassed against thee.

9:8 O Lord, to us belongeth confusion of face, to our kings, to our princes, and to our fathers, because we have sinned against thee.

9:9 To the Lord our God belong mercies and forgivenesses, though we have rebelled against him; 9:10 Neither have we obeyed the voice of the LORD our God, to walk in his laws, which he set before us by his servants the prophets.

9:11 Yea, all Israel have transgressed thy law, even by departing, that they might not obey thy voice; therefore the curse is poured upon us, and the oath that is written in the law of Moses the servant of God, because we have sinned against him.

9:12 And he hath confirmed his words, which he spake against us, and against our judges that judged us, by bringing upon us a great evil: for under the whole heaven hath not been done as hath been done upon Jerusalem.

9:13 As it is written in the law of Moses, all this evil is come upon us: yet made we not our prayer before the LORD our God, that we might turn from our iniquities, and understand thy truth.

9:14 Therefore hath the LORD watched upon the evil, and brought it upon us: for the LORD our God is righteous in all his works which he doeth: for we obeyed not his voice.

9:15 And now, O Lord our God, that hast brought thy people forth out of the land of Egypt with a mighty hand, and hast gotten thee renown, as at this day; we have sinned, we have done wickedly.

9:16 O LORD, according to all thy righteousness, I beseech thee, let thine anger and thy fury be turned away from thy city Jerusalem, thy holy mountain: because for our sins, and for the iniquities of our fathers, Jerusalem and thy people are become a reproach to all that are about us.

9:17 Now therefore, O our God, hear the prayer of thy servant, and his supplications, and cause thy face to shine upon thy sanctuary that is desolate, for the Lord's sake.

9:18 O my God, incline thine ear, and hear; open thine eyes, and behold our desolations, and the city which is called by thy name: for we do not present our supplications before thee for our righteousnesses, but for thy great mercies.

9:19 O Lord, hear; O Lord, forgive; O Lord, hearken and do; defer not, for thine own sake, O my God: for thy city and thy people are called by thy name.

9:20 And whiles I was speaking, and praying, and confessing my sin and the sin of my people Israel, and presenting my supplication before the LORD my God for the holy mountain of my God; 9:21 Yea, whiles I was speaking in prayer, even the man Gabriel, whom I had seen in the vision at the beginning, being caused to fly swiftly, touched me about the time of the evening oblation.

9:22 And he informed me, and talked with me, and said, O Daniel, I am now come forth to give thee skill and understanding.

9:23 At the beginning of thy supplications the commandment came forth, and I am come to shew thee; for thou art greatly beloved: therefore understand the matter, and consider the vision.

9:24 Seventy weeks are determined upon thy people and upon thy holy city, to finish the transgression, and to make an end of sins, and to make reconciliation for iniquity, and to bring in everlasting righteousness, and to seal up the vision and prophecy, and to anoint the most Holy.

9:25 Know therefore and understand, that from the going forth of the commandment to restore and to build Jerusalem unto the Messiah the Prince shall be seven weeks, and threescore and two weeks: the street shall be built again, and the wall, even in troublous times.

9:26 And after threescore and two weeks shall Messiah be cut off, but not for himself: and the people of the prince that shall come shall destroy the city and the sanctuary; and the end thereof shall be with a flood, and unto the end of the war desolations are determined.

9:27 And he shall confirm the covenant with many for one week: and in the midst of the week he shall cause the sacrifice and the oblation to cease, and for the overspreading of abominations he shall make it desolate, even until the consummation, and that determined shall be poured upon the desolate.

10

10:1 In the third year of Cyrus king of Persia a thing was revealed unto Daniel, whose name was called Belteshazzar; and the thing was true, but the time appointed was long: and he understood the thing, and had understanding of the vision.

10:2 In those days I Daniel was mourning three full weeks.

10:3 I ate no pleasant bread, neither came flesh nor wine in my mouth, neither did I anoint myself at all, till three whole weeks were fulfilled.

10:4 And in the four and twentieth day of the first month, as I was by the side of the great river, which is Hiddekel; 10:5 Then I lifted up mine eyes, and looked, and behold a certain man clothed in linen, whose loins were girded with fine gold of Uphaz: 10:6 His body also was like the beryl, and his face as the appearance of lightning, and his eyes as lamps of fire, and his arms and his feet like in colour to polished brass, and the voice of his words like the voice of a multitude.

10:7 And I Daniel alone saw the vision: for the men that were with me saw not the vision; but a great quaking fell upon them, so that they fled to hide themselves.

10:8 Therefore I was left alone, and saw this great vision, and there remained no strength in me: for my comeliness was turned in me into corruption, and I retained no strength.

10:9 Yet heard I the voice of his words: and when I heard the voice of his words, then was I in a deep sleep on my face, and my face toward the ground.

10:10 And, behold, an hand touched me, which set me upon my knees and upon the palms of my hands.

10:11 And he said unto me, O Daniel, a man greatly beloved, understand the words that I speak unto thee, and stand upright: for unto thee am I now sent.

And when he had spoken this word unto me, I stood trembling.

10:12 Then said he unto me, Fear not, Daniel: for from the first day that thou didst set thine heart to understand, and to chasten thyself before thy God, thy words were heard, and I am come for thy words.

10:13 But the prince of the kingdom of Persia withstood me one and twenty days: but, lo, Michael, one of the chief princes, came to help me; and I remained there with the kings of Persia.

10:14 Now I am come to make thee understand what shall befall thy people in the latter days: for yet the vision is for many days.

10:15 And when he had spoken such words unto me, I set my face toward the ground, and I became dumb.

10:16 And, behold, one like the similitude of the sons of men touched my lips: then I opened my mouth, and spake, and said unto him that stood before me, O my lord, by the vision my sorrows are turned upon me, and I have retained no strength.

10:17 For how can the servant of this my lord talk with this my lord? for as for me, straightway there remained no strength in me, neither is there breath left in me.

10:18 Then there came again and touched me one like the appearance of a man, and he strengthened me, 10:19 And said, O man greatly beloved, fear not: peace be unto thee, be strong, yea, be strong. And when he had spoken unto me, I was strengthened, and said, Let my lord speak; for thou hast strengthened me.

10:20 Then said he, Knowest thou wherefore I come unto thee? and now will I return to fight with the prince of Persia: and when I am gone forth, lo, the prince of Grecia shall come.

10:21 But I will shew thee that which is noted in the scripture of truth: and there is none that holdeth with me in these things, but Michael your prince.

11

11:1 Also I in the first year of Darius the Mede, even I, stood to confirm and to strengthen him.

11:2 And now will I shew thee the truth. Behold, there shall stand up yet three kings in Persia; and the fourth shall be far richer than they all: and by his strength through his riches he shall stir up all against the realm of Grecia.

11:3 And a mighty king shall stand up, that shall rule with great dominion, and do according to his will.

11:4 And when he shall stand up, his kingdom shall be broken, and shall be divided toward the four winds of heaven; and not to his posterity, nor according to his dominion which he ruled: for his kingdom shall be plucked up, even for others beside those.

11:5 And the king of the south shall be strong, and one of his princes; and he shall be strong above him, and have dominion; his dominion shall be a great dominion.

11:6 And in the end of years they shall join themselves together; for the king's daughter of the south shall come to the king of the north to make an agreement: but she shall not retain the power of the arm; neither shall he stand, nor his arm: but she shall be given up, and they that brought her, and he that begat her, and he that strengthened her in these times.

11:7 But out of a branch of her roots shall one stand up in his estate, which shall come with an army, and shall enter into the fortress of the king of the north, and shall deal against them, and shall prevail: 11:8 And shall also carry captives into Egypt their gods, with their princes, and with their precious vessels of silver and of gold; and he shall continue more years than the king of the north.

11:9 So the king of the south shall come into his kingdom, and shall return into his own land.

11:10 But his sons shall be stirred up, and shall assemble a multitude of great forces: and one shall certainly come, and overflow, and pass through: then shall he return, and be stirred up, even to his fortress.

11:11 And the king of the south shall be moved with choler, and shall come forth and fight with him, even with the king of the north: and he shall set forth a great multitude; but the multitude shall be given into his hand.

11:12 And when he hath taken away the multitude, his heart shall be lifted up; and he shall cast down many ten thousands: but he shall not be strengthened by it.

11:13 For the king of the north shall return, and shall set forth a multitude greater than the former, and shall certainly come after certain years with a great army and with much riches.

11:14 And in those times there shall many stand up against the king of the south: also the robbers of thy people shall exalt themselves to establish the vision; but they shall fall.

11:15 So the king of the north shall come, and cast up a mount, and take the most fenced cities: and the arms of the south shall not withstand, neither his chosen people, neither shall there be any strength to withstand.

11:16 But he that cometh against him shall do according to his own will, and none shall stand before him: and he shall stand in the glorious land, which by his hand shall be consumed.

11:17 He shall also set his face to enter with the strength of his whole kingdom, and upright ones with him; thus shall he do: and he shall give him the daughter of women, corrupting her: but she shall not stand on his side, neither be for him.

11:18 After this shall he turn his face unto the isles, and shall take many: but a prince for his own behalf shall cause the reproach offered by him to cease; without his own reproach he shall cause it to turn upon him.

11:19 Then he shall turn his face toward the fort of his own land: but he shall stumble and fall, and not be found.

11:20 Then shall stand up in his estate a raiser of taxes in the glory of the kingdom: but within few days he shall be destroyed, neither in anger, nor in battle.

11:21 And in his estate shall stand up a vile person, to whom they shall not give the honour of the kingdom: but he shall come in peaceably, and obtain the kingdom by flatteries.

11:22 And with the arms of a flood shall they be overflown from before him, and shall be broken; yea, also the prince of the covenant.

11:23 And after the league made with him he shall work deceitfully: for he shall come up, and shall become strong with a small people.

11:24 He shall enter peaceably even upon the fattest places of the province; and he shall do that which his fathers have not done, nor his fathers' fathers; he shall scatter among them the prey, and spoil, and riches: yea, and he shall forecast his devices against the strong holds, even for a time.

11:25 And he shall stir up his power and his courage against the king of the south with a great army; and the king of the south shall be stirred up to battle with a very great and mighty army; but he shall not stand: for they shall forecast devices against him.

11:26 Yea, they that feed of the portion of his meat shall destroy him, and his army shall overflow: and many shall fall down slain.

11:27 And both of these kings' hearts shall be to do mischief, and they shall speak lies at one table; but it shall not prosper: for yet the end shall be at the time appointed.

11:28 Then shall he return into his land with great riches; and his heart shall be against the holy covenant; and he shall do exploits, and return to his own land.

11:29 At the time appointed he shall return, and come toward the south; but it shall not be as the former, or as the latter.

11:30 For the ships of Chittim shall come against him: therefore he shall be grieved, and return, and have indignation against the holy covenant: so shall he do; he shall even return, and have intelligence with them that forsake the holy covenant.

11:31 And arms shall stand on his part, and they shall pollute the sanctuary of strength, and shall take away the daily sacrifice, and they shall place the abomination that maketh desolate.

11:32 And such as do wickedly against the covenant shall he corrupt by flatteries: but the people that do know their God shall be strong, and do exploits.

11:33 And they that understand among the people shall instruct many: yet they shall fall by the sword, and by flame, by captivity, and by spoil, many days.

11:34 Now when they shall fall, they shall be holpen with a little help: but many shall cleave to them with flatteries.

11:35 And some of them of understanding shall fall, to try them, and to purge, and to make them white, even to the time of the end: because it is yet for a time appointed.

11:36 And the king shall do according to his will; and he shall exalt himself, and magnify himself above every god, and shall speak marvellous things against the God of gods, and shall prosper till the indignation be accomplished: for that that is determined shall be done.

11:37 Neither shall he regard the God of his fathers, nor the desire of women, nor regard any god: for he shall magnify himself above all.

11:38 But in his estate shall he honour the God of forces: and a god whom his fathers knew not shall he honour with gold, and silver, and with precious stones, and pleasant things.

11:39 Thus shall he do in the most strong holds with a strange god, whom he shall acknowledge and increase with glory: and he shall cause them to rule over many, and shall divide the land for gain.

11:40 And at the time of the end shall the king of the south push at him: and the king of the north shall come against him like a whirlwind, with chariots, and with horsemen, and with many ships; and he shall enter into the countries, and shall overflow and pass over.

11:41 He shall enter also into the glorious land, and many countries shall be overthrown: but these shall escape out of his hand, even Edom, and Moab, and the chief of the children of Ammon.

11:42 He shall stretch forth his hand also upon the countries: and the land of Egypt shall not escape.

11:43 But he shall have power over the treasures of gold and of silver, and over all the precious things of Egypt: and the Libyans and the Ethiopians shall be at his steps.

11:44 But tidings out of the east and out of the north shall trouble him: therefore he shall go forth with great fury to destroy, and utterly to make away many.

11:45 And he shall plant the tabernacles of his palace between the seas in the glorious holy mountain; yet he shall come to his end, and none shall help him.

12

12:1 And at that time shall Michael stand up, the great prince which standeth for the children of thy people: and there shall be a time of trouble, such as never was since there was a nation even to that same time: and at that time thy people shall be delivered, every one that shall be found written in the book.

12:2 And many of them that sleep in the dust of the earth shall awake, some to everlasting life, and some to shame and everlasting contempt.

12:3 And they that be wise shall shine as the brightness of the firmament; and they that turn many to righteousness as the stars for ever and ever.

12:4 But thou, O Daniel, shut up the words, and seal the book, even to the time of the end: many shall run to and fro, and knowledge shall be increased.

12:5 Then I Daniel looked, and, behold, there stood other two, the one on this side of the bank of the river, and the other on that side of the bank of the river.

12:6 And one said to the man clothed in linen, which was upon the waters of the river, How long shall it be to the end of these wonders? 12:7 And I heard the man clothed in linen, which was upon the waters of the river, when he held up his right hand and his left hand unto heaven, and sware by him that liveth for ever that it shall be for a time, times, and an half; and when he shall have accomplished to scatter the power of the holy people, all these things shall be finished.

12:8 And I heard, but I understood not: then said I, O my Lord, what shall be the end of these things? 12:9 And he said, Go thy way, Daniel: for the words are closed up and sealed till the time of the end.

12:10 Many shall be purified, and made white, and tried; but the wicked shall do wickedly: and none of the wicked shall understand; but the wise shall understand.

12:11 And from the time that the daily sacrifice shall be taken away, and the abomination that maketh desolate set up, there shall be a thousand two hundred and ninety days.

12:12 Blessed is he that waiteth, and cometh to the thousand three hundred and five and thirty days.

12:13 But go thou thy way till the end be: for thou shalt rest, and stand in thy lot at the end of the days.

THE PROPHECY OF DANIEL

DOUAY RHEIMS

DANIEL, whose name signifies THE JUDGMENT OF GOD, was of the royal blood of the kings of Juda: and one of those that were first of all carried away into captivity. He was so renowned for wisdom and knowledge, that it became a proverb among the Babylonians, AS WISE AS DANIEL (Ezech. 28.3). And his holiness was so great from his very childhood, that at the time when he was as yet but a young man, he is joined by the SPIRIT of GOD with NOE and JOB, as three persons most eminent for virtue and sanctity, Ezech. 14.

He is not commonly numbered by the Hebrews among THE PROPHETS: because he lived at court, and in high station in the world: but if we consider his many clear predictions of things to come, we shall find that no one better deserves the name and title of A PROPHET: which also has been given him by the SON of GOD himself, Matt. 24, Mark 13., Luke 21.

Daniel Chapter 1

Daniel and his companions are taken into the palace of the king of Babylon: they abstain from his meat and wine, and succeed better with pulse and water. Their excellence and wisdom.

1:1. In the third year of the reign of Joakim, king of Juda, Nabuchodonosor, king of Babylon, came to Jerusalem, and beseiged it.
1:2. And the Lord delivered into his hands Joakim, the king of Juda, and part of the vessels of the house of God: and he carried them away into the land of Sennaar, to the house of his god, and the vessels he brought into the treasure house of his god.
His god... Bel or Belus, the principal idol of the Chaldeans.
1:3. And the king spoke to Asphenez, the master of the eunuchs, that he should bring in some of the children of Israel, and of the king's seed, and of the princes,
1:4. Children in whom there was no blemish, well favoured, and skilful in all wisdom, acute in knowledge, and instructed in science, and such as might stand in the king's palace, that he might teach them the learning, and tongue of the Chaldeans.

1:5. And the king appointed them a daily provision, of his own meat, and of the wine of which he drank himself, that being nourished three years, afterwards they might stand before the king.

1:6. Now there was among them of the children of Juda, Daniel, Ananias, Misael, and Azarias.

1:7. And the master of the eunuchs gave them names: to Daniel, Baltassar: to Ananias, Sidrach: to Misael, Misach: and to Azarias, Abdenago.

1:8. But Daniel purposed in his heart that he would not be defiled with the king's table, nor with the wine which he drank: and he requested the master of the eunuchs that he might not be defiled.

Be defiled, etc... Viz., either by eating meat forbidden by the law, or which had before been offered to idols.

1:9. And God gave to Daniel grace and mercy in the sight of the prince of the eunuchs.

1:10. And the prince of the eunuchs said to Daniel: I fear my lord, the king, who hath appointed you meat and drink: who if he should see your faces leaner than those of the other youths, your equals, you shall endanger my head to the king.

1:11. And Daniel said to Malasar, whom the prince of the eunuchs had appointed over Daniel, Ananias, Misael, and Azarias:

1:12. Try, I beseech thee, thy servants for ten days, and let pulse be given us to eat, and water to drink:

Pulse... That is, pease, beans, and such like.

1:13. And look upon our faces, and the faces of the children that eat of the king's meat: and as thou shalt see, deal with thy servants.

1:14. And when he had heard these words, he tried them for ten days.

1:15. And after ten days, their faces appeared fairer and fatter than all the children that ate of the king's meat.

1:16. So Malasar took their portions, and the wine that they should drink: and he gave them pulse.

1:17. And to these children God gave knowledge, and understanding in every book, and wisdom: but to Daniel the understanding also of all visions and dreams.

1:18. And when the days were ended, after which the king had ordered they should be brought in: the prince of the eunuchs brought them in before Nabuchodonosor.

1:19. And when the king had spoken to them, there were not found among them all such as Daniel, Ananias, Misael, and Azarias: and they stood in the king's presence.

1:20. And in all matters of wisdom and understanding, that the king enquired of them, he found them ten times better than all the diviners, and wise men, that were in all his kingdom.

1:21. And Daniel continued even to the first year of king Cyrus.

Daniel Chapter 2

Daniel, by divine revelation, declares the dream of Nabuchodonosor, and the interpretation of it. He is highly honoured by the king.

2:1. In the second year of the reign of Nabuchodonosor, Nabuchodonosor had a dream, and his spirit was terrified, and his dream went out of his mind.

The second year... Viz., from the death of his father Nabopolassar; for he had reigned before as partner with his father in the empire.

2:2. Then the king commanded to call together the diviners and the wise men, and the magicians, and the Chaldeans: to declare to the king his dreams: so they came and stood before the king.

The Chaldeeans... That is, the astrologers, that pretended to divine by stars.

2:3. And the king said to them: I saw a dream: and being troubled in mind I know not what I saw.

2:4. And the Chaldeans answered the king in Syriac: O king, live for ever: tell to thy servants thy dream, and we will declare the interpretation thereof.

2:5. And the king, answering, said to the Chaldeans: The thing is gone out of my mind: unless you tell me the dream, and the meaning thereof, you shall be put to death, and your houses shall be confiscated.

2:6. but if you tell the dream, and the meaning of it, you shall receive of me rewards, and gifts, and great honour: therefore, tell me the dream, and the interpretation thereof.

2:7. They answered again and said: Let the king tell his servants the dream, and we will declare the interpretation of it.

2:8. The king answered and said: I know for certain, that you seek to gain time, since you know that the thing is gone from me.

2:9. If, therefore, you tell me not the dream, there is one sentence concerning you, that you have also framed a lying interpretation, and full of deceit, to speak before me till the time pass away. Tell me, therefore, the dream, that I may know that you also give a true interpretation thereof.

2:10. Then the Chaldeans answered before the king, and said: There is no man upon earth, that can accomplish thy word, O king; neither doth any king, though great and mighty, ask such a thing of any diviner, or wise man, or Chaldean.

2:11. For the thing that thou asketh, O king, is difficult: nor can any one be found that can shew it before the king, except the gods, whose conversation is not with men.

2:12. Upon hearing this, the king in fury, and in great wrath, commanded that all the wise men of Babylon should be put to death.

2:13. And the decree being gone forth, the wise men were slain: and Daniel and his companions were sought for, to be put to death.

2:14. Then Daniel inquired concerning the law and the sentence, of Arioch, the general of the king's army, who was gone forth to kill the wise men of Babylon.

2:15. And he asked him that had received the orders of the king, why so cruel a sentence was gone forth from the face of the king. And when Arioch had told the matter to Daniel,

2:16. Daniel went in, and desired of the king, that he would give him time to resolve the question, and declare it to the king.

2:17. And he went into his house, and told the matter to Ananias, and Misael, and Azarias, his companions:

2:18. To the end that they should ask mercy at the face of the God of heaven, concerning this secret, and that Daniel and his companions might not perish with the rest of the wise men of Babylon.

2:19. Then was the mystery revealed to Daniel by a vision in the night: and Daniel blessed the God of heaven,

2:20. And speaking, he said: Blessed be the name of the Lord from eternity and for evermore: for wisdom and fortitude are his.

2:21. And he changeth times and ages: taketh away kingdoms, and establisheth them: giveth wisdom to the wise, and knowledge to them that have understanding:

2:22. He revealeth deep and hidden things, and knoweth what is in darkness: and light is with him.

2:23. To thee, O God of our fathers, I give thanks, and I praise thee: because thou hast given me wisdom and strength: and now thou hast shewn me what we desired of thee, for thou hast made known to us the king's discourse.

2:24. After this Daniel went in to Arioch, to whom the king had given orders to destroy the wise men of Babylon, and he spoke thus to him: Destroy not the wise men of Babylon: bring me in before the king, and I will tell the solution to the king.

2:25. Then Arioch in haste brought in Daniel to the king, and said to him: I have found a man of the children of the captivity of Juda, that will resolve the question to the king.

2:26. The king answered, and said to Daniel, whose name was Baltassar: Thinkest thou indeed that thou canst tell me the dream that I saw, and the interpretation thereof?

2:27. And Daniel made answer before the king, and said: The secret that the king desireth to know, none of the wise men, or the philosophers, or the diviners, or the soothsayers, can declare to the king.

2:28. But there is a God in heaven that revealeth mysteries, who hath shewn to thee, O king Nabuchodonosor, what is to come to pass in the latter times. Thy dream, and the visions of thy head upon thy bed, are these:

2:29. Thou, O king, didst begin to think in thy bed, what should come to pass hereafter: and he that revealeth mysteries shewed thee what shall come to pass.

2:30. To me also this secret is revealed, not by any wisdom that I have more than all men alive: but that the interpretation might be made manifest to the king, and thou mightest know the thought of thy mind.

2:31. Thou, O king, sawest, and behold there was as it were a great statue: this statue, which was great and high, tall of stature, stood before thee, and the look thereof was terrible.

2:32. The head of this statue was of fine gold, but the breast and the arms of silver, and the belly and the thighs of brass.

2:33. And the legs of iron, the feet part of iron and part of clay.

2:34. Thus thou sawest, till a stone was cut out of a mountain without hands: and it struck the statue upon the feet thereof that were of iron and clay, and broke them in pieces.

2:35. Then was the iron, the clay, the brass, the silver, and the gold broken to pieces together, and became like the chaff of a summer's threshing floor, and they were carried away by the wind: and there was no place found for them: but the stone that struck the statue became a great mountain, and filled the whole earth.

2:36. This is the dream: we will also tell the interpretation thereof before thee, O king.

2:37. Thou art a king of kings: and the God of heaven hath given thee a kingdom, and strength, and power, and glory:

2:38. And all places wherein the children of men, and the beasts of the field do dwell: he hath also given the birds of the air into thy hand, and hath put all things under thy power: thou, therefore, art the head of gold.

2:39. And after thee shall rise up another kingdom, inferior to thee, of silver: and another third kingdom of brass, which shall rule over all the world.

Another kingdom... Viz., that of the Medes and Persians. Ibid. Third kingdom... Viz., that of Alexander the Great.

2:40. And the fourth kingdom shall be as iron. As iron breaketh into pieces, and subdueth all things, so shall that break, and destroy all these.

The fourth kingdom, etc... Some understand this of the successors of Alexander, the kings of Syria and Egypt, others of the Roman empire, and its civil wars.

2:41. And whereas thou sawest the feet, and the toes, part of potter's clay, and part of iron: the kingdom shall be divided, but yet it shall take its origin from the iron, according as thou sawest the iron mixed with the miry clay.

2:42. And as the toes of the feet were part of iron, and part of clay: the kingdom shall be partly strong, and partly broken.

2:43. And whereas thou sawest the iron mixed with miry clay, they shall be mingled indeed together with the seed of man, but they shall not stick fast one to another, as iron cannot be mixed with clay.

2:44. But in the days of those kingdoms, the God of heaven will set up a kingdom that shall never by destroyed, and his kingdom shall not be delivered up to another people: and it shall break in pieces, and shall consume all these kingdoms: and itself shall stand for ever.

A kingdom... Viz., the kingdom of Christ in the Catholic Church which cannot be destroyed.

2:45. According as thou sawest, that the stone was cut out of the mountain without hands, and broke in pieces the clay and the iron, and the brass, and the silver, and the gold, the great God hath shewn the king what shall come to pass hereafter, and the dream is true, and the interpretation thereof is faithful.

2:46. Then king Nabuchodonosor fell on his face, and worshipped Daniel, and commanded that they should offer in sacrifice to him victims and incense.

2:47. And the king spoke to Daniel, and said: Verily, your God is the God of gods, and Lord of kings, and a revealer of hidden things: seeing thou couldst discover this secret.

2:48. Then the king advanced Daniel to a high station, and gave him many and great gifts: and he made him governor over all the provinces of Babylon: and chief of the magistrates over all the wise men of Babylon.

2:49. And Daniel requested of the king, and he appointed Sidrach, Misach, and Abdenago, over the works of the province of Babylon: but Daniel himself was in the king's palace.

Daniel Chapter 3

Nabuchodonosor set up a golden statue; which he commands all to adore: the three children for refusing to do it are cast into the fiery furnace; but are not hurt by the flames. Their prayer and canticle of praise.

3:1. King Nabuchodonosor made a statue of gold, of sixty cubits high, and six cubits broad, and he set it up in the plain of Dura, of the province of Babylon.

3:2. Then Nabuchodonosor, the king, sent to call together the nobles, the magistrates, and the judges, the captains, the rulers, and governors, and all the chief men of the provinces, to come to the dedication of the statue which king Nabuchodonosor had set up.

3:3. Then the nobles, the magistrates, and the judges, the captains, and rulers, and the great men that were placed in authority, and all the princes of the provinces, were gathered together to come to the dedication of the statue, which king Nabuchodonosor had set up. And they stood before the statue which king Nabuchodonosor had set up.

3:4. Then a herald cried with a strong voice: To you it is commanded, O nations, tribes and languages:

3:5. That in the hour that you shall hear the sound of the trumpet, and of the flute, and of the harp, of the sackbut, and of the psaltery, and of the symphony, and of all kind of music, ye fall down and adore the golden statue which king Nabuchodonosor hath set up.

3:6. But if any man shall not fall down and adore, he shall the same hour be cast into a furnace of burning fire.

3:7. Upon this, therefore, at the time when all the people heard the sound of the trumpet, the flute, and the harp, of the sackbut, and the psaltery, of the symphony, and of all kind of music, all the nations, tribes, and languages fell down and adored the golden statue which king Nabuchodonosor had set up.

3:8. And presently at that very time some Chaldeans came and accused the Jews,

3:9. And said to king Nabuchodonosor: O king, live for ever:

3:10. Thou, O king, hast made a decree, that every man that shall hear the sound of the trumpet, the flute, and the harp, of the sackbut, and the psaltery, of the symphony, and of all kind of music, shall prostrate himself, and adore the golden statue:

3:11. And that if any man shall not fall down and adore, he should be cast into a furnace of burning fire.

3:12. Now there are certain Jews, whom thou hast set over the works of the province of

Babylon, Sidrach, Misach, and Abdenago: these men, O king, have slighted thy decree: they worship not thy gods, nor do they adore the golden statue which thou hast set up.

3:13. Then Nabuchodonosor in fury, and in wrath, commanded that Sidrach, Misach, ad Abdenago should be brought: who immediately were brought before the king.

3:14. And Nabuchodonosor, the king, spoke to them, and said: Is it true, O Sidrach, Misach, and Abdenago, that you do not worship my gods, nor adore the golden statue that I have set up?

3:15. Now, therefore, if you be ready, at what hour soever, you shall hear the sound of the trumpet, flute, harp, sackbut, and psaltery, and symphony, and of all kind of music, prostrate yourselves, and adore the statue which I have made: but if you do not adore, you shall be cast the same hour into the furnace of burning fire: and who is the God that shall deliver you out of my hand?

3:16. Sidrach, Misach, and Abdenago, answered, and said to king Nabuchodonosor: We have no occasion to answer thee concerning this matter.

3:17. For behold our God, whom we worship, is able to save us from the furnace of burning fire, and to deliver us out of thy hands, O king.

3:18. But if he will not, be it known to thee, O king, that we will not worship thy gods, nor adore the golden statue which thou hast set up.

3:19. Then was Nabuchodonosor filled with fury: and the countenance of his face was changed against Sidrach, Misach, and Abdenago, and he commanded that the furnace should be heated seven times more than it had been accustomed to be heated.

3:20. And he commanded the strongest men that were in his army, to bind the feet of Sidrach, Misach, and Abdenago, and to cast them into the furnace of burning fire.

3:21. And immediately these men were bound, and were cast into the furnace of burning fire, with their coats, and their caps, and their shoes, and their garments.

3:22. For the king's commandment was urgent, and the furnace was heated exceedingly. And the flame of the fire slew those men that had cast in Sidrach, Misach, and Abdenago.

3:23. But these three men, that is, Sidrach, Misach, and Abdenago, fell down bound in the midst of the furnace of burning fire.

3:24. And they walked in the midst of the flame, praising God, and blessing the Lord.

And they walked, etc... Here St. Jerome takes notice, that from this verse, to ver. 91, was not in the Hebrew in his time. But as it was in all the Greek Bibles, (which were originally translated from the Hebrew,) it is more than probable that it had been formerly in the Hebrew or rather in the Chaldaic, in which the book of Daniel was written. But this is certain: that it is, and has been of old, received by the church, and read as canonical scripture in her liturgy, and divine offices.

3:25. Then Azarias standing up, prayed in this manner, and opening his mouth in the midst of the fire, he said:

3:26. Blessed art thou, O Lord, the God of our fathers, and thy name is worthy of praise, and glorious for ever:

3:27. For thou art just in all that thou hast done to us, and all thy works are true, and thy ways right, and all thy judgments true.

3:28. For thou hast executed true judgments in all the things that thou hast brought upon us, and upon Jerusalem, the holy city of our fathers: for according to truth and judgment, thou hast brought all these things upon us for our sins.

3:29. For we have sinned, and committed iniquity, departing from thee: and we have trespassed in all things:

3:30. And we have not hearkened to thy commandments, nor have we observed nor done as thou hadst commanded us, that it might go well with us.

3:31. Wherefore, all that thou hast brought upon us, and every thing that thou hast done to us, thou hast done in true judgment:

3:32. And thou hast delivered us into the hands of our enemies that are unjust, and most wicked, and prevaricators, and to a king unjust, and most wicked beyond all that are upon the earth.

3:33. And now we cannot open our mouths: we are become a shame, and a reproach to thy servants, and to them that worship thee.

3:34. Deliver us not up for ever, we beseech thee, for thy name's sake, and abolish not thy covenant.

3:35. And take not away thy mercy from us, for the sake of Abraham, thy beloved, and Isaac, thy servant, and Israel, thy holy one:

3:36. To whom thou hast spoken, promising that thou wouldst multiply their seed as the stars of heaven, and as the sand that is on the sea shore.

3:37. For we, O Lord, are diminished more than any nation, and are brought low in all the earth this day for our sins.

3:38. Neither is there at this time prince, or leader, or prophet, or holocaust, or sacrifice, or oblation, or incense, or place of first fruits before thee,

3:39. That we may find thy mercy: nevertheless, in a contrite heart and humble spirit let us be accepted.

3:40. As in holocausts of rams, and bullocks, and as in thousands of fat lambs: so let our sacrifice be made in thy sight this day, that it may please thee: for there is no confusion to them that trust in thee.

3:41. And now we follow thee with all our heart, and we fear thee, and seek thy face.

3:42. Put us not to confusion, but deal with us according to thy meekness, and according to the multitude of thy mercies.

3:43. And deliver us, according to thy wonderful works, and give glory to thy name, O Lord:

3:44. And let all them be confounded that shew evils to thy servants, let them be confounded in all thy might, and let their strength be broken:

3:45. And let them know that thou art the Lord, the only God, and glorious over all the world.

3:46. Now the king's servants that had cast them in, ceased not to heat the furnace with brimstone and tow, and pitch, and dry sticks,

3:47. And the flame mounted up above the furnace nine and forth cubits:

3:48. And it broke forth, and burnt such of the Chaldeans as it found near the furnace.

3:49. But the angel of the Lord went down with Azarias and his companions into the furnace: and he drove the flame of the fire out of the furnace,

3:50. And made the midst of the furnace like the blowing of a wind bringing dew, and the fire touched them not at all, nor troubled them, nor did them any harm.

3:51. Then these three, as with one mouth, praised and glorified and blessed God, in the furnace, saying:

3:52. Blessed art thou, O Lord, the God of our fathers; and worthy to be praised, and glorified, and exalted above all for ever: and blessed is the holy name of thy glory: and worthy to be praised and exalted above all, in all ages.

3:53. Blessed art thou in the holy temple of thy glory: and exceedingly to be praised and exalted above all for ever.

3:55. Blessed art thou that beholdest the depths, and sittest upon the cherubims: and worthy to be praised and exalted above all for ever.

3:56. Blessed art thou in the firmament of heaven: and worthy of praise, and glorious for ever.

3:57. All ye works of the Lord, bless the Lord: praise and exalt him above all for ever.

3:58. O ye angels of the Lord, bless the Lord: praise and exalt him above all for ever.

3:59. O ye heavens, bless the Lord: praise and exalt him above all for ever.

3:60. O all ye waters that are above the heavens, bless the Lord: praise and exalt him above all for ever.

3:61. O all ye powers of the Lord, bless the Lord: praise and exalt him above all for ever.

3:62. O ye sun and moon, bless the Lord: praise and exalt him above all for ever.
3:63. O ye stars of heaven, bless the Lord: praise and exalt him above all for ever.
3:64. O every shower and dew, bless ye the Lord: praise and exalt him above all for ever.
3:65. O all ye spirits of God, bless the Lord: praise and exalt him above all for ever.
3:66. O ye fire and heat, bless the Lord: praise and exalt him above all for ever.
3:67. O ye cold and heat, bless the Lord, praise and exalt him above all for ever.
3:68. O ye dews and hoar frost, bless the Lord: praise and exalt him above all for ever.
3:69. O ye frost and cold, bless the Lord: praise and exalt him above all for ever.
3:70. O ye ice and snow, bless the Lord: praise and exalt him above all for ever.
3:71. O ye nights and days, bless the Lord: praise and exalt him above all for ever.
3:72. O ye light and darkness, bless the Lord: praise and exalt him above all for ever.
3:73. O ye lightnings and clouds, bless the Lord: praise and exalt him above all for ever.
3:74. O let the earth bless the Lord: let it praise and exalt him above all for ever.
3:76. O all ye things that spring up in the earth, bless the Lord: praise and exalt him above all for ever.
3:77. O ye fountains, bless the Lord: praise and exalt him above all for ever.
3:78. O ye seas and rivers, bless the Lord: praise and exalt him above all for ever.
3:79. O ye whales, and all that move in the waters, bless the Lord: praise and exalt him above all for ever.
3:80. O all ye fowls of the air, bless the Lord: praise and exalt him above all for ever.
3:81. O all ye beasts and cattle, bless the Lord: praise and exalt him above all for ever.
3:82. O ye sons of men, bless the Lord: praise and exalt him above all for ever.
3:83. O let Israel bless the Lord: let them praise and exalt him above all for ever.
3:84. O ye priests of the Lord, bless the Lord: praise and exalt him above all for ever.
3:85. O ye servants of the Lord, bless the Lord: praise and exalt him above all for ever.
3:86. O ye spirits and souls of the just, bless the Lord: praise and exalt him above all for ever.
3:87. O ye holy and humble of heart, bless the Lord: praise and exalt him above all for ever.
3:88. O Ananias, Azarias, Misael, bless ye the Lord: praise and exalt him above all for ever. For he hath delivered us from hell, ad saved us out of the hand of death, and delivered us out of the midst of the burning flame, and saved us out of the midst of the fire.
3:89. O give thanks to the Lord, because he is good: because his mercy endureth for ever and ever.
3:90. O all ye religious, bless the Lord, the God of gods: praise him, and give him thanks, because his mercy endureth for ever and ever.
3:91. Then Nabuchodonosor, the king, was astonished, and rose up in haste, and said to his nobles: Did we not cast three men bound into the midst of the fire? They answered the king, and said: True, O king.
3:92. He answered, and said: Behold, I see four men loose, and walking in the midst of the fire, and there is no hurt in them, and the form of the fourth is like the son of God.
3:93. Then Nabuchodonosor came to the door of the burning fiery furnace, and said: Sidrach, Misach, and Abdenago, ye servants of the most high God, go ye forth, and come. And immediately Sidrach, Misach, and Abdenago, went out from the midst of the fire.
3:94. And the nobles, and the magistrates, and the judges, and the great men of the king, being gathered together, considered these men, that the fire had no power on their bodies, and that not a hair of their head had been singed, nor their garments altered, nor the smell of the fire had passed on them.
3:95. Then Nabuchodonosor breaking forth, said: Blessed be the God of them, to wit, of Sidrach, Misach, and Abdenago, who hath sent his angel, and delivered his servants that believed in him: and they changed the king's word, and delivered up their bodies, that they might not serve nor adore any god except their own God.
3:96. By me, therefore, this decree is made: That every people, tribe, and tongue, which shall speak blasphemy against the God of Sidrach, Misach, and Abdenago, shall be destroyed, and their houses laid waste: for there is no other God that can save in this manner.

3:97. Then the king promoted Sidrach, Misach, and Abdenago, in the province of Babylon.
3:98. Nabuchodonosor, the king, to all peoples, nations, and tongues, that dwell in all the earth, peace be multiplied unto you.

Nabuchodonosor, etc. These last three verses are a kind of preface to the following chapter, which is written in the style of an epistle from the king.

3:99. The most high God hath wrought signs and wonders towards me. It hath seemed good to me, therefore, to publish
3:100. His signs, because they are great: and his wonders, because they are mighty: and his kingdom is an everlasting kingdom, and his power to all generations.

Daniel Chapter 4

Nabuchodonosor's dream, by which the judgments of God are denounced against him for his pride, is interpreted by Daniel, and verified by the event.

4:1. I, Nabuchodonosor, was at rest in my house, and flourishing in my palace:
4:2. I saw a dream that affrighted me: and my thoughts in my bed, and the visions of my head, troubled me.
4:3. Then I set forth a decree, that all the wise men of Babylon should be brought in before me, and that they should shew me the interpretation of the dream.
4:4. Then came in the diviners, the wise men, the Chaldeans, and the soothsayers, and I told the dream before them: but they did not shew me the interpretation thereof.
4:5. Till their colleague, Daniel, came in before me, whose name is Baltassar, according to the name of my god, who hath in him the spirit of the holy gods: and I told the dream before him.

Baltassar, according to the name of my god... He says this, because the name of Baltassar, or Belteshazzar, is derived from the name of Bel, the chief god of the Babylonians.

4:6. Baltassar, prince of the diviners, because I know that thou hast in thee the spirit of the holy gods, and that no secret is impossible to thee, tell me the visions of my dreams that I have seen, and the interpretation of them?
4:7. This was the vision of my head in my bed: I saw, and behold a tree in the midst of the earth, and the height thereof was exceeding great.
4:8. The tree was great and strong, and the height thereof reached unto heaven: the sight thereof was even to the ends of all the earth.
4:9. Its leaves were most beautiful, and its fruit exceeding much: and in it was food for all: under it dwelt cattle and beasts, and in the branches thereof the fowls of the air had their abode: and all flesh did eat of it.
4:10. I saw in the vision of my head upon my bed, and behold a watcher, and a holy one came down from heaven.

A watcher... A vigilant angel, perhaps the guardian of Israel.

4:11. He cried aloud, and said thus: Cut down the tree, and chop off the branches thereof: shake off its leaves, and scatter its fruits: let the beasts fly away that are under it, and the birds from its branches.
4:12. Nevertheless, leave the stump of its roots in the earth, and let it be tied with a band of iron and of brass, among the grass, that is without, and let it be wet with the dew of heaven, and let its protion be with the wild beasts in the grass of the earth.
4:13. Let his heart be changed from man's, and let a beast's heart be given him: and let seven

times pass over him.

Let his heart be changed, etc... It does not appear by scripture that Nabuchodonosor was changed from human shape; much less that he was changed into an ox; but only that he lost his reason, and became mad; and in this condition remained abroad in the company of beasts, eating grass like an ox, till his hair grew in such manner as to resemble the feathers of eagles, and his nails to be like birds' claws.

4:14. This is the decree by the sentence of the watchers, and the word and demand of the holy ones: till the living know, that the most High ruleth in the kingdom of men: and he will give it to whomsoever it shall please him, and he will appoint the basest man over it.

4:15. I, king Nabuchodonosor, saw this dream: thou, therefore, O Baltassar, tell me quickly the interpretation: for all the wise men of my kingdom are not able to declare the meaning of it to me: but thou art able, because the spirit of the holy gods is in thee.

4:16. Then Daniel, whose name was Baltassar, began silently to think within himself for about one hour: and his thought troubled him. But the king answering, said: Baltassar, let not the dream and the interpretation thereof trouble thee. Baltassar answered, and said: My lord, the dream be to them that hate thee, and the interpretation thereof to thy enemies.

4:17. The tree which thou sawest, which was high and strong, whose height reached to the skies, and the sight thereof into all the earth:

4:18. And the branches thereof were most beautiful, and its fruit exceeding much, and in it was food for all, under which the beasts of the field dwelt, and the birds of the air had their abode in its branches.

4:19. It is thou, O king, who art grown great, and become mighty: for thy greatness hath grown, and hath reached to heaven, and thy power unto the ends of the earth.

4:20. And whereas the king saw a watcher, and a holy one come down from heaven, and say: Cut down the tree, and destroy it, but leave the stump of the roots thereof in the earth, and let it be bound with iron and brass, among the grass without, and let it be sprinkled with the dew of heaven, and let his feeding be with the wild beasts, till seven times pass over him.

4:21. This is the interpretation of the sentence of the most High, which is come upon my lord, the king.

4:22. They shall cast thee out from among men, and thy dwelling shall be with cattle, and with wild beasts, and thou shalt eat grass, as an ox, and shalt be wet with the dew of heaven: and seven times shall pass over thee, till thou know that the most High ruleth over the kingdom of men, and giveth it to whomsoever he will.

4:23. But whereas he commanded, that the stump of the roots thereof, that is, of the tree, should be left: thy kingdom shall remain to thee, after thou shalt have known that power is from heaven.

4:24. Wherefore, O king, let my counsel be acceptable to thee, and redeem thou thy sins with alms, and thy iniquities with works of mercy to the poor: perhaps he will forgive thy offences.

4:25. All these things came upon king Nabuchodonosor.

4:26. At the end of twelve months he was walking in the palace of Babylon.

4:27. And the king answered, and said: Is not this the great Babylon, which I have built, to be the seat of the kingdom, by the strength of my power, and in the glory of my excellence?

4:28. And while the word was yet in the king's mouth, a voice came down from heaven: To thee, O king Nabuchodonosor, it is said: Thy kingdom shall pass from thee.

4:29. And they shall cast thee out from among men, and thy dwelling shall be with cattle and wild beasts: thou shalt eat grass like an ox, and seven times shall pass over thee, till thou know that the most High ruleth in the kingdom of men, and giveth it to whomsoever he will.

4:30. The same hour the word was fulfilled upon Nabuchodonosor, and he was driven away from among men, and did eat grass, like an ox, and his body was wet with the dew of heaven: till his hairs grew like the feathers of eagles, and his nails like birds' claws.

4:31. Now at the end of the days, I, Nabuchodonosor, lifted up my eyes to heaven, and my sense was restored to me: and I blessed the most High, and I praised and glorified him that liveth for ever: for his power is an everlasting power, and his kingdom is to all generations.

4:32. And all the inhabitants of the earth are reputed as nothing before him: for he doth according to his will, as well with the powers of heaven, as among the inhabitants of the earth: and there is none that can resist his hand, and say to him: Why hast thou done it?

4:33. At the same time my sense returned to me, and I came to the honour and glory of my kingdom: and my shape returned to me: and my nobles, and my magistrates, sought for me, and I was restored to my kingdom: and greater majesty was added to me.

4:34. Therefore I, Nabuchodonosor, do now praise, and magnify, and glorify the King of heaven: because all his works are true, and his ways judgments, and them that walk in pride he is able to abase.

I, Nabuchodonosor, do now, etc... From this place some commentators infer that this king became a true convert, and dying not long after, was probably saved.

Daniel Chapter 5

Baltasar's profane banquet: his sentence is denounced by a handwriting on the wall, which Daniel reads and interprets.

5:1. Baltasar, the king, made a great feast for a thousand of his nobles: and every one drank according to his age.

Baltasar... He is believed to be the same as Nabonydus, the last of the Chaldean kings, grandson to Nabuchodonosor. He is called his son, ver. 2, 11, etc., according to the style of the scriptures, because he was a descendant from him.

5:2. And being now drunk, he commanded that they should bring the vessels of gold and silver, which Nabuchodonosor, his father, had brought away out of the temple, that was in Jerusalem, that the king and his nobles, and his wives, and his concubines, might drink in them.

5:3. Then were the golden and silver vessels brought, which he had brought away out of the temple that was in Jeursalem: and the king and his nobles, his wives, and his concubines, drank in them.

5:4. They drank wine, and praised their gods of gold, and of silver, of brass, of iron, and of wood, and of stone.

5:5. In the same hour there appeared fingers, as it were of the hand of a man, writing over against the candlestick, upon the surface of the wall of the king's palace: and the king beheld the joints of the hand that wrote.

5:6. Then was the king's countenance changed, and his thoughts troubled him: and the joints of his loins were loosed, and his knees struck one against the other.

5:7. And the king cried out aloud to bring in the wise men, the Chaldeans, and the soothsayers. And the king spoke, and said to the wise men of Babylon: Whosoever shall read this writing, and shall make known to me the interpretation thereof, shall be clothed with purple, and shall have a golden chain on his neck, and shall be the third man in my kingdom.

5:8. Then came in all the king's wise men, but they could neither read the writing, nor declare the interpretation to the king.

5:9. Wherewith king Baltasar was much troubled, and his countenance was changed: and his nobles also were troubled.

5:10. Then the queen, on occasion of what had happened to the king, and his nobles, came into the banquet-house: and she spoke, and said: O king, live for ever: let not thy thoughts trouble thee, neither let thy countenance be changed.

The queen... Not the wife, but the mother of the king.

5:11. There is a man in thy kingdom that hath the spirit of the holy gods in him: and in the days of thy father knowledge and wisdom were found in him: for king Nabuchodonosor, thy father, appointed him prince of the wise men, enchanters, Chaldeans, and soothsayers, thy father, I say, O king:

5:12. Because a greater spirit, and knowledge, and understanding, and interpretation of dreams, and shewing of secrets, and resolving of difficult things, were found in him, that is, in Daniel: whom the king named Baltassar. Now, therefore, let Daniel be called for, and he will tell the interpretation.

5:13. Then Daniel was brought in before the king. And the king spoke, and said to him: Art thou Daniel, of the children of the captivity of Juda, whom my father, the king, brought out of Judea?

5:14. I have heard of thee, that thou hast the spirit of the gods, and excellent knowledge, and understanding, and wisdom are found in thee.

5:15. And now the wise men, the magicians, have come in before me, to read this writing, and shew me the interpretation thereof; and they could not declare to me the meaning of this writing.

5:16. But I have heard of thee, that thou canst interpret obscure things, and resolve difficult things: now if thou art able to read the writing, and to shew me the interpretation thereof, thou shalt be clothed with purple, and shalt have a chain of gold about thy neck, and shalt be the third prince in my kingdom.

5:17. To which Daniel made answer, and said before the king: thy rewards be to thyself, and the gifts of thy house give to another: but the writing I will read to thee, O king, and shew thee the interpretation thereof.

5:18. O king, the most high God gave to Nabuchodonosor, thy father, a kingdom, and greatness, and glory, and honour.

5:19. And for the greatness that he gave to him, all people, tribes, and languages trembled, and were afraid of him: whom he would, he slew: and whom he would, he destroyed: and whom he would, he set up: and whom he would, he brought down.

5:20. But when his heart was lifted up, and his spirit hardened unto pride, he was put down from the throne of his kingdom, and his glory was taken away.

5:21. And he was driven out from the the sons of men, and his heart was made like the beasts, and his dwelling was with the wild asses, and he did eat grass like an ox, and his body was wet with the dew of heaven: till he knew that the most High ruled in the kingdom of men, and that he will set over it whomsoever it shall please him.

5:22. Thou also, his son, O Baltasar, hast not humbled thy heart, whereas thou knewest all these things:

5:23. But hast lifted thyself up against the Lord of heaven: and the vessels of his house have been brought before thee: and thou, and thy nobles, and thy wives, and thy concubines, have drunk wine in them: and thou hast praised the gods of silver, and of gold, and of brass, of iron, and of wood, and of stone, that neither see, nor hear, nor feel: but the God who hath thy breath in his hand, and all thy ways, thou hast not glorified.

5:24. Wherefore, he hath sent the part of the hand which hath written this that is set down.

5:25. And this is the writing that is written: MANE, THECEL, PHARES.

5:26. And this is the interpretation of the word. MANE: God hath numbered thy kingdom, and hath finished it.

5:27. THECEL: thou art weighed in the balance, and art found wanting.

5:28. PHARES: thy kingdom is divided, and is given to the Medes and Persians.

5:29. Then by the king's command, Daniel was clothed with purple, and a chain of gold was put about his neck: and it was proclaimed of him that he had power as the third man in the kingdom.

5:30. The same night Baltasar, the Chaldean king, was slain.

5:31. And Darius, the Mede, succeeded to the kingdom, being threescore and two years old. Darius... He is called Cyaxares by the historians; and was the son of Astyages, and uncle to Cyrus.

Daniel Chapter 6

Daniel is promoted by Darius: his enemies procure a law forbidding prayer; for the transgression of this law Daniel is cast into the lions' den: but miraculously delivered.

6:1. It seemed good to Darius, and he appointed over the kingdom a hundred and twenty governors, to be over his whole kingdom.
6:2. And three princes over them of whom Daniel was one: that the governors might give an account to them, and the king might have no trouble.
6:3. And Daniel excelled all the princes, and governors: because a greater spirit of God was in him.
6:4. And the king thought to set him over all the kingdom; whereupon the princes, and the governors, sought to find occasion against Daniel, with regard to the king: and they could find no cause, nor suspicion, because he was faithful, and no fault, nor suspicion was found in him.
6:5. Then these men said: We shall not find any occasion against this Daniel, unless perhaps concerning the law of his God.
6:6. Then the princes, and the governors, craftily suggested to the king, and spoke thus unto him: King Darius, live for ever:
6:7. All the princes of the kingdom, the magistrates, and governors, the senators, and judges, have consulted together, that an imperial decree, and an edict be published: That whosoever shall ask any petition of any god, or man, for thirty days, but of thee, O king, shall be cast into the den of the lions.
6:8. Now, therefore, O king, confirm the sentence, and sign the decree: that what is decreed by the Medes and Persians may not be altered, nor any man be allowed to transgress it.
6:9. So king Darius set forth the decree, and established it.
6:10. Now, when Daniel knew this, that is to say, that the law was made, he went into his house: and opening the windows in his upper chamber towards Jerusalem, he knelt down three times a day, and adored and gave thanks before his God, as he had been accustomed to do before.
6:11. Wherefore those men carefully watching him, found Daniel praying and making supplication to his God.
6:12. And they came and spoke to the king concerning the edict: O king, hast thou not decreed, that every man that should make a request to any of the gods, or men, for thirty days, but to thyself, O king, should be cast into the den of the lions? And the king answered them, saying: The word is true, according to the decree of the Medes and Persians, which it is not lawful to violate.
6:13. Then they answered, and said before the king: Daniel, who is of the children of the captivity of Juda, hath not regarded thy law, nor the decree that thou hast made: but three times a day he maketh his prayer.
6:14. Now when the king had heard these words, he was very much grieved, and in behalf of Daniel he set his heart to deliver him, and even till sunset he laboured to save him.
6:15. But those men perceiving the king's design, said to him: Know thou, O king, that the law of the Medes and Persians is, that no decree which the king hath made, may be altered.
6:16. Then the king commanded, and they brought Daniel, and cast him into the den of the lions. And the king said to Daniel: Thy God, whom thou always servest, he will deliver thee.
6:17. And a stone was brought, and laid upon the mouth of the den: which the king sealed with his own ring, and with the ring of his nobles, that nothing should be done against Daniel.

6:18. And the king went away to his house, and laid himself down without taking supper, and meat was not set before him, and even sleep departed from him.

6:19. Then the king rising very early in the morning, went in haste to the lions' den:

6:20. And coming near to the den, cried with a lamentable voice to Daniel, and said to him: Daniel, servant of the living God, hath thy God, whom thou servest always, been able, thinkest thou, to deliver thee from the lions?

6:21. And Daniel answering the king, said: O king, live for ever:

6:22. My God hath sent his angel, and hath shut up the mouths of the lions, and they have not hurt me: forasmuch as before him justice hath been found in me: yea, and before thee, O king, I have done no offence.

6:23. Then was the king exceeding glad for him, and he commanded that Daniel should be taken out of the den: and Daniel was taken out of the den, and no hurt was found in him, because he believed in his God.

6:24. And by the king's commandment, those men were brought that had accused Daniel: and they were cast into the lions' den, they and their children, and their wives: and they did not reach the bottom of the den, before the lions caught them, and broke all their bones in pieces.

6:25. Then king Darius wrote to all people, tribes, and languages, dwelling in the whole earth: PEACE be multiplied unto you.

6:26. It is decreed by me, that in all my empire and my kingdom, all men dread and fear the God of Daniel. For he is the living and eternal God for ever: and his kingdom shall not be destroyed, and his power shall be for ever.

6:27. He is the deliverer, and saviour, doing signs and wonders in heaven, and in earth: who hath delivered Daniel out of the lions' den.

6:28. Now Daniel continued unto the reign of Darius, and the reign of Cyrus, the Persian.

Daniel Chapter 7

Daniel's vision of the four beasts, signifying four kingdoms: of God sitting on his throne: and of the opposite kingdoms of Christ and Antichrist.

7:1. In the first year of Baltasar, king of Babylon, Daniel saw a dream: and the vision of his head was upon his bed: and writing the dream, he comprehended it in a few words: and relating the sum of it in short, he said:

7:2. I saw in my vision by night, and behold the four winds of the heavens strove upon the great sea.

7:3. And four great beasts, different one from another, came up out of the sea.

Four great beasts... Viz., the Chaldean, Persian, Grecian, and Roman empires. But some rather choose to understand the fourth beast of the successors of Alexander the Great, more especially of them that reigned in Asia and Syria.

7:4. The first was like a lioness, and had the wings of an eagle: I beheld till her wings were plucked off, and she was lifted up from the earth, and stood upon her feet as a man, and the heart of a man was given to her.

7:5. And behold another beast, like a bear, stood up on one side: and there were three rows in the mouth thereof, and in the teeth thereof, and thus they said to it: Arise, devour much flesh.

7:6. After this I beheld, and lo, another like a leopard, and it had upon it four wings, as of a fowl, and the beast had four heads, and power was given to it.

7:7. After this I beheld in the vision of the night, and lo, a fourth beast, terrible and wonderful, and exceeding strong, it had great iron teeth, eating and breaking in pieces, and treading down the rest with his feet: and it was unlike to the other beasts which I had seen before it, and had ten horns.

Ten horns... That is, ten kingdoms, (as Apoc. 17.12,) among which the empire of the fourth beast shall be parcelled. Or ten kings of the number of the successors of Alexander; as figures of such as shall be about the time of Antichrist.

7:8. I considered the horns, and behold another little horn sprung out of the midst of them: and three of the first horns were plucked up at the presence thereof: and behold eyes like the eyes of a man were in this horn, and a mouth speaking great things.

Another little horn... This is commonly understood of Antichrist. It may also be applied to that great persecutor Antiochus Epiphanes, as a figure of Antichrist.

7:9. I beheld till thrones were placed, and the ancient of days sat: his garment was white as snow, and the hair of his head like clean wool: his throne like flames of fire: the wheels of it like a burning fire.

7:10. A swift stream of fire issued forth from before him: thousands of thousands ministered to him, and ten thousand times a hundred thousand stood before him: the judgment sat, and the books were opened.

7:11. I beheld, because of the voice of the great words which that horn spoke: and I saw that the beast was slain, and the body thereof was destroyed, and given to the fire to be burnt:

7:12. And that the power of the other beasts was taken away: and that times of life were appointed them for a time, and a time.

7:13. I beheld, therefore, in the vision of the night, and lo, one like the Son of man came with the clouds of heaven, and he came even to the ancient of days: and they presented him before him.

7:14. And he gave him power, and glory, and a kingdom: and all peoples, tribes, and tongues shall serve him: his power is an everlasting power that shall not be taken away: and his kingdom that shall not be destroyed.

7:15. My spirit trembled; I, Daniel, was affrighted at these things, and the visions of my head troubled me.

7:16. I went near to one of them that stood by, and asked the truth of him concerning all these things, and he told me the interpretation of the words, and instructed me:

7:17. These four great beasts, are four kingdoms, which shall arise out of the earth.

7:18. But the saints of the most high God shall take the kingdom: and they shall possess the kingdom for ever and ever.

7:19. After this I would diligently learn concerning the fourth beast, which was very different from all, and exceeding terrible: his teeth and claws were of iron: he devoured and broke in pieces, and the rest he stamped upon with his feet:

7:20. And concerning the ten horns that he had on his head: and concerning the other that came up, before which three horns fell: and of that horn that had eyes, and a mouth speaking great things, and was greater than the rest.

7:21. I beheld, and lo, that horn made war against the saints, and prevailed over them,

7:22. Till the ancient of days came and gave judgment to the saints of the most High, and the time came, and the saints obtained the kingdom.

7:23. And thus he said: The fourth beast shall be the fourth kingdom upon earth, which shall be greater than all the kingdoms, and shall devour the whole earth, and shall tread it down, and break it in pieces.

7:24. And the ten horns of the same kingdom, shall be ten kings: and another shall rise up after them, and he shall be mightier than the former, and he shall bring down three kings.

7:25. And he shall speak words against the High One, and shall crush the saints of the most High: and he shall think himself able to change times and laws, and they shall be delivered into his hand until a time, and times, and half a time.

A time, and times, and half a time... That is, three years and a half; which is supposed to be the length of the duration of the persecution of Antichrist.

7:26. And a judgment shall sit, that his power may be taken away, and be broken in pieces, and perish even to the end.

7:27. And that the kingdom, and power, and the greatness of the kingdom, under the whole heaven, may be given to the people of the saints of the most High: whose kingdom is an everlasting kingdom, and all kings shall serve him, and shall obey him.

7:28. Hitherto is the end of the word. I, Daniel, was much troubled with my thoughts, and my countenance was changed in me: but I kept the word in my heart.

Daniel Chapter 8

Daniel's vision of the ram and the he goat interpreted by the angel Gabriel.

8:1. In the third year of the reign of king Baltasar, a vision appeared to me. I, Daniel, after what I had seen in the beginning,

8:2. Saw in my vision when I was in the castle of Susa, which is in the province of Elam: and I saw in the vision that I was over the gate of Ulai.

8:3. And I lifted up my eyes, and saw: and behold a ram stood before the water, having two high horns, and one higher than the other, and growing up. Afterward

A ram... The empire of the Medes and Persians.

8:4. I saw the ram pushing with his horns against the west, and against the north, and against the south: and no beasts could withstand him, nor be delivered out of his hand: and he did according to his own will, and became great.

8:5. And I understood: and behold a he goat came from the west on the face of the whole earth, and he touched not the ground, and the he goat had a notable horn between his eyes.

A he goat... The empire of the Greeks, or Macedonians. Ibid. He touched not the ground... He conquered all before him, with so much rapidity, that he seemed rather to fly, than to walk upon the earth.-Ibid. A notable horn... Alexander the Great.

8:6. And he went up to the ram that had the horns, which I had seen standing before the gate, and he ran towards him in the force of his strength.

8:7. And when he was come near the ram, he was enraged against him, and struck the ram: and broke his two horns, and the ram cound not withstand him: and when he had cast him down on the ground, he stamped upon him, and none could deliver the ram out of his hand.

8:8. And the he goat became exceeding great: and when he was grown, the great horn was broken, and there came up four horns under it towards the four winds of heaven.

Four horns... Seleucus, Antigonus, Philip, and Ptolemeus, the successors of Alexander, who divided his empire among them.

8:9. And out of one of them came forth a little horn: and it became great against the south, and against the east, and against the strength.

A little horn... Antiochus Epiphanes, a descendant of Seleucus. He grew against the south, and the east, by his victories over the kings of Egypt and Armenia: and against the strength, that is, against Jerusalem and the people of God.

8:10. And it was magnified even unto the strength of heaven: and it threw down of the strength, and of the stars, and trod upon them.

Unto the strength of heaven... or, against the strength of heaven. So are here called the army of the Jews, the people of God.

8:11. And it was magnified even to the prince of the strength: and it took away from him the continual sacrifice, and cast down the place of his sanctuary.

8:12. And strength was given him against the continual sacrifice, because of sins: and truth shall be cast down on the ground, and he shall do and shall prosper.

8:13. And I heard one of the saints speaking, and one saint said to another I know not to whom, that was speaking: How long shall be the vision, concerning the continual sacrifice, and the sin of the desolation that is made: and the sanctuary, and the strength be trodden under foot?

8:14. And he said to him: Unto evening and morning two thousand three hundred days: and the sanctuary shall be cleansed.

Unto evening and morning two thousand three hundred days... That is, six years and almost four months: which was the whole time from the beginning of the persecution of Antiochus till his death.

8:15. And it came to pass when I, Daniel, saw the vision, and sought the meaning, that behold there stood before me as it were the appearance of a man.

8:16. And I heard the voice of a man between Ulai: and he called, and said: Gabriel, make this man to understand the vision.

8:17. And he came, and stood near where I stood: and when he was come, I fell on my face, trembling, and he said to me: Understand, O son of man, for in the time of the end the vision shall be fulfilled.

8:18. And when he spoke to me, I fell flat on the ground: and he touched me, and set me upright.

8:19. And he said to me: I will shew thee what things are to come to pass in the end of the malediction: for the time hath its end.

8:20. The ram, which thou sawest with horns, is the king of the Medes and Persians.

8:21. And the he goat, is the king of the Greeks, and the great horn that was between his eyes, the same is the first king.

8:22. But whereas when that was borken, there arose up four for it, four kings shall rise up of his nation, but not with his strength.

8:23. And after their reign, when iniquities shall be grown up, there shall arise a king of a shameless face, and understanding dark sentences.

8:24. And his power shall be strengthened, but not by his own force: and he shall lay all things waste, and shall prosper, and do more than can be believed. And he shall destroy the mighty, and the people of the saints,

8:25. According to his will, and craft shall be successful in his hand: and his heart shall be puffed up, and in the abundance of all things he shall kill many: and he shall rise up aginst the prince of princes, and shall be broken without hand.

8:26. And the vision of the evening and the morning, which was told, is true: thou, therefore, seal up the vision, because it shall come to pass after many days.

8:27. And I, Daniel, languished, and was sick for some days: and when I was risen up, I did the king's business, and I was astonished at the vision, and there was none that could interpret it.

Daniel Chapter 9

Daniel's confession and prayer: Gabriel informs him concerning the seventy weeks to the coming of Christ.

9:1. In the first year of Darius, the son of Assuerus, of the seed of the Medes, who reigned over the kingdom of the Chaldeans:

9:2. The first year of his reign I, Daniel, understood by books the number of the years, concerning which the word of the Lord came to Jeremias, the prophet, that seventy years should be accomplished of the desolation of Jerusalem.

9:3. And I set my face to the Lord, my God, to pray and make supplication with fasting, and sackcloth, and ashes.

9:4. And I prayed to the Lord, my God, and I made my confession, and said: I beseech thee, O Lord God, great and terrible, who keepest the covenant, and mercy to them that love thee, and keep thy commandments.

9:5. We have sinned, we have committed iniquity, we have done wickedly, and have revolted: and we have gone aside from thy commandments, and thy judgments.

9:6. We have not hearkened to thy servants, the prophets, that have spoken in thy name to our kings, to our princes, to our fathers, and to all the people of the land.

9:7. To thee, O Lord, justice: but to us confusion of face, as at this day to the men of Juda, and to the inhabitants of Jerusalem, and to all Israel, to them that are near, and to them that are far off, in all the countries whither thou hast driven them, for their iniquities, by which they have sinned against thee.

9:8. O Lord, to us belongeth confusion of face, to our princes, and to our fathers, that have sinned.

9:9. But to thee, the Lord our God, mercy and forgiveness, for we have departed from thee:

9:10. And we have not hearkened to the voice of the Lord, our God, to walk in his law, which he set before us by his servants, the prophets.

9:11. And all Israel have transgressed thy law, and have turned away from hearing thy voice, and the malediction, and the curse, which is written in the book of Moses, the servant of God, is fallen upon us, because we have sinned against him.

9:12. And he hath confirmed his words which he spoke against us, and against our princes that judged us, that he would bring in upon us a great evil, such as never was under all the heaven, according to that which hath been done in Jerusalem.

9:13. As it is written in the law of Moses, all this evil is come upon us: and we entreated not thy face, O Lord our God, that we might turn from our iniquities, and think on thy truth.

9:14. And the Lord hath watched upon the evil, and hath brought it upon us: the Lord, our God, is just in all his works which he hath done: for we have not hearkened to his voice.

9:15. And now, O Lord, our God, who hast brought forth thy people out of the land of Egypt, with a strong hand, and hast made thee a name as at this day: we have sinned, we have committed iniquity,

9:16. O Lord, against all thy justice: let thy wrath and thy indignation be turned away, I beseech thee, from thy city, Jerusalem, and from thy holy mountain. For by reason of our sins, and the iniquities of our fathers, Jerusalem, and thy people, are a reproach to all that are round about us.

9:17. Now, therefore, O our God, hear the supplication of thy servant, and his prayers: and shew thy face upon thy sanctuary, which is desolate, for thy own sake.

9:18. Incline, O my God, thy ear, and hear: open thy eyes, and see our desolation, and the city upon which thy name is called: for it is not for our justifications that we present our prayers before thy face, but for the multitude of thy tender mercies.

9:19. O Lord, hear: O Lord, be appeased: hearken, and do: delay not, for thy own sake, O my God: because thy name is invocated upon thy city, and upon thy people.

9:20. Now while I was yet speaking, and praying, and confessing my sins, and the sins of my people of Israel, and presenting my supplications in the sight of my God, for the holy mountain of my God:

9:21. As I was yet speaking in prayer, behold the man, Gabriel, whom I had seen in the vision at the beginning, flying swiftly, touched me at the time of the evening sacrifice.

The man Gabriel... The angel Gabriel in the shape of a man.

9:22. And he instructed me, and spoke to me, and said: O Daniel, I am now come forth to teach thee, and that thou mightest understand.

9:23. From the beginning of thy prayers the word came forth: and I am come to shew it to thee, because thou art a man of desires: therefore, do thou mark the word, and understand the vision.

Man of desires... that is, ardently praying for the Jews then in captivity.

9:24. Seventy weeks are shortened upon thy people, and upon thy holy city, that transgression may be finished, and sin may have an end, and iniquity may be abolished; and everlasting justice may be brought; and vision and prophecy may be fulfilled; and the Saint of saints may be anointed.

Seventy weeks... Viz., of years, (or seventy times seven, that is, 490 years,) are shortened; that is, fixed and determined, so that the time shall be no longer.

9:25. Know thou, therefore, and take notice: that from the going forth of the word, to build up Jerusalem again, unto Christ, the prince, there shall be seven weeks, and sixty-two weeks: and the street shall be built again, and the walls, in straitness of times.

From the going forth of the word, etc... That is, from the twentieth year of king Artaxerxes, when by his commandment Nehemias rebuilt the walls of Jerusalem, 2 Esd. 2. From which time, according to the best chronology, there were just sixty-nine weeks of years, that is, 483 years to the baptism of Christ, when he first began to preach and execute the office of Messias.-Ibid. In straitness of times... angustia temporum: which may allude both to the difficulties and opposition they met with in building: and to the shortness of the time in which they finished the wall, viz., fifty-two days.

9:26. And after sixty-two weeks Christ shall be slain: and the people that shall deny him shall not be his. And a people, with their leader, that shall come, shall destroy the city, and the sanctuary: and the end thereof shall be waste, and after the end of the war the appointed desolation.

A people with their leader... The Romans under Titus.

9:27. And he shall confirm the covenant with many, in one week: and in the half of the week the victim and the sacrifice shall fail: and there shall be in the temple the abomination of desolation: and the desolation shall continue even to the consummation, and to the end.

In the half of the week... or, in the middle of the week, etc. Because Christ preached three years and a half: and then by his sacrifice upon the cross abolished all the sacrifices of the law.-Ibid. The abomination of desolation... Some understand this of the profanation of the temple by the crimes of the Jews, and by the bloody faction of the zealots.

Others of the bringing in thither the ensigns and standard of the pagan Romans. Others, in fine, distinguish three different times of desolation: viz., that under Antiochus; that when the temple was destroyed by the Romans; and the last near the end of the world under Antichrist. To all which, as they suppose, this prophecy may have a relation.

Daniel Chapter 10

Daniel having humbled himself by fasting and penance seeth a vision, with which he is much terrified; but he is comforted by an angel.

10:1. In the third year of Cyrus, king of the Persians, a word was revealed to Daniel, surnamed Baltassar, and a true word, and great strength: and he understood the word: for there is need of understanding in a vision.

10:2. In those days I, Daniel, mourned the days of three weeks.

10:3. I ate no desirable bread, and neither flesh, nor wine, entered into my mouth, neither was I anointed with ointment: till the days of three weeks were accomplished.

10:4. And in the four and twentieth day of the first month, I was by the great river, which is the Tigris.

10:5. And I lifted up my eyes, and I saw: and behold a man clothed in linen, and his loins were girded with the finest gold:

10:6. And his body was like the chrysolite, and his face as the appearance of lightning, and his eyes as a burning lamp: and his arms, and all downward even to the feet, like in appearance to glittering brass: and the voice of his word like the voice of a multitude.

10:7. And I, Daniel alone, saw the vision: for the men that were with me saw it not: but an exceeding great terror fell upon them, and they fled away, and hid themselves.

10:8. And I, being left alone, saw this great vision: and there remained no strength in me, and the appearance of my countenance was changed in me, and I fainted away, and retained no strength.

10:9. And I heard the voice of his words: and when I heard I lay in a consternation upon my face, and my face was close to the ground.

10:10. And behold a hand touched me, and lifted me up upon my knees, and upon the joints of my hands.

10:11. And he said to me: Daniel, thou man of desires, understand the words that I speak to thee, and stand upright: for I am sent now to thee. And when he had said this word to me, I stood trembling.

10:12. And he said to me: Fear not, Daniel: for from the first day that thou didst set thy heart to understand, to afflict thyself in the sight of thy God, thy words have been heard: and I am come for thy words.

10:13. But the prince of the kingdom of the Persians resisted me one and twenty days: and behold Michael, one of the chief princes, came to help me, and I remained there by the king of the Persians.

The prince, etc... That is, the angel guardian of Persia: who according to his office, seeking the spiritual good of the Persians was desirous that many of the Jews should remain among them.

10:14. But I am come to teach thee what things shall befall thy people in the latter days, for as yet the vision is for days.

10:15. And when he was speaking such words to me, I cast down my countenance to the ground, and held my peace.

10:16. And behold as it were the likeness of a son of man touched my lips: then I opened my mouth and spoke, and said to him that stood before me: O my lord, at the sight of thee my joints are loosed, and no strength hath remained in me.

10:17. And how can the servant of my lord speak with my lord? for no strength remaineth in me; moreover, my breath is stopped.

10:18. Therefore, he that looked like a man, touched me again, and strengthened me.

10:19. And he said: Fear not, O man of desires, peace be to thee: take courage, and be strong. And when he spoke to me, I grew strong, and I said: Speak, O my lord, for thou hast strengthened me.

10:20. And he said: Dost thou know wherefore I am come to thee? And now I will return, to fight against the prince of the Persians. When I went forth, there appeared the prince of the Greeks coming.

10:21. But I will tell thee what is set down in the scripture of truth: and none is my helper in all these things, but Michael your prince.

Michael your prince... The guardian general of the church of God.

Daniel Chapter 11

The angel declares to Daniel many things to come, with regard to the Persian and Grecian kings: more especially with regard to Antiochus as a figure of Antichrist.

11:1. And from the first year of Darius, the Mede, I stood up, that he might be strengthened, and confirmed.

11:2. And now I will shew thee the truth. Behold, there shall stand yet three kings in Persia, and the fourth shall be enriched exceedingly above them all: and when he shall be grown mighty by his riches, he shall stir up all against the kingdom of Greece.

Three kings... Viz., Cambyses, Smerdes Magus, and Darius, the son of Hystaspes.-Ibid. The fourth... Xerxes.

11:3. But there shall rise up a strong king, and shall rule with great power: and he shall do what he pleaseth.

A strong king... Alexander.

11:4. And when he shall come to his height, his kingdom shall be broken, and it shall be divided towards the four winds of the heaven: but not to his posterity, nor according to his pwoer with wheich he ruled. For his kingdom shall be rent in pieces, even for strangers, besides these.

11:5. And the king of the south shall be strengthened, and one of his princes shall prevail over him, and he shall rule with great power: for his dominions shall be great.

The king of the south... Ptolemeus the son of Lagus, king of Egypt, which lies south of Jerusalem.-Ibid. One of his princes... that is, one of Alexander's princes, shall prevail over him: that is, shall be stronger than the king of Egypt. He speaks of Seleucus Nicator, king of Asia and Syria, whose successors are here called the kings of the north, because their dominions lay to the north in respect to Jerusalem.

11:6. And after the end of years they shall be in league together: and the daughter of the king of the south shall come to the king of the north to make friendship, but she shall not obtain the strength of the arm, neither shall her seed stand: and she shall be given up, and her young men that brought her, and they that strengthened her in these times.

The daughter of the king of the south... Viz., Berenice, daughter of Ptolemeus Philadelphus, given in marriage to Antiochus Theos, grandson of Seleucus.

11:7. And a plant of the bud of her roots shall stand up: and he shall come with an army, and shall enter into the province of the king of the north: and he shall abuse them, and shall prevail.

A plant, etc... Ptolemeus Evergetes, the son of Philadelphus.

11:8. And he shall also carry away captive into Egypt their gods, and their graven things, and their precious vessels of gold and silver: he shall prevail aginst the king of the north.

The king of the north... Seleucus Callinicus.

11:9. And the king of the south shall enter into the kingdom, and shall return to his own land.
11:10. And his sons shall be provoked, and they shall assemble a multitude of great forces: and he shall come with haste like a flood: and he shall return, and be stirred up, and he shall join battle with his force.

His sons... Seleucus Ceraunius, and Antiochus the Great, the sons of Callinicus.-Ibid. He shall come... Viz., Antiochus the Great.

11:11. And the king of the south being provoked, shall go forth, and shall fight against the king of the north, and shall prepare an exceeding great multitude, and a multitude shall be given into his hands.

The king of the south... Ptolemeus Philopator, son of Evergetes.

11:12. And he shall take a multitude, and his heart shall be lifted up, and he shall cast down many thousands: but he shall not prevail.
11:13. For the king of the north shall return, and shall prepare a multitude much greater than before: and in the end of times, and years, he shall come in haste with a great army, and much riches.
11:14. And in those times many shall rise up against the king of the south, and the children of prevaricators of thy people shall lift up themselves to fulfil the vision, and they shall fall.
11:15. And the king of the north shall come, and shall cast up a mount, and shall take the best fenced citits: and the arms of the south shall not withstand, and his chosen ones shall rise up to resist, and they shall not have strength.
11:16. And he shall come upon him, and do according to his pleasure, and there shall be none to stand against his face: and he shall stand in the glorious land, and it shall be

consumed by his hand.

He shall come upon him... Viz., Antiochus shall come upon the king of the south.-Ibid. The glorious land... Judea.

11:17. And he shall set his face to come to possess all his kingdom, and he shall make upright conditions with him: and he shall give him a daughter of women, to overthrow it: and she shall not stand, neither shall she be for him.

All his kingdom... Viz., all the kingdom of Ptolemeus Epiphanes, son of Philopator.-Ibid. A daughter of women... That is, a most beautiful woman, viz., his daughter Cleopatra.-Ibid. To overthrow it... Viz., the kingdom of Epiphanes: but his policy shall not succeed; for Cleopatra shall take more to heart the interest of her husband, than that of her father.

11:18. And he shall turn his face to the islands, and shall take many: and he shall cause the prince of his reproach to cease, and his reproach shall be turned upon him.

The prince of his reproach... Scipio the Roman general, called the prince of his reproach, because he overthrew Antiochus, and obliged him to submit to very dishonourable terms, before he would cease from the war.

11:19. And he shall turn his face to the empire of his own land, and he shall stumble, and fall, ans shall not be found.
11:20. And there shall stand up in his place one most vile, and unworthy of kingly honour: and in a few days he shall be destroyed, not in rage nor in battle.

One most vile... Seleucus Philopator, who sent Heliodorus to plunder the temple: and was shortly after slain by the same Heliodorus.

11:21. And there shall stand up in his place one despised, and the kingly honour shall not be given him: and he shall come privately, and shall obtain the kingdom by fraud.

One despised... Viz., Antiochus Epiphanes, who at first was despised and not received for king. What is here said of this prince, is accommodated by St. Jerome and others to Antichrist; of whom this Antiochus was a figure.

11:22. And the arms of the fighter shall be overcome before his face, and shall be broken: yea, also the prince of the covenant.

Of the fighter... That is, of them that shall oppose him, and shall fight against him.-Ibid. The prince of the covenant... or, of the league. The chief of them that conspired against him: or the king of Egypt his most powerful adversary.

11:23. And after friendships, he will deal deceitfully with him: and he shall go up, and shall overcome with a small people.
11:24. And he shall enter into rich and plentiful cities: and he shall do that which his fathers never did, nor his fathers' fathers: he shall scatter their spoils, and their prey, and their riches, and shall forecast devices against the best fenced places: and this until a time.
11:25. And his strength, and his heart, shall be stirred up aginst the king of the south, with a great army: and the king of the south shall be stirred up to battle with many and very strong succours: and they shall not stand, for they shall form designs against him.

The king... Ptolemeus Philometor.

11:26. And they that eat bread with him, shall destroy him, and his army shall be overthrown: and many shall fall down slain.

11:27. And the heart of the two kings shall be to do evil, and they shall speak lies at one table, and they shall not prosper: because as yet the end is unto another time.

11:28. And he shall return into his land with much riches: and his heart shall be aginst the holy covenant, and he shall succeed, and shall return into his own land.

11:29. At the time appointed he shall return, and he shall come to the south, but the latter time shall not be like the former.

11:30. And the galleys and the Romans shall come upon him, and he shall be struck, and shall return, and shall have indignation against thecovenant of the sanctuary, and he shall succeed: and he shall returnm, and shall devise against them that haave forsaken the covenant of the sanctuary.

The galleys and the Romans... Popilius, and the other Roman ambassadors, who came in galleys, and obliged him to depart from Egypt.

11:31. And arms shall stand on his part, and they shall defile the sanctuary of strength, and shall take away the continual sacrifice: and they shall place there the abomination unto desolation.

They shall place there the abomination, etc... The idol of Jupiter Olympius, which Antiochus ordered to be set up in the sanctuary of the temple: which is here called the sanctuary of strength, from the Almighty that was worshipped there.

11:32. And such as deal wickedly against the covenant shall deceitfully dissemble: but the people that know their God shall prevail and succeed.

11:33. And they that are learned among the people shall teach many: and they shall fall by the sword, and by fire, and by captivity, and by spoil for many days.

11:34. And when they shall have fallen, they shall be relieved with a small help: and many shall be joined to them deceitfully.

11:35. And some of thelearned shall fall, that they may be tried, and may be chosen, and made white, even to the appointed time: because yet there shall be another time.

11:36. And the king shall do according to his will, and he shall be lifted up, and shall magnify himself against every god: and he shall speak great things against the God of gods, and shall prosper, till the wrath be accomplished. For the determination is made.

11:37. And he shall make no account of the God of his fathers: and he shall follow the lust of women, and he shall not regard any gods: for he shall rise up against all things.

11:38. But he shall worship the god Maozim, in his place: and a god whom his fathers knew not, he shall worship with gold, and silver, and precious stones, and things of great price.

The god Maozim... That is, the god of forces or strong holds.

11:39. And he shall do this to fortify Maozim with a strange god, whom he hath acknowledged, and he shall increase glory, and shall give them power over many, and shall divide the land gratis.

And he shall increase glory, etc... He shall bestow honours, riches and lands, upon them that shall worship his god.

11:40. And at the time prefixed the king of the south shall fight against him, and the king of the north shall come against him like a tempest, with chariots, and with horsemen, and with a great navy, and he shall enter into the countries, and shall destroy, and pass through.

11:41. And he shall enter into the glorious land, ansd many shall fall: and these only shakll be saved out of his hand, Edom, and Moab, and the principality of the children of Ammon.

11:42. And he shall lay his hand upon the lands: and the land of Egypt shall not escape.

11:43. And he shall have power over the treasures of gold, and of silver, and all the precious things of Egypt: and he shall pass through Lybia, and Ethiopia.

11:44. And tidings out of the east, and out of the north, shall trouble him: and he shall come with a great multitude to destroy and slay many.

11:45. And he shall fix his tabernacle, Apadno, between the seas, upon a glorious and holy mountain: and he shall come even to the top thereof, and none shall help him.

Apadno... Some take it for the proper name of a place: others, from the Hebrew, translate it his palace.

Daniel Chapter 12

Michael shall stand up for the people of God: with other things relating to Antichrist, and the end of the world.

12:1. But at that time shall Michael rise up, the great prince, who standeth for the children of thy people: and a time shall come, such as never was from the time that nations began, even until that time.

And at that time shall thy people be saved, every one that shall be found written in the book.

12:2. And many of those that sleep in the dust of the earth, shall awake: some unto life everlasting, and others unto reproach, to see it always.

12:3. But they that are learned, shall shine as the brightness of the firmament: and they that instruct many to justice, as stars for all eternity.

Learned... Viz., in the law of God and true wisdom, which consists in knowing and loving God.

12:4. But thou, O Daniel, shut up the words, and seal the book, even to the time appointed: many shall pass over, and knowledge shall be manifold.

12:5. And I, Daniel, looked, and behold as it were two others stood: one on this side upon the bank of the river, and another on that side, on the other bank of the river.

12:6. And I said to the man that was clothed in linen, that stood upon the waters of the river: How long shall it be to the end of these wonders?

12:7. And I heard the man that was clothed in linen, that stood upon the waters of the river, when he had lifted up his right hand, and his left hand to heaven, and had sworn by him that liveth for ever, that it should be unto a time, and times, and half a time. And when the scattering of the band of the holy people shall be accomplished, all these things shall be finished.

12:8. And I heard, and understood not. And I said: O my lord, what shall be after these things?

12:9. And he said: Go, Daniel, because the words are shut up, and sealed until the appointed time.

12:10. Many shall be chosen, and made white, and shall be tried as fire: and the wicked shall deal wickedly, and none of the wicked shall understand, but the learned shall understand.

12:11. And from the time when the continual sacrifice shall be taken away, and the abomination unto desolation shall be set up, there shall be a thousand two hundred ninety days.

12:12. Blessed is he that waitedth, and cometh unto a thousand three hundred thirty-five days.

12:13. But go thou thy ways until the time appointed: and thou shalt rest, and stand in thy lot unto the end of the days.

Daniel Chapter 13

The history of Susanna and the two elders.

This history of Susanna, in all the ancient Greek and Latin Bibles, was placed in the beginning of the book of Daniel: till St. Jerome, in his translation, detached it from thence; because he did not find it in the Hebrew: which is also the case of the history of Bel and the Dragon. But both the one and the other are received by the Catholic Church: and were from the very beginning a part of the Christian Bible.

13:1. Now there was a man that dwelt in Babylon, and his name was Joakim:

13:2. And he took a wife, whose name was Susanna, the daughter of Helcias, a bery beautiful woman, and one that feared God.

13:3. For her parents being just, had instructed their daughter according to the law of Moses.

13:4. Now Joakim was very rich, and had an orchard near his house: and the Jews resorted to him, because he was the most honourable of them all.

13:5. And there were two of the ancients of the people appointed judges that year, of whom the Lord said: That iniquity came out from Babylon, from the ancient judges, that seemed to govern the people.

13:6. These men frequented the house of Joakim, and all that hand any maters of judgment came to them.

13:7. And when the people departed away at noon, Susanna went in, and walked in her husband's orchard.

13:8. And the old men saw her going in every day, and walking: and they were inflamed with lust towards her:

13:9. And they perverted their own mind, and turned away their eyes, that they might not look unto heaven, nor remember just judgments.

13:10. So they were both wounded with the love of her, yet they did not make known their grief one to the other.

13:11. For they were ashamed to declare to one another their lust, being desirous to have to do with her:

13:12. And they watched carefully every day to see her. And one said to the other:

13:13. Let us now go home, for it is dinner time. So going out, they departed one from another.

13:14. And turning back again, they came both to the same place: and asking one another the cause, they acknowledged their lust: and then they agreed together upon a time, when they might find her alone.

13:15. And it fell out, as they watched a fit day, she went in on a time, as yesterday and the day before, with two maids only, and was desirous to wash herself in the orchard: for it was hot weather.

13:16. And there was nobody there, but the two old men that had hid themselves, and were beholding her.

13:17. So she said to the maids: Bring me oil, and washing balls, and shut the doors of the orchard, that I may wash me.

13:18. And they did as she bade them: and they shut the doors of the orchard, and went out by a back door to fetch what she had commanded them, and they knew not that the elders were hid within.

13:19. Now when the maids were gone forth, the two elders arose, and ran to her, and said:

13:20. Behold the doors of the orchard are shut, and nobody seeth us, and we are in love with thee: wherefore consent to us, and lie with us.

13:21. But if thou wilt not, we will bear witness against thee, that a young man was with thee, and therefore thou didst send away thy maids form thee.

13:22. Susanna sighed, and said: I am straitened on every side: for if I do this thing, it is death to me: and if I do it not, I shall not escape your hands.

13:23. But it is better for me to fall into your hands without doing it, than to sin in the sight of the Lord.

13:24. With that Susanna cried out with a loud voice: and the elders also cried out against her.

13:25. And one of them ran to the door of the orchard, and opened it.

13:26. So when the servants of the house heard the cry in the orchard, they rushed in by the back door, to see what was the matter.

13:27. But after the old men had spoken, the servants were greatly ashamed: for never had there been any such word said of Susanna. And on the next day,

13:28. When the people were come to Joakim, her husband, the two elders also came full of wicked device against Susanna, to put her to death.

13:29. And they said before the people: Send to Susanna, daughter of Helcias, the wife of Joakim. And presently they sent.

13:30. And she came with her parents, and children and all her kindred.

13:31. Now Susanna was exceeding delicate, and beautiful to behold.

13:32. But those wicked men commanded that her face should be uncovered, (for she was covered) that so at least they might be satisfied with her beauty.

13:33. Therefore her friends, and all her acquaintance wept.

13:34. But the two elders rising up in the midst of the people, laid their hands upon her head.

13:35. And she weeping, looked kup to heaven, for her heart had confidence in the Lord.

13:36. And the elders said: As we walked in the orchard alone, this woman came in with two maids, and shut the doors of the orchard, ans sent away the maids from her.

13:37. Then a young man that was there hid came to her, and lay with her.

13:38. But we that were in a corner of the orchard, seeing this wickedness, ran up to them, and we saw them lie together.

13:39. And him indeed we could not take, because he was stronger than us, and opening the doors, he leaped out:

13:40. But having taken this woman, we asked who the young man was, but she would not tell us: of this thing we are witnesses.

13:41. The multitude believed them, as being the elders, and the judges of the people, and they condemned her to death.

13:42. Then Susanna cried out with a loud voice, and said: O eternal God, who knowest hidden things, who knowest all things before they come to pass,

13:43. Thou knowest that they have borne false witness against me: and behold I must die, whereas I have done none of these things, which these men have maliciously forged against me.

13:44. And the Lord heard her voice.

13:45. And when she was led to be put to death, the Lord raised up the holy spirit of a young boy, whose name was Daniel:

13:46. And he cried out with a loud voice: I am clear from the blood of this woman.

13:47. Then all the people turning themselves towards him, said: What meaneth this word that thou hast spoken?

13:48. But he standing in the midst of them, said: Are ye so foolish, ye children of Israel, that without examination or knowledge of the truth, you have condemned a daughter of Israel?

13:49. Return to judgment, for they have borne false witness against her.

13:50. So all the people turned again in haste, and the old men said to him: Come, and sit thou down among us, and shew it us: seeing God hath given thee the honour of old age.

13:51. And Daniel said to the people: Separate these two far from one another, and I will examine them.

13:52. So when they were put asunder one from the other, he called one of them, and said to him: O thou that art grown old in evil days, now are thy sins come out, which thou hast committed before:

13:53. In judging unjust judgments, oppressing the innocent, and letting the guilty to go free, whereas the Lord saith: The innocent and the just thou shalt not kill.

13:54. Now then if thou sawest her, tell me under what tree thou sawest them conversing together. He said. Under a mastic tree.

13:55. And Daniel said: Welll hast thou lide against thy own head: for behold the angel of God having recieved the sentence of him, shall cut thee in two.

13:56. And having put him aside, he commanded that the other should come, and he said to him: O thou seed of Chanaan, and not of Juda, beauty hath deceived tee, and lust hath perverted thy heart:

13:57. Thus did you do to the daughters of Israel, and they for fear conversed with you: but a daughter of Juda would not abide your wickedness.

13:58. Now, therefore, tell me, under what tree didst thou take them conversing together. And he answered: Under a holm tree.

13:59. And Daniel said to him: Well hast thou also lied against thy own head: for the angel of the Lord waiteth with a sword to cut thee in two, and to destroy you.

13:60. With that all the assembly cried out with a loud voice, and they blessed God, who saveth them that trust in him.

13:61. And they rose up against the two elders, (for Daniel had convicted them of false witness by their own mouth) and they did to them as they had maliciously dealt against their neighbour,

13:62. To fulfil the law of Moses: and they put them to death, and innocent blood was saved in that day.

13:63. But Helcias, and his wife, praised God, for their daughter, Susanna, with Joakim, her husband, and all her kindred, because there was no dishonesty found in her.

13:64. And Daniel became great in the sight of the people from that day, and thence forward.

13:65. And king Astyages was gathered to his fathers; and Cyrus, the Persian, received his kingdom.

Daniel Chapter 14

The history of Bel, and of the great serpent worshipped by the Babylonians.

14:1. And Daniel was the king's guest, and was honoured above all his friends.

The king's guest... It seems most probable, that the king here spoken of was Evilmerodach, the son and successor of Nabuchodonosor, and a great favourer of the Jews.

14:2. Now the Babylonians had an idol called Bel: and there was spent upon him every day twelve great measures of fine flour, and forty sheep, and six vessels of wine.

14:3. The king also worshipped him, and went every day to adore him: but Daniel adored his God. And the king said to him: Why dost thou not adore Bel?

14:4. And he answered, and said to him: Because I do not worship idols made with hands, but the living God, that created heaven and earth, and hath power over all flesh.

14:5. And the king said to him: Doth not Bel seem to thee to be a living god? Seest thou not how much he eateth and drinketh every day?

14:6. Then Daniel smiled, and siad: O king, be not deceived: for this is but clay within, and brass without, neither hath he eaten at any time.

14:7. And the king being angry, called for his priests, and siad to them: If you tell me not who it is that eateth up these expenses, you shall die.

14:8. But if you can shew that Bel eateth these things, Daniel shall die, because he hath blasphemed against Bel. And Daniel said to the king: Be it done according to thy word.

14:9. Now the priests of Bel were seventy, beside their wives, and little ones, and children. And the king went with Daniel into the temple of Bel.

14:10. And the priests of Bel said: Behold, we go out: and do thou, O king, set on the meats, and make ready the wine, and shut the door fast, and seal it with thy own ring:

14:11. And when thou comest in the morning, if thou findest not that Bel hath eaten up all, we will suffer death, or else Daniel, that hath lied against us.

14:12. And they little regarded it, because they had made under the table a secret entrance, and they always came in by it, and consumed those things.

14:13. So it came to pass after they were gone out, the king set the meats before Bel: and Daniel commanded his servants, and they brought ashes, and he sifted them all over the temple before the king: and going forth, they shut the door, and having sealed it with the king's ring, they departed.

14:14. But the priests went in by night, according to their custom, with their wives, and their children: and they eat and drank up all.

14:15. And the king arose early in the morning, and Daniel with him.

14:16. And the king said: Are the seals whole, Daniel? And he answered: They lare whole, O king.

14:17. And as soon as he had opened the door, the king looked upon the table, and cried out with a loud voice: Great art thou, O Bel, and there is not any deceit with thee.

14:18. And Daniel laughed: and he held the king, that he should not go in: and he said: Behold the pavement, mark whose footsteps these are.

14:19. And the king said: I see the footsteps of men, and women, and children. And the king was angry.

14:20. Then he took the priests, and their wives, and their children: and they shewed him the private doors by which they came in, and consumed the things that were on the table.

14:21. The king, therefore, put them to death, and delivered Bel into the power of Daniel: who destroyed him and his temple.

14:22. And there was a great dragon in that place, and the Babylonians worshipped him.

14:23. And the king said to Daniel: Behold, thou canst not say now, that this is not a living god: adore him, therefore.

14:24. And Daniel said: I adore the Lord, my God: for he is the living God: but that is no living god.

14:25. But give me leave, O king, and I will kill this dreagon without sword or club. And the king said, I give thee leave.

14:26. Then Daniel took pitch, and fat, and hair, and boiled them together: and he made lumps, and put them into the dragon's mouth, and the dragon burst asunder. And he said: Behold him whom you worship.

14:27. And when the Babylonians had heard this, they took great indignation: and being gathered together against the king, they said: The king is become a Jew. He hath destroyed Bel, he hath killed the dragon, and he hath put the priests to death.

14:28. And they came to the king, and said: Deliver us Daniel, or else we will destroy thee and thy house.

14:29. And the king saw that they pressed upon him violently: and being constrained by necessity: he delivered Daniel to them.

14:30. And they cast him into the den of lions, and he was there six days.

The den of lions... Daniel was twice cast into the den of lions; one under Darius the Mede, because he had transgressed the king's edict, by praying three times a day: and another time under Evilmerodach by a sedition of the people. This time he remained six days in the lions' den; the other time only one night.

14:31. And in the den there were seven lions, and they had given to them two carcasses every day, and two sheep: but then they were not given unto them, that they might devour

Daniel.

14:32. Now there was in Judea a prophet called Habacuc, and he had boiled pottage, and had broken bread in a bowl: and was going into the field, to carry it to the reapers.

Habacuc... The same, as some think whose prophecy is found among the lesser prophets but others believe him to be different.

14:33. And the angel of the Lord said to Habacuc: Carry the dinner which thou hast into Babylon, to Daniel, who is in the lions' den.

14:34. And Habacuc said: Lord, I never saw Babylon, nor do I know the den.

14:35. And the angel of the Lord took him by the top of his head, and carried him by the hair of his head, and set him in Babylon, over the den, in the force of his spirit.

14:36. And Habacuc cried, saying: O Daniel, thou servant of God, take the dinner that God hath sent thee.

14:37. And Daniel said, Thou hast remembered me, O God, and thou hast not forsaken them that love thee.

14:38. And Daniel arose, and eat. And the angel of the Lord presently set Habacuc again in his own place.

14:39. And upon the seventh day the king came to bewail Daniel: and he came to the den, and looked in, and behold Daniel was sitting in the midst of the lions.

14:40. And the king cried out with a loud voice, saying: Great art thou, O Lord, the God of DAniel. And he drew him out of the lions' den.

14:41. But those that had been the cause of his destruction, he cast into the den, and they were devoured in a moment before him.

14:42. Then the king said: Let all the inhabitants of the whole earth fear the God of Daniel: for he is the Saviour, working signs, and wonders in the earth: who hath delivered Daniel out of the lions' den.

THE BOOK OF DANIEL

AMERICAN STANDARD BIBLE

1

1 In the third year of the reign of Jehoiakim king of Judah came Nebuchadnezzar king of Babylon unto Jerusalem, and besieged it.

2 And the Lord gave Jehoiakim king of Judah into his hand, with part of the vessels of the house of God; and he carried them into the land of Shinar to the house of his god: and he brought the vessels into the treasure-house of his god.

3 And the king spake unto Ashpenaz the master of his eunuchs, that he should bring in certain of the children of Israel, even of the seed royal and of the nobles;

4 youths in whom was no blemish, but well-favored, and skilful in all wisdom, and endued with knowledge, and understanding science, and such as had ability to stand in the king's palace; and that he should teach them the learning and the tongue of the Chaldeans.

5 And the king appointed for them a daily portion of the king's dainties, and of the wine which he drank, and that they should be nourished three years; that at the end thereof they should stand before the king.

6 Now among these were, of the children of Judah, Daniel, Hananiah, Mishael, and Azariah.

7 And the prince of the eunuchs gave names unto them: unto Daniel he gave the name of Belteshazzar; and to Hananiah, of Shadrach; and to Mishael, of Meshach; and to Azariah, of Abed-nego.

8 But Daniel purposed in his heart that he would not defile himself with the king's dainties, nor with the wine which he drank: therefore he requested of the prince of the eunuchs that he might not defile himself.

9 Now God made Daniel to find kindness and compassion in the sight of the prince of the eunuchs.

10 And the prince of the eunuchs said unto Daniel, I fear my lord the king, who hath appointed your food and your drink: for why should he see your faces worse looking than the youths that are of your own age? so would ye endanger my head with the king.

11 Then said Daniel to the steward whom the prince of the eunuchs had appointed over Daniel, Hananiah, Mishael, and Azariah:

12 Prove thy servants, I beseech thee, ten days; and let them give us pulse to eat, and water to drink.

13 Then let our countenances be looked upon before thee, and the countenance of the youths that eat of the king's dainties; and as thou seest, deal with thy servants.

14 So he hearkened unto them in this matter, and proved them ten days.

15 And at the end of ten days their countenances appeared fairer, and they were fatter in flesh, than all the youths that did eat of the king's dainties.

16 So the steward took away their dainties, and the wine that they should drink, and gave them pulse.

17 Now as for these four youths, God gave them knowledge and skill in all learning and wisdom: and Daniel had understanding in all visions and dreams.

18 And at the end of the days which the king had appointed for bringing them in, the prince of the eunuchs brought them in before Nebuchadnezzar.

19 And the king communed with them; and among them all was found none like Daniel, Hananiah, Mishael, and Azariah: therefore stood they before the king.

20 And in every matter of wisdom and understanding, concerning which the king inquired of them, he found them ten times better than all the magicians and enchanters that were in all his realm.

21 And Daniel continued even unto the first year of king Cyrus.

2

1 And in the second year of the reign of Nebuchadnezzar, Nebuchadnezzar dreamed dreams; and his spirit was troubled, and his sleep went from him.

2 Then the king commanded to call the magicians, and the enchanters, and the sorcerers, and the Chaldeans, to tell the king his dreams. So they came in and stood before the king.

3 And the king said unto them, I have dreamed a dream, and my spirit is troubled to know the dream.

4 Then spake the Chaldeans to the king in the Syrian language, O king, live for ever: tell thy servants the dream, and we will show the interpretation.

5 The king answered and said to the Chaldeans, The thing is gone from me: if ye make not known unto me the dream and the interpretation thereof, ye shall be cut in pieces, and your houses shall be made a dunghill.

6 But if ye show the dream and the interpretation thereof, ye shall receive of me gifts and rewards and great honor: therefore show me the dream and the interpretation thereof.

7 They answered the second time and said, Let the king tell his servants the dream, and we will show the interpretation.

8 The king answered and said, I know of a certainty that ye would gain time, because ye see the thing is gone from me.

9 But if ye make not known unto me the dream, there is but one law for you; for ye have prepared lying and corrupt words to speak before me, till the time be changed: therefore tell me the dream, and I shall know that ye can show me the interpretation thereof.

10 The Chaldeans answered before the king, and said, There is not a man upon the earth that can show the king's matter, forasmuch as no king, lord, or ruler, hath asked such a thing of any magician, or enchanter, or Chaldean.

11 And it is a rare thing that the king requireth, and there is no other that can show it before the king, except the gods, whose dwelling is not with flesh.

12 For this cause the king was angry and very furious, and commanded to destroy all the wise men of Babylon.

13 So the decree went forth, and the wise men were to be slain; and they sought Daniel and his companions to be slain.

14 Then Daniel returned answer with counsel and prudence to Arioch the captain of the king's guard, who was gone forth to slay the wise men of Babylon;

15 he answered and said to Arioch the king's captain, Wherefore is the decree so urgent from the king? Then Arioch made the thing known to Daniel.

16 And Daniel went in, and desired of the king that he would appoint him a time, and he would show the king the interpretation.

17 Then Daniel went to his house, and made the thing known to Hananiah, Mishael, and Azariah, his companions:

18 that they would desire mercies of the God of heaven concerning this secret; that Daniel and his companions should not perish with the rest of the wise men of Babylon.

19 Then was the secret revealed unto Daniel in a vision of the night. Then Daniel blessed the God of heaven.

20 Daniel answered and said, Blessed be the name of God for ever and ever; for wisdom and might are his.

21 And he changeth the times and the seasons; he removeth kings, and setteth up kings; he giveth wisdom unto the wise, and knowledge to them that have understanding;

22 he revealeth the deep and secret things; he knoweth what is in the darkness, and the light dwelleth with him.

23 I thank thee, and praise thee, O thou God of my fathers, who hast given me wisdom and might, and hast now made known unto me what we desired of thee; for thou hast made known unto us the king's matter.

24 Therefore Daniel went in unto Arioch, whom the king had appointed to destroy the wise men of Babylon; he went and said thus unto him: Destroy not the wise men of Babylon; bring me in before the king, and I will show unto the king the interpretation.

25 Then Arioch brought in Daniel before the king in haste, and said thus unto him, I have found a man of the children of the captivity of Judah, that will make known unto the king the interpretation.

26 The king answered and said to Daniel, whose name was Belteshazzar, Art thou able to make known unto me the dream which I have seen, and the interpretation thereof?

27 Daniel answered before the king, and said, The secret which the king hath demanded can neither wise men, enchanters, magicians, nor soothsayers, show unto the king;

28 but there is a God in heaven that revealeth secrets, and he hath made known to the king Nebuchadnezzar what shall be in the latter days. Thy dream, and the visions of thy head upon thy bed, are these:

29 as for thee, O king, thy thoughts came into thy mind upon thy bed, what should come to pass hereafter; and he that revealeth secrets hath made known to thee what shall come to pass.

30 But as for me, this secret is not revealed to me for any wisdom that I have more than any living, but to the intent that the interpretation may be made known to the king, and that thou mayest know the thoughts of thy heart.

31 Thou, O king, sawest, and, behold, a great image. This image, which was mighty, and whose brightness was excellent, stood before thee; and the aspect thereof was terrible.

32 As for this image, its head was of fine gold, its breast and its arms of silver, its belly and its thighs of brass,

33 its legs of iron, its feet part of iron, and part of clay.

34 Thou sawest till that a stone was cut out without hands, which smote the image upon its feet that were of iron and clay, and brake them in pieces.

35 Then was the iron, the clay, the brass, the silver, and the gold, broken in pieces together, and became like the chaff of the summer threshing-floors; and the wind carried them away, so that no place was found for them: and the stone that smote the image became a great mountain, and filled the whole earth.

36 This is the dream; and we will tell the interpretation thereof before the king.

37 Thou, O king, art king of kings, unto whom the God of heaven hath given the kingdom, the power, and the strength, and the glory;

38 and wheresoever the children of men dwell, the beasts of the field and the birds of the heavens hath he given into thy hand, and hath made thee to rule over them all: thou art the head of gold.

39 And after thee shall arise another kingdom inferior to thee; and another third kingdom of brass, which shall bear rule over all the earth.

40 And the fourth kingdom shall be strong as iron, forasmuch as iron breaketh in pieces and subdueth all things; and as iron that crusheth all these, shall it break in pieces and crush.

41 And whereas thou sawest the feet and toes, part of potters' clay, and part of iron, it shall be a divided kingdom; but there shall be in it of the strength of the iron, forasmuch as thou sawest the iron mixed with miry clay.

42 And as the toes of the feet were part of iron, and part of clay, so the kingdom shall be partly strong, and partly broken.

43 And whereas thou sawest the iron mixed with miry clay, they shall mingle themselves with the seed of men; but they shall not cleave one to another, even as iron doth not mingle with clay.

44 And in the days of those kings shall the God of heaven set up a kingdom which shall never be destroyed, nor shall the sovereignty thereof be left to another people; but it shall break in pieces and consume all these kingdoms, and it shall stand for ever.

45 Forasmuch as thou sawest that a stone was cut out of the mountain without hands, and that it brake in pieces the iron, the brass, the clay, the silver, and the gold; the great God hath made known to the king what shall come to pass hereafter: and the dream is certain, and the interpretation thereof sure.

46 Then the king Nebuchadnezzar fell upon his face, and worshipped Daniel, and commanded that they should offer an oblation and sweet odors unto him.

47 The king answered unto Daniel, and said, Of a truth your God is the God of gods, and the Lord of kings, and a revealer of secrets, seeing thou hast been able to reveal this secret.

48 Then the king made Daniel great, and gave him many great gifts, and made him to rule over the whole province of Babylon, and to be chief governor over all the wise men of Babylon.

49 And Daniel requested of the king, and he appointed Shadrach, Meshach, and Abed-nego, over the affairs of the province of Babylon: but Daniel was in the gate of the king.

3

1 Nebuchadnezzar the king made an image of gold, whose height was threescore cubits, and the breadth thereof six cubits: he set it up in the plain of Dura, in the province of Babylon.

2 Then Nebuchadnezzar the king sent to gather together the satraps, the deputies, and the governors, the judges, the treasurers, the counsellors, the sheriffs, and all the rulers of the provinces, to come to the dedication of the image which Nebuchadnezzar the king had set up.

3 Then the satraps, the deputies, and the governors, the judges, the treasurers, the counsellors, the sheriffs, and all the rulers of the provinces, were gathered together unto the dedication of the image that Nebuchadnezzar the king had set up; and they stood before the image that Nebuchadnezzar had set up.

4 Then the herald cried aloud, To you it is commanded, O peoples, nations, and languages,

5 that at what time ye hear the sound of the cornet, flute, harp, sackbut, psaltery, dulcimer, and all kinds of music, ye fall down and worship the golden image that Nebuchadnezzar the king hath set up;

6 and whoso falleth not down and worshippeth shall the same hour be cast into the midst of a burning fiery furnace.

7 Therefore at that time, when all the peoples heard the sound of the cornet, flute, harp, sackbut, psaltery, and all kinds of music, all the peoples, the nations, and the languages, fell down and worshipped the golden image that Nebuchadnezzar the king had set up.

8 Wherefore at that time certain Chaldeans came near, and brought accusation against the Jews.

9 They answered and said to Nebuchadnezzar the king, O king, live for ever.

10 Thou, O king, hast made a decree, that every man that shall hear the sound of the cornet, flute, harp, sackbut, psaltery, and dulcimer, and all kinds of music, shall fall down and worship the golden image;

11 and whoso falleth not down and worshippeth, shall be cast into the midst of a burning fiery furnace.

12 There are certain Jews whom thou hast appointed over the affairs of the province of Babylon: Shadrach, Meshach, and Abed-nego; these men, O king, have not regarded thee: they serve not thy gods, nor worship the golden image which thou hast set up.

13 Then Nebuchadnezzar in his rage and fury commanded to bring Shadrach, Meshach, and Abed-nego. Then they brought these men before the king.

14 Nebuchadnezzar answered and said unto them, Is it of purpose, O Shadrach, Meshach, and Abed-nego, that ye serve not my god, nor worship the golden image which I have set up?

15 Now if ye be ready that at what time ye hear the sound of the cornet, flute, harp, sackbut, psaltery, and dulcimer, and all kinds of music, ye fall down and worship the image which I have made, well: but if ye worship not, ye shall be cast the same hour into the midst of a burning fiery furnace; and who is that god that shall deliver you out of my hands?

16 Shadrach, Meshach, and Abed-nego answered and said to the king, O Nebuchadnezzar, we have no need to answer thee in this matter.

17 If it be so, our God whom we serve is able to deliver us from the burning fiery furnace; and he will deliver us out of thy hand, O king.

18 But if not, be it known unto thee, O king, that we will not serve thy gods, nor worship the golden image which thou hast set up.

19 Then was Nebuchadnezzar full of fury, and the form of his visage was changed against Shadrach, Meshach, and Abed-nego: therefore he spake, and commanded that they should heat the furnace seven times more than it was wont to be heated.

20 And he commanded certain mighty men that were in his army to bind Shadrach, Meshach, and Abed-nego, and to cast them into the burning fiery furnace.

21 Then these men were bound in their hosen, their tunics, and their mantles, and their other garments, and were cast into the midst of the burning fiery furnace.

22 Therefore because the king's commandment was urgent, and the furnace exceeding hot, the flame of the fire slew those men that took up Shadrach, Meshach, and Abed-nego.

23 And these three men, Shadrach, Meshach, and Abed-nego, fell down bound into the midst of the burning fiery furnace.

24 Then Nebuchadnezzar the king was astonished, and rose up in haste: he spake and said unto his counsellors, Did not we cast three men bound into the midst of the fire? They answered and said unto the king, True, O king.

25 He answered and said, Lo, I see four men loose, walking in the midst of the fire, and they have no hurt; and the aspect of the fourth is like a son of the gods.

26 Then Nebuchadnezzar came near to the mouth of the burning fiery furnace: he spake and said, Shadrach, Meshach, and Abed-nego, ye servants of the Most High God, come forth, and come hither. Then Shadrach, Meshach, and Abed-nego came forth out of the midst of the fire.

27 And the satraps, the deputies, and the governors, and the king's counsellors, being gathered together, saw these men, that the fire had no power upon their bodies, nor was the hair of their head singed, neither were their hosen changed, nor had the smell of fire passed on them.

28 Nebuchadnezzar spake and said, Blessed be the God of Shadrach, Meshach, and Abed-nego, who hath sent his angel, and delivered his servants that trusted in him, and have changed the king's word, and have yielded their bodies, that they might not serve nor worship any god, except their own God.

29 Therefore I make a decree, that every people, nation, and language, which speak anything

amiss against the God of Shadrach, Meshach, and Abed-nego, shall be cut in pieces, and their houses shall be made a dunghill; because there is no other god that is able to deliver after this sort.

30 Then the king promoted Shadrach, Meshach, and Abed-nego in the province of Babylon.

4

1 Nebuchadnezzar the king, unto all the peoples, nations, and languages, that dwell in all the earth: Peace be multiplied unto you.

2 It hath seemed good unto me to show the signs and wonders that the Most High God hath wrought toward me.

3 How great are his signs! and how mighty are his wonders! his kingdom is an everlasting kingdom, and his dominion is from generation to generation.

4 I, Nebuchadnezzar, was at rest in my house, and flourishing in my palace.

5 I saw a dream which made me afraid; and the thoughts upon my bed and the visions of my head troubled me.

6 Therefore made I a decree to bring in all the wise men of Babylon before me, that they might make known unto me the interpretation of the dream.

7 Then came in the magicians, the enchanters, the Chaldeans, and the soothsayers; and I told the dream before them; but they did not make known unto me the interpretation thereof.

8 But at the last Daniel came in before me, whose name was Belteshazzar, according to the name of my god, and in whom is the spirit of the holy gods: and I told the dream before him, saying,

9 O Belteshazzar, master of the magicians, because I know that the spirit of the holy gods is in thee, and no secret troubleth thee, tell me the visions of my dream that I have seen, and the interpretation thereof.

10 Thus were the visions of my head upon my bed: I saw, and, behold, a tree in the midst of the earth; and the height thereof was great.

11 The tree grew, and was strong, and the height thereof reached unto heaven, and the sight thereof to the end of all the earth.

12 The leaves thereof were fair, and the fruit thereof much, and in it was food for all: the beasts of the field had shadow under it, and the birds of the heavens dwelt in the branches thereof, and all flesh was fed from it.

13 I saw in the visions of my head upon my bed, and, behold, a watcher and a holy one came down from heaven.

14 He cried aloud, and said thus, Hew down the tree, and cut off its branches, shake off its leaves, and scatter its fruit: let the beasts get away from under it, and the fowls from its branches.

15 Nevertheless leave the stump of its roots in the earth, even with a band of iron and brass, in the tender grass of the field; and let it be wet with the dew of heaven: and let his portion be with the beasts in the grass of the earth:

16 let his heart be changed from man's, and let a beast's heart be given unto him; and let seven times pass over him.

17 The sentence is by the decree of the watchers, and the demand by the word of the holy ones; to the intent that the living may know that the Most High ruleth in the kingdom of men, and giveth it to whomsoever he will, and setteth up over it the lowest of men.

18 This dream I, king Nebuchadnezzar, have seen; and thou, O Belteshazzar, declare the interpretation, forasmuch as all the wise men of my kingdom are not able to make known unto me the interpretation; but thou art able; for the spirit of the holy gods is in thee.

19 Then Daniel, whose name was Belteshazzar, was stricken dumb for a while, and his thoughts troubled him. The king answered and said, Belteshazzar, let not the dream, or the interpretation, trouble thee. Belteshazzar answered and said, My lord, the dream be to them that hate thee, and the interpretation thereof to thine adversaries.

20 The tree that thou sawest, which grew, and was strong, whose height reached unto heaven, and the sight thereof to all the earth;

21 whose leaves were fair, and the fruit thereof much, and in it was food for all; under which the beasts of the field dwelt, and upon whose branches the birds of the heavens had their habitation:

22 it is thou, O king, that art grown and become strong; for thy greatness is grown, and reacheth unto heaven, and thy dominion to the end of the earth.

23 And whereas the king saw a watcher and a holy one coming down from heaven, and saying, Hew down the tree, and destroy it; nevertheless leave the stump of the roots thereof in the earth, even with a band of iron and brass, in the tender grass of the field, and let it be wet with the dew of heaven: and let his portion be with the beasts of the field, till seven times pass over him;

24 this is the interpretation, O king, and it is the decree of the Most High, which is come upon my lord the king:

25 that thou shalt be driven from men, and thy dwelling shall be with the beasts of the field, and thou shalt be made to eat grass as oxen, and shalt be wet with the dew of heaven, and seven times shall pass over thee; till thou know that the Most High ruleth in the kingdom of men, and giveth it to whomsoever he will.

26 And whereas they commanded to leave the stump of the roots of the tree; thy kingdom shall be sure unto thee, after that thou shalt have known that the heavens do rule.

27 Wherefore, O king, let my counsel be acceptable unto thee, and break off thy sins by righteousness, and thine iniquities by showing mercy to the poor; if there may be a lengthening of thy tranquillity.

28 All this came upon the king Nebuchadnezzar.

29 At the end of twelve months he was walking in the royal palace of Babylon.

30 The king spake and said, Is not this great Babylon, which I have built for the royal dwelling-place, by the might of my power and for the glory of my majesty?

31 While the word was in the king's mouth, there fell a voice from heaven, saying, O king Nebuchadnezzar, to thee it is spoken: The kingdom is departed from thee:

32 and thou shalt be driven from men; and they dwelling shall be with the beasts of the field; thou shalt be made to eat grass as oxen; and seven times shall pass over thee; until thou know that the Most High ruleth in the kingdom of men, and giveth it to whomsoever he will.

33 The same hour was the thing fulfilled upon Nebuchadnezzar: and he was driven from men, and did eat grass as oxen, and his body was wet with the dew of heaven, till his hair was grown like eagles' feathers, and his nails like birds' claws.

34 And at the end of the days I, Nebuchadnezzar, lifted up mine eyes unto heaven, and mine understanding returned unto me, and I blessed the Most High, and I praised and honored him that liveth for ever; for his dominion is an everlasting dominion, and his kingdom from generation to generation.

35 And all the inhabitants of the earth are reputed as nothing; and he doeth according to his will in the army of heaven, and among the inhabitants of the earth; and none can stay his hand, or say unto him, What doest thou?

36 At the same time mine understanding returned unto me; and for the glory of my kingdom, my majesty and brightness returned unto me; and my counsellors and my lords sought unto me; and I was established in my kingdom, and excellent greatness was added unto me.

37 Now I, Nebuchadnezzar, praise and extol and honor the King of heaven; for all his works are truth, and his ways justice; and those that walk in pride he is able to abase.

5

1 Belshazzar the king made a great feast to a thousand of his lords, and drank wine before

the thousand.

2 Belshazzar, while he tasted the wine, commanded to bring the golden and silver vessels which Nebuchadnezzar his father had taken out of the temple which was in Jerusalem; that the king and his lords, his wives and his concubines, might drink therefrom.

3 Then they brought the golden vessels that were taken out of the temple of the house of God which was at Jerusalem; and the king and his lords, his wives and his concubines, drank from them.

4 They drank wine, and praised the gods of gold, and of silver, of brass, of iron, of wood, and of stone.

5 In the same hour came forth the fingers of a man's hand, and wrote over against the candlestick upon the plaster of the wall of the king's palace: and the king saw the part of the hand that wrote.

6 Then the king's countenance was changed in him, and his thoughts troubled him; and the joints of his loins were loosed, and his knees smote one against another.

7 The king cried aloud to bring in the enchanters, the Chaldeans, and the soothsayers. The king spake and said to the wise men of Babylon, Whosoever shall read this writing, and show me the interpretation thereof, shall be clothed with purple, and have a chain of gold about his neck, and shall be the third ruler in the kingdom.

8 Then came in all the king's wise men; but they could not read the writing, nor make known to the king the interpretation.

9 Then was king Belshazzar greatly troubled, and his countenance was changed in him, and his lords were perplexed.

10 Now the queen by reason of the words of the king and his lords came into the banquet house: the queen spake and said, O king, live forever; let not thy thoughts trouble thee, nor let thy countenance be changed.

11 There is a man in thy kingdom, in whom is the spirit of the holy gods; and in the days of thy father light and understanding and wisdom, like the wisdom of the gods, were found in him; and the king Nebuchadnezzar thy father, the king, I say, thy father, made him master of the magicians, enchanters, Chaldeans, and soothsayers;

12 forasmuch as an excellent spirit, and knowledge, and understanding, interpreting of dreams, and showing of dark sentences, and dissolving of doubts, were found in the same Daniel, whom the king named Belteshazzar. Now let Daniel be called, and he will show the interpretation.

13 Then was Daniel brought in before the king. The king spake and said unto Daniel, Art thou that Daniel, who art of the children of the captivity of Judah, whom the king my father brought out of Judah?

14 I have heard of thee, that the spirit of the gods is in thee, and that light and understanding and excellent wisdom are found in thee.

15 And now the wise men, the enchanters, have been brought in before me, that they should read this writing, and make known unto me the interpretation thereof; but they could not show the interpretation of the thing.

16 But I have heard of thee, that thou canst give interpretations, and dissolve doubts; now if thou canst read the writing, and make known to me the interpretation thereof, thou shalt be clothed with purple, and have a chain of gold about thy neck, and shalt be the third ruler in the kingdom.

17 Then Daniel answered and said before the king, Let thy gifts be to thyself, and give thy rewards to another; nevertheless I will read the writing unto the king, and make known to him the interpretation.

18 O thou king, the Most High God gave Nebuchadnezzar thy father the kingdom, and greatness, and glory, and majesty:

19 and because of the greatness that he gave him, all the peoples, nations, and languages trembled and feared before him: whom he would he slew, and whom he would he kept alive; and whom he would he raised up, and whom he would he put down.

20 But when his heart was lifted up, and his spirit was hardened so that he dealt proudly, he was deposed from his kingly throne, and they took his glory from him:

21 and he was driven from the sons of men, and his heart was made like the beasts', and his dwelling was with the wild asses; he was fed with grass like oxen, and his body was wet with the dew of heaven; until he knew that the Most High God ruleth in the kingdom of men, and that he setteth up over it whomsoever he will.

22 And thou his son, O Belshazzar, hast not humbled thy heart, though thou knewest all this,

23 but hast lifted up thyself against the Lord of heaven; and they have brought the vessels of his house before thee, and thou and thy lords, thy wives and thy concubines, have drunk wine from them; and thou hast praised the gods of silver and gold, of brass, iron, wood, and stone, which see not, nor hear, nor know; and the God in whose hand thy breath is, and whose are all thy ways, hast thou not glorified.

24 Then was the part of the hand sent from before him, and this writing was inscribed.

25 And this is the writing that was inscribed: MENE, MENE, TEKEL, UPHARSIN.

26 This is the interpretation of the thing: MENE; God hath numbered thy kingdom, and brought it to an end;

27 TEKEL; thou art weighed in the balances, and art found wanting.

28 PERES; thy kingdom is divided, and given to the Medes and Persians.

29 Then commanded Belshazzar, and they clothed Daniel with purple, and put a chain of gold about his neck, and made proclamation concerning him, that he should be the third ruler in the kingdom.

30 In that night Belshazzar the Chaldean King was slain.

31 And Darius the Mede received the kingdom, being about threescore and two years old.

6

1 It pleased Darius to set over the kingdom a hundred and twenty satraps, who should be throughout the whole kingdom;

2 and over them three presidents, of whom Daniel was one; that these satraps might give account unto them, and that the king should have no damage.

3 Then this Daniel was distinguished above the presidents and the satraps, because an excellent spirit was in him; and the king thought to set him over the whole realm.

4 Then the presidents and the satraps sought to find occasion against Daniel as touching the kingdom; but they could find no occasion nor fault, forasmuch as he was faithful, neither was there any error or fault found in him.

5 Then said these men, We shall not find any occasion against this Daniel, except we find it against him concerning the law of his God.

6 Then these presidents and satraps assembled together to the king, and said thus unto him, King Darius, live for ever.

7 All the presidents of the kingdom, the deputies and the satraps, the counsellors and the governors, have consulted together to establish a royal statute, and to make a strong interdict, that whosoever shall ask a petition of any god or man for thirty days, save of thee, O king, he shall be cast into the den of lions.

8 Now, O king, establish the interdict, and sign the writing, that it be not changed, according to the law of the Medes and Persians, which altereth not.

9 Wherefore king Darius signed the writing and the interdict.

10 And when Daniel knew that the writing was signed, he went into his house (now his windows were open in his chamber toward Jerusalem) and he kneeled upon his knees three times a day, and prayed, and gave thanks before his God, as he did aforetime.

11 Then these men assembled together, and found Daniel making petition and supplication before his God.

12 Then they came near, and spake before the king concerning the king's interdict: Hast

thou not signed an interdict, that every man that shall make petition unto any god or man within thirty days, save unto thee, O king, shall be cast into the den of lions? The king answered and said, The thing is true, according to the law of the Medes and Persians, which altereth not.

13 Then answered they and said before the king, That Daniel, who is of the children of the captivity of Judah, regardeth not thee, O king, nor the interdict that thou hast signed, but maketh his petition three times a day.

14 Then the king, when he heard these words, was sore displeased, and set his heart on Daniel to deliver him; and he labored till the going down of the sun to rescue him.

15 Then these men assembled together unto the king, and said unto the king, Know, O king, that it is a law of the Medes and Persians, that no interdict nor statute which the king establisheth may be changed.

16 Then the king commanded, and they brought Daniel, and cast him into the den of lions. Now the king spake and said unto Daniel, Thy God whom thou servest continually, he will deliver thee.

17 And a stone was brought, and laid upon the mouth of the den; and the king sealed it with his own signet, and with the signet of his lords; that nothing might be changed concerning Daniel.

18 Then the king went to his palace, and passed the night fasting; neither were instruments of music brought before him: and his sleep fled from him.

19 Then the king arose very early in the morning, and went in haste unto the den of lions.

20 And when he came near unto the den to Daniel, he cried with a lamentable voice; the king spake and said to Daniel, O Daniel, servant of the living God, is thy God, whom thou servest continually, able to deliver thee from the lions?

21 Then said Daniel unto the king, O king, live for ever.

22 My God hath sent his angel, and hath shut the lions' mouths, and they have not hurt me; forasmuch as before him innocency was found in me; and also before thee, O king, have I done no hurt.

23 Then was the king exceeding glad, and commanded that they should take Daniel up out of the den. So Daniel was taken up out of the den, and no manner of hurt was found upon him, because he had trusted in his God.

24 And the king commanded, and they brought those men that had accused Daniel, and they cast them into the den of lions, them, their children, and their wives; and the lions had the mastery of them, and brake all their bones in pieces, before they came to the bottom of the den.

25 Then king Darius wrote unto all the peoples, nations, and languages, that dwell in all the earth: Peace be multiplied unto you.

26 I make a decree, that in all the dominion of my kingdom men tremble and fear before the God of Daniel; for he is the living God, and stedfast for ever, And his kingdom that which shall not be destroyed; and his dominion shall be even unto the end.

27 He delivereth and rescueth, and he worketh signs and wonders in heaven and in earth, who hath delivered Daniel from the power of the lions.

28 So this Daniel prospered in the reign of Darius, and in the reign of Cyrus the Persian.

7

1 In the first year of Belshazzar king of Babylon Daniel had a dream and visions of his head upon his bed: then he wrote the dream and told the sum of the matters.

2 Daniel spake and said, I saw in my vision by night, and, behold, the four winds of heaven brake forth upon the great sea.

3 And four great beasts came up from the sea, diverse one from another.

4 The first was like a lion, and had eagle's wings: I beheld till the wings thereof were plucked, and it was lifted up from the earth, and made to stand upon two feet as a man; and a man's

heart was given to it.

5 And, behold, another beast, a second, like to a bear; and it was raised up on one side, and three ribs were in its mouth between its teeth: and they said thus unto it, Arise, devour much flesh.

6 After this I beheld, and, lo, another, like a leopard, which had upon its back four wings of a bird; the beast had also four heads; and dominion was given to it.

7 After this I saw in the night-visions, and, behold, a fourth beast, terrible and powerful, and strong exceedingly; and it had great iron teeth; it devoured and brake in pieces, and stamped the residue with its feet: and it was diverse from all the beasts that were before it; and it had ten horns.

8 I considered the horns, and, behold, there came up among them another horn, a little one, before which three of the first horns were plucked up by the roots: and, behold, in this horn were eyes like the eyes of a man, and a mouth speaking great things.

9 I beheld till thrones were placed, and one that was ancient of days did sit: his raiment was white as snow, and the hair of his head like pure wool; his throne was fiery flames, and the wheels thereof burning fire.

10 A fiery stream issued and came forth from before him: thousands of thousands ministered unto him, and ten thousand times ten thousand stood before him: the judgment was set, and the books were opened.

11 I beheld at that time because of the voice of the great words which the horn spake; I beheld even till the beast was slain, and its body destroyed, and it was given to be burned with fire.

12 And as for the rest of the beasts, their dominion was taken away: yet their lives were prolonged for a season and a time.

13 I saw in the night-visions, and, behold, there came with the clouds of heaven one like unto a son of man, and he came even to the ancient of days, and they brought him near before him.

14 And there was given him dominion, and glory, and a kingdom, that all the peoples, nations, and languages should serve him: his dominion is an everlasting dominion, which shall not pass away, and his kingdom that which shall not be destroyed.

15 As for me, Daniel, my spirit was grieved in the midst of my body, and the visions of my head troubled me.

16 I came near unto one of them that stood by, and asked him the truth concerning all this. So he told me, and made me know the interpretation of the things.

17 These great beasts, which are four, are four kings, that shall arise out of the earth.

18 But the saints of the Most High shall receive the kingdom, and possess the kingdom for ever, even for ever and ever.

19 Then I desired to know the truth concerning the fourth beast, which was diverse from all of them, exceeding terrible, whose teeth were of iron, and its nails of brass; which devoured, brake in pieces, and stamped the residue with its feet;

20 and concerning the ten horns that were on its head, and the other horn which came up, and before which three fell, even that horn that had eyes, and a mouth that spake great things, whose look was more stout than its fellows.

21 I beheld, and the same horn made war with the saints, and prevailed against them;

22 until the ancient of days came, and judgment was given to the saints of the Most High, and the time came that the saints possessed the kingdom.

23 Thus he said, The fourth beast shall be a fourth kingdom upon earth, which shall be diverse from all the kingdoms, and shall devour the whole earth, and shall tread it down, and break it in pieces.

24 And as for the ten horns, out of this kingdom shall ten kings arise: and another shall arise after them; and he shall be diverse from the former, and he shall put down three kings.

25 And he shall speak words against the Most High, and shall wear out the saints of the Most High; and he shall think to change the times and the law; and they shall be given into

his hand until a time and times and half a time.

26 But the judgment shall be set, and they shall take away his dominion, to consume and to destroy it unto the end.

27 And the kingdom and the dominion, and the greatness of the kingdoms under the whole heaven, shall be given to the people of the saints of the Most High: his kingdom is an everlasting kingdom, and all dominions shall serve and obey him.

28 Here is the end of the matter. As for me, Daniel, my thoughts much troubled me, and my countenance was changed in me: but I kept the matter in my heart.

8

1 In the third year of the reign of king Belshazzar a vision appeared unto me, even unto me, Daniel, after that which appeared unto me at the first.

2 And I saw in the vision; now it was so, that when I saw, I was in Shushan the palace, which is in the province of Elam; and I saw in the vision, and I was by the river Ulai.

3 Then I lifted up mine eyes, and saw, and, behold, there stood before the river a ram which had two horns: and the two horns were high; but one was higher than the other, and the higher came up last.

4 I saw the ram pushing westward, and northward, and southward; and no beasts could stand before him, neither was there any that could deliver out of his hand; but he did according to his will, and magnified himself.

5 And as I was considering, behold, a he-goat came from the west over the face of the whole earth, and touched not the ground: and the goat had a notable horn between his eyes.

6 And he came to the ram that had the two horns, which I saw standing before the river, and ran upon him in the fury of his power.

7 And I saw him come close unto the ram, and he was moved with anger against him, and smote the ram, and brake his two horns; and there was no power in the ram to stand before him; but he cast him down to the ground, and trampled upon him; and there was none that could deliver the ram out of his hand.

8 And the he-goat magnified himself exceedingly: and when he was strong, the great horn was broken; and instead of it there came up four notable horns toward the four winds of heaven.

9 And out of one of them came forth a little horn, which waxed exceeding great, toward the south, and toward the east, and toward the glorious land.

10 And it waxed great, even to the host of heaven; and some of the host and of the stars it cast down to the ground, and trampled upon them.

11 Yea, it magnified itself, even to the prince of the host; and it took away from him the continual burnt-offering, and the place of his sanctuary was cast down.

12 And the host was given over to it together with the continual burnt-offering through transgression; and it cast down truth to the ground, and it did its pleasure and prospered.

13 Then I heard a holy one speaking; and another holy one said unto that certain one who spake, How long shall be the vision concerning the continual burnt-offering, and the transgression that maketh desolate, to give both the sanctuary and the host to be trodden under foot?

14 And he said unto me, Unto two thousand and three hundred evenings and mornings; then shall the sanctuary be cleansed.

15 And it came to pass, when I, even I Daniel, had seen the vision, that I sought to understand it; and, behold, there stood before me as the appearance of a man.

16 And I heard a man's voice between the banks of the Ulai, which called, and said, Gabriel, make this man to understand the vision.

17 So he came near where I stood; and when he came, I was affrighted, and fell upon my face: but he said unto me, Understand, O son of man; for the vision belongeth to the time of the end.

18 Now as he was speaking with me, I fell into a deep sleep with my face toward the ground; but he touched me, and set me upright.

19 And he said, Behold, I will make thee know what shall be in the latter time of the indignation; for it belongeth to the appointed time of the end.

20 The ram which thou sawest, that had the two horns, they are the kings of Media and Persia.

21 And the rough he-goat is the king of Greece: and the great horn that is between his eyes is the first king.

22 And as for that which was broken, in the place whereof four stood up, four kingdoms shall stand up out of the nation, but not with his power.

23 And in the latter time of their kingdom, when the transgressors are come to the full, a king of fierce countenance, and understanding dark sentences, shall stand up.

24 And his power shall be mighty, but not by his own power; and he shall destroy wonderfully, and shall prosper and do his pleasure; and he shall destroy the mighty ones and the holy people.

25 And through his policy he shall cause craft to prosper in his hand; and he shall magnify himself in his heart, and in their security shall he destroy many: he shall also stand up against the prince of princes; but he shall be broken without hand.

26 And the vision of the evenings and mornings which hath been told is true: but shut thou up the vision; for it belongeth to many days to come.

27 And I, Daniel, fainted, and was sick certain days; then I rose up, and did the king's business: and I wondered at the vision, but none understood it.

9

1 In the first year of Darius the son of Ahasuerus, of the seed of the Medes, who was made king over the realm of the Chaldeans,

2 in the first year of his reign I, Daniel, understood by the books the number of the years whereof the word of Jehovah came to Jeremiah the prophet, for the accomplishing of the desolations of Jerusalem, even seventy years.

3 And I set my face unto the Lord God, to seek by prayer and supplications, with fasting and sackcloth and ashes.

4 And I prayed unto Jehovah my God, and made confession, and said, Oh, Lord, the great and dreadful God, who keepeth covenant and lovingkindness with them that love him and keep his commandments,

5 we have sinned, and have dealt perversely, and have done wickedly, and have rebelled, even turning aside from thy precepts and from thine ordinances;

6 neither have we hearkened unto thy servants the prophets, that spake in thy name to our kings, our princes, and our fathers, and to all the people of the land.

7 O Lord, righteousness belongeth unto thee, but unto us confusion of face, as at this day; to the men of Judah, and to the inhabitants of Jerusalem, and unto all Israel, that are near, and that are far off, through all the countries whither thou hast driven them, because of their trespass that they have trespassed against thee.

8 O Lord, to us belongeth confusion of face, to our kings, to our princes, and to our fathers, because we have sinned against thee.

9 To the Lord our God belong mercies and forgiveness; for we have rebelled against him;

10 neither have we obeyed the voice of Jehovah our God, to walk in his laws, which he set before us by his servants the prophets.

11 Yea, all Israel have transgressed thy law, even turning aside, that they should not obey thy voice: therefore hath the curse been poured out upon us, and the oath that is written in the law of Moses the servant of God; for we have sinned against him.

12 And he hath confirmed his words, which he spake against us, and against our judges that judged us, by bringing upon us a great evil; for under the whole heaven hath not been done

as hath been done upon Jerusalem.

13 As it is written in the law of Moses, all this evil is come upon us: yet have we not entreated the favor of Jehovah our God, that we should turn from our iniquities, and have discernment in thy truth.

14 Therefore hath Jehovah watched over the evil, and brought it upon us; for Jehovah our God is righteous in all his works which he doeth, and we have not obeyed his voice.

15 And now, O Lord our God, that hast brought thy people forth out of the land of Egypt with a mighty hand, and hast gotten thee renown, as at this day; we have sinned, we have done wickedly.

16 O Lord, according to all thy righteousness, let thine anger and thy wrath, I pray thee, be turned away from thy city Jerusalem, thy holy mountain; because for our sins, and for the iniquities of our fathers, Jerusalem and thy people are become a reproach to all that are round about us.

17 Now therefore, O our God, hearken unto the prayer of thy servant, and to his supplications, and cause thy face to shine upon thy sanctuary that is desolate, for the Lord's sake.

18 O my God, incline thine ear, and hear; open thine eyes, and behold our desolations, and the city which is called by thy name: for we do not present our supplications before thee for our righteousness, but for thy great mercies' sake.

19 O Lord, hear; O Lord, forgive; O Lord, hearken and do; defer not, for thine own sake, O my God, because thy city and thy people are called by thy name.

20 And while I was speaking, and praying, and confessing my sin and the sin of my people Israel, and presenting my supplication before Jehovah my God for the holy mountain of my God;

21 yea, while I was speaking in prayer, the man Gabriel, whom I had seen in the vision at the beginning, being caused to fly swiftly, touched me about the time of the evening oblation.

22 And he instructed me, and talked with me, and said, O Daniel, I am now come forth to give thee wisdom and understanding.

23 At the beginning of thy supplications the commandment went forth, and I am come to tell thee; for thou art greatly beloved: therefore consider the matter, and understand the vision.

24 Seventy weeks are decreed upon thy people and upon thy holy city, to finish transgression, and to make an end of sins, and to make reconciliation for iniquity, and to bring in everlasting righteousness, and to seal up vision and prophecy, and to anoint the most holy.

25 Know therefore and discern, that from the going forth of the commandment to restore and to build Jerusalem unto the anointed one, the prince, shall be seven weeks, and threescore and two weeks: it shall be built again, with street and moat, even in troublous times.

26 And after the threescore and two weeks shall the anointed one be cut off, and shall have nothing: and the people of the prince that shall come shall destroy the city and the sanctuary; and the end thereof shall be with a flood, and even unto the end shall be war; desolations are determined.

27 And he shall make a firm covenant with many for one week: and in the midst of the week he shall cause the sacrifice and the oblation to cease; and upon the wing of abominations shall come one that maketh desolate; and even unto the full end, and that determined, shall wrath be poured out upon the desolate.

10

1 In the third year of Cyrus king of Persia a thing was revealed unto Daniel, whose name was called Belteshazzar; and the thing was true, even a great warfare: and he understood the thing, and had understanding of the vision.

2 In those days I, Daniel, was mourning three whole weeks.

3 I ate no pleasant bread, neither came flesh nor wine into my mouth, neither did I anoint myself at all, till three whole weeks were fulfilled.

4 And in the four and twentieth day of the first month, as I was by the side of the great river, which is Hiddekel,

5 I lifted up mine eyes, and looked, and, behold, a man clothed in linen, whose loins were girded with pure gold of Uphaz:

6 his body also was like the beryl, and his face as the appearance of lightning, and his eyes as flaming torches, and his arms and his feet like unto burnished brass, and the voice of his words like the voice of a multitude.

7 And I, Daniel, alone saw the vision; for the men that were with me saw not the vision; but a great quaking fell upon them, and they fled to hide themselves.

8 So I was left alone, and saw this great vision, and there remained no strength in me; for my comeliness was turned in me into corruption, and I retained no strength.

9 Yet heard I the voice of his words; and when I heard the voice of his words, then was I fallen into a deep sleep on my face, with my face toward the ground.

10 And, behold, a hand touched me, which set me upon my knees and upon the palms of my hands.

11 And he said unto me, O Daniel, thou man greatly beloved, understand the words that I speak unto thee, and stand upright; for unto thee am I now sent. And when he had spoken this word unto me, I stood trembling.

12 Then said he unto me, Fear not, Daniel; for from the first day that thou didst set thy heart to understand, and to humble thyself before thy God, thy words were heard: and I am come for thy words' sake.

13 But the prince of the kingdom of Persia withstood me one and twenty days; but, lo, Michael, one of the chief princes, came to help me: and I remained there with the kings of Persia.

14 Now I am come to make thee understand what shall befall thy people in the latter days; for the vision is yet for many days:

15 and when he had spoken unto me according to these words, I set my face toward the ground, and was dumb.

16 And, behold, one in the likeness of the sons of men touched my lips: then I opened my mouth, and spake and said unto him that stood before me, O my lord, by reason of the vision my sorrows are turned upon me, and I retain no strength.

17 For how can the servant of this my lord talk with this my lord? for as for me, straightway there remained no strength in me, neither was there breath left in me.

18 Then there touched me again one like the appearance of a man, and he strengthened me.

19 And he said, O man greatly beloved, fear not: peace be unto thee, be strong, yea, be strong. And when he spake unto me, I was strengthened, and said, Let my lord speak; for thou hast strengthened me.

20 Then said he, Knowest thou wherefore I am come unto thee? and now will I return to fight with the prince of Persia: and when I go forth, lo, the prince of Greece shall come.

21 But I will tell thee that which is inscribed in the writing of truth: and there is none that holdeth with me against these, but Michael your prince.

11

1 And as for me, in the first year of Darius the Mede, I stood up to confirm and strengthen him.

2 And now will I show thee the truth. Behold, there shall stand up yet three kings in Persia; and the fourth shall be far richer than they all: and when he is waxed strong through his riches, he shall stir up all against the realm of Greece.

3 And a mighty king shall stand up, that shall rule with great dominion, and do according to

his will.

4 And when he shall stand up, his kingdom shall be broken, and shall be divided toward the four winds of heaven, but not to his posterity, nor according to his dominion wherewith he ruled; for his kingdom shall be plucked up, even for others besides these.

5 And the king of the south shall be strong, and one of his princes; and he shall be strong above him, and have dominion; his dominion shall be a great dominion.

6 And at the end of years they shall join themselves together; and the daughter of the king of the south shall come to the king of the north to make an agreement: but she shall not retain the strength of her arm; neither shall he stand, nor his arm; but she shall be given up, and they that brought her, and he that begat her, and he that strengthened her in those times.

7 But out of a shoot from her roots shall one stand up in his place, who shall come unto the army, and shall enter into the fortress of the king of the north, and shall deal against them, and shall prevail.

8 And also their gods, with their molten images, and with their goodly vessels of silver and of gold, shall he carry captive into Egypt; and he shall refrain some years from the king of the north.

9 And he shall come into the realm of the king of the south, but he shall return into his own land.

10 And his sons shall war, and shall assemble a multitude of great forces, which shall come on, and overflow, and pass through; and they shall return and war, even to his fortress.

11 And the king of the south shall be moved with anger, and shall come forth and fight with him, even with the king of the north; and he shall set forth a great multitude, and the multitude shall be given into his hand.

12 And the multitude shall be lifted up, and his heart shall be exalted; and he shall cast down tens of thousands, but he shall not prevail.

13 And the king of the north shall return, and shall set forth a multitude greater than the former; and he shall come on at the end of the times, even of years, with a great army and with much substance.

14 And in those times there shall many stand up against the king of the south: also the children of the violent among thy people shall lift themselves up to establish the vision; but they shall fall.

15 So the king of the north shall come, and cast up a mound, and take a well-fortified city: and the forces of the south shall not stand, neither his chosen people, neither shall there be any strength to stand.

16 But he that cometh against him shall do according to his own will, and none shall stand before him; and he shall stand in the glorious land, and in his hand shall be destruction.

17 And he shall set his face to come with the strength of his whole kingdom, and with him equitable conditions; and he shall perform them: and he shall give him the daughter of women, to corrupt her; but she shall not stand, neither be for him.

18 After this shall he turn his face unto the isles, and shall take many: but a prince shall cause the reproach offered by him to cease; yea, moreover, he shall cause his reproach to turn upon him.

19 Then he shall turn his face toward the fortresses of his own land; but he shall stumble and fall, and shall not be found.

20 Then shall stand up in his place one that shall cause an exactor to pass through the glory of the kingdom; but within few days he shall be destroyed, neither in anger, nor in battle.

21 And in his place shall stand up a contemptible person, to whom they had not given the honor of the kingdom: but he shall come in time of security, and shall obtain the kingdom by flatteries.

22 And the overwhelming forces shall be overwhelmed from before him, and shall be broken; yea, also the prince of the covenant.

23 And after the league made with him he shall work deceitfully; for he shall come up, and shall become strong, with a small people.

24 In time of security shall he come even upon the fattest places of the province; and he shall do that which his fathers have not done, nor his fathers' fathers; he shall scatter among them prey, and spoil, and substance: yea, he shall devise his devices against the strongholds, even for a time.

25 And he shall stir up his power and his courage against the king of the south with a great army; and the king of the south shall war in battle with an exceeding great and mighty army; but he shall not stand; for they shall devise devices against him.

26 Yea, they that eat of his dainties shall destroy him, and his army shall overflow; and many shall fall down slain.

27 And as for both these kings, their hearts shall be to do mischief, and they shall speak lies at one table: but it shall not prosper; for yet the end shall be at the time appointed.

28 Then shall he return into his land with great substance; and his heart shall be against the holy covenant; and he shall do his pleasure, and return to his own land.

29 At the time appointed he shall return, and come into the south; but it shall not be in the latter time as it was in the former.

30 For ships of Kittim shall come against him; therefore he shall be grieved, and shall return, and have indignation against the holy covenant, and shall do his pleasure: he shall even return, and have regard unto them that forsake the holy covenant.

31 And forces shall stand on his part, and they shall profane the sanctuary, even the fortress, and shall take away the continual burnt-offering, and they shall set up the abomination that maketh desolate.

32 And such as do wickedly against the covenant shall he pervert by flatteries; but the people that know their God shall be strong, and do exploits.

33 And they that are wise among the people shall instruct many; yet they shall fall by the sword and by flame, by captivity and by spoil, many days.

34 Now when they shall fall, they shall be helped with a little help; but many shall join themselves unto them with flatteries.

35 And some of them that are wise shall fall, to refine them, and to purify, and to make them white, even to the time of the end; because it is yet for the time appointed.

36 And the king shall do according to his will; and he shall exalt himself, and magnify himself above every god, and shall speak marvellous things against the God of gods; and he shall prosper till the indignation be accomplished; for that which is determined shall be done.

37 Neither shall he regard the gods of his fathers, nor the desire of women, nor regard any god; for he shall magnify himself above all.

38 But in his place shall he honor the god of fortresses; and a god whom his fathers knew not shall he honor with gold, and silver, and with precious stones, and pleasant things.

39 And he shall deal with the strongest fortresses by the help of a foreign god: whosoever acknowledgeth him he will increase with glory; and he shall cause them to rule over many, and shall divide the land for a price.

40 And at the time of the end shall the king of the south contend with him; and the king of the north shall come against him like a whirlwind, with chariots, and with horsemen, and with many ships; and he shall enter into the countries, and shall overflow and pass through.

41 He shall enter also into the glorious land, and many countries shall be overthrown; but these shall be delivered out of his hand: Edom, and Moab, and the chief of the children of Ammon.

42 He shall stretch forth his hand also upon the countries; and the land of Egypt shall not escape.

43 But he shall have power over the treasures of gold and of silver, and over all the precious things of Egypt; and the Libyans and the Ethiopians shall be at his steps.

44 But tidings out of the east and out of the north shall trouble him; and he shall go forth with great fury to destroy and utterly to sweep away many.

45 And he shall plant the tents of his palace between the sea and the glorious holy mountain;

yet he shall come to his end, and none shall help him.

12

1 And at that time shall Michael stand up, the great prince who standeth for the children of thy people; and there shall be a time of trouble, such as never was since there was a nation even to that same time: and at that time thy people shall be delivered, every one that shall be found written in the book.

2 And many of them that sleep in the dust of the earth shall awake, some to everlasting life, and some to shame and everlasting contempt.

3 And they that are wise shall shine as the brightness of the firmament; and they that turn many to righteousness as the stars for ever and ever.

4 But thou, O Daniel, shut up the words, and seal the book, even to the time of the end: many shall run to and fro, and knowledge shall be increased.

5 Then I, Daniel, looked, and, behold, there stood other two, the one on the brink of the river on this side, and the other on the brink of the river on that side.

6 And one said to the man clothed in linen, who was above the waters of the river, How long shall it be to the end of these wonders?

7 And I heard the man clothed in linen, who was above the waters of the river, when he held up his right hand and his left hand unto heaven, and sware by him that liveth for ever that it shall be for a time, times, and a half; and when they have made an end of breaking in pieces the power of the holy people, all these things shall be finished.

8 And I heard, but I understood not: then said I, O my lord, what shall be the issue of these things?

9 And he said, Go thy way, Daniel; for the words are shut up and sealed till the time of the end.

10 Many shall purify themselves, and make themselves white, and be refined; but the wicked shall do wickedly; and none of the wicked shall understand; but they that are wise shall understand.

11 And from the time that the continual burnt-offering shall be taken away, and the abomination that maketh desolate set up, there shall be a thousand and two hundred and ninety days.

12 Blessed is he that waiteth, and cometh to the thousand three hundred and five and thirty days.

13 But go thou thy way till the end be; for thou shalt rest, and shalt stand in thy lot, at the end of the days.

DANIEL

BIBLE IN BASIC ENGLISH

1

1 In the third year of the rule of Jehoiakim, king of Judah, Nebuchadnezzar, king of Babylon, came to Jerusalem, shutting it in with his forces.

2 And the Lord gave into his hands Jehoiakim, king of Judah, with some of the vessels of the house of God; and he took them away into the land of Shinar to the house of his god; and he put the vessels into the store-house of his god.

3 And the king gave orders to Ashpenaz, the captain of his unsexed servants, to take in some of the children of Israel, certain of the king's family, and those of high birth;

4 Young men who were strong and healthy, good-looking, and trained in all wisdom, having a good education and much knowledge, and able to take positions in the king's house; and to have them trained in the writing and language of the Chaldaeans.

5 And a regular amount of food and wine every day from the king's table was ordered for them by the king; and they were to be cared for for three years so that at the end of that time they might take their places before the king.

6 And among these there were, of the children of Judah, Daniel, Hananiah, Mishael, and Azariah.

7 And the captain of the unsexed servants gave them names; to Daniel he gave the name of Belteshazzar, to Hananiah the name of Shadrach, to Mishael the name of Meshach, and to Azariah the name of Abed-nego.

8 And Daniel had come to the decision that he would not make himself unclean with the king's food or wine; so he made a request to the captain of the unsexed servants that he might not make himself unclean.

9 And God put into the heart of the captain of the unsexed servants kind feelings and pity for Daniel.

10 And the captain of the unsexed servants said to Daniel, I am in fear of my lord the king, who has given orders about your food and your drink; what if he sees you looking less happy than the other young men of your generation? then you would have put my head in danger from the king.

11 Then Daniel said to the keeper in whose care the captain of the unsexed servants had put Daniel, Hananiah, Mishael, and Azariah:

12 Put your servants to the test for ten days; let them give us grain for our food and water for our drink.

13 Then take a look at our faces and the faces of the young men who have food from the king's table; and, having seen them, do to your servants as it seems right to you.

14 So he gave ear to them in this thing and put them to the test for ten days.

15 And at the end of ten days their faces seemed fairer and they were fatter in flesh than all the young men who had their food from the king's table.

16 So the keeper regularly took away their meat and the wine which was to have been their drink, and gave them grain.

17 Now as for these four young men, God gave them knowledge and made them expert in all book-learning and wisdom: and Daniel was wise in all visions and dreams.

18 Now at the end of the time fixed by the king for them to go in, the captain of the unsexed servants took them in to Nebuchadnezzar.

19 And the king had talk with them; and among them all there was no one like Daniel, Hananiah, Mishael, and Azariah; so they were given places before the king.

20 And in any business needing wisdom and good sense, about which the king put questions to them, he saw that they were ten times better than all the wonder-workers and users of secret arts in all his kingdom.

21 And Daniel went on till the first year of King Cyrus.

2

1 In the second year of the rule of Nebuchadnezzar, Nebuchadnezzar had dreams; and his spirit was troubled and his sleep went from him.

2 Then the king gave orders that the wonder-workers, and the users of secret arts, and those who made use of evil powers, and the Chaldaeans, were to be sent for to make clear to the king his dreams. So they came and took their places before the king.

3 And the king said to them, I have had a dream, and my spirit is troubled by the desire to have the dream made clear to me.

4 Then the Chaldaeans said to the king in the Aramaean language, O King, have life for ever: give your servants an account of your dream, and we will make clear to you the sense of it.

5 The king made answer and said to the Chaldaeans, This is my decision: if you do not make clear to me the dream and the sense of it, you will be cut in bits and your houses made waste.

6 But if you make clear the dream and the sense of it, you will have from me offerings and rewards and great honour: so make clear to me the dream and the sense of it.

7 A second time they said in answer, Let the king give his servants an account of his dream, and we will make clear the sense.

8 The king made answer and said, I am certain that you are attempting to get more time, because you see that my decision is fixed;

9 That if you do not make my dream clear to me there is only one fate for you: for you have made ready false and evil words to say before me till the times are changed: so give me an account of the dream, and I will be certain that you are able to make the sense of it clear.

10 Then the Chaldaeans said to the king in answer, There is not a man on earth able to make clear the king's business; for no king, however great his power, has ever made such a request to any wonder-worker or user of secret arts or Chaldaean.

11 The king's request is a very hard one, and there is no other who is able to make it clear to the king, but the gods, whose living-place is not with flesh.

12 Because of this the king was angry and full of wrath, and gave orders for the destruction of all the wise men of Babylon.

13 So the order went out that the wise men were to be put to death; and they were looking for Daniel and his friends to put them to death.

14 Then Daniel gave an answer with wisdom and good sense to Arioch, the captain of the

king's armed men, who had gone out to put to death the wise men of Babylon;

15 He made answer and said to Arioch, O captain of the king, why is the king's order so cruel? Then Arioch gave Daniel an account of the business.

16 And Daniel went in and made a request to the king to give him time and he would make clear the sense of his dream to the king.

17 And Daniel went to his house and gave his friends Hananiah, Mishael, and Azariah the news:

18 So that they might make a request for the mercy of the God of heaven in the question of this secret; so that Daniel and his friends might not come to destruction with the rest of the wise men of Babylon.

19 Then the secret was made clear to Daniel in a vision of the night. And Daniel gave blessing to the God of heaven.

20 And Daniel said in answer, May the name of God be praised for ever and ever: for wisdom and strength are his:

21 By him times and years are changed: by him kings are taken away and kings are lifted up: he gives wisdom to the wise, and knowledge to those whose minds are awake:

22 He is the unveiler of deep and secret things: he has knowledge of what is in the dark, and the light has its living-place with him.

23 I give you praise and worship, O God of my fathers, who have given me wisdom and strength, and have now made clear to me what we were requesting from you: for you have given us knowledge of the king's business.

24 For this reason Daniel went to Arioch, to whom the king had given orders for the destruction of the wise men of Babylon, and said to him, Do not put to death the wise men of Babylon: take me in before the king and I will make clear to him the sense of the dream.

25 Then Arioch quickly took Daniel in before the king, and said to him, Here is a man from among the prisoners of Judah, who will make clear to the king the sense of the dream.

26 The king made answer and said to Daniel, whose name was Belteshazzar, Are you able to make clear to me the dream which I saw and its sense?

27 Then Daniel said in answer to the king, No wise men, or users of secret arts, or wonder-workers, or readers of signs, are able to make clear to the king the secret he is searching for;

28 But there is a God in heaven, the unveiler of secrets, and he has given to King Nebuchadnezzar knowledge of what will take place in the last days. Your dreams and the visions of your head on your bed are these:

29 As for you, O King, the thoughts which came to you on your bed were of what will come about after this: and the unveiler of secrets has made clear to you what is to come.

30 As for me, this secret is not made clear to me because of any wisdom which I have more than any living man, but in order that the sense of the dream may be made clear to the king, and that you may have knowledge of the thoughts of your heart.

31 You, O King, were looking, and a great image was there. This image, which was very great, and whose glory was very bright, was placed before you: its form sent fear into the heart.

32 As for this image, its head was made of the best gold, its breast and its arms were of silver, its middle and its sides were of brass,

33 Its legs of iron, its feet were in part of iron and in part of potter's earth.

34 While you were looking at it, a stone was cut out, but not by hands, and it gave the image a blow on its feet, which were of iron and earth, and they were broken in bits.

35 Then the iron and the earth, the brass and the silver and the gold, were smashed together, and became like the dust on the floors where grain is crushed in summer; and the wind took them away so that no sign of them was to be seen: and the stone which gave the image a blow became a great mountain, covering all the earth.

36 This is the dream; and we will make clear to the king the sense of it.

37 You, O King, king of kings, to whom the God of heaven has given the kingdom, the power, and the strength, and the glory,

38 Wherever the children of men are living; into whose hands he has given the beasts of the field and the birds of heaven, and has made you ruler over them all, you are the head of gold.

39 And after you another kingdom, lower than you, will come to power; and a third kingdom, of brass, ruling over all the earth.

40 And the fourth kingdom will be strong as iron: because, as all things are broken and overcome by iron, so it will have the power of crushing and smashing down all the earth.

41 And as you saw the feet and toes, part of potter's work and part of iron, there will be a division in the kingdom; but there will be some of the strength of iron in it, because you saw the iron mixed with the potter's earth.

42 And as the toes of the feet were in part of iron and in part of earth, so part of the kingdom will be strong and part of it will readily be broken.

43 And as you saw the iron mixed with earth, they will give their daughters to one another as wives: but they will not be united one with another, even as iron is not mixed with earth.

44 And in the days of those kings, the God of heaven will put up a kingdom which will never come to destruction, and its power will never be given into the hands of another people, and all these kingdoms will be broken and overcome by it, but it will keep its place for ever.

45 Because you saw that a stone was cut out of the mountain without hands, and that by it the iron and the brass and the earth and the silver and the gold were broken to bits, a great God has given the king knowledge of what is to take place in the future: the dream is fixed, and its sense is certain.

46 Then King Nebuchadnezzar, falling down on his face, gave worship to Daniel, and gave orders for an offering and spices to be given to him;

47 And the king made answer to Daniel and said, Truly, your God is a God of gods and a Lord of kings, and an unveiler of secrets, for you have been able to make this secret clear.

48 Then the king made Daniel great, and gave him offerings in great number, and made him ruler over all the land of Babylon, and chief over all the wise men of Babylon.

49 And at Daniel's request, the king gave Shadrach, Meshach, and Abed-nego authority over the business of the land of Babylon: but Daniel was kept near the king's person.

3

1 Nebuchadnezzar the king made an image of gold, sixty cubits high and six cubits wide: he put it up in the valley of Dura, in the land of Babylon.

2 And Nebuchadnezzar the king sent to get together all the captains, the chiefs, the rulers, the wise men, the keepers of public money, the judges, the overseers, and all the rulers of the divisions of the country, to come to see the unveiling of the image which Nebuchadnezzar the king had put up.

3 Then the captains, the chiefs, the rulers, the wise men, the keepers of public money, the judges, the overseers, and all the rulers of the divisions of the country, came together to see the unveiling of the image which Nebuchadnezzar the king had put up; and they took their places before the image which Nebuchadnezzar had put up.

4 Then one of the king's criers said in a loud voice, To you the order is given, O peoples, nations, and languages,

5 That when the sound of the horn, pipe, harp, trigon, psaltery, bagpipe, and all sorts of instruments, comes to your ears, you are to go down on your faces in worship before the image of gold which Nebuchadnezzar the king has put up:

6 And anyone not falling down and worshipping will that same hour be put into a burning and flaming fire.

7 So at that time, all the people, when the sound of the horn, pipe, harp, trigon, psaltery, and all sorts of instruments, came to their ears, went down on their faces in worship before the image of gold which Nebuchadnezzar the king had put up.

8 At that time certain Chaldaeans came near and made a statement against the Jews.

9 They made answer and said to Nebuchadnezzar the king, O King, have life for ever.

10 You, O King, have given an order that every man, when the sound of the horn, pipe, harp, trigon, psaltery, bagpipe, and all sorts of instruments, comes to his ears, is to go down on his face in worship before the image of gold:

11 And anyone not falling down and worshipping is to be put into a burning and flaming fire.

12 There are certain Jews whom you have put over the business of the land of Babylon, Shadrach, Meshach, and Abed-nego; these men have not given attention to you, O King: they are not servants of your gods or worshippers of the gold image which you have put up.

13 Then Nebuchadnezzar in his wrath and passion gave orders for Shadrach, Meshach, and Abed-nego to be sent for. Then they made these men come in before the king.

14 Nebuchadnezzar made answer and said to them, Is it true, O Shadrach, Meshach, and Abed-nego, that you will not be servants of my god or give worship to the image of gold which I have put up?

15 Now if you are ready, on hearing the sound of the horn, pipe, harp, trigon, psaltery, bagpipe, and all sorts of instruments, to go down on your faces in worship before the image which I have made, it is well: but if you will not give worship, that same hour you will be put into a burning and flaming fire; and what god is there who will be able to take you out of my hands?

16 Shadrach, Meshach, and Abed-nego, answering Nebuchadnezzar the king, said, There is no need for us to give you an answer to this question.

17 If our God, whose servants we are, is able to keep us safe from the burning and flaming fire, and from your hands, O King, he will keep us safe.

18 But if not, be certain, O King, that we will not be the servants of your gods, or give worship to the image of gold which you have put up.

19 Then Nebuchadnezzar was full of wrath, and the form of his face was changed against Shadrach, Meshach, and Abed-nego: and he gave orders that the fire was to be heated up seven times more than it was generally heated.

20 And he gave orders to certain strong men in his army to put cords on Shadrach, Meshach and Abed-nego and put them into the burning and flaming fire.

21 Then these men had cords put round them as they were, in their coats, their trousers, their hats, and their clothing, and were dropped into the burning and flaming fire.

22 And because the king's order was not to be put on one side, and the heat of the fire was so great, the men who took up Shadrach, Meshach, and Abed-nego were burned to death by the flame of the fire.

23 And these three men, Shadrach, Meshach, and Abed-nego, with the cords about them, went down into the burning and flaming fire.

24 Then King Nebuchadnezzar, full of fear and wonder, got up quickly, and said to his wise men, Did we not put three men in cords into the fire? and they made answer and said to the king, True, O King.

25 He made answer and said, Look! I see four men loose, walking in the middle of the fire, and they are not damaged; and the form of the fourth is like a son of the gods.

26 Then Nebuchadnezzar came near the door of the burning and flaming fire: he made answer and said, Shadrach, Meshach, and Abed-nego, you servants of the Most High God, come out and come here. Then Shadrach, Meshach, and Abed-nego came out of the fire.

27 And the captains, the chiefs, and the rulers, and the king's wise men who had come together, saw these men, over whose bodies the fire had no power, and not a hair of their heads was burned, and their coats were not changed, and there was no smell of fire about them.

28 Nebuchadnezzar made answer and said, Praise be to the God of Shadrach, Meshach, and Abed-nego, who has sent his angel and kept his servants safe who had faith in him, and who put the king's word on one side and gave up their bodies to the fire, so that they might not be servants or worshippers of any other god but their God.

29 And it is my decision that any people, nation, or language saying evil against the God of Shadrach, Meshach, and Abed-nego, will be cut to bits and their houses made waste: because there is no other god who is able to give salvation such as this.

30 Then the king gave Shadrach, Meshach, and Abed-nego even greater authority in the land of Babylon.

4

1 Nebuchadnezzar the king, to all the peoples, nations, and languages living in all the earth: May your peace be increased.

2 It has seemed good to me to make clear the signs and wonders which the Most High God has done with me.

3 How great are his signs! and how full of power are his wonders! his kingdom is an eternal kingdom and his rule goes on from generation to generation.

4 I, Nebuchadnezzar, was at rest in my place, and all things were going well for me in my great house:

5 I saw a dream which was a cause of great fear to me; I was troubled by the images of my mind on my bed, and by the visions of my head.

6 And I gave orders for all the wise men of Babylon to come in before me so that they might make clear to me the sense of my dream.

7 Then the wonder-workers, the users of secret arts, the Chaldaeans, and the readers of signs came in to me: and I put the dream before them but they did not make clear the sense of it to me.

8 But at last Daniel came in before me, he whose name was Belteshazzar, after the name of my god, and in whom is the spirit of the holy gods: and I put the dream before him, saying,

9 O Belteshazzar, master of the wonder-workers, because I am certain that the spirit of the holy gods is in you, and you are troubled by no secret; this is the dream which I saw: make clear to me its sense.

10 On my bed I saw a vision: there was a tree in the middle of the earth, and it was very high.

11 And the tree became tall and strong, stretching up to heaven, and to be seen from the ends of the earth:

12 Its leaves were fair and it had much fruit, and in it was food enough for all: the beasts of the field had shade under it, and the birds of heaven were resting in its branches, and it gave food to all living things.

13 In the visions of my head on my bed I saw a watcher, a holy one, coming down from heaven,

14 Crying out with a loud voice; and this is what he said: Let the tree be cut down and its branches broken off; let its leaves be taken off and its fruit sent in every direction: let the beasts get away from under it and the birds from its branches:

15 But keep its broken end and its roots still in the earth, even with a band of iron and brass; let him have the young grass of the field for food, and let him be wet with the dew of heaven, and let his part be with the beasts.

16 Let his heart be changed from that of a man, and the heart of a beast be given to him; and let seven times go by him.

17 This order is fixed by the watchers, and the decision is by the word of the holy ones: so that the living may be certain that the Most High is ruler over the kingdom of men, and gives it to any man at his pleasure, lifting up over it the lowest of men.

18 This dream I, King Nebuchadnezzar, saw; and do you, O Belteshazzar, make clear the sense of it, for all the wise men of my kingdom are unable to make the sense of it clear to me; but you are able, for the spirit of the holy gods is in you.

19 Then Daniel, whose name was Belteshazzar, was at a loss for a time, his thoughts troubling him. The king made answer and said, Belteshazzar, do not be troubled by the

dream or by the sense of it. Belteshazzar, answering, said, My lord, may the dream be about your haters, and its sense about those who are against you.

20 The tree which you saw, which became tall and strong, stretching up to heaven and seen from the ends of the earth;

21 Which had fair leaves and much fruit, and had in it food for all; under which the beasts of the field were living, and in the branches of which the birds of heaven had their resting-places:

22 It is you, O King, who have become great and strong: for your power is increased and stretching up to heaven, and your rule to the end of the earth.

23 And as for the vision which the king saw of a watcher, a holy one, coming down from heaven, saying, Let the tree be cut down and given to destruction;

24 This is the sense of it, O King, and it is the decision of the Most High which has come on my lord the king:

25 That they will send you out from among men, to be with the beasts of the field; they will give you grass for your food like the oxen, and you will be wet with the dew of heaven, and seven times will go by you, till you are certain that the Most High is ruler in the kingdom of men, and gives it to any man at his pleasure.

26 And as they gave orders to let the broken end and the roots of the tree be, so your kingdom will be safe for you after it is clear to you that the heavens are ruling.

27 For this cause, O King, let my suggestion be pleasing to you, and let your sins be covered by righteousness and your evil-doing by mercy to the poor, so that the time of your well-being may be longer.

28 All this came to King Nebuchadnezzar.

29 At the end of twelve months he was walking on the roof of his great house in Babylon.

30 The king made answer and said, Is this not great Babylon, which I have made for the living-place of kings, by the strength of my power and for the glory of my honour?

31 While the word was still in the king's mouth, a voice came down from heaven, saying, O King Nebuchadnezzar, to you it is said: The kingdom has gone from you:

32 And they will send you out from among men, to be with the beasts of the field; they will give you grass for your food like the oxen, and seven times will go by you, till you are certain that the Most High is ruler in the kingdom of men, and gives it to any man at his pleasure.

33 That very hour the order about Nebuchadnezzar was put into effect: and he was sent out from among men, and had grass for his food like the oxen, and his body was wet with the dew of heaven, till his hair became long as eagles' feathers and his nails like those of birds.

34 And at the end of the days, I, Nebuchadnezzar, lifting up my eyes to heaven, got back my reason, and, blessing the Most High, I gave praise and honour to him who is living for ever, whose rule is an eternal rule and whose kingdom goes on from generation to generation.

35 And all the people of the earth are as nothing: he does his pleasure in the army of heaven and among the people of the earth: and no one is able to keep back his hand, or say to him, What are you doing?

36 At the same time my reason came back to me; and for the glory of my kingdom, my honour and my great name came back to me; and my wise men and my lords were turned to me again; and I was made safe in my kingdom and had more power than before.

37 Now I, Nebuchadnezzar, give worship and praise and honour to the King of heaven; for all his works are true and his ways are right: and those who go in pride he is able to make low.

5

1 Belshazzar the king made a great feast for a thousand of his lords, drinking wine before the thousand.

2 Belshazzar, while he was overcome with wine, gave orders for them to put before him the gold and silver vessels which Nebuchadnezzar, his father, had taken from the Temple in

Jerusalem; so that the king and his lords, his wives and his other women, might take their drink from them.

3 Then they took in the gold and silver vessels which had been in the Temple of the house of God at Jerusalem; and the king and his lords, his wives and his other women, took wine from them.

4 They took their wine and gave praise to the gods of gold and silver, of brass and iron and wood and stone.

5 In that very hour the fingers of a man's hand were seen, writing opposite the support for the light on the white wall of the king's house, and the king saw the part of the hand which was writing.

6 Then the colour went from the king's face, and he was troubled by his thoughts; strength went from his body, and his knees were shaking.

7 The king, crying out with a loud voice, said that the users of secret arts, the Chaldaeans, and the readers of signs, were to be sent for. The king made answer and said to the wise men of Babylon, Whoever is able to make out this writing, and make clear to me the sense of it, will be clothed in purple and have a chain of gold round his neck, and will be a ruler of high authority in the kingdom.

8 Then all the king's wise men came in: but they were not able to make out the writing or give the sense of it to the king.

9 Then King Belshazzar was greatly troubled and the colour went from his face, and his lords were at a loss.

10 The queen, because of the words of the king and his lords, came into the house of the feast: the queen made answer and said, O King, have life for ever; do not be troubled by your thoughts or let the colour go from your face:

11 There is a man in your kingdom in whom is the spirit of the holy gods; and in the days of your father, light and reason like the wisdom of the gods were seen in him: and King Nebuchadnezzar, your father, made him master of the wonder-workers, and the users of secret arts, and the Chaldaeans, and the readers of signs;

12 Because a most special spirit, and knowledge and reason and the power of reading dreams and unfolding dark sayings and answering hard questions, were seen to be in him, even in Daniel (named Belteshazzar by the king): now let Daniel be sent for, and he will make clear the sense of the writing.

13 Then they took Daniel in before the king; the king made answer and said to Daniel, So you are that Daniel, of the prisoners of Judah, whom my father took out of Judah.

14 And I have had news of you, that the spirit of the gods is in you, and that light and reason and special wisdom have been seen in you.

15 And now the wise men, the users of secret arts, have been sent in before me for the purpose of reading this writing and making clear to me the sense of it: but they are not able to make clear the sense of the thing:

16 And I have had news of you, that you have the power of making things clear, and of answering hard questions: now if you are able to make out the writing and give me the sense of it, you will be clothed in purple and have a gold chain round your neck and be a ruler of high authority in the kingdom.

17 Then Daniel made answer and said to the king, Keep your offerings for yourself, and give your rewards to another; but I, after reading the writing to the king, will give him the sense of it.

18 As for you, O King, the Most High God gave to Nebuchadnezzar, your father, the kingdom and great power and glory and honour:

19 And because of the great power he gave him, all peoples and nations and languages were shaking in fear before him: some he put to death and others he kept living, at his pleasure, lifting up some and putting others down as it pleased him.

20 But when his heart was lifted up and his spirit became hard with pride, he was put down from his place as king, and they took his glory from him:

21 And he was sent out from among the sons of men; and his heart was made like the beasts', and he was living with the asses of the fields; he had grass for his food like the oxen, and his body was wet with the dew of heaven, till he was certain that the Most High is ruler in the kingdom of men, and gives power over it to anyone at his pleasure.

22 And you, his son, O Belshazzar, have not kept your heart free from pride, though you had knowledge of all this;

23 But you have been lifting yourself up against the Lord of heaven, and they have put the vessels of his house before you, and you and your lords, your wives and your women, have taken wine in them; and you have given praise to gods of silver and gold, of brass and iron and wood and stone, who are without the power of seeing or hearing, and without knowledge: and to the God in whose hand your breath is, and whose are all your ways, you have not given glory;

24 Then the part of the hand was sent out from before him, and this writing was recorded.

25 And this is the writing which was recorded, Mene, tekel, peres.

26 This is the sense of the words: Mene; your kingdom has been numbered by God and ended.

27 Tekel; you have been put in the scales and seen to be under weight.

28 Peres; your kingdom has been cut up and given to the Medes and Persians.

29 Then, by the order of Belshazzar, they put a purple robe on Daniel, and a gold chain round his neck, and a public statement was made that he was to be a ruler of high authority in the kingdom.

30 That very night Belshazzar, the king of the Chaldaeans, was put to death.

31 And Darius the Mede took the kingdom, being then about sixty-two years old.

6

1 Darius was pleased to put over the kingdom a hundred and twenty captains, who were to be all through the kingdom;

2 And over them were three chief rulers, of whom Daniel was one; and the captains were to be responsible to the chief rulers, so that the king might undergo no loss.

3 Then this Daniel did his work better than the chief rulers and the captains, because there was a special spirit in him; and it was the king's purpose to put him over all the kingdom.

4 Then the chief rulers and the captains were looking for some cause for putting Daniel in the wrong in connection with the kingdom, but they were unable to put forward any wrongdoing or error against him; because he was true, and no error or wrong was to be seen in him.

5 Then these men said, We will only get a reason for attacking Daniel in connection with the law of his God.

6 Then these chief rulers and the captains came to the king and said to him, O King Darius, have life for ever.

7 All the chief rulers of the kingdom, the chiefs and the captains, the wise men and the rulers, have made a common decision to put in force a law having the king's authority, and to give a strong order, that whoever makes any request to any god or man but you, O King, for thirty days, is to be put into the lions' hole.

8 Now, O King, put the order in force, signing the writing so that it may not be changed, like the law of the Medes and Persians which may not come to an end.

9 For this reason King Darius put his name on the writing and the order.

10 And Daniel, on hearing that the writing had been signed, went into his house; (now he had windows in his room on the roof opening in the direction of Jerusalem;) and three times a day he went down on his knees in prayer and praise before his God, as he had done before.

11 Then these men were watching and saw Daniel making prayers and requesting grace before his God.

12 Then they came near before the king and said, O King, have you not put your name to an order that any man who makes a request to any god or man but you, O King, for thirty days, is to be put into the lions' hole? The king made answer and said, The thing is fixed by the law of the Medes and Persians which may not come to an end.

13 Then they made answer and said before the king, Daniel, one of the prisoners of Judah, has no respect for you, O King, or for the order signed by you, but three times a day he makes his prayer to God.

14 When this thing came to the king's ears, it was very evil to him, and his heart was fixed on keeping Daniel safe, and till the going down of the sun he was doing everything in his power to get him free.

15 Then these men said to the king, Be certain, O King, that by the law of the Medes and Persians no order or law which the king has put into force may be changed.

16 Then the king gave the order, and they took Daniel and put him into the lions' hole. The king made answer and said to Daniel, Your God, whose servant you are at all times, will keep you safe.

17 Then they got a stone and put it over the mouth of the hole, and it was stamped with the king's stamp and with the stamp of the lords, so that the decision about Daniel might not be changed.

18 Then the king went to his great house, and took no food that night, and no ... were placed before him, and his sleep went from him.

19 Then very early in the morning the king got up and went quickly to the lions' hole.

20 And when he came near the hole where Daniel was, he gave a loud cry of grief; the king made answer and said to Daniel, O Daniel, servant of the living God, is your God, whose servant you are at all times, able to keep you safe from the lions?

21 Then Daniel said to the king, O King, have life for ever.

22 My God has sent his angel to keep the lions' mouths shut, and they have done me no damage: because I was seen to be without sin before him; and further, before you, O King, I have done no wrong.

23 Then the king was very glad, and gave orders for them to take Daniel up out of the hole. So Daniel was taken up out of the hole and he was seen to be untouched, because he had faith in his God.

24 And at the king's order, they took those men who had said evil against Daniel, and put them in the lions' hole, with their wives and their children; and they had not got to the floor of the hole before the lions overcame them and all their bones were broken.

25 Then King Darius sent a letter to all the peoples, nations, and languages, living in all the earth: May your peace be increased.

26 It is my order that in all the kingdom of which I am ruler, men are to be shaking with fear before the God of Daniel: for he is the living God, unchanging for ever, and his kingdom is one which will never come to destruction, his rule will go on to the end.

27 He gives salvation and makes men free from danger, and does signs and wonders in heaven and earth, who has kept Daniel safe from the power of the lions.

28 So this Daniel did well in the kingdom of Darius and in the kingdom of Cyrus the Persian.

7

1 In the first year of Belshazzar, king of Babylon, Daniel saw a dream, and visions came into his head on his bed: then he put the dream in writing.

2 I had a vision by night, and saw the four winds of heaven violently moving the great sea.

3 And four great beasts came up from the sea, different one from another.

4 The first was like a lion and had eagle's wings; while I was watching its wings were pulled off, and it was lifted up from the earth and placed on two feet like a man, and a man's heart was given to it.

5 And I saw another beast, like a bear, and it was lifted up on one side, and three side-bones were in its mouth, between its teeth: and they said to it, Up! take much flesh.

6 After this I saw another beast, like a leopard, which had on its back four wings like those of a bird; and the beast had four heads, and the power of a ruler was given to it.

7 After this, in my vision of the night, I saw a fourth beast, a thing causing fear and very troubling, full of power and very strong; and it had great iron teeth: it took its food, crushing some of it to bits and stamping down the rest with its feet: it was different from all the beasts before it; and it had ten horns.

8 I was watching the horns with care, and I saw another coming up among them, a little one, before which three of the first horns were pulled up by the roots: and there were eyes like a man's eyes in this horn, and a mouth saying great things.

9 I went on looking till the seats of kings were placed, and one like a very old man took his seat: his clothing was white as snow, and the hair of his head was like clean wool; his seat was flames of fire and its wheels burning fire.

10 A stream of fire was flowing and coming out from before him: a thousand thousands were his servants, and ten thousand times ten thousand were in their places before him: the judge was seated and the books were open.

11 Then I saw--because of the voice of the great words which the horn said--I saw till the beast was put to death, and its body was given to destruction, and the beast was given to the burning of fire.

12 As for the rest of the beasts, their authority was taken away: but they let them go on living for a measure of time.

13 I saw in visions of the night, and there was coming with the clouds of heaven one like a man, and he came to the one who was very old, and they took him near before him.

14 And to him was given authority and glory and a kingdom; and all peoples, nations, and languages were his servants: his authority is an eternal authority which will not come to an end, and his kingdom is one which will not come to destruction.

15 As for me, Daniel, my spirit was pained because of this, and the visions of my head were troubling me.

16 I came near to one of those who were waiting there, questioning him about what all this was. And he said to me that he would make clear to me the sense of these things.

17 These great beasts are four kings who will be cut off from the earth.

18 But the saints of the Most High will take the kingdom, and it will be theirs for ever, even for ever and ever.

19 Then it was my desire to have certain knowledge about the fourth beast, which was different from all the others, a cause of great fear, whose teeth were of iron and his nails of brass; who took his food, crushing some of it to bits and stamping on the rest with his feet;

20 And about the ten horns on his head and the other which came up, causing the fall of three; that horn which had eyes, and a mouth saying great things, which seemed to be greater than the other horns.

21 And I saw how that horn made war on the saints and overcame them,

22 Till he came, who was very old, and the decision was made and the authority was given to the saints of the Most High; and the time came when the saints took the kingdom.

23 This is what he said: The fourth beast is a fourth kingdom which will come on earth, different from all the kingdoms, and it will overcome all the earth, crushing it down and smashing it.

24 And as for the ten horns, out of this kingdom ten kings will come to power; and after them another will come up: he will be different from the first ones and will put down three kings.

25 And he will say words against the Most High, attempting to put an end to the saints of the Most High; and he will have the idea of changing times and law; and the saints will be given into his hands for a time and times and half a time.

26 But the judge will be seated, and they will put an end to his authority, to overcome it and

send complete destruction on it.

27 And the kingdom and the authority and the power of the kingdoms under all the heaven will be given to the people of the saints of the Most High: his kingdom is an eternal kingdom, and all powers will be his servants and do his pleasure.

28 Here is the end of the account. As for me, Daniel, I was greatly troubled by my thoughts, and the colour went from my face: but I kept the thing in my heart.

8

1 In the third year of the rule of Belshazzar the king, a vision was seen by me, Daniel, after the one I saw at first.

2 And I saw in the vision; and when I saw it, I was in the strong town Shushan, which is in the country of Elam; and in the vision I was by the water-door of the Ulai.

3 And lifting up my eyes, I saw, there before the stream, a male sheep with two horns: and the two horns were high, but one was higher than the other, the higher one coming up last.

4 I saw the sheep pushing to the west and to the north and to the south; and no beasts were able to keep their place before him, and no one was able to get people out of his power; but he did whatever his pleasure was and made himself great.

5 And while I was giving thought to this, I saw a he-goat coming from the west over the face of all the earth without touching the earth: and the he-goat had a great horn between his eyes.

6 And he came to the two-horned sheep which I saw before the stream, rushing at him in the heat of his power.

7 And I saw him come right up to the sheep, and he was moved with wrath against him, attacking the sheep so that his two horns were broken; and the sheep had not strength to keep his place before him, but was pushed down on the earth and crushed under his feet: and there was no one to get the sheep out of his power.

8 And the he-goat became very great: and when he was strong, the great horn was broken, and in its place came up four other horns turned to the four winds of heaven.

9 And out of one of them came another horn, a little one, which became very great, stretching to the south and to the east and to the beautiful land.

10 And it became great, even as high as the army of heaven, pulling down some of the army, even of the stars, to the earth and crushing them under its feet.

11 It made itself great, even as great as the lord of the army; and by it the regular burned offering was taken away, and the place overturned and the holy place made waste.

12 ... against the regular burned offering; and ... crushed down to the earth, and it did its pleasure and things went well for it.

13 Then there came to my ears the voice of a holy one talking; and another holy one said to that certain one who was talking, How long will the vision be while the regular burned offering is taken away, and the unclean thing causing fear is put up, and the holy place crushed under foot?

14 And he said to him, For two thousand, three hundred evenings and mornings; then the holy place will be made clean.

15 And it came about that when I, Daniel, had seen this vision, I had a desire for the sense of it to be unfolded; and I saw one before me in the form of a man.

16 And the voice of a man came to my ears between the sides of the Ulai, crying out and saying, Gabriel, make the vision clear to this man.

17 So he came and took his place near where I was; and when he came, I was full of fear and went down on my face: but he said to me, Let it be clear to you, O son of man; for the vision has to do with the time of the end.

18 Now while he was talking to me, I went into a deep sleep with my face to the earth: but touching me, he put me on my feet where I had been.

19 And he said, See, I will make clear to you what is to come in the later time of the wrath:

for it has to do with the fixed time of the end.

20 The sheep which you saw with two horns, they are the kings of Media and Persia.

21 And the he-goat is the king of Greece: and the great horn between his eyes is the first king.

22 And as for that which was broken, in place of which four came up, four kingdoms will come up from his nation, but not with his power.

23 And in the later years of their kingdom, when their evil doings have become complete, there will come up a king full of pride and expert in dark sayings.

24 And his power will be great, and he will be purposing strange things. And all will go well for him and he will do his pleasure; and he will send destruction on the strong ones.

25 And his designs will be turned against the holy people, causing deceit to do well in his hand; in his heart he will make himself great, and send destruction on numbers who are living unconscious of their danger; and he will put himself up against the prince of princes; but he will be broken, though not by men's hands.

26 And the vision of evenings and mornings which has been talked of is true: and keep the vision secret; for it has to do with the far-off future.

27 And I, Daniel, was ill for some days; then I got up and did the king's business: and I was full of wonder at the vision, but no one was able to give the sense of it.

9

1 In the first year of Darius, the son of Ahasuerus, of the seed of the Medes, who was made king over the kingdom of the Chaldaeans;

2 In the first year of his rule, I, Daniel, saw clearly from the books the number of years given by the word of the Lord to the prophet Jeremiah, in which the making waste of Jerusalem was to be complete, that is, seventy years.

3 And turning my face to the Lord God, I gave myself up to prayer, requesting his grace, going without food, in haircloth and dust.

4 And I made prayer to the Lord my God, putting our sins before him, and said, O Lord, the great God, greatly to be feared. keeping your agreement and mercy with those who have love for you and do your orders;

5 We are sinners, acting wrongly and doing evil; we have gone against you, turning away from your orders and from your laws:

6 We have not given ear to your servants the prophets, who said words in your name to our kings and our rulers and our fathers and all the people of the land.

7 O Lord, righteousness is yours, but shame is on us, even to this day; and on the men of Judah and the people of Jerusalem, and on all Israel, those who are near and those who are far off, in all the countries where you have sent them because of the sin which they have done against you.

8 O Lord, shame is on us, on our kings and our rulers and our fathers, because of our sin against you.

9 With the Lord our God are mercies and forgiveness, for we have gone against him;

10 And have not given ear to the voice of the Lord our God to go in the way of his laws which he put before us by the mouth of his servants the prophets.

11 And all Israel have been sinners against your law, turning away so as not to give ear to your voice: and the curse has been let loose on us, and the oath recorded in the law of Moses, the servant of God, for we have done evil against him.

12 And he has given effect to his words which he said against us and against those who were our judges, by sending a great evil on us: for under all heaven there has not been done what has been done to Jerusalem.

13 As it was recorded in the law of Moses, all this evil has come on us: but we have made no prayer for grace from the Lord our God that we might be turned from our evil doings and come to true wisdom.

14 So the Lord has been watching over this evil and has made it come on us: for the Lord our God is upright in all his acts which he has done, and we have not given ear to his voice.

15 And now, O Lord our God, who took your people out of the land of Egypt with a strong hand and made a great name for yourself even to this day; we are sinners, we have done evil.

16 O Lord, because of your righteousness, let your wrath and your passion be turned away from your town Jerusalem, your holy mountain: because, through our sins and the evil-doing of our fathers, Jerusalem and your people have become a cause of shame to all who are round about us.

17 And now, give ear, O our God, to the prayer of your servant and to his request for grace, and let your face be shining on your holy place which is made waste, because of your servants, O Lord.

18 O my God, let your ear be turned and give hearing; let your eyes be open and see how we have been made waste and the town which is named by your name: for we are not offering our prayers before you because of our righteousness, but because of your great mercies.

19 O Lord, give ear; O Lord, have forgiveness; O Lord, take note and do; let there be no more waiting; for the honour of your name, O my God, because your town and your people are named by your name.

20 And while I was still saying these words in prayer, and putting my sins and the sins of my people Israel before the Lord, and requesting grace from the Lord my God for the holy mountain of my God;

21 Even while I was still in prayer, the man Gabriel, whom I had seen in the vision at first when my weariness was great, put his hand on me about the time of the evening offering.

22 And teaching me and talking to me he said, O Daniel, I have come now to give you wisdom.

23 At the first word of your prayer a word went out, and I have come to give you knowledge; for you are a man dearly loved: so give thought to the word and let the vision be clear to you.

24 Seventy weeks have been fixed for your people and your holy town, to let wrongdoing be complete and sin come to its full limit, and for the clearing away of evil-doing and the coming in of eternal righteousness: so that the vision and the word of the prophet may be stamped as true, and to put the holy oil on a most holy place.

25 Have then the certain knowledge that from the going out of the word for the building again of Jerusalem till the coming of a prince, on whom the holy oil has been put, will be seven weeks: in sixty-two weeks its building will be complete, with square and earthwork.

26 And at the end of the times, even after the sixty-two weeks, one on whom the holy oil has been put will be cut off and have no ...; and the town and the holy place will be made waste together with a prince; and the end will come with an overflowing of waters, and even to the end there will be war; the making waste which has been fixed.

27 And a strong order will be sent out against the great number for one week; and so for half of the week the offering and the meal offering will come to an end; and in its place will be an unclean thing causing fear; till the destruction which has been fixed is let loose on him who has made waste.

10

1 In the third year of Cyrus, king of Persia, a secret was unfolded to Daniel, whose name was Belteshazzar; and the thing was true, even a hard work: and he had knowledge of it, and the vision was clear to him.

2 In those days I, Daniel, gave myself up to grief for three full weeks.

3 I had no pleasing food, no meat or wine came into my mouth, and I put no oil on my body till three full weeks were ended.

4 And on the twenty-fourth day of the first month I was by the side of the great river;

5 And lifting up my eyes I saw the form of a man clothed in a linen robe, and round him

there was a band of gold, of the best gold:

6 And his body was like the beryl, and his face had the look of a thunder-flame, and his eyes were like burning lights, and his arms and feet like the colour of polished brass, and the sound of his voice was like the sound of an army.

7 And I, Daniel, was the only one who saw the vision, for the men who were with me did not see it; but a great shaking came on them and they went in flight to take cover.

8 So I was by myself, and I saw this great vision, and all my strength went from me; and the colour went from my face.

9 But the sound of his words came to my ears, and on hearing his voice I went into a deep sleep with my face to the earth.

10 Then a hand gave me a touch, awaking me, and putting me on my knees and my hands.

11 And he said to me, O Daniel, you man dearly loved, take in the sense of the words I say to you and get up on to your feet: for to you I am now sent; and when he had said this to me I got on to my feet, shaking with fear.

12 Then he said to me, Have no fear, Daniel; for from the first day when you gave your heart to getting wisdom and making yourself poor in spirit before your God, your words have come to his ears: and I have come because of your words.

13 But the angel of the kingdom of Persia put himself against me for twenty-one days; but Michael, one of the chief angels, came to my help; and when I came he was still there with the angel of the kings of Persia.

14 Now I have come to give you knowledge of the fate of your people in the later days; for there is still a vision for the days.

15 And after he had said these words to me, I kept my face turned to the earth and was unable to say anything.

16 Then one whose form was like the sons of men put his finger on my lips; and opening my mouth, I said to him who was before me, O my lord, because of the vision my pains have come on me, and I have no more strength.

17 For how may this servant of my lord have talk with my lord? for, as for me, straight away my strength went from me and there was no breath in my body.

18 Then again one having the form of a man put his hand on me and gave me strength.

19 And he said to me, O man greatly loved, have no fear: peace be with you, be strong and let your heart be lifted up. And at his words I became strong, and said, Let my lord say on, for you have given me strength.

20 Then he said, It is clear to you why I have come to you. And now I will give you an account of what is recorded in the true writings:

21 But I am going back to make war with the angel of Persia, and when I am gone, the angel of Greece will come. And there is no one on my side against these, but Michael, your angel.

11

1 And as for me, in the first year of Darius the Mede I was on his side to make his position safe and make him strong.

2 And now I will make clear to you what is true. There are still three kings to come in Persia, and the fourth will have much greater wealth than all of them: and when he has become strong through his wealth, he will put his forces in motion against all the kingdoms of Greece.

3 And a strong king will come to power, ruling with great authority and doing whatever is his pleasure.

4 And when he has become strong, his kingdom will be broken and parted to the four winds of heaven; but not to his offspring, for it will be uprooted; and his kingdom will be for the others and not for these: but not with the same authority as his.

5 And the king of the south will be strong, but one of his captains will be stronger than he and will be ruler; and his rule will be a great rule.

6 And at the end of years they will be joined together; and the daughter of the king of the south will come to the king of the north to make an agreement: but she will not keep the strength of her arm; and his offspring will not keep their place; but she will be uprooted, with those who were the cause of her coming, and her son, and he who took her in those times

7 But out of a branch from her roots one will come up to take his place, who will come against the army, forcing his way into the strong place of the king of the north, and he will take them in hand and overcome them:

8 And their gods and their metal images and their fair vessels of silver and gold he will take away into the south; and for some years he will keep away from the king of the north.

9 And he will come into the kingdom of the king of the south, but he will go back to his land.

10 And his son will make war, and will get together an army of great forces, and he will make an attack on him, overflowing and going past: and he will again take the war even to his strong place.

11 And the king of the south will be moved with wrath, and will come out and make war on him, on this same king of the north: and he will get together a great army, but the army will be given into his hand.

12 And the army will be taken away, and his heart will be uplifted: he will be the cause of the downfall of tens of thousands, but he will not be strong.

13 And again the king of the north will get together an army greater than the first; and he will make an attack on him at the end of years, with a great army and much wealth.

14 In those times, a number will take up arms against the king of the south: and the children of the violent among your people will be lifting themselves up to make the vision come true; but it will be their downfall.

15 So the king of the north will come, and put up earthworks and take a well-armed town: and the forces of the king of the south will make an attempt to keep their position, even the best of his army, but they will not have strength to do so.

16 And he who comes against him will do his pleasure, and no one will be able to keep his place before him: he will take up his position in the beautiful land and in his hand there will be destruction.

17 And it will be his purpose to come with the strength of all his kingdom, but in place of this he will make an agreement with him; and he will give him the daughter of women to send destruction on it; but this will not take place or come about.

18 After this, his face will be turned to the islands, and he will take a number of them: but a chief, by his destruction, will put an end to the shame offered by him; and more than this, he will make his shame come back on him.

19 Then his face will be turned to the strong places of his land: but his way will be stopped, causing his downfall, and he will not be seen again.

20 Then his place will be taken by one who will send out a man with the glory of a king to get wealth together; but after a short time destruction will overtake him, but not in wrath or in the fight.

21 And his place will be taken by a low person, to whom the honour of the kingdom had not been given: but he will come in time of peace and will get the kingdom by fair words.

22 And his forces will be completely taken away from before him and broken; and even the ruler of the agreement will have the same fate.

23 And from the time when they make an agreement with him, he will be working falsely: for he will take up arms suddenly with a small force,

24 Against fertile places, and will make waste a part of the country; and he will do what his fathers have not done, or his fathers' fathers; he will make distribution among them of goods taken in war and by force, and of property: he will even make designs against the strong places for a time.

25 And he will put in motion his power and his strength against the king of the south with a

great army; and the king of the south will go to war with a very great and strong army: but he will be forced to give way, because of their designs against him;

26 And his fears will overcome him and be the cause of his downfall, and his army will come to complete destruction, and a great number will be put to the sword.

27 And as for these two kings, their hearts will be fixed on doing evil and they will say false words at one table; but it will come to nothing: for the end will be at the time fixed.

28 And he will go back to his land with great wealth; and his heart will be against the holy agreement; and he will do his pleasure and go back to his land.

29 At the time fixed he will come back and come into the south; but in the later time it will not be as it was before.

30 For those who go out from the west will come against him, and he will be in fear and will go back, full of wrath against the holy agreement; and he will do his pleasure: and he will go back and be united with those who have given up the holy agreement.

31 And armies sent by him will take up their position and they will make unclean the holy place, even the strong place, and take away the regular burned offering and put in its place an unclean thing causing fear.

32 And those who do evil against the agreement will be turned to sin by his fair words: but the people who have knowledge of their God will be strong and do well.

33 And those who are wise among the people will be the teachers of the mass of the people: but they will come to their downfall by the sword and by the flame, being made prisoners and undergoing loss for a long time.

34 Now at the time of their downfall they will have a little help, but numbers will be joined to them in the town, and in their separate heritages.

35 And some of those who are wise will have wisdom in testing themselves and making themselves clean, till the time of the end: for it is still for the fixed time.

36 And the king will do his pleasure; he will put himself on high, lifting himself over every god, and saying things to be wondered at against the God of gods; and all will be well for him till the wrath is complete; for what has been purposed will be done.

37 He will have no respect for the gods of his fathers or for the god desired by women; he will have no respect for any god: for he will put himself on high over all.

38 But in place of this he will give honour to the god of armed places, and to a god of whom his fathers had no knowledge he will give honour with gold and silver and jewels and things to be desired.

39 And he will make use of the people of a strange god to keep his strongest places; to those whom he takes note of he will give high honour: and he will make them rulers over the mass of the people, and will make division of the land for a price.

40 And at the time of the end, the king of the south will make an attack on him: and the king of the north will come against him like a storm-wind, with war-carriages and horsemen and numbers of ships; and he will go through many lands like overflowing waters.

41 And he will come into the beautiful land, and tens of thousands will be overcome: but these will be kept from falling into his hands: Edom and Moab and the chief of the children of Ammon.

42 And his hand will be stretched out on the countries: and the land of the south will not be safe from him.

43 But he will have power over the stores of gold and silver, and over all the valued things of the south: and the Libyans and the Ethiopians will be at his steps.

44 But he will be troubled by news from the east and from the north; and he will go out in great wrath, to send destruction on, and put an end to, great numbers.

45 He will put the tents of his great house between the sea and the beautiful holy mountain: but he will come to his end with no helper.

12

1 And at that time Michael will take up his place, the great angel, who is the supporter of the children of your people: and there will be a time of trouble, such as there never was from the time there was a nation even till that same time: and at that time your people will be kept safe, everyone who is recorded in the book.

2 And a number of those who are sleeping in the dust of the earth will come out of their sleep, some to eternal life and some to eternal shame.

3 And those who are wise will be shining like the light of the outstretched sky; and those by whom numbers have been turned to righteousness will be like the stars for ever and ever.

4 But as for you, O Daniel, let the words be kept secret and the book rolled up and kept shut till the time of the end: numbers will be going out of the way and troubles will be increased.

5 Then I, Daniel, looking, saw two others, one at the edge of the river on this side and one at the edge of the river on that side.

6 And I said to the man clothed in linen, who was over the waters of the river, How long will it be to the end of these wonders?

7 Then in my hearing the man clothed in linen, who was over the river, lifting up his right hand and his left hand to heaven, took an oath by him who is living for ever that it would be a time, times, and a half; and when the power of the crusher of the holy people comes to an end, all these things will be ended.

8 And the words came to my ears, but the sense of them was not clear to me: then I said, O my lord, what is the sense of these things?

9 And he said, Go on your way, Daniel: for the words are secret and shut up till the time of the end;

10 Till a number are tested and make themselves clean; and the evil-doers will do evil; for not one of the evil-doers will have knowledge; but all will be made clear to those who are wise.

11 And from the time when the regular burned offering is taken away, and an unclean thing causing fear is put up, there will be a thousand, two hundred and ninety days.

12 A blessing will be on the man who goes on waiting, and comes to the thousand, three hundred and thirty-five days.

13 But you, go on your way and take your rest: for you will be in your place at the end of the days.

DANIEL

WEBSTER BIBLE

1:1 In the third year of the reign of Jehoiakim king of Judah came Nebuchadnezzar king of Babylon to Jerusalem, and besieged it.

1:2 And the Lord gave Jehoiakim king of Judah into his hand, with part of the vessels of the house of God: which he carried into the land of Shinar to the house of his god; and he brought the vessels into the treasure-house of his god.

1:3 And the king spoke to Ashpenaz the master of his eunuchs, that he should bring certain of the children of Israel, and of the king's seed, and of the princes;

1:4 Children in whom was no blemish, but of good appearance, and skillful in all wisdom, and intelligent in knowledge, and understanding science, and such as had ability in them to stand in the king's palace, and whom they might teach the learning and the language of the Chaldeans.

1:5 And the king appointed them a daily provision of the king's food, and of the wine which he drank: so nourishing them three years, that at the end of them they might stand before the king.

1:6 Now among these were of the children of Judah, Daniel, Hananiah, Mishael, and Azariah:

1:7 To whom the prince of the eunuchs gave names: for he gave to Daniel the name of Belteshazzar; and to Hananiah, of Shadrach; and to Mishael, of Meshach; and to Azariah, of Abed-nego.

1:8 But Daniel purposed in his heart that he would not defile himself with the portion of the king's food, nor with the wine which he drank: therefore he requested of the prince of the eunuchs that he might not defile himself.

1:9 Now God had brought Daniel into favor and tender love with the prince of the eunuchs.

1:10 And the prince of the eunuchs said to Daniel, I fear my lord the king, who hath appointed your provision and your drink: for why should he see your faces more meager than the children who are of your sort? then will ye make me endanger my head to the king.

1:11 Then said Daniel to Melzar, whom the prince of the eunuchs had set over Daniel, Hananiah, Mishael, and Azariah,

1:12 Prove thy servants, I beseech thee, ten days; and let them give us pulse to eat, and water to drink.

1:13 Then let our countenances be looked upon before thee, and the countenances of the children that eat of the portion of the king's provision: and as thou seest, deal with thy servants.

1:14 So he consented to them in this matter, and proved them ten days.

1:15 And at the end of ten days their countenances appeared fairer and fatter in flesh than all the children who ate the portion of the king's provision.

1:16 Thus Melzar took away the portion of their food, and the wine that they should drink, and gave them pulse.

1:17 As for these four children, God gave them knowledge and skill in all learning and wisdom: and Daniel had understanding in all visions and dreams.

1:18 Now at the end of the days that the king had said he should bring them in, then the prince of the eunuchs brought them in before Nebuchadnezzar.

1:19 And the king communed with them; and among them all was found none like Daniel, Hananiah, Mishael, and Azariah: therefore they stood before the king.

1:20 And in all matters of wisdom and understanding, that the king inquired of them, he found them ten times superior to all the magicians and astrologers that were in all his realm.

1:21 And Daniel continued even to the first year of king Cyrus.

2:1 And in the second year of the reign of Nebuchadnezzar, Nebuchadnezzar dreamed dreams, with which his spirit was troubled, and his sleep broke from him.

2:2 Then the king commanded to call the magicians, and the astrologers, and the sorcerers, and the Chaldeans, to show the king his dream. So they came and stood before the king.

2:3 And the king said to them, I have dreamed a dream, and my spirit was troubled to know the dream.

2:4 Then the Chaldeans spoke to the king in Syriac, O king, live for ever: tell thy servants the dream, and we will show the interpretation.

2:5 The king answered and said to the Chaldeans, The thing is gone from me: if ye will not make known to me the dream, with the interpretation of it, ye shall be cut in pieces, and your houses shall be made a dunghill.

2:6 But if ye shall show the dream, and the interpretation of it, ye shall receive of me gifts and rewards and great honor: therefore show me the dream, and the interpretation of it.

2:7 They answered again and said, Let the king tell his servants the dream, and we will show the interpretation of it.

2:8 The king answered and said, I know of certainty that ye would gain the time, because ye see the thing is gone from me.

2:9 But if ye will not make known to me the dream, there is but one decree for you: for ye have prepared lying and corrupt words to speak before me, till the time be changed: therefore tell me the dream, and I shall know that ye can show me the interpretation of it.

2:10 The Chaldeans answered before the king, and said, There is not a man upon the earth that can show the king's matter: therefore there is no king, lord, nor ruler, that hath asked such things of any magician, or astrologer, or Chaldean.

2:11 And it is a rare thing that the king requireth, and there is no other that can show it before the king, except the gods, whose dwelling is not with flesh.

2:12 For this cause the king was angry and very furious, and commanded to destroy all the wise men of Babylon.

2:13 And the decree went forth that the wise men should be slain; and they sought Daniel and his fellows to be slain.

2:14 Then Daniel answered with counsel and wisdom to Arioch the captain of the king's guard, who had gone forth to slay the wise men of Babylon:

2:15 He answered and said to Arioch the king's captain, Why is the decree so hasty from the king? Then Arioch made the thing known to Daniel.

2:16 Then Daniel went in, and desired of the king that he would give him time, and that he would show the king the interpretation.

2:17 Then Daniel went to his house, and made the thing known to Hananiah, Mishael, and Azariah, his companions:

2:18 That they would desire mercies of the God of heaven concerning this secret; that Daniel and his companions should not perish with the rest of the wise men of Babylon.

2:19 Then was the secret revealed to Daniel in a night vision. Then Daniel blessed the God of heaven.

2:20 Daniel answered and said, Blessed be the name of God for ever and ever: for wisdom and might are his:

2:21 And he changeth the times and the seasons; he removeth kings, and setteth up kings; he giveth wisdom to the wise, and knowledge to them that know understanding:

2:22 He revealeth the deep and secret things: he knoweth what is in the darkness, and the light dwelleth with him.

2:23 I thank thee, and praise thee, O thou God of my fathers, who hast given me wisdom and might, and hast made known to me now what we desired of thee: for thou hast now made known to us the king's matter.

2:24 Therefore Daniel went into Arioch, whom the king had ordained to destroy the wise men of Babylon: he went and said thus to him; Destroy not the wise men of Babylon: bring me in before the king, and I will show to the king the interpretation.

2:25 Then Arioch brought in Daniel before the king in haste, and said thus to him, I have found a man of the captives of Judah, that will make known to the king the interpretation.

2:26 The king answered and said to Daniel, whose name was Belteshazzar, Art thou able to make known to me the dream which I have seen, and the interpretation of it?

2:27 Daniel answered in the presence of the king, and said, The secret which the king hath demanded, the wise men, the astrologers, the magicians, the sooth-sayers, cannot show to the king;

2:28 But there is a God in heaven that revealeth secrets, and maketh known to the king Nebuchadnezzar what shall be in the latter days. Thy dream, and the visions of thy head upon thy bed, are these;

2:29 As for thee, O king, thy thoughts came into thy mind upon thy bed, what should come to pass hereafter: and he that revealeth secrets maketh known to thee what shall come to pass.

2:30 But as for me, this secret is not revealed to me for any wisdom that I have more than any living, but for their sakes that shall make known the interpretation to the king, and that thou mayest know the thoughts of thy heart.

2:31 Thou, O king, sawest, and behold a great image. This great image, whose brightness was excellent, stood before thee; and its form was terrible.

2:32 The head of this image was of fine gold, his breast and his arms of silver, his belly and his thighs of brass,

2:33 His legs of iron, his feet part of iron and part of clay.

2:34 Thou sawest till a stone was cut out without hands, which smote the image upon his feet that were of iron and clay, and broke them to pieces.

2:35 Then was the iron, the clay, the brass, the silver, and the gold, broken to pieces together, and became like the chaff of the summer threshing-floors; and the wind carried them away, that no place was found for them: and the stone that smote the image became a great mountain, and filled the whole earth.

2:36 This is the dream; and we will tell the interpretation of it before the king.

2:37 Thou, O king, art a king of kings: for the God of heaven hath given thee a kingdom, power, and strength, and glory.

2:38 And wherever the children of men dwell, the beasts of the field and the fowls of the heaven hath he given into thy hand, and hath made thee ruler over them all. Thou art this head of gold.

2:39 And after thee shall arise another kingdom inferior to thee, and another third kingdom of brass, which shall bear rule over all the earth.

2:40 And the fourth kingdom shall be strong as iron: forasmuch as iron breaketh in pieces and subdueth all things: and as iron that breaketh all these, shall it break in pieces and bruise.

2:41 And whereas thou sawest the feet and toes, part of potter's clay, and part of iron, the kingdom shall be divided; but there shall be in it of the strength of the iron, forasmuch as thou sawest the iron mixed with the miry clay.

2:42 And as the toes of the feet were part of iron, and part of clay, so the kingdom shall be partly strong, and partly broken.

2:43 And whereas thou sawest iron mixed with miry clay, they shall mingle themselves with the seed of men: but they shall not cleave one to another, even as iron is not mixed with clay.

2:44 And in the days of these kings shall the God of heaven set up a kingdom, which shall never be destroyed: and the kingdom shall not be left to other people, but it shall break in pieces and consume all these kingdoms, and it shall stand for ever.

2:45 Forasmuch as thou sawest that the stone was cut out of the mountain, without hands, and that it broke in pieces the iron, the brass, the clay, the silver, and the gold; the great God hath made known to the king what shall come to pass hereafter: and the dream is certain, and the interpretation of it sure.

2:46 Then the king Nebuchadnezzar fell upon his face, and worshiped Daniel, and commanded that they should offer an oblation and sweet odors to him.

2:47 The king answered to Daniel, and said, Of a truth it is, that your God is a God of gods, and a Lord of kings, and a revealer of secrets, seeing thou couldst reveal this secret.

2:48 Then the king made Daniel a great man, and gave him many great gifts, and made him ruler over the whole province of Babylon, and chief of the governors over all the wise men of Babylon.

2:49 Then Daniel requested of the king, and he set Shadrach, Meshach, and Abed-nego, over the affairs of the province of Babylon: but Daniel sat in the gate of the king.

3:1 Nebuchadnezzar the king made an image of gold, whose hight was sixty cubits, and the breadth of it six cubits: he set it up in the plain of Dura, in the province of Babylon.

3:2 Then Nebuchadnezzar the king sent to convene the princes, the governors, and the captains, the judges, the treasurers, the counselors, the sherifs, and all the rulers of the provinces, to come to the dedication of the image which Nebuchadnezzar the king had set up.

3:3 Then the princes, the governors, and captains, the judges, the treasurers, the counselors, the sherifs, and all the rulers of the provinces, were assembled to the dedication of the image that Nebuchadnezzar the king had set up; and they stood before the image that Nebuchadnezzar had set up.

3:4 Then a herald cried aloud, To you it is commanded, O people, nations, and languages,

3:5 That at what time ye hear the sound of the cornet, flute, harp, sackbut, psaltery, dulcimer, and all kinds of music, ye fall down and worship the golden image that Nebuchadnezzar the king hath set up.

3:6 And whoever shall not fall down and worship shall the same hour be cast into the midst of a burning fiery furnace.

3:7 Therefore at that time, when all the people heard the sound of the cornet, flute, harp, sackbut, psaltery, and all kinds of music, all the people, the nations, and the languages, fell down and worshiped the golden image that Nebuchadnezzar the king had set up.

3:8 Wherefore at that time certain Chaldeans came near, and accused the Jews.

3:9 They spoke and said to the king Nebuchadnezzar, O king, live for ever.

3:10 Thou, O king, hast made a decree, that every man that shall hear the sound of the cornet, flute, harp, sackbut, psaltery, and dulcimer, and all kinds of music, shall fall down and worship the golden image:

3:11 And whoever shall not fall down and worship, that he shall be cast into the midst of a burning fiery furnace.

3:12 There are certain Jews whom thou hast set over the affairs of the province of Babylon, Shadrach, Meshach, and Abed-nego; these men, O king, have not regarded thee: they serve not thy gods, nor worship the golden image which thou hast set up.

3:13 Then Nebuchadnezzar in his rage and fury commanded to bring Shadrach, Meshach, and Abed-nego. Then they brought these men before the king.

3:14 Nebuchadnezzar spoke and said to them, Is it true, O Shadrach, Meshach, and Abed-nego, do ye not serve my gods, nor worship the golden image which I have set up?

3:15 Now if ye be ready that at what time ye hear the sound of the cornet, flute, harp, sackbut, psaltery, and dulcimer, and all kinds of music, ye fall down and worship the image which I have made; well: but if ye worship not, ye shall be cast the same hour into the midst of a burning fiery furnace; and who is that God that shall deliver you out of my hands?

3:16 Shadrach, Meshach, and Abed-nego, answered and said to the king, O Nebuchadnezzar, we are not careful to answer thee in this matter.

3:17 If it is so, our God whom we serve is able to deliver us from the burning fiery furnace, and he will deliver us out of thy hand, O king.

3:18 But if not, be it known to thee, O king, that we will not serve thy gods, nor worship the golden image which thou hast set up.

3:19 Then was Nebuchadnezzar full of fury, and the form of his visage was changed against Shadrach, Meshach, and Abed-nego: therefore he spoke, and commanded that they should heat the furnace seven times more than it was wont to be heated.

3:20 And he commanded the most mighty men that were in his army to bind Shadrach, Meshach, and Abed-nego, and to cast them into the burning fiery furnace.

3:21 Then these men were bound in their coats, their hose, and their hats, and their other garments, and were cast into the midst of the burning fiery furnace.

3:22 Therefore because the king's commandment was urgent, and the furnace exceeding hot, the flame of the fire killed those men that took up Shadrach, Meshach, and Abed-nego.

3:23 And these three men, Shadrach, Meshach, and Abed-nego, fell down bound into the midst of the burning fiery furnace.

3:24 Then Nebuchadnezzar the king was astonished, and rose up in haste, and spoke, and said to his counselors, Did we not cast three men bound into the midst of the fire? They answered and said to the king, True, O king.

3:25 He answered and said, Lo, I see four men loose, walking in the midst of the fire, and they have no hurt: and the form of the fourth is like the son of God.

3:26 Then Nebuchadnezzar came near to the mouth of the burning fiery furnace, and spoke, and said, Shadrach, Meshach, and Abed-nego, ye servants of the most high God, come forth, and come hither. Then Shadrach, Meshach, and Abed-nego, came forth from the midst of the fire.

3:27 And the princes, governors, and captains, and the king's counselors, being assembled, saw these men, upon whose bodies the fire had no power, nor was a hair of their head singed, neither were their coats changed, nor had the smell of fire passed upon them.

3:28 Then Nebuchadnezzar spoke, and said, Blessed be the God of Shadrach, Meshach, and Abed-nego, who hath sent his angel, and delivered his servants that trusted in him, and have changed the king's word, and yielded their bodies, that they might not serve nor worship any god, except their own God.

3:29 Therefore I make a decree, that every people, nation, and language, which speak any thing amiss against the God of Shadrach, Meshach, and Abed-nego, shall be cut in pieces, and their houses shall be made a dunghill: because there is no other god that can deliver after this sort.

3:30 Then the king promoted Shadrach, Meshach, and Abed-nego, in the province of Babylon.

4:1 Nebuchadnezzar the king, to all people, nations, and languages, that dwell in all the earth; Peace be multiplied to you.

4:2 I thought it good to show the signs and wonders that the high God hath wrought towards me.

4:3 How great are his signs! and how mighty are his wonders! his kingdom is an everlasting kingdom, and his dominion is from generation to generation.

4:4 I Nebuchadnezzar was at rest in my house, and flourishing in my palace:

4:5 I saw a dream which made me afraid, and the thoughts upon my bed and the visions of my head troubled me.

4:6 Therefore I made a decree to bring in all the wise men of Babylon before me, that they might make known to me the interpretation of the dream.

4:7 Then came in the magicians, the astrologers, the Chaldeans, and the sooth-sayers: and I told the dream before them; but they did not make known to me the interpretation of it.

4:8 But at the last Daniel came in before me, whose name is Belteshazzar, according to the name of my God, and in whom is the spirit of the holy gods: and before him I told the dream, saying,

4:9 O Belteshazzar, master of the magicians, because I know that the spirit of the holy gods is in thee, and no secret troubleth thee, tell me the visions of my dream that I have seen, and the interpretation of it.

4:10 Thus were the visions of my head in my bed; I saw, and behold a tree in the midst of the earth, and its hight was great.

4:11 The tree grew, and was strong, and its hight reached to heaven, and the sight of it to the end of all the earth:

4:12 Its leaves were fair, and its fruit abundant, and in it was food for all: the beasts of the field had shade under it, and the fowls of heaven dwelt among its boughs, and all flesh was fed from it.

4:13 I saw in the visions of my head upon my bed, and behold, a watcher and a holy one came down from heaven;

4:14 He cried aloud, and said thus, Hew down the tree, and cut off its branches, shake off its leaves, and scatter its fruit: let the beasts escape from under it, and the fowls from its branches.

4:15 Nevertheless leave the stump of its roots in the earth, even with a band of iron and brass, in the tender grass of the field; and let it be wet with the dew of heaven, and let its portion be with the beasts in the grass of the earth.

4:16 Let his heart be changed from man's, and let a beast's heart be given to him; and let seven times pass over him.

4:17 This matter is by the decree of the watchers, and the demand by the word of the holy ones: to the intent that the living may know that the most High ruleth in the kingdom of men, and giveth it to whomsoever he will, and setteth up over it the basest of men.

4:18 This dream I king Nebuchadnezzar have seen. Now thou, O Belteshazzar, declare the interpretation of it, forasmuch as all the wise men of my kingdom are not able to make known to me the interpretation: but thou art able; for the spirit of the holy gods is in thee.

4:19 Then Daniel, whose name was Belteshazzar, was astonished for one hour, and his thoughts troubled him. The king spoke, and said, Belteshazzar, let not the dream, or the interpretation of it, trouble thee. Belteshazzar answered, and said, My lord, the dream be to them that hate thee, and the interpretation of it to thy enemies.

4:20 The tree that thou sawest, which grew, and was strong, whose hight reached to the heaven, and the sight of it to all the earth;

4:21 Whose leaves were fair, and the fruit of it abundant, and in it was food for all; under which the beasts of the field dwelt, and upon whose branches the fowls of heaven had their habitation:

4:22 It is thou, O king, that art grown and become strong: for thy greatness is grown, and reacheth to heaven, and thy dominion to the end of the earth.

4:23 And whereas the king saw a watcher and a holy one coming down from heaven, and saying, Hew the tree down, and destroy it; yet leave the stump of its roots in the earth, even with a band of iron and brass, in the tender grass of the field; and let it be wet with the dew of heaven, and let its portion be with the beasts of the field, till seven times shall pass over him;

4:24 This is the interpretation, O king, and this is the decree of the most High, which is come upon my lord the king:

4:25 That they shall drive thee from men, and thy dwelling shall be with the beasts of the field, and they shall make thee to eat grass as oxen, and they shall wet thee with the dew of heaven, and seven times shall pass over thee, till thou shalt know that the most High ruleth in the kingdom of men, and giveth it to whomsoever he will.

4:26 And whereas they commanded to leave the stump of the tree roots; thy kingdom shall be sure to thee, after that thou shalt have known that the heavens do rule.

4:27 Wherefore, O king, let my counsel be acceptable to thee, and break off thy sins by righteousness, and thy iniquities by showing mercy to the poor; if it may be a lengthening of thy tranquillity.

4:28 All this came upon the king Nebuchadnezzar.

4:29 At the end of twelve months he walked in the palace of the kingdom of Babylon.

4:30 The king spoke, and said, Is not this great Babylon, that I have built for the house of the kingdom by the might of my power, and for the honor of my majesty?

4:31 While the word was in the king's mouth, there fell a voice from heaven, saying, O king Nebuchadnezzar, to thee it is spoken; The kingdom hath departed from thee.

4:32 And they shall drive thee from men, and thy dwelling shall be with the beasts of the field: they shall make thee to eat grass as oxen, and seven times shall pass over thee, until thou shalt know that the most High ruleth in the kingdom of men, and giveth it to whomsoever he will.

4:33 The same hour was the thing fulfilled upon Nebuchadnezzar: and he was driven from men, and ate grass as oxen, and his body was wet with the dew of heaven, till his hairs were grown like eagles' feathers, and his nails like birds' claws.

4:34 And at the end of the days I Nebuchadnezzar lifted up my eyes to heaven, and my understanding returned to me, and I blessed the most High, and I praised and honored him that liveth for ever, whose dominion is an everlasting dominion, and his kingdom is from generation to generation:

4:35 And all the inhabitants of the earth are reputed as nothing: and he doeth according to his will in the army of heaven, and among the inhabitants of the earth: and none can stay his hand, or say to him, What doest thou?

4:36 At the same time my reason returned to me; and for the glory of my kingdom, my honor and brightness returned to me; and my counselors and my lords sought to me; and I was established in my kingdom, and excellent majesty was added to me.

4:37 Now I Nebuchadnezzar praise and extol and honor the King of heaven, all whose works are truth, and his ways judgment: and those that walk in pride he is able to abase.

5:1 Belshazzar the king made a great feast to a thousand of his lords, and drank wine before the thousand.

5:2 Belshazzar, while he tasted the wine, commanded to bring the golden and silver vessels which his father Nebuchadnezzar had taken out of the temple which was in Jerusalem; that the king, and his princes, his wives, and his concubines, might drink in them.

5:3 Then they brought the golden vessels that were taken out of the temple of the house of God which was at Jerusalem; and the king, and his princes, his wives, and his concubines, drank in them.

5:4 They drank wine, and praised the gods of gold, and of silver, of brass, of iron, of wood, and of stone.

5:5 In the same hour came forth fingers of a man's hand, and wrote over against the candlestick upon the plaster of the wall of the king's palace: and the king saw the part of the hand that wrote.

5:6 Then the king's countenance was changed, and his thoughts troubled him, so that the joints of his loins were loosed, and his knees smote one against another.

5:7 The king cried aloud to bring in the astrologers, the Chaldeans, and the sooth-sayers. And the king spoke and said to the wise men of Babylon, Whoever shall read this writing, and show me the interpretation of it, shall be clothed with scarlet, and have a chain of gold about his neck, and shall be the third ruler in the kingdom.

5:8 Then came in all the king's wise men: but they could not read the writing, nor make known to the king the interpretation of it.

5:9 Then was the king Belshazzar greatly troubled, and his countenance was changed in him, and his lords were astonished.

5:10 Now the queen by reason of the words of the king and his lords came into the banquet house: and the queen spoke and said, O king, live for ever: let not thy thoughts trouble thee, nor let thy countenance be changed:

5:11 There is a man in thy kingdom, in whom is the spirit of the holy gods; and in the days of thy father light and understanding and wisdom, like the wisdom of the gods, was found in him; whom the king Nebuchadnezzar thy father, the king, I say, thy father, made master of the magicians, astrologers, Chaldeans, and sooth-sayers;

5:12 Forasmuch as an excellent spirit, and knowledge, and understanding, the interpreting of dreams, and showing of hard sentences, and dissolving of doubts, were found in the same Daniel, whom the king named Belteshazzar: now let Daniel be called, and he will show the interpretation.

5:13 Then was Daniel brought in before the king. And the king spoke and said to Daniel, Art thou that Daniel, who art of the children of the captivity of Judah, whom the king my father brought out of Judea?

5:14 I have even heard of thee, that the spirit of the gods is in thee, and that light and understanding and excellent wisdom is found in thee.

5:15 And now the wise men, the astrologers, have been brought in before me, that they should read this writing, and make known to me the interpretation of it, but they could not show the interpretation of the thing:

5:16 And I have heard of thee, that thou canst make interpretations, and dissolve doubts: now if thou canst read the writing, and make known to me the interpretation of it, thou shalt be clothed with scarlet, and have a chain of gold about thy neck, and shalt be the third ruler in the kingdom.

5:17 Then Daniel answered and said before the king, Let thy gifts be to thyself, and give thy rewards to another; yet I will read the writing to the king, and make known to him the interpretation.

5:18 O thou king, the most high God gave Nebuchadnezzar thy father a kingdom, and majesty, and glory, and honor:

5:19 And for the majesty that he gave him, all people, nations, and languages, trembled and feared before him: whom he would he slew; and whom he would he kept alive; and whom he would he set up; and whom he would he put down.

5:20 But when his heart was lifted up, and his mind hardened in pride, he was deposed from his kingly throne, and they took his glory from him:

5:21 And he was driven from the sons of men; and his heart was made like the beasts, and his dwelling was with the wild asses: they fed him with grass like oxen, and his body was wet with the dew of heaven; till he knew that the most high God ruleth in the kingdom of men, and that he appointeth over it whomsoever he will.

5:22 And thou his son, O Belshazzar, hast not humbled thy heart, though thou knewest all this;

5:23 But hast lifted up thyself against the Lord of heaven; and they have brought the vessels of his house before thee, and thou, and thy lords, thy wives, and thy concubines, have drank wine in them; and thou hast praised the gods of silver, and gold, of brass, iron, wood, and stone, which see not, nor hear, nor know: and the God in whose hand thy breath is, and whose are all thy ways, thou hast not glorified.

5:24 Then was the part of the hand sent from him; and this writing was written.

5:25 And this is the writing that was written, MENE, MENE, TEKEL, UPHARSIN.

5:26 This is the interpretation of the thing: MENE; God hath numbered thy kingdom, and finished it.

5:27 TEKEL; Thou art weighed in the balances, and art found wanting.

5:28 PERES; Thy kingdom is divided, and given to the Medes and Persians.

5:29 Then commanded Belshazzar, and they clothed Daniel with scarlet, and put a chain of gold about his neck, and made a proclamation concerning him, that he should be the third ruler in the kingdom.

5:30 In that night was Belshazzar the king of the Chaldeans slain.

5:31 And Darius the Median took the kingdom, being about sixty and two years old.

6:1 It pleased Darius to set over the kingdom a hundred and twenty princes, who should be over the whole kingdom;

6:2 And over these three presidents; of whom Daniel was first: that the princes might give accounts to them, and the king should have no damage.

6:3 Then this Daniel was preferred above the presidents and princes, because an excellent spirit was in him; and the king thought to set him over the whole realm.

6:4 Then the presidents and princes sought to find occasion against Daniel concerning the kingdom; but they could find no occasion nor fault; forasmuch as he was faithful, neither was there any error or fault found in him.

6:5 Then said these men, We shall not find any occasion against this Daniel, except we find it against him concerning the law of his God.

6:6 Then these presidents and princes assembled to the king, and said thus to him, King Darius, live for ever.

6:7 All the presidents of the kingdom, the governors, and the princes, the counselors, and the captains, have consulted together to establish a royal statute, and to make a firm decree, that whoever shall ask a petition of any God or man for thirty days, save of thee, O king, he shall be cast into the den of lions.

6:8 Now, O king, establish the decree, and sign the writing, that it may not be changed, according to the law of the Medes and Persians, which altereth not.

6:9 Wherefore king Darius signed the writing and the decree.

6:10 Now when Daniel knew that the writing was signed, he went into his house; and his windows being open in his chamber towards Jerusalem, he kneeled upon his knees three times a day, and prayed, and gave thanks before his God, as he did before.

6:11 Then these men assembled, and found Daniel praying and making supplication before his God.

6:12 Then they came near, and spoke before the king concerning the king's decree; Hast thou not signed a decree, that every man that shall ask a petition of any God or man within thirty days, save of thee, O king, shall be cast into the den of lions? The king answered and said, The thing is true, according to the law of the Medes and Persians, which altereth not.

6:13 Then they answered and said before the king, That Daniel, who is of the children of the captivity of Judah, regardeth not thee, O king, nor the decree that thou hast signed, but maketh his petition three times a day.

6:14 Then the king, when he heard these words, was much displeased with himself, and set his heart on Daniel to deliver him: and he labored till the setting of the sun to deliver him.

6:15 Then these men assembled to the king, and said to the king, Know, O king, that the law of the Medes and Persians is, That no decree nor statute which the king establisheth may be changed.

6:16 Then the king commanded, and they brought Daniel, and cast him into the den of lions. Now the king spoke and said to Daniel, Thy God whom thou servest continually, he will deliver thee.

6:17 And a stone was brought, and laid upon the mouth of the den; and the king sealed it with his own signet, and with the signet of his lords; that the purpose might not be changed concerning Daniel.

6:18 Then the king went to his palace, and passed the night fasting: neither were instruments of music brought before him: and his sleep went from him.

6:19 Then the king arose very early in the morning, and went in haste to the den of lions.

6:20 And when he came to the den, he cried with a lamentable voice to Daniel: and the king spoke and said to Daniel, O Daniel, servant of the living God, is thy God, whom thou servest continually, able to deliver thee from the lions?

6:21 Then said Daniel to the king, O king, live for ever.

6:22 My God hath sent his angel, and hath shut the lions' mouths, that they have not hurt me: forasmuch as before him innocence was found in me; and also before thee, O king, have I done no hurt.

6:23 Then was the king exceeding glad for him, and commanded that they should take Daniel out of the den. So Daniel was taken out of the den, and no manner of hurt was found upon him, because he believed in his God.

6:24 And the king commanded, and they brought those men who had accused Daniel, and they cast them into the den of lions, them, their children, and their wives; and the lions had the mastery of them, and broke all their bones in pieces before they came to the bottom of the den.

6:25 Then king Darius wrote to all people, nations, and languages, that dwell in all the earth; Peace be multiplied to you.

6:26 I make a decree, That in every dominion of my kingdom men tremble and fear before the God of Daniel: for he is the living God, and steadfast for ever, and his kingdom that which shall not be destroyed, and his dominion shall be even to the end.

6:27 He delivereth and rescueth, and he worketh signs and wonders in heaven and on earth, who hath delivered Daniel from the power of the lions.

6:28 So this Daniel prospered in the reign of Darius, and in the reign of Cyrus the Persian.

7:1 In the first year of Belshazzar king of Babylon, Daniel had a dream and visions of his head upon his bed: then he wrote the dream, and told the sum of the matters.

7:2 Daniel spoke and said, I saw in my vision by night, and behold, the four winds of heaven strove upon the great sea.

7:3 And four great beasts came up from the sea, diverse one from another.

7:4 The first was like a lion, and had eagles' wings: I beheld till its wings were plucked, and it was lifted up from the earth, and made to stand upon the feet as a man, and a man's heart was given to it.

7:5 And behold another beast, a second, like a bear, and it raised itself on one side, and it had three ribs in the mouth of it between the teeth of it: and they said thus to it, Arise, devour much flesh.

7:6 After this I beheld, and lo another, like a leopard, which had upon the back of it four wings of a fowl; the beast had also four heads; and dominion was given to it.

7:7 After this I saw in the night visions, and behold a fourth beast, dreadful and terrible, and strong exceedingly; and it had great iron teeth: it devoured and broke in pieces, and stamped the residue with its feet: and it was diverse from all the beasts that were before it; and it had ten horns.

7:8 I considered the horns, and behold, there came up among them another little horn, before whom there were three of the first horns plucked up by the roots: and behold, in this horn were eyes like the eyes of a man, and a mouth speaking great things.

7:9 I beheld till the thrones were cast down, and the Ancient of days did sit, whose garment was white as snow, and the hair of his head like the pure wool: his throne was like the fiery flame, and his wheels as burning fire.

7:10 A fiery stream issued and came forth from before him: thousand thousands ministered to him, and ten thousand times ten thousand stood before him: the judgment was set and the books were opened.

7:11 I beheld then because of the voice of the great words which the horn spoke: I beheld even till the beast was slain, and his body destroyed, and given to the burning flame.

7:12 As concerning the rest of the beasts, they had their dominion taken away: yet their lives were prolonged for a season and time.

7:13 I saw in the night visions, and behold, one like the son of man came with the clouds of heaven, and came to the Ancient of days, and they brought him near before him.

7:14 And there was given him dominion, and glory, and a kingdom, that all people, nations, and languages, should serve him: his dominion is an everlasting dominion, which shall not pass away, and his kingdom that which shall not be destroyed.

7:15 I Daniel was grieved in my spirit in the midst of my body, and the visions of my head troubled me.

7:16 I came near to one of them that stood by, and asked him the truth of all this. So he told me, and made me know the interpretation of the things.

7:17 These great beasts, which are four, are four kings, which shall arise out of the earth.

7:18 But the saints of the most High shall take the kingdom, and possess the kingdom for ever, even for ever and ever.

7:19 Then I would know the truth of the fourth beast, which was diverse from all the others, exceeding dreadful, whose teeth were of iron, and his nails of brass; which devoured, broke in pieces, and stamped the residue with his feet;

7:20 And of the ten horns that were in his head, and of the other which came up, and before whom three fell; even of that horn that had eyes, and a mouth that spoke very great things, whose look was more stout than his fellows.

7:21 I beheld, and the same horn made war with the saints, and prevailed against them;

7:22 Until the Ancient of days came, and judgment was given to the saints of the most High; and the time came that the saints possessed the kingdom.

7:23 Thus he said, The fourth beast shall be the fourth kingdom upon earth, which shall be diverse from all kingdoms, and shall devour the whole earth, and shall tread it down, and break it in pieces.

7:24 And the ten horns out of this kingdom are ten kings that shall arise: and another shall rise after them; and he shall be diverse from the first, and he shall subdue three kings.

7:25 And he shall speak great words against the most High, and shall wear out the saints of the most High, and think to change times and laws: and they shall be given into his hand until a time and times and the dividing of time.

7:26 But the judgment shall sit, and they shall take away his dominion to consume and to destroy it to the end.

7:27 And the kingdom and dominion, and the greatness of the kingdom under the whole heaven, shall be given to the people of the saints of the most High, whose kingdom is an everlasting kingdom, and all dominions shall serve and obey him.

7:28 Hitherto is the end of the matter. As for me Daniel, my cogitations much troubled me, and my countenance changed in me: but I kept the matter in my heart.

8:1 In the third year of the reign of king Belshazzar a vision appeared to me, even to me, Daniel, after that which appeared to me at the first.

8:2 And I saw in a vision; and it came to pass, when I saw, that I was at Shushan in the palace, which is in the province of Elam; and I saw in a vision, and I was by the river Ulai.

8:3 Then I lifted up my eyes, and saw, and behold, there stood before the river a ram which had two horns: and the two horns were high; but one was higher than the other, and the higher came up last.

8:4 I saw the ram pushing westward, and northward, and southward; so that no beasts might stand before him, neither was there any that could deliver out of his hand; but he did according to his will, and became great.

8:5 And as I was considering, behold, a he-goat came from the west on the face of the whole earth, and touched not the ground: and the goat had a notable horn between his eyes.

8:6 And he came to the ram that had two horns, which I had seen standing before the river, and ran to him in the fury of his power.

8:7 And I saw him come close to the ram, and he was moved with anger against him, and smote the ram, and broke his two horns: and there was no power in the ram to stand before him, but he cast him down to the ground, and stamped upon him: and there was none that could deliver the ram out of his hand.

8:8 Therefore the he-goat became very great: and when he was strong, the great horn was broken; and in its stead came up four notable ones towards the four winds of heaven.

8:9 And out of one of them came forth a little horn, which became exceeding great, towards the south, and towards the east, and towards the pleasant land.

8:10 And it grew great, even to the host of heaven; and it cast down some of the host and of the stars to the ground, and stamped upon them.

8:11 Yes, he magnified himself even to the prince of the host, and by him the daily sacrifice was taken away, and the place of his sanctuary was cast down.

8:12 And a host was given him against the daily sacrifice by reason of transgression, and it cast down the truth to the ground; and it practiced, and prospered.

8:13 Then I heard one saint speaking, and another saint said to that certain saint who spoke, How long shall be the vision concerning the daily sacrifice, and the transgression of desolation, to give both the sanctuary and the host to be trodden under foot?

8:14 And he said to me, Until two thousand and three hundred days; then shall the sanctuary be cleansed.

8:15 And it came to pass, when I, even I Daniel, had seen the vision, and sought for the meaning, then behold, there stood before me as the appearance of a man.

8:16 And I heard a man's voice between the banks of Ulai, which called, and said, Gabriel, make this man to understand the vision.

8:17 So he came near where I stood: and when he came, I was afraid, and fell upon my face: but he said to me, Understand, O son of man: for at the time of the end shall be the vision.

8:18 Now as he was speaking with me, I was in a deep sleep on my face towards the ground: but he touched me, and set me upright.

8:19 And he said, Behold, I will make thee know what shall be in the last end of the indignation: for at the time appointed the end shall be.

8:20 The ram which thou sawest having two horns are the kings of Media and Persia.

8:21 And the rough goat is the king of Grecia: and the great horn that is between his eyes is the first king.

8:22 Now that being broken, whereas four stood up in its place, four kingdoms shall stand up out of the nation, but not in his power.

8:23 And in the latter time of their kingdom, when the transgressors are come to the full, a king of fierce countenance, and understanding dark sentences, shall stand up.

8:24 And his power shall be mighty, but not by his own power: and he shall destroy wonderfully, and shall prosper, and practice, and shall destroy the mighty and the holy people.

8:25 And through his policy also he shall cause craft to prosper in his hand; and he shall magnify himself in his heart, and by peace shall destroy many: he shall also stand up against the Prince of princes; but he shall be broken without hand.

8:26 And the vision of the evening and the morning which was told is true: wherefore shut thou up the vision; for it shall be for many days.

8:27 And I Daniel fainted, and was sick certain days; afterward I rose, and did the king's business; and I was astonished at the vision, but none understood it.

9:1 In the first year of Darius the son of Ahasuerus, of the seed of the Medes, who was made king over the realm of the Chaldeans;

9:2 In the first year of his reign, I Daniel understood by books the number of the years, concerning which the word of the LORD came to Jeremiah the prophet, that he would accomplish seventy years in the desolations of Jerusalem.

9:3 And I set my face to the Lord God, to seek by prayer and supplications, with fasting, and sackcloth, and ashes:

9:4 And I prayed to the LORD my God, and made my confession, and said, O Lord, the great and dreadful God, keeping the covenant and mercy to them that love him, and to them that keep his commandments;

9:5 We have sinned, and have committed iniquity, and have done wickedly, and have rebelled, even by departing from thy precepts and from thy judgments:

9:6 Neither have we hearkened to thy servants the prophets, who spoke in thy name to our kings, our princes, and our fathers, and to all the people of the land.

9:7 O Lord, righteousness belongeth to thee, but to us confusion of faces, as at this day; to the men of Judah, and to the inhabitants of Jerusalem, and to all Israel, that are near, and that are far off, through all the countries whither thou hast driven them, because of their trespass that they have trespassed against thee.

9:8 O Lord, to us belongeth confusion of face, to our kings, to our princes, and to our fathers, because we have sinned against thee.

9:9 To the Lord our God belong mercies and forgivenesses, though we have rebelled against him;

9:10 Neither have we obeyed the voice of the LORD our God, to walk in his laws, which he set before us by his servants the prophets.

9:11 And all Israel have transgressed thy law, even by departing, that they might not obey thy voice; therefore the curse is poured upon us, and the oath that is written in the law of Moses the servant of God, because we have sinned against him.

9:12 And he hath confirmed his words, which he spoke against us, and against our judges that judged us, by bringing upon us a great evil: for under the whole heaven it hath not been done as it hath been done upon Jerusalem.

9:13 As it is written in the law of Moses, all this evil is come upon us: yet we have not made our prayer before the LORD our God, that we might turn from our iniquities, and understand thy truth.

9:14 Therefore hath the LORD watched upon the evil, and brought it upon us: for the LORD our God is righteous in all his works which he doeth: for we have not obeyed his voice.

9:15 And now, O Lord our God, that hast brought thy people out of the land of Egypt with a mighty hand, and hast obtained thee renown, as at this day; we have sinned, we have done wickedly.

9:16 O Lord, according to all thy righteousness, I beseech thee, let thy anger and thy fury be turned away from thy city Jerusalem, thy holy mountain: because for our sins and for the iniquities of our fathers, Jerusalem and thy people have become a reproach to all that are about us.

9:17 Now therefore, O our God, hear the prayer of thy servant, and his supplications, and cause thy face to shine upon thy sanctuary that is desolate, for the Lord's sake.

9:18 O my God, incline thy ear, and hear; open thy eyes, and behold our desolations, and the city which is called by thy name: for we do not present our supplications before thee for our righteousnesses, but for thy great mercies.

9:19 O Lord, hear; O Lord, forgive; O Lord, hearken and do; defer not, for thy own sake, O my God: for thy city and thy people are called by thy name.

9:20 And while I was speaking, and praying, and confessing my sin, and the sin of my people Israel, and presenting my supplication before the LORD my God for the holy mountain of my God;

9:21 Yes, while I was speaking in prayer, even the man Gabriel, whom I had seen in the vision at the beginning, being caused to fly swiftly, touched me about the time of the evening oblation.

9:22 And he informed me, and talked with me, and said, O Daniel, I am now come forth to give thee skill and understanding.

9:23 At the beginning of thy supplications the commandment came forth, and I am come to show thee; for thou art greatly beloved: therefore understand the matter, and consider the vision.

9:24 Seventy weeks are determined upon thy people and upon thy holy city to finish the transgression, and to make an end of sins, and to make reconciliation for iniquity, and to bring in everlasting righteousness, and to seal up the vision and prophecy, and to anoint the most Holy.

9:25 Know therefore and understand, that from the going forth of the commandment to restore and to build Jerusalem to the Messiah the Prince shall be seven weeks, and sixty and two weeks: the street shall be built again, and the wall, even in troublous times.

9:26 And after sixty and two weeks shall Messiah be cut off, but not for himself: and the people of the prince that shall come shall destroy the city and the sanctuary; and its end shall be with a flood, and to the end of the war desolations are determined.

9:27 And he shall confirm the covenant with many for one week: and in the midst of the week he shall cause the sacrifice and the oblation to cease, and for the overspreading of abominations, he shall make it desolate, even until the consummation, and that determined shall be poured upon the desolate.

10:1 In the third year of Cyrus king of Persia, a thing was revealed to Daniel, whose name was called Belteshazzar; and the thing was true, but the time appointed was long: and he understood the thing, and had understanding of the vision.

10:2 In those days I Daniel was mourning three full weeks.

10:3 I ate no pleasant bread, neither came flesh nor wine in my mouth, neither did I anoint myself at all, till three whole weeks were fulfilled.

10:4 And in the four and twentieth day of the first month, as I was by the side of the great river, which is Hiddekel;

10:5 Then I lifted up my eyes, and looked, and behold a certain man clothed in linen, whose loins were girded with fine gold of Uphaz:

10:6 His body also was like the beryl, and his face as the appearance of lightning, and his eyes as lamps of fire, and his arms and his feet like in color to polished brass, and the voice of his words like the voice of a multitude.

10:7 And I Daniel alone saw the vision: for the men that were with me saw not the vision: but a great quaking fell upon them, so that they fled to hide themselves.

10:8 Therefore I was left alone, and saw this great vision, and there remained no strength in me: for my comeliness was turned in me into corruption, and I retained no strength.

10:9 Yet I heard the voice of his words: and when I heard the voice of his words, then I was in a deep sleep on my face, and my face toward the ground.

10:10 And behold, a hand touched me, which set me upon my knees and upon the palms of my hands.

10:11 And he said to me, O Daniel, a man greatly beloved, understand the words that I speak to thee, and stand upright: for to thee I am now sent. And when he had spoken this word to me, I stood trembling.

10:12 Then said he to me, Fear not, Daniel: for from the first day that thou didst set thy heart to understand, and to chasten thyself before thy God, thy words were heard, and I am come for thy words.

10:13 But the prince of the kingdom of Persia withstood me one and twenty days: but lo, Michael, one of the chief princes, came to help me; and I remained there with the kings of Persia.

10:14 Now I have come to make thee understand what shall befall thy people in the latter days: for yet the vision is for many days.

10:15 And when he had spoken such words to me, I set my face towards the ground, and I became dumb.

10:16 And behold, one like the similitude of the sons of men touched my lips: then I opened my mouth, and spoke, and said to him that stood before me, O my lord, by the vision my sorrows are turned upon me, and I have retained no strength.

10:17 For how can the servant of this my lord talk with this my lord? for as for me, immediately there remained no strength in me, neither is there breath left in me.

10:18 Then there came again and touched me one like the appearance of a man, and he strengthened me,

10:19 And said, O man greatly beloved, fear not: peace be to thee, be strong, yes, be strong.

And when he had spoken to me, I was strengthened, and said, Let my lord speak; for thou hast strengthened me.

10:20 Then said he, Knowest thou for what cause I come to thee? and now will I return to fight with the prince of Persia: and when I am gone forth, lo, the prince of Grecia shall come.

10:21 But I will show thee that which is noted in the scripture of truth: and there is none that holdeth with me in these things, but Michael your prince.

11:1 Also I, in the first year of Darius the Mede, even I, stood to confirm and to strengthen him.

11:2 And now will I show thee the truth. Behold, there shall stand up yet three kings in Persia; and the fourth shall be far richer than they all: and by his strength through his riches he shall stir up all against the realm of Grecia.

11:3 And a mighty king shall stand up, that shall rule with great dominion, and do according to his will.

11:4 And when he shall stand up, his kingdom shall be broken, and shall be divided towards the four winds of heaven; and not to his posterity, nor according to his dominion which he ruled: for his kingdom shall be plucked up, even for others beside those.

11:5 And the king of the south shall be strong, and one of his princes; and he shall be strong above him, and have dominion; his dominion shall be a great dominion.

11:6 And in the end of years they shall join themselves together; for the king's daughter of the south shall come to the king of the north to make an agreement: but she shall not retain the power of the arm; neither shall he stand, nor his arm: but she shall be given up, and they that brought her, and he that begat her, and he that strengthened her in these times.

11:7 But out of a branch of her roots shall one stand up in his estate, who shall come with an army, and shall enter into the fortress of the king of the north, and shall deal against them, and shall prevail:

11:8 And shall also carry captives into Egypt their gods, with their princes, and with their precious vessels of silver and of gold; and he shall continue more years than the king of the north.

11:9 So the king of the south shall come into his kingdom, and shall return into his own land.

11:10 But his sons shall be stirred up, and shall assemble a multitude of great forces: and one shall certainly come, and overflow, and pass through: then shall he return, and be stirred up, even to his fortress.

11:11 And the king of the south shall be moved with wrath, and shall come forth and fight with him, even with the king of the north: and he shall set forth a great multitude; but the multitude shall be given into his hand.

11:12 And when he hath taken away the multitude, his heart shall be lifted up; and he shall cast down many ten thousands: but he shall not be strengthened by it.

11:13 For the king of the north shall return, and shall set forth a multitude greater than the former, and shall certainly come after certain years with a great army and with much riches.

11:14 And in those times there shall many stand up against the king of the south: also the robbers of thy people shall exalt themselves to establish the vision; but they shall fall.

11:15 So the king of the north shall come, and cast up a mount, and take the most fortified cities: and the arms of the south shall not withstand, neither his chosen people, neither shall there be any strength to withstand.

11:16 But he that cometh against him shall do according to his own will, and none shall stand before him: and he shall stand in the glorious land, which by his hand shall be consumed.

11:17 He shall also set his face to enter with the strength of his whole kingdom, and upright ones with him; thus shall he do: and he shall give him the daughter of women, corrupting her: but she shall not stand on his side, neither be for him.

11:18 After this shall he turn his face to the isles, and shall take many: but a prince for his own behalf shall cause the reproach offered by him to cease; without his own reproach he shall cause it to turn upon him.

11:19 Then he shall turn his face towards the fort of his own land: but he shall stumble and fall, and not be found.

11:20 Then shall stand up in his estate a raiser of taxes in the glory of the kingdom: but within few days he shall be destroyed, neither in anger, nor in battle.

11:21 And in his estate shall stand up a vile person, to whom they shall not give the honor of the kingdom: but he shall come in peaceably, and obtain the kingdom by flatteries.

11:22 And with the arms of a flood shall they be overflowed from before him, and shall be broken; yes, also the prince of the covenant.

11:23 And after the league made with him he shall work deceitfully: for he shall come up, and shall become strong with a small people.

11:24 He shall enter peaceably even upon the fattest places of the province; and he shall do that which his fathers have not done, nor his fathers' fathers; he shall scatter among them the prey, and spoil, and riches: yes, and he shall forecast his devices against the strong holds, even for a time.

11:25 And he shall stir up his power and his courage against the king of the south with a great army; and the king of the south shall be stirred up to battle with a very great and mighty army; but he shall not stand: for they shall forecast devices against him.

11:26 Yes, they that feed of the portion of his provisions shall destroy him, and his army shall overflow: and many shall fall down slain.

11:27 And both these kings hearts shall be to do mischief, and they shall speak lies at one table; but it shall not prosper: for yet the end shall be at the time appointed.

11:28 Then shall he return into his land with great riches; and his heart shall be against the holy covenant; and he shall do exploits, and return to his own land.

11:29 At the time appointed he shall return, and come towards the south; but it shall not be as the former, or as the latter.

11:30 For the ships of Chittim shall come against him: therefore he shall be grieved, and return, and have indignation against the holy covenant: so shall he do; he shall even return, and have intelligence with them that forsake the holy covenant.

11:31 And arms shall stand on his part, and they shall pollute the sanctuary of strength, and shall take away the daily sacrifice, and they shall place the abomination that maketh desolate.

11:32 And such as do wickedly against the covenant shall he corrupt by flatteries: but the people that know their God shall be strong, and do exploits.

11:33 And they that understand among the people shall instruct many: yet they shall fall by the sword, and by flame, by captivity, and by spoil, many days.

11:34 Now when they shall fall, they shall be assisted with a little help: but many shall cleave to them with flatteries.

11:35 And some of them of understanding shall fall, to try them, and to purge, and to make them white, even to the time of the end: because it is yet for a time appointed.

11:36 And the king shall do according to his will; and he shall exalt himself, and magnify himself above every god, and shall speak marvelous things against the God of gods, and shall prosper till the indignation be accomplished: for that which is determined shall be done.

11:37 Neither shall he regard the God of his fathers, nor the desire of women, nor regard any god: for he shall magnify himself above all.

11:38 But in his estate shall he honor the God of forces: and a god whom his fathers knew not shall he honor with gold, and silver, and with precious stones, and pleasant things.

11:39 Thus shall he do in the most strong holds with a strange god, whom he shall acknowledge and increase with glory: and he shall cause them to rule over many, and shall divide the land for gain.

11:40 And at the time of the end shall the king of the south push at him: and the king of the north shall come against him like a whirlwind, with chariots, and with horsemen, and with many ships; and he shall enter into the countries, and shall overflow and pass over.

11:41 He shall enter also into the glorious land, and many countries shall be overthrown: but these shall escape out of his hand, even Edom, and Moab, and the chief of the children of Ammon.

11:42 He shall stretch forth his hand also upon the countries: and the land of Egypt shall not escape.

11:43 But he shall have power over the treasures of gold and of silver, and over all the precious things of Egypt: and the Libyans and the Cushites shall be at his steps.

11:44 But tidings out of the east and out of the north shall trouble him: therefore he shall go forth with great fury to destroy, and utterly to make away many.

11:45 And he shall plant the tabernacles of his palace between the seas in the glorious holy mountain: yet he shall come to his end, and none shall help him.

12:1 And at that time shall Michael stand up, the great prince who standeth for the children of thy people: and there shall be a time of trouble, such as never was since there was a nation even to that same time: and at that time thy people shall be delivered, every one that shall be found written in the book.

12:2 And many of them that sleep in the dust of the earth shall awake, some to everlasting life, and some to shame and everlasting contempt.

12:3 And they that are wise shall shine as the brightness of the firmament; and they that turn many to righteousness as the stars for ever and ever.

12:4 But thou, O Daniel, shut up the words, and seal the book, even to the time of the end: many shall run to and fro, and knowledge shall be increased.

12:5 Then I Daniel looked, and behold, there stood other two, the one on this side of the bank of the river, and the other on that side of the bank of the river.

12:6 And one said to the man clothed in linen, who was upon the waters of the river, How long shall it be to the end of these wonders?

12:7 And I heard the man clothed in linen, who was upon the waters of the river, when he held up his right hand and his left hand to heaven, and swore by him that liveth for ever, that it shall be for a time, times, and a half; and when he shall have accomplished to scatter the power of the holy people, all these things shall be finished.

12:8 And I heard, but I understood not: then said I, O my Lord, what shall be the end of these things?

12:9 And he said, Go thy way Daniel: for the words are closed up and sealed till the time of the end.

12:10 Many shall be purified, and made white, and tried; but the wicked shall do wickedly: and none of the wicked shall understand; but the wise shall understand.

12:11 And from the time that the daily sacrifice shall be taken away, and the abomination that maketh desolate set up, there shall be a thousand two hundred and ninety days.

12:12 Blessed is he that waiteth, and cometh to the thousand three hundred and five and thirty days.

12:13 But go thou thy way till the end: for thou shalt rest, and stand in thy lot at the end of the days.

COMMENTARY

MATTHEW HENRY

Introduction

THE book of Ezekiel left the affairs of Jerusalem under a doleful aspect, all in ruins, but with a joyful prospect of all in glory again. This of Daniel fitly follows. Ezekiel told us what was seen, and what was foreseen, by him in the former years of the captivity: Daniel tells us what was seen, and foreseen, in the latter years of the captivity. When God employs different hands, yet it is about the same work. And it was a comfort to the poor captives that they had first one prophet among them and then another, to show them how long, and a sign that God had not quite cast them off. Let us enquire, I. Concerning this prophet His Hebrew name was Daniel, which signifies the judgment of God; his Chaldean name was Belteshazzar. He was of the tribe of Judah, and, as it should seem, of the royal family. He was betimes eminent for wisdom and piety. Ezekiel, his contemporary, but much his senior, speaks of him as an oracle when thus he upbraids the king of Tyre with his conceitedness of himself: Thou art wiser then Daniel. He is likewise there celebrated for success in prayer, when Noah, Daniel, and Job are reckoned as three men that had the greatest interest in heaven of any. He began betimes to be famous, and continued long so. Some of the Jewish rabbin are loth to acknowledge him to be a prophet of the higher form, and therefore rank his book among the Hagiographa, not among the prophecies, and would not have their disciples pay much regard to it. One reason they pretend is because he did not live such a mean mortified life as Jeremiah and some other of the prophets did, but lived like a prince, and was a prime-minister of state; whereas we find him persecuted as other prophets were and mortifying himself as other prophets did, when he ate no pleasant bread and fainting sick when he was under the power of the Spirit of prophecy. Another reason they pretend is because he wrote his book in a heathen country, and there had his visions, and not in the land of Israel; but, for the same reason, Ezekiel also must be expunged out of the roll of prophets. But the true reason is that he speaks so plainly of the time of the Messiah's coming that the Jews cannot avoid the conviction of it and therefore do not care to hear of it. But Josephus calls him one of the greatest of the prophets, nay, the angel Gabriel calls him a man greatly beloved. He lived long an active life in the courts and councils of some of the greatest monarchs the world ever had, Nebuchadnezzar, Cyrus, Darius; for we mistake of we confine the privilege of an intercourse with heaven to speculative men, or those that spend their time in contemplation; no, who was more intimately acquainted with the mind of God than Daniel, a courtier, a statesman, and a man of business? The Spirit, as the wind, blows where it lists. And, if those that have much to do in the world plead that as an excuse for the infrequency and slightness of their converse with God, Daniel will condemn them. Some have thought that he returned to Jerusalem, and was one of the masters of the Greek synagogue; but nothing of that appears in scripture; it is therefore generally concluded that he died in Persia at Susan, where he lived to be very old. II. Concerning this book. The first six chapters of it are historical, and are plain and easy; the last six are prophetical, and in them are many things dark, and hard to be understood, which yet would be more intelligible if we had a more complete history of the nations, and especially the Jewish nation, from Daniel's time to the coming of the Messiah. Our Saviour intimates the difficulty of apprehending the sense of Daniel's prophecies when, speaking of them, he says, Let him that readeth understand. The first chapter, and the first three verses of the second chapter, are in Hebrew; thence to the eighth chapter is in the Chaldee dialect; and thence to the end is in Hebrew. Mr. Broughton observes that, as the Chaldeans were kind to Daniel, and gave cups of cold water to him when he requested it, rather than the king's wine, God would not have them lose their reward, but made that language which they taught him to have honour in his writings through all the world, unto this day. Daniel, according to his computation, continues the holy story from the first surprising of Jerusalem by the Chaldean Babel, when he himself was carried away captive, until the last destruction of it by Rome, the mystical Babel, for so far forward his predictions look. The fables of Susannah, and of Bel and the Dragon, in both which Daniel is made a party, are apocryphal stories, which we think we have no reason to give any credit to, they being never found in the Hebrew or Chaldee, but only in the Greek, nor ever admitted by the Jewish church. There are some both of the histories and of the prophecies of this book that bear date in the latter end of the Chaldean monarchy, and others of both that are dated in the beginning of the Persian monarchy. But both Nebuchadnezzar's dream, which Daniel interpreted, and his own visions, point at the Grecian and Roman monarchies, and very particularly at the Jews' troubles under Antiochus, which it would be of great use to them to prepare for; as his fixing the very time for the coming of the Messiah was of use to all those that waited for the consolation of Israel, and is to us, for the confirming of our belief, That this is he who should come, and we are to look for no other.

Chapter 1

This chapter gives us a more particular account of the beginning of Daniel's life, his original and education, than we have of any other of the prophets. Isaiah, Jeremiah, and Ezekiel, began immediately with divine visions; but Daniel began with the study of human learning, and was afterwards honoured with divine visions; such variety of methods has God taken in training up men for the service of his church. We have here, I. Jehoiakim's first captivity (v.1, v.2), in which Daniel, with others of the seed-royal, was carried to Babylon. II. The choice made of Daniel, and some other young men, to be brought up in the Chaldean literature, that they might be fitted to serve the government, and the provision made for them (v.3-7). III. Their pious refusal to eat the portion of the king's meat, and their determining to live upon pulse and water, which, having tried it, the master of the eunuchs allowed them to do, finding that it agreed very well with them IV. Their wonderful improvement, above all their fellows, in wisdom and knowledge.

Verses 1-7

We have in these verses an account, I. Of the first descent which Nebuchadnezzar, king of Babylon, in the first year of his reign, made upon Judah and Jerusalem, in the third year of the reign of Jehoiakim, and his success in that expedition: He besieged Jerusalem, soon made himself master of it, seized the king, took whom he pleased and what he pleased away with him, and then left Jehoiakim to reign as tributary to him, which he did about eight years longer, but then rebelled, and it was his ruin. Now from this first captivity most interpreters think the seventy years are to be dated, though Jerusalem was not destroyed, nor the captivity completed, till about nineteen years after, In that first year Daniel was carried to Babylon, and there continued the whole seventy years, during which time all nations shall serve Nebuchadnezzar, and his son, and his son's son . This one prophet therefore saw within the compass of his own time the rise, reign, and ruin of that monarchy; so that it was res unius aetatis—the affair of a single age, such short-lived things are the kingdoms of the earth; but the kingdom of heaven is everlasting. The righteous, that see them taking root, shall see their fall. Mr. Broughton observes the proportion of times in God's government since the coming out of Egypt: thence to their entering Canaan forty years, thence seven years to the dividing of the land, thence seven Jubilees to the first year of Samuel, in whom prophecy began, thence to this first year of the captivity seven seventies of years, 490 (ten Jubilees), thence to the return one seventy, thence to the death of Christ seven seventies more, thence to the destruction of Jerusalem forty years.II. The improvement he made of this success. He did not destroy the city or kingdom, but did that which just accomplished the first threatening of mischief by Babylon. It was denounced against Hezekiah, for showing his treasures to the king of Babylon's ambassadors, that the treasures and the children should be carried away, and, if they had been humbled and reformed by this, hitherto the king of Babylon's power and success should have gone, but no further. If less judgments do the work, God will not send greater; but, if not, he will heat the furnace seven times hotter. Let us see what was now done.

1. The vessels of the sanctuary were carried away, part of them. They fondly trusted to the temple to defend them, though they went on in their iniquity. And now, to show them the vanity of that confidence, the temple is first plundered. Many of the holy vessels which used to be employed in the service of God were taken away by the king of Babylon, those of them, it is likely, which were most valuable, and he brought them as trophies of victory to the house of his god, to whom, with a blind devotion, he gave praise of his success; and having appropriated these vessels, in token of gratitude, to his god, he put them in the treasury of his temple. See the righteousness of God; his people had brought the images of other gods into his temple, and now he suffers the vessels of the temple to be carried into the treasuries of those other gods. Note, When men profane the vessels of the sanctuary with their sins it is just with God to profane them by his judgments. It is probable that the treasures of the king's house were rifled, as was foretold, but particular mention is made of the taking away of the vessels of the sanctuary because we shall find afterwards that the profanation of them was that which filled up the measure of the Chaldeans' iniquity . But observe, It was only part of them that went now; some were left them yet upon trial, to see if they would take the right course to prevent the carrying away of the remainder. The children and young men, especially such as were of noble or royal extraction, that were sightly and promising, and of good natural parts, were carried away. Thus was the iniquity of the fathers visited upon the children. These were taken away by Nebuchadnezzar, (1.) As trophies, to be made a show of for the evidencing and magnifying of his success. (2.) As hostages for the fidelity of their parents in their own land, who would be concerned to conduct themselves well that their children might have the better treatment. (3.) As a seed to serve him. He took them away to train them up for employments and preferments under him, either out of an unaccountable affectation, which great men often have, to be attended by foreigners, though they be blacks, rather than by those of their own nation, or because he knew that there were no such witty, sprightly, ingenious young men to be found among his Chaldeans as abounded among the youth of Israel; and, if that were so, it was much for the honour of the Jewish nation, as of an uncommon genius above other people, and a fruit of the blessing. But it was a shame that a people who had so much wit should have so little wisdom and

grace. Now observe, [1.]

The directions which the king of Babylon gave for the choice of these youths. They must not choose such as were deformed in body, but comely and well-favoured, whose countenances were indexes of ingenuity and good humour. But that is not enough; they must be skilful in all wisdom, and cunning, or well-seen in knowledge, and understanding science, such as were quick and sharp, and could give a ready and intelligent account of their own country and of the learning they had hitherto been brought up in. He chose such as were young, because they would be pliable and tractable, would forget their own people and incorporate with the Chaldeans. He had an eye to what he designed them for; they must be such as had ability in them to stand in the king's palace, not only to attend his royal person, but to preside in his affairs. This is an instance of the policy of this rising monarch, now in the beginning of his reign, and was a good omen of his prosperity, that he was in care to raise up a succession of persons fit for public business. He did not, like Ahasuerus, appoint them to choose him out young women for the service of his government. It is the interest of princes to have wise men employed under them; it is therefore their wisdom to take care for the finding out and training up of such. It is the misery of this world that so many who are fit for public stations are buried in obscurity, and so many who are unfit for them are preferred to them. [2.]

The care which he took concerning them. First, For their education. He ordered that they should be taught the learning and tongue of the Chaldeans. They are supposed to be wise and knowing young men, and yet they must be further taught. Give instructions to a wise man and he will increase in learning. Note, Those that would do good in the world when they grow up must learn when they are young. That is the learning age; if that time be lost, it will hardly be redeemed. It does not appear that Nebuchadnezzar designed they should learn the unlawful arts that were used among the Chaldeans, magic and divination; if he did, Daniel and his fellows would not defile themselves with them. Nay, we do not find that he ordered them to be taught the religion of the Chaldeans, by which it appears That he was at this time no bigot; if men were skilful and faithful, and fit for his business, it was not material to him what religion they were of, provided they had but some religion. They must be trained up in the language and laws of the country, in history, philosophy, and mathematics, in the arts of husbandry, war, and navigation, in such learning as might qualify them to serve their generation.

Note, It is real service to the public to provide for the good education of the youth. Secondly, For their maintenance. He provided for them three years, not only necessaries, but dainties for their encouragement in their studies. They had daily provision of the king's meat, and of the wine which he drank. This was an instance of his generosity and humanity; though they were captives, he considered their birth and quality, their spirit and genius, and treated them honourably, and studied to make their captivity easy to them. There is a respect due to those who are well-born and bred when they have fallen into distress. With a liberal education there should be a liberal maintenance.

III. A particular account of Daniel and his fellows. They were of the children of Judah, the royal tribe, and probably of the house of David, which had grown a numerous family; and God told Hezekiah that of the children that should issue from him some should be taken and made eunuchs, or chamberlains, in the palace of the king of Babylon. The prince of the eunuchs changed the names of Daniel and his fellows, partly to show his authority over them and their subjection to him, and partly in token of their being naturalized and made Chaldeans. Their Hebrew names, which they received at their circumcision, had something of God, or Jah, in them: Daniel—God is my Judge; Hananiah—The grace of the Lord; Mishael—He that is the strong God; Azariah—The Lord is a help. To make them forget the

God of their fathers, the guide of their youth, they give them names that savour of the Chaldean idolatry. Belteshazzar signifies the keeper of the hidden treasures of Bel; Shadrach —The inspiration of the sun, which the Chaldeans worshipped; Meshach —Of the goddess Shach, under which name Venus was worshipped; Abed-nego, The servant of the shining fire, which they worshipped also. Thus, though they would not force them from the religion of their fathers to that of their conquerors, yet they did what they could by fair means insensibly to wean them from the former and instil the latter into them. Yet see how comfortably they were provided for; though they suffered for their fathers' sins they were preferred for their own merits, and the land of their captivity was made more comfortable to them than the land of their nativity at this time would have been.

Verses 8-16

We observe here, very much to our satisfaction, I. That Daniel was a favourite with the prince of the eunuchs as Joseph was with the keeper of the prison; he had a tender love for him. No doubt Daniel deserved it, and recommended himself by his ingenuity and sweetness of temper (he was greatly beloved); and yet it is said here that it was God that brought him into favour with the prince of the eunuchs, for every one does not meet with acceptance according to his merits. Note, The interest which we think we make for ourselves we must acknowledge to be God's gift, and must ascribe to him the glory of it. Whoever are in favour, it is God that has brought them into favour; and it is by him that they find good understanding. Herein was again verified That work. He made them to be pitied of all those that carried them captives. Let young ones know that the way to be acceptable is to be tractable and dutiful.

II. That Daniel was still firm to his religion. They had changed his name, but they could not change his nature. Whatever they pleased to call him, he still retained the spirit of an Israelite indeed. He would apply his mind as closely as any of them to his books, and took pains to make himself master of the learning and tongue of the Chaldeans, but he was resolved that he would not defile himself with the portion of the king's meat, he would not meddle with it, nor with the wine which he drank. And having communicated his purpose, with the reasons of it, to his fellows, they concurred in the same resolution, as appears. This was not out of sullenness, or peevishness, or a spirit of contradiction, but from a principle of conscience. Perhaps it was not in itself unlawful for them to eat of the king's meat or to drink of his wine.

But, 1. They were scrupulous concerning the meat, lest it should be sinful. Sometimes such meat would be set before them as was expressly forbidden by their law, as swine's flesh; or they were afraid lest it should have been offered in sacrifice to an idol, or blessed in the name of an idol. The Jews were distinguished from other nations very much by their meats and these pious young men, being in a strange country, thought themselves obliged to keep up the honour of their being a peculiar people. Though they could not keep up their dignity as princes, they would not lose it as Israelites; for on that they most valued themselves Note, When God's people are in Babylon they have need to take special care that they partake not in her sins. Providence seemed to lay this meat before them; being captives they must eat what they could get and must not disoblige their masters; yet, if the command be against it, they must abide by that. Though Providence says, Kill and eat, conscience says, Not so, Lord, for nothing common or unclean has come into my mouth. 2. They were jealous over themselves, lest, though it should not be sinful in itself, it should be an occasion of sin to them, lest, by indulging their appetites with these dainties, they should grow sinful, voluptuous, and in love with the pleasures of Babylon. They had learned David's prayer, Let me not eat of their dainties, and Solomon's precept, Be not desirous of dainties, for they are deceitful meat and accordingly they form their resolution. Note, It is very much the praise of all, and especially of young people, to be dead to the delights of sense, not to covet them, not to relish them, but to look upon them with indifference. Those that would excel in wisdom and piety must learn betimes to keep under the body and bring it into subjection. 3. However, they thought it unseasonable now, when Jerusalem was in distress, and they themselves were in captivity. They had no heart to drink wine in bowls, so much were they grieved for the affliction of Joseph. Though they had royal blood in their veins, yet they did not think it proper to have royal dainties in their mouths when they were thus brought low. Note, It becomes us to be humble under humbling providences. Call me not Naomi; call me Marah. See the benefit of affliction; by the account Jeremiah gives of the princes and great men now at Jerusalem it appears that they were very corrupt and wicked, and defiled themselves with things offered to idols, while these young gentlemen that were in captivity would not defile themselves, no, not with their portion of the king's meat. How much better is it with those that retain their integrity in the depths of affliction than with those that retain their iniquity in the heights of prosperity! Observe, The great thing that Daniel avoided was defiling himself with the pollutions of sin; that is the thing we should be more afraid of than of any outward trouble. Daniel, having taken up this resolution, requested of the prince of the eunuchs that he might not defile himself, not only that he might not be compelled to do it, but that he might not be tempted to do it, that the bait might not be laid before him, that he might not see the portion appointed him of the king's meat, nor look upon the wine when it was red. It will be easier to keep the temptation at a distance than to suffer it to come near and then be forced to put a knife to our throat. Note, We cannot better improve our interest in any with whom we have found favour than by making use of them to keep us from sin. III. That God wonderfully owned him herein. When Daniel requested that he might have none of the king's meat or wine set before him the prince of the eunuchs objected that, if he and his fellows were not found in as good case as any of their companions, he should be in danger of having anger and of losing his head. Daniel, to satisfy him that there would be no danger of any bad consequence, desires the matter might be put to a trial. He applies himself further to the under-officer, Melzar, or the steward: "Prove us for ten days; during that time let us have nothing but pulse to eat, nothing but herbs and fruits, or parched peas or lentils, and nothing but water to drink, and see how we can live upon that, and proceed accordingly.".

People will not believe the benefit of abstemiousness and a spare diet, nor how much it contributes to the health of the body, unless they try it. Trial was accordingly made. Daniel and his fellows lived for ten days upon pulse and water, hard fare for young men of genteel extraction and education, and which one would rather expect they should have indented against than petitioned for; but at the end of the ten days they were compared with the other children, and were found fairer and fatter in flesh, of a more healthful look and better complexion, than all those who did eat the portion of the king's meat. This was in part a natural effect of their temperance, but it must be ascribed to the special blessing of God, which will make a little to go a great way, a dinner of herbs better than a stalled ox. By this it appears that man lives not by bread alone; pulse and water shall be the most nourishing food if God speak the word. See what it is to keep ourselves pure from the pollutions of sin; it is the way to have that comfort and satisfaction which will be health to the navel and marrow to the bones, while the pleasures of sin are rottenness to the bones. IV. That his master countenanced him. The steward did not force them to eat against their consciences, but, as they desired, gave them pulse and water, the pleasures of which they enjoyed, and we have reason to think were not envied the enjoyment. Here is a great example of temperance and contentment with mean things; and (as Epicurus said) "he that lives according to nature will never be poor, but he that lives according to opinion will never be rich."

This wonderful abstemiousness of these young men in the days of their youth contributed to the fitting of them, 1. For their eminent services. Hereby they kept their minds clear and unclouded, and fit for contemplation, and saved for the best employments a great deal both of time and thought; and thus they prevented those diseases which indispose men for the business of age that owe their rise to the intemperances of youth. 2. For their eminent sufferings. Those that had thus inured themselves to hardship, and lived a life of self-denial and mortification, could the more easily venture upon the fiery furnace and the den of lions, rather than sin against God.

Verses 17-21

Concerning Daniel and his fellows we have here, I. Their great attainments in learning. They were very sober and diligent, and studied hard; and we may suppose their tutors, finding them of an uncommon capacity, took a great deal of pains with them, but, after all, their achievements are ascribed to God only. It was he that gave them knowledge and skill in all learning and wisdom; for every good and perfect gift is from above, from the Father of the lights. It is the Lord our God that gives men power to get this wealth; the mind is furnished only by him that formed it. The great learning which God gave these four children was, 1. A balance for their losses. They had, for the iniquity of their fathers, been deprived of the honours and pleasures that would have attended their noble extraction; but, to make them amends for that, God, in giving them learning, gave them better honours and pleasures than those they had been deprived of. 2. A recompence for their integrity. They kept to their religion, even in the minutest instances of it, and would not so much as defile themselves with the king's meat or wine, but became, in effect, Nazarites; and now God rewarded them for it with eminency in learning; for God gives to a man that is good in his sight, wisdom, and knowledge, and joy with them . To Daniel he gave a double portion; he had understanding in visions and dreams; he knew how to interpret dreams, as Joseph, not by rules of art, such as are pretended to be given by the oneiro critics, but by a divine sagacity and wisdom which God gave him. Nay, he was endued with a prophetic spirit, by which he was enabled to converse with God, and to receive the notices of divine things in dreams and visions . According to this gift given to Daniel, we find him, in this book, all along employed about dreams and visions, interpreting or entertaining them; for, as every one has received the gift, so shall he have an opportunity, and so should he have a heart, to minister the same .II. Their great acceptance with the king. After three years spent in their education (they being of some maturity, it is likely, when they came, perhaps about twenty years old) they were presented to the king with the rest that were of their standing. And the king examined them and communed with them himself. He could do it, being a man of parts and learning himself, else he would not have come to be so great; and he would do it, for it is the wisdom of princes, in the choice of the persons they employ, to see with their own eyes, to exercise their own judgment, and not trust too much to the representation of others.

The king examined them not so much in the languages, in the rules of oratory or poetry, as in all matters of wisdom and understanding, the rules of prudence and true politics; he enquired into their judgment about the due conduct of human life and public affairs; not "Were they wits?" but, "Were they wise?" And he not only found them to excel the young candidates for preferment that were of their own standing, but found that they had more understanding than the ancients, than all their teachers . So far was the king from being partial to his own countrymen, to seniors, to those of his own religion and of an established reputation, that he freely owned that, upon trial, he found those poor young captive Jews ten times wiser and better than all the magicians that were in all his realm. He was soon aware of something extraordinary in these young men, and, which gave him a surprising satisfaction, was soon aware that a little of their true divinity was preferable to a great deal of the divination he had been used to. What is the chaff to the wheat? what are the magicians' rods to Aaron's? There was no comparison between them. These four young students were better, were ten times better, than all the old practitioners, put them all together, that were in all his realm, and we may be sure that they were not a few.

This contempt did God pour upon the pride of the Chaldeans, and this honour did he put upon the low estate of his own people; and thus did he make not only these persons, but the rest of their nation for their sakes, the more respected in the land of their captivity. Lastly, This judgment being given concerning them, they stood before the king they attended in the presence-chamber, nay, and in the council-chamber, for to see the king's face is the periphrasis of a privy-counsellor . This confirms Solomon's observation, Seest thou a mandiligent in his business, sober and humble? he shall stand before kings; he shall not stand before mean men. Industry is the way to preferment. How long the other three were about the court we are not told; but Daniel, for his part, continued to the first year of Cyrus , though not always alike in favour and reputation. He lived and prophesied after the first year of Cyrus; but that is mentioned to intimate that he lived to see the deliverance of his people out of their captivity and their return to their own land. Note, Sometimes God favours his servants that mourn with Zion in her sorrows to let them live to see better times with the church than they saw in the beginning of their days and to share with her in her joys.

Chapter 2

It was said (ch. i. 17) that Daniel had understanding in dreams; and here we have an early and eminent instance of it, which soon made him famous in the court of Babylon, as Joseph by the same means came to be so in the court of Egypt. This chapter is a history, but it is the history of a prophecy, by a dream and the interpretation of it. Pharaoh's dream, and Joseph's interpretation of it, related only to the years of plenty and famine and the interest of God's Israel in them; but Nebuchadnezzar's dream here, and Daniel's interpretation of that, look much higher, to the four monarchies, and the concerns of Israel in them, and the kingdom of the Messiah, which should be set up in the world upon the ruins of them. In this chapter we have, I. The great perplexity that Nebuchadnezzar was put into by a dream which he had forgotten, and his command to the magicians to tell him what it was, which they could not pretend to do, ver. 1-11. II. Orders given for the destroying of all the wise men of Babylon, and of Daniel among the rest, with his fellows, ver. 12-15. III. The discovery of this secret to him, in answer to prayer, and the thanksgiving he offered up to God thereupon, ver. 16-23. IV. His admission to the king, and the discovery he made to him both of his dream and of the interpretation of it, ver. 24-45. V. The great honour which Nebuchadnezzar put upon Daniel, in recompence for this service, and the preferment of his companions with him, ver. 46-49.

Nebuchadnezzar's Forgotten Dream. (b. c. 603.)

1 And in the second year of the reign of Nebuchadnezzar Nebuchadnezzar dreamed dreams, wherewith his spirit was troubled, and his sleep brake from him. 2 Then the king commanded to call the magicians, and the astrologers, and the sorcerers, and the Chaldeans, for to show the king his dreams. So they came and stood before the king. 3 And the king said unto them, I have dreamed a dream, and my spirit was troubled to know the dream. 4 Then spake the Chaldeans to the king in Syriac, O king, live for ever: tell thy servants the dream, and we will show the interpretation. 5 The king answered and said to the Chaldeans, The thing is gone from me: if ye will not make known unto me the dream, with the interpretation thereof, ye shall be cut in pieces, and your houses shall be made a dunghill. 6 But if ye show the dream, and the interpretation thereof, ye shall receive of me gifts and rewards and great honour: therefore show me the dream, and the interpretation thereof. 7 They answered again and said, Let the king tell his servants the dream, and we will show the interpretation of it. 8 The king answered and said, I know of certainty that ye would gain

the time, because ye see the thing is gone from me. 9 But if ye will not make known unto me the dream, there is but one decree for you: for ye have prepared lying and corrupt words to speak before me, till the time be changed: therefore tell me the dream, and I shall know that ye can show me the interpretation thereof. 10 The Chaldeans answered before the king, and said, There is not a man upon the earth that can show the king's matter: therefore there is no king, lord, nor ruler, that asked such things at any magician, or astrologer, or Chaldean. 11 And it is a rare thing that the king requireth, and there is none other that can show it before the king, except the gods, whose dwelling is not with flesh. 12 For this cause the king was angry and very furious, and commanded to destroy all the wise men of Babylon. 13 And the decree went forth that the wise men should be slain; and they sought Daniel and his fellows to be slain.

We meet with a great difficulty in the date of this story; it is said to be in the second year of the reign of Nebuchadnezzar, v. 1. Now Daniel was carried to Babylon in his first year, and, it should seem, he was three years under tutors and governors before he was presented to the king, ch. i. 5. How then could this happen in the second year? Perhaps, though three years were appointed for the education of other children, yet Daniel was so forward that he was taken into business when he had been but one year at school, and so in the second year he became thus considerable. Some make it to be the second year after he began to reign alone, but the fifth or sixth year since he began to reign in partnership with his father. Some read it, and in the second year, (the second after Daniel and his fellows stood before the king), in the kingdom of Nebuchadnezzar, or in his reign, this happened; as Joseph, in the second year after his skill in dreams, showed and expounded Pharaoh's, so Daniel, in the second year after he commenced master in that art, did this service. I would much rather take it some of these ways than suppose, as some do, that it was in the second year after he had conquered Egypt, which was the thirty-sixth year of his reign, because it appears by what we meet with in Ezekiel, that Daniel was famous both for wisdom and prevalence in prayer long before that; and therefore this passage, or story, which shows how he came to be so eminent for both these must be laid early in Nebuchadnezzar's reign.

Now here we may observe,

I. The perplexity that Nebuchadnezzar was in by reason of a dream which he had dreamed but had forgotten (v. 1): He dreamed dreams, that is, a dream consisting of divers distinct parts, or which filled his head as much as if it had been many dreams. Solomon speaks of a multitude of dreams, strangely incoherent, in which there are divers vanities, Eccl. v. 7. This dream of Nebuchadnezzar's had nothing in the thing itself but what might be paralleled in many a common dream, in which are often represented to men things as foreign as are here mentioned; but there was something in the impression it made upon him which carried with it an incontestable evidence of its divine original and its prophetic significancy. Note, The greatest of men are not exempt from, nay, they lie most open to, those cares and troubles of mind which disturb their repose in the night, while the sleep of the labouring man is sweet and sound, and the sleep of the sober temperate man free from confused dreams.

The abundance of the rich will not suffer them to sleep at all for care, and the excesses of gluttons and drunkards will not suffer them to sleep quietly for dreaming. But this recorded here was not from natural causes. Nebuchadnezzar was a troubler of God's Israel, but God here troubled him; for he that made the soul can make his sword to approach to it. He had his guards about him, but they could not keep trouble from his spirit. We know not the uneasiness of many that live in great pomp, and, one would think, in pleasure, too. We look into their houses, and are tempted to envy them; but, could we look into their hearts, we should pity them rather. All the treasures and all the delights of the children of men, which this mighty monarch had command of, could not procure him a little repose, when by reason of the trouble of his mind his sleep broke from him. But God gives his beloved sleep, who return to him as their rest.

II. The trial that he made of his magicians and astrologers whether they could tell him what his dream was, which he had forgotten. They were immediately sent for, to show the king his dreams, v. 2. There are many things which we retain the impressions of, and yet have lost the images of the things; though we cannot tell what the matter was, we know how we were affected with it; so it was with this king. His dream had slipped out of his mind, and he could not possibly recollect it, but he was confident he should know it if he heard it again. God ordered it so that Daniel might have the more honour, and, in him, the God of Daniel.

Note, God sometimes serves his own purposes by putting things out of men's minds as well as by putting things into their minds. The magicians, it is likely, were proud of their being sent for into the king's bed-chamber, to give him a taste of their office, not doubting but it would be for their honour. He tells them that he had dreamed a dream, v. 3. They speak to him in the Syriac tongue, which was then the same with the Chaldee, but now they differ much. And henceforward Daniel uses that language, or dialect of the Hebrew, for the same reason that those words, Jer. x. 11, are in that language because designed to convince the Chaldeans of the folly of their idolatry and to bring them to the knowledge and worship of the true and living God, which the stories of these chapters have a direct tendency to. But ch. viii. and forward, being intended for the comfort of the Jews, is written in their peculiar language. They, in their answer, complimented the king with their good wishes, desired him to tell his dream, and undertook with all possible assurance to interpret it, v. 4. But the king insisted upon it that they must tell him the dream itself, because he had forgotten it and could not tell it to them.

And, if they could not do this, they should all be put to death as deceivers (v. 5), themselves cut to pieces and their houses made a dunghill. If they could, they should be rewarded and preferred, v. 6. And they knew, as Balaam did concerning Balak, that he was able to promote them to great honour, and give them that wages of unrighteousness which, like him, they loved so dearly. No question therefore that they will do their utmost to gratify the king; if they do not, it is not for want of good-will, but for want of power, Providence so ordering it that the magicians of Babylon might now be as much confounded and put to shame as of old the magicians of Egypt had been, that, how much soever his people were both in Egypt and Babylon vilified and made contemptible, his oracles might in both be magnified and made honourable, by the silencing of those that set up in competition with them. The magicians, having reason on their side, insist upon it that the king must tell them the dream, and then, if they do not tell him the interpretation of it, it is their fault, v. 7. But arbitrary power is deaf to reason. The king falls into a passion, gives them hard words, and, without any colour of reason, suspects that they could tell him but would not; and instead of upbraiding them with impotency, and the deficiency of their art, as he might justly have done, he charges them with a combination to affront him: You have prepared lying and corrupt words to speak before me. How unreasonable and absurd is this imputation! If they had undertaken to tell him what his dream was, and had imposed upon him with a sham, he might have charged them with lying and corrupt words; but to say this of them when they honestly confessed their own weakness only shows what senseless things indulged passions are, and how apt great men are to think it is their prerogative to pursue their humour in defiance of reason and equity, and all the dictates of both. When the magicians begged of him to tell them the dream, though the request was highly rational and just, he tells them that they did but dally with him, to gain time (v. 8), till the time be changed (v. 9), either till the king's desire to know his dream be over, and he grown indifferent whether he be told it or no, though now he is so hot upon it, or till they may hope he has so perfectly forgotten his dream (the remaining shades of which are slipping from him apace as he catches at them) that they may tell him what they please and make him believe it was his dream, and, when the thing which is going, is quite gone from him, as it will be in a little time, he will not be able to disprove them. And therefore, without delay, they must tell him the dream. In vain do they plead, 1. That there is no man on earth that can retrieve the king's dream, v. 10. There are settled rules by which to discover what the meaning of the dream was; whether they will hold or no is the question. But never were any rules offered to be given by which to discover what the dream was; they cannot work unless they have something to work upon. They acknowledge that the gods may indeed declare unto man what is his thought (Amos iv. 13), for God understands our thoughts afar off (Ps. cxxxix. 2), what they will be before we think them, what they are when we do not regard them, what they have been when we have forgotten them. But those who can do this are gods, that have not their dwelling with flesh (v. 11), and it is they alone that can do this.

As for men, their dwelling is with flesh; the wisest and greatest of men are clouded with a veil of flesh, which quite obstructs and confounds all their acquaintance with spirit, and their powers and operations; but the gods, that are themselves pure spirit, know what is in man. See here an instance of the ignorance of these magicians, that they speak of many gods, whereas there is but one and can be but one infinite; yet see their knowledge of that which even the light of nature teaches and the works of nature prove, that there is a God, who is a Spirit, and perfectly knows the spirits of men and all their thoughts, so as it is not possible that any man should. This confession of the divine omniscience is here extorted from these idolaters, to the honour of God and their own condemnation, who though they knew there is a God in heaven, to whom all hearts are open, all desires known, and from whom no secret is hid, yet offered up their prayers and praises to dumb idols, that have eyes and see not, ears and hear not. 2. That there is no king on earth that would expect or require such a thing, v. 10. This intimates that they were kings, lords, and potentates, not ordinary people, that the magicians had most dealings with, and at whose devotion they were, while the oracles of God and the gospel of Christ are dispensed to the poor. Kings and potentates have often required unreasonable things of their subjects, but they think that never any required so unreasonable a thing as this, and therefore hope his imperial majesty will not insist upon it. But it is all in vain; when passion is in the throne reason is under foot: He was angry and very furious, v. 12. Note, It is very common for those that will not be convinced by reason to be provoked and exasperated by it, and to push on with fury what they cannot support with equity.

III. The doom passed upon all the magicians of Babylon. There is but one decree for them all (v. 9); they all stand condemned without exception or distinction. The decree has gone forth, they must every man of them be slain (v. 13), Daniel and his fellows (though they knew nothing of the matter) not excepted. See here, 1. What are commonly the unjust proceedings of arbitrary power. Nebuchadnezzar is here a tyrant in true colours, speaking death when he cannot speak sense, and treating those as traitors whose only fault is that they would serve him, but cannot. 2. What is commonly the just punishment of pretenders. How unrighteous soever Nebuchadnezzar was in this sentence, as to the ringleaders in the imposture, God was righteous. Those that imposed upon men, in pretending to do what they could not do, are now sentenced to death for not being able to do what they did not pretend to.

The Dream Revealed to Daniel; Daniel's Thanksgiving. (b. c. 603.)

14 Then Daniel answered with counsel and wisdom to Arioch the captain of the king's guard, which was gone forth to slay the wise men of Babylon: 15 He answered and said to Arioch the king's captain, Why is the decree so hasty from the king? Then Arioch made the thing known to Daniel. 2:15 Then Daniel went in, and desired of the king that he would give him time, and that he would show the king the interpretation.   17 Then Daniel went to his

house, and made the thing known to Hananiah, Mishael, and Azariah, his companions: 18 That they would desire mercies of the God of heaven concerning this secret; that Daniel and his fellows should not perish with the rest of the wise men of Babylon. 19 Then was the secret revealed unto Daniel in a night vision. Then Daniel blessed the God of heaven. 20 Daniel answered and said, Blessed be the name of God for ever and ever: for wisdom and might are his: 21 And he changeth the times and the seasons: he removeth kings, and setteth up kings: he giveth wisdom unto the wise, and knowledge to them that know understanding: 22 He revealeth the deep and secret things: he knoweth what is in the darkness, and the light dwelleth with him. 23 I thank thee, and praise thee, O thou God of my fathers, who hast given me wisdom and might, and hast made known unto me now what we desired of thee: for thou hast now made known unto us the king's matter.

When the king sent for his wise men to tell them his dream, and the interpretation of it (v. 2), Daniel, it seems, was not summoned to appear among them; the king, though he was highly pleased with him when he examined him, and thought him ten times wiser than the rest of his wise men, yet forgot him when he had most occasion for him; and no wonder, when all was done in a heat, and nothing with a cool and deliberate thought. But Providence so ordered it; that the magicians being nonplussed might be the more taken notice of, and so the more glory might redound to the God of Daniel. But, though Daniel had not the honour to be consulted with the rest of the wise men, contrary to all law and justice, by an undistinguishing sentence, he stands condemned with them, and till he has notice brought him to prepare for execution he knows nothing of the matter. How miserable is the case of those who live under arbitrary government, as this of Nebuchadnezzar's! How happy are we, whose lives are under the protection of the law and methods of justice, and lie not thus at the mercy of a peevish and capricious prince!

We have found already, in Ezekiel, that Daniel was famous both for prudence and prayer; as a prince he had power with God and by man; by prayer he had power with God, by prudence he had power with man, and in both he prevailed. Thus did he find favour and good understanding in the sight of both, and in these verses we have a remarkable instance of both.

I. Daniel by prudence knew how to deal with men, and he prevailed with them. When Arioch, the captain of the guard, that was appointed to slay all the wise men of Babylon, the whole college of them, seized Daniel (for the sword of tyranny, like the sword of war, devours one as well as another), he answered with counsel and wisdom (v. 14); he did not fall into a passion, and reproach the king as unjust and barbarous, much less did he contrive how to make resistance, but mildly asked, Why is the decree so hasty? v. 15. And whereas the rest of the wise men had insisted upon it that it was utterly impossible for him ever to have his demand gratified, which did but make him more outrageous, Daniel undertakes, if he may but have a little time allowed him, to give the king all the satisfaction he desired, v. 16. The king, being now sensible of his error in not sending for Daniel sooner, whose character he began to recollect, was soon prevailed upon to respite the judgment, and make trial of Daniel. Note, The likeliest method to turn away wrath, even the wrath of a king, which is as the messenger of death, is by a soft answer, by that yielding which pacifies great offences; thus, though where the word of a king is there is power, yet even that word may be repelled, and that so as to be repealed; and so some read it here (v. 14):Then Daniel returned, and stayed the counsel and edict, through Arioch, the king's provost-marshal.

II. Daniel knew how by prayer to converse with God, and he found favour with him, both in petition and in thanksgiving, which are the two principal parts of prayer. Observe,

1. His humble petition for this mercy, that God would discover to him what was the king's dream, and the interpretation of it. When he had gained time he did not go to consult with the rest of the wise men whether there was anything in their art, in their books, that might be of use in this matter, but went to his house, there to be alone with God, for from him alone, who is the Father of lights, he expected this great gift. Observe, (1.) He did not only pray for

this discovery himself, but he engaged his companions to pray for it too. He made the thing known to those who had been all along his bosom-friends and associates, requesting that they would desire mercy of God concerning this secret, v. 17, 18. Though Daniel was probably their senior, and every way excelled them, yet he engaged them as partners with him in this matter, Vis unita fortior—The union of forces produces greater force. See Esth. iv. 16. Note, Praying friends are valuable friends; it is good to have an intimacy with and an interest in those that have fellowship with God and an interest at the throne of grace; and it well becomes the greatest and best of men to desire the assistance of the prayers of others for them.

St. Paul often entreats his friends to pray for him. Thus we must show that we put a value upon our friends, upon prayer, upon their prayers. (2.) He was particular in this prayer, but had an eye to, and a dependence upon, the general mercy of God: That they would desire the mercies of the God of heaven concerning this secret, v. 18. We ought in prayer to look up to God as the God of heaven, a God above us, and who has dominion over us, to whom we owe adoration and allegiance, a God of power, who can do everything. Our savior has taught us to pray to God as our Father in heaven. And, whatever good we pray for, our dependence must be upon the mercies of God for it, and an interest in those mercies we must desire; we can expect nothing by way of recompence for our merits, but all as the gift of God's mercies. They desired mercy concerning this secret. Note, Whatever is the matter of our care must be the matter of our prayer; we must desire mercy of God concerning this thing and the other thing that occasions us trouble and fear. God gives us leave to be humbly free with him, and in prayer to enter into the detail of our wants and burdens. Secret things belong to the Lord our God, and therefore, if there be any mercy we stand in need of that concerns a secret, to him we must apply; and, though we cannot in faith pray for miracles, yet we may in faith pray to him who has all hearts in his hand, and who in his providence does wonders without miracles, for the discovery of that which is out of our view and the obtaining of that which is out of our reach, as far as is for his glory and our good, believing that to him nothing is hidden, nothing is hard. (3.) Their plea with God was the imminent peril they were in; they desired mercy of God in this matter, that so Daniel and his fellows might not perish with the rest of the wise men of Babylon, that the righteous might not be destroyed with the wicked. Note, When the lives of good and useful men are in danger it is time to be earnest with God for mercy for them, as for Peter in prison, Acts xii. 5. (4.) The mercy which Daniel and his fellows prayed for was bestowed. The secret was revealed unto Daniel in a night-vision, v. 19. Some think he dreamed the same dream, when he was asleep, that Nebuchadnezzar had dreamed; it should rather seem that when he was awake, and continuing instant in prayer, and watching in the same, the dream itself, and the interpretation of it, were communicated to him by the ministry of an angel, abundantly to his satisfaction. Note, The effectual fervent prayer of righteous men avails much. There are mysteries and secrets which by prayer we are let into; with that key the cabinets of heaven are unlocked, for Christ has said, Thus knock, and it shall be opened unto you.

2. His grateful thanksgiving for this mercy when he had received it: Then Daniel blessed the God of heaven, v. 19. He did not stay till he had told it to the king, and seen whether he would own it to be his dream or no, but was confident that it was so, and that he had gained his point, and therefore he immediately turned his prayers into praises. As he had prayed in a full assurance that God would do this for him, so he gave thanks in a full assurance that he had done it; and in both he had an eye to God as the God of heaven. His prayer was not recorded, but his thanksgiving is. Observe,

(1.) The honour he gives to God in this thanksgiving, which he studies to do in a great variety and copiousness of expression: Blessed be the name of God for ever and ever. There is that for ever in God which is to be blessed and praised; it is unchangeably and eternally in him. And it is to be blessed for ever and ever; as the matter of praise is God's eternal perfection, so the work of praise shall be everlastingly in the doing.

[1.] He gives to God the glory of what he is in himself: Wisdom and might are his, wisdom and courage (so some); whatever is fit to be done he will do; whatever he will do he can do, he dares do, and he will be sure to do it in the best manner, for he has infinite wisdom to design and contrive and infinite power to execute and accomplish. With him are strength and wisdom, which in men are often parted.

[2.] He gives him the glory of what he is to the world of mankind. He has a universal influence and agency upon all the children of men, and all their actions and affairs. Are the times changed? Is the posture of affairs altered? Does every thing lie open to mutability? It is God that changes the times and the seasons, and the face of them. No change comes to pass by chance, but according to the will and counsel of God. Are those that were kings removed and deposed? Do they abdicate? Are they laid aside? It is God that removes kings. Are the poor raised out of the dust, to be set among princes? It is God that sets up kings; and the making and unmaking of kings is a flower of his crown who is the fountain of all power, King of kings and Lord of lords. Are there men that excel others in wisdom, philosophers and statesmen, that think above the common rate, contemplative penetrating men? It is God that gives wisdom to the wise, whether they be so wise as to acknowledge it or no; they have it not of themselves, but it is he that gives knowledge to those that know understanding, which is a good reason why we should not be proud of our knowledge, and why we should serve and honour God with it and make it our business to know him.

[3.] He gives him the glory of this particular discovery. He praises him, First, For that he could make such a discovery (v. 22): He reveals the deep and secret things which are hidden from the eyes of all living. It was he that revealed to man what is true wisdom when none else could (Job xxvii. 27, 28); it is he that reveals things to come to his servants and prophets. He does himself perfectly discern and distinguish that which is most closely and most industriously concealed, for he will bring into judgment every secret thing; the truth will be evident in the great day. He knows what is in the darkness, and what is done in the darkness, for that hides not from him, Ps. cxxxix. 11, 12. The light dwells with him, and he dwells in the light (1 Tim. vi. 16), and yet, as to us, he makes darkness his pavilion. Some understand it of the light of prophecy and divine revelation, which dwells with God and is derived from him; for he is the Father of lights, of all lights; they are all at home in him. Secondly, For that he had made this discovery to him. Here he has an eye to God as the God of his fathers; for, though the Jews were now captives in Babylon, yet they were beloved for their father's sake. He praises God, who is the fountain of wisdom and might, for the wisdom and might he had given him, wisdom to know this great secret and might to bear the discovery. Note, What wisdom and might we have we must acknowledge to be God's gift. Thou hast made this known to me, v. 23. What was hidden from the celebrated Chaldeans, who made the interpreting of dreams their profession, is revealed to Daniel, a captive-Jew, a babe, much their junior. God would hereby put honour upon the Spirit of prophecy just when he was putting contempt upon the spirit of divination. Was Daniel thus thankful to God for making known that to him which was the saving of the lives of him and his fellows? Much more reason have we to be thankful to him for making known to us the great salvation of the soul, to us and not to the world, to us and not to the wise and prudent.

(2.) The respect he puts upon his companions in this thanksgiving. Though it was by his prayers principally that this discovery was obtained, and to him that it was made, yet he owns their partnership with him, both in praying for it (it is what we desired of thee) and in enjoying it—Thou hast made known unto us the king's matter. Either they were present with Daniel when the discovery was made to him, or as soon as he knew it he told it them (heureka, heureka—I have found it, I have found it), that those who had assisted him with their prayers might assist him in their praises; his joining them with him is an instance of his humility and modesty, which well become those that are taken into communion with God. Thus St. Paul sometimes joins Sylvanus, Timotheus, or some other minister, with himself in the inscriptions to many of his epistles. Note, What honour God puts upon us we should be willing that our brethren may share with us in.

Nebuchadnezzar's Dream. (b. c. 603.)

24 Therefore Daniel went in unto Arioch, whom the king had ordained to destroy the wise men of Babylon: he went and said thus unto him; Destroy not the wise men of Babylon: bring me in before the king, and I will show unto the king the interpretation.   25 Then Arioch brought in Daniel before the king in haste, and said thus unto him, I have found a man of the captives of Judah, that will make known unto the king the interpretation.   26 The king answered and said to Daniel, whose name was Belteshazzar, Art thou able to make known unto me the dream which I have seen, and the interpretation thereof?   27 Daniel answered in the presence of the king, and said, The secret which the king hath demanded cannot the wise men, the astrologers, the magicians, the soothsayers, show unto the king; 28 But there is a God in heaven that revealeth secrets, and maketh known to the king Nebuchadnezzar what shall be in the latter days. Thy dream, and the visions of thy head upon thy bed, are these;   29 As for thee, O king, thy thoughts came into thy mind upon thy bed, what should come to pass hereafter: and he that revealeth secrets maketh known to thee what shall come to pass.   30 But as for me, this secret is not revealed to me for any wisdom that I have more than any living, but for their sakes that shall make known the interpretation to the king, and that thou mightest know the thoughts of thy heart.

We have here the introduction to Daniel's declaring the dream, and the interpretation of it.

I. He immediately bespoke the reversing of the sentence against the wise men of Babylon, v. 24. He went with all speed to Arioch, to tell him that his commission was now superseded: Destroy not the wise men of Babylon. Though there were those of them perhaps that deserved to die, as magicians, by the law of God, yet here that which they stood condemned for was not a crime worth of death or of bonds, and therefore let them not die, and be unjustly destroyed, but let them live, and be justly shamed, as having been nonplussed and unable to do that which a prophet of the Lord could do. Note, Since God shows common kindness to the evil and good, we should do so too, and be ready to save the lives of even bad men, Matt. v. 45. A good man is a common good. To Paul in the ship God gave the souls of all that sailed with him; they were saved for his sake. To Daniel was owing the preservation of all the wise men, who yet rendered not according to the benefit done to them, ch. iii. 8.

II. He offered his service, with great assurance, to go to the king, and tell him his dream and the interpretation of it, and was admitted accordingly, v. 24, 25. Arioch brought him in haste to the king, hoping to ingratiate himself by introducing Daniel; he pretends he had sought him to interpret the king's dream, whereas really it was to execute upon him the king's sentence that he sought him. But courtiers' business is every way to humour the prince and make their own services acceptable.

III. He contrived as much as might be to reflect shame upon the magicians, and to give honour to God, upon this occasion. The king owned that it was a bold undertaking, and questioned whether he could make it good (v. 26): Art thou able to make known unto me the dream? What! Such a babe in this knowledge, such a stripling as thou are, wilt thou undertake that which thy seniors despair of doing? The less likely it appeared to the king that Daniel should do this the more God was glorified in enabling him to do it. Note, In transmitting divine revelation to the children of men it has been God's usual way to make use of the weak and foolish things and persons of the world, and such as were despised and despaired of, to confound the wise and mighty, that the excellency of the power might be of him, 1 Cor. i. 27, 28. Daniel from this takes occasion, 1. To put the king out of conceit with his magicians and soothsayers, whom he had such great expectations from (v. 27): "This secret they cannot show to the king; it is out of their power; the rules of their art will not reach to it. Therefore let not the king be angry with them for not doing that which they cannot do; but rather despise them, and cast them off, because they cannot do it." Broughton reads it generally: "This secret no sages, astrologers, enchanters, or entrail-cookers, can show unto the king; let not the king therefore consult them any more." Note, The experience we have of the inability of all creatures to give us satisfaction should lessen our esteem of them, and lower our expectations from them. They are baffled in their pretensions; we are baffled in our hopes from them. Hitherto they come, and no further; let us therefore say to them, as Job to his friends, Now you are nothing; miserable comforters are you all. 2. To bring him to the knowledge of the one only living and true God, the God whom Daniel worshipped: "Though they cannot find out the secret, let not the king despair of having it found out, for there is a God in heaven that reveals secrets," v. 28. Note, The insufficiency of creatures should drive us to the all-sufficiency of the Creator. There is a God in heaven (and it is well for us there is) who can do that for us, and make known that to us, which none on earth can, particularly the secret history of the work of redemption and the secret designs of God's love to us therein, the mystery which was hidden from ages and generations; divine revelation helps us out where human reason leaves us quite at a loss, and makes known that, not only to kings, but to the poor of this world, which none of the philosophers or politicians of the heathens, with all their oracles and arts of divination to help them, could ever pretend to give us any light into, Rom. xvi. 25, 26.

IV. He confirmed the king in his opinion that the dream he was thus solicitous to recover the idea of was really well worth enquiring after, that it was of great value and of vast consequence, not a common dream, the idle disport of a ludicrous and luxuriant fancy, which was not worth remembering or telling again, but that it was a divine discovery, a ray of light darted into his mind from the upper world, relating to the great affairs and revolutions of this lower world. God in it made known to the king what should be in the latter days (v. 28), that is, in the times that were to come, reaching as far as the setting up of Christ's kingdom in the world, which was to be in the latter days, Heb. i. 1. And again (v. 29): "The thoughts which came into thy mind were not the repetitions of what had been before, as our dreams usually are"—

Omnia quae sensu volvuntur vota diurno
Tempore sopito reddit amica quies—
The sentiments which we indulge throughout the day
often mingle with the grateful slumbers of the night.
Claudian.

"But they were predictions of what should come to pass hereafter, which he that reveals secrets makes known unto thee; and therefore thou art in the right in taking the hint and pursuing it thus." Note, Things that are to come to pass hereafter are secret things, which God only can reveal; and what he has revealed of those things, especially with reference to the last days of all, to the end of time, ought to be very seriously and diligently enquired into and considered by every one of us. Some think that the thoughts which are said to have come into the king's mind upon his bed, what should come to pass hereafter, were his own thoughts when he was awake. Just before he fell asleep, and dreamed this dream, he was musing in his own mind what would be the issue of his growing greatness, what his kingdom would hereafter come to; and so the dream was an answer to those thoughts. What discoveries God intends to make he thus prepares men for.

V. He solemnly professes that he could not pretend to have merited from God the favour of this discovery, or to have obtained it by any sagacity of his own (v. 30): "But, as for me, this secret is not found out by me, but is revealed to me, and that not for any wisdom that I have more than any living, to qualify me for the receiving of such a discovery." Note, It well becomes those whom God has highly favoured and honoured to be very humble and low in their own eyes, to lay aside all opinion of their own wisdom and worthiness, that God alone may have all the praise of the good they are, and have, and do, and that all may be attributed to the freeness of his good-will towards them and the fulness of his good work in them. The secret was made known to him not for his own sake, but,

1. For the sake of his people, for their sakes that shall make known the interpretation to the king, that is, for the sake of his brethren and companions in tribulation, who had by their prayers helped him to obtain this discovery, and so might be said to make known the interpretation—that their lives might be spared, that they might come into favour and be preferred, and all the people of the Jews might fare the better, in their captivity, for their sakes. Note, Humble men will be always ready to think that what God does for them and by them is more for the sake of others than for their own.

2. For the sake of his prince; and some read the former clause in this sense, "Not for any wisdom of mine, but that the king may know the interpretation, and that thou mightest know the thoughts of thy heart, that thou mightest have satisfaction given thee as to what thou wast before considering, and thereby instruction given thee how to behave towards the church of God." God revealed this thing to Daniel that he might make it known to the king. Prophets receive that they may give, that the discoveries made to them may not be lodged with themselves, but communicated to the persons that are concerned.

Nebuchadnezzar's Dream Interpreted. (b. c. 603.)

31 Thou, O king, sawest, and behold a great image. This great image, whose brightness was excellent, stood before thee; and the form thereof was terrible. 32 This image's head was of fine gold, his breast and his arms of silver, his belly and his thighs of brass, 33 His legs of iron, his feet part of iron and part of clay. 34 Thou sawest till that a stone was cut out without hands, which smote the image upon his feet that were of iron and clay, and brake them to pieces. 35 Then was the iron, the clay, the brass, the silver, and the gold, broken to pieces together, and became like the chaff of the summer threshing-floors; and the wind carried them away, that no place was found for them: and the stone that smote the image became a great mountain, and filled the whole earth. 36 This is the dream; and we will tell the interpretation thereof before the king. 37 Thou, O king, art a king of kings: for the God of heaven hath given thee a kingdom, power, and strength, and glory. 38 And wheresoever the children of men dwell, the beasts of the field and the fowls of the heaven hath he given into thine hand, and hath made thee ruler over them all. Thou art this head of gold. 39 And after thee shall arise another kingdom inferior to thee, and another third kingdom of brass, which shall bear rule over all the earth. 40 And the fourth kingdom shall be strong as iron: forasmuch as iron breaketh in pieces and subdueth all things: and as iron that breaketh all these, shall it break in pieces and bruise. 41 And whereas thou sawest the feet and toes, part of potters' clay, and part of iron, the kingdom shall be divided; but there shall be in it of the strength of the iron, forasmuch as thou sawest the iron mixed with miry clay. 42 And as the toes of the feet were part of iron, and part of clay, so the kingdom shall be partly strong, and partly broken. 43 And whereas thou sawest iron mixed with miry clay, they shall mingle themselves with the seed of men: but they shall not cleave one to another, even as iron is not mixed with clay. 44 And in the days of these kings shall the God of heaven set up a kingdom, which shall never be destroyed: and the kingdom shall not be left to other people, but it shall break in pieces and consume all these kingdoms, and it shall stand for ever. 45 Forasmuch as thou sawest that the stone was cut out of the mountain without hands, and that it brake in pieces the iron, the brass, the clay, the silver, and the gold; the great God hath

made known to the king what shall come to pass hereafter: and the dream is certain, and the interpretation thereof sure.

Daniel here gives full satisfaction to Nebuchadnezzar concerning his dream and the interpretation of it. That great prince had been kind to this poor prophet in his maintenance and education; he had been brought up at the king's cost, preferred at court, and the land of his captivity had hereby been made much easier to him than to others of his brethren. And now the king is abundantly repaid for all the expense he had been at upon him; and for receiving this prophet, though not in the name of a prophet, he had a prophet's reward, such a reward as a prophet only could give, and for which that wealthy mighty prince was now glad to be beholden to him. Here is,

I. The dream itself, v. 31, 45. Nebuchadnezzar perhaps was an admirer of statues, and had his palace and gardens adorned with them; however, he was a worshipper of images, and now behold a great image is set before him in a dream, which might intimate to him what the images were which he bestowed so much cost upon, and paid such respect to; they were mere dreams. The creatures of fancy might do as well to please the fancy. By the power of imagination he might shut his eyes, and represent to himself what forms he thought fit, and beautify them at his pleasure, without the expense and trouble of sculpture. This was the image of a man erect: It stood before him, as a living man; and, because those monarchies which were designed to be represented by it were admirable in the eyes of their friends, the brightness of this image was excellent; and because they were formidable to their enemies, and dreaded by all about them, the form of this image is said to be terrible; both the features of the face and the postures of the body made it so. But that which was most remarkable in this image was the different metals of which it was composed—the head of gold (the richest and most durable metal), the breast and arms of silver (the next to it in worth), the belly and sides (or thighs) of brass, the legs of iron (still baser metals), and lastly the feet part of iron and part of clay. See what the things of this world are; the further we go in them the less valuable they appear. In the life of a man youth is a head of gold, but it grows less and less worthy of our esteem; and old age is half clay; a man is then as good as dead. It is so with the world; later ages degenerate. The first age of the Christian church, of the reformation, was a head of gold; but we live in an age that is iron and clay. Some allude to this in the description of a hypocrite, whose practice is not agreeable to his knowledge. He has a head of gold, but feet of iron and clay: he knows his duty, but does it not. Some observe that in Daniel's visions the monarchies were represented by four beasts (ch. vii.), for he looked upon that wisdom from beneath, by which they were turned to be earthly and sensual, and a tyrannical power, to have more in it of the beast than of the man, and so the vision agreed with his notions of the thing. But to Nebuchadnezzar, a heathen prince, they were represented by a gay and pompous image of a man, for he was an admirer of the kingdoms of this world and the glory of them. To him the sight was so charming that he was impatient to see it again. But what became of this image? The next part of the dream shows it to us calcined, and brought to nothing. He saw a stone cut out of the quarry by an unseen power, without hands, and this stone fell upon the feet of the image, that were of iron and clay, and broke them to pieces; and then the image must fall of course, and so the gold, and silver, and brass, and iron, were all broken to pieces together, and beaten so small that they became like the chaff of the summer threshing-floors, and there were not to be found any the least remains of them; but the stone cut out of the mountain became itself a great mountain, and filled the earth. See how God can bring about great effects by weak and unlikely causes; when he pleases a little one shall become a thousand. Perhaps the destruction of this image of gold, and silver, and brass, and iron, might be intended to signify the abolishing of idolatry out of the world in due time. The idols of the heathen are silver and gold, as this image was, and they shall perish from off the earth and from under these heavens, Jer. x. 11; Isa. ii. 18. And whatever power destroys idolatry is in the ready way to magnify and exalt itself, as this stone, when it had broken the image to pieces, became a great mountain.

II. The interpretation of this dream. Let us now see what is the meaning of this. It was from God, and therefore from him it is fit that we take the explication of it. It should seem, Daniel had his fellows with him, and speaks for them as well as for himself, when he says, We will tell the interpretation, v. 36.

Now,

1. This image represented the kingdoms of the earth that should successively bear rule among the nations and have influence on the affairs of the Jewish church. The four monarchies were not represented by four distinct statues, but by one image, because they were all of one and the same spirit and genius, and all more or less against the church. It was the same power, only lodged in four different nations, the two former lying eastward of Judea, the two latter westward. (1.) The head of gold signified the Chaldean monarchy, which was now in being (v. 37, 38): Thou, O king! art (or rather, shalt be) a king of kings, a universal monarch, to whom many kings and kingdoms shall be tributaries; or, Thou art the highest of kings on earth at this time (as a servant of servants is the meanest servant); thou dost outshine all other kings. But let him not attribute his elevation to his own politics or fortitude. No; it is the God of heaven that has given thee a kingdom, power, and strength, and glory, a kingdom that exercises great authority, stands firmly, and shines brightly, acts by a puissant army with an arbitrary power.

Note, The greatest of princes have no power but what is given them from above. The extent of his dominion is set forth (v. 38), that wheresoever the children of men dwell, in all the nations of that part of the world, he was ruler over them all, over them and all that belonged to them, all their cattle, not only those which they had a property in, but those that were ferae naturae—wild, the beasts of the field and the fowls of the heaven. He was lord of all the woods, forests, and chases, and none were allowed to hunt or fowl without his leave. Thus "thou art the head of gold; thou, and thy son, and thy son's son, for seventy years." Compare this with Jer. xxv. 9, 11, especially Jer. xxvii. 5-7. There were other powerful kingdoms in the world at this time, as that of the Scythians; but it was the kingdom of Babylon that reigned over the Jews, and that began the government which continued in the succession here described till Christ's time. It is called a head, for its wisdom, eminency, and absolute power, a head of gold for its wealth (Isa. xiv. 4); it was a golden city. Some make this monarchy to begin in Nimrod, and so bring into it all the Assyrian kings, about fifty monarchs in all, and compute that it lasted above 1600 years. But it had not been so long a monarchy of such vast extent and power as is here described, nor any thing like it; therefore others make only Nebuchadnezzar, Evil-merodach, and Belshazzar, to belong to this head of gold; and a glorious high throne they had, and perhaps exercised a more despotic power than any of the kings that went before them. Nebuchadnezzar reigned forty-five years current, Evil-merodach twenty-three years current, and Belshazzar three. Babylon was their metropolis, and Daniel was with them upon the spot during the seventy years. (2.) The breast and arms of silver signified the monarchy of the Medes and Persians, of which the king is told no more than this, There shall arise another kingdom inferior to thee (v. 39), not so rich, powerful, or victorious. This kingdom was founded by Darius the Mede and Cyrus the Persian, in alliance with each other, and therefore represented by two arms, meeting in the breast. Cyrus was himself a Persian by his father, a Mede by his mother. Some reckon that this second monarchy lasted 130 years, others 204 years. The former computation agrees best with the scripture chronology. (3.) The belly and thighs of brass signified the monarchy of the Grecians, founded by Alexander, who conquered Darius Codomannus, the last of the Persian emperors. This is the third kingdom, of brass, inferior in wealth and extent of dominion to the Persian monarchy, but in Alexander himself it shall by the power of the sword bear rule over all the earth; for Alexander boasted that he had conquered the world, and then sat down and wept because he had not another world to conquer. (4.) The legs and feet of iron signified the Roman monarchy. Some make this to signify the latter part of the Grecian monarchy, the two empires of Syria and Egypt, the former governed by the family of the Seleucidae, from Seleucus, the latter by that of the Lagidae, from Ptolemaeus Lagus; these they make the two legs and feet of this image: Grotius, and Junius, and Broughton, go this way. But it has been the more received opinion that it is the Roman monarchy that is here intended, because it was in the time of that monarchy, and when it was at its height, that the kingdom of Christ was set up in the world by the preaching of the everlasting gospel. The Roman kingdom was strong as iron (v. 40), witness the prevalency of that kingdom against all that contended with it for many ages. That kingdom broke in pieces the Grecian empire and afterwards quite destroyed the nation of the Jews. Towards the latter end of the Roman monarchy it grew very weak, and branched into ten kingdoms, which were as the toes of these feet. Some of these were weak as clay, others strong as iron, v. 42. Endeavours were used to unite and cement them for the strengthening of the empire, but in vain: They shall not cleave one to another, v. 43. This empire divided the government for a long time between the senate and the people, the nobles and the commons, but they did not entirely coalesce. There were civil wars between Marius and Sylla, Caesar and Pompey, whose parties were as iron and clay. Some refer this to the declining times of that empire, when, for the strengthening of the empire against the irruptions of the barbarous nations, the branches of the royal family intermarried; but the politics had not the desired effect, when the day of the fall of that empire came.

2. The stone cut out without hands represented the kingdom of Jesus Christ, which should be set up in the world in the time of the Roman empire, and upon the ruins of Satan's kingdom in the kingdoms of the world. This is the stone cut out of the mountain without hands, for it should be neither raised nor supported by human power or policy; no visible hand should act in the setting of it up, but it should be done invisibly by the Spirit of the Lord of hosts. This was the stone which the builders refused, because it was not cut out by their hands, but it has now become the head-stone of the corner. (1.) The gospel-church is a kingdom, which Christ is the sole and sovereign monarch of, in which he rules by his word and Spirit, to which he gives protection and law, and from which he receives homage and tribute. It is a kingdom not of this world, and yet set up in it; it is the kingdom of God among men. (2.) The God of heaven was to set up this kingdom, to give authority to Christ to execute judgment, to set him as King upon his holy hill of Zion, and to bring into obedience to him a willing people. Being set up by the God of heaven, it is often in the New Testament called the kingdom of heaven, for its original is from above and its tendency is upwards. (3.) It was to be set up in the days of these kings, the kings of the fourth monarchy, of which particular notice is taken (Luke ii. 1), That Christ was born when, by the decree of the emperor of Rome, all the world was taxed, which was a plain indication that that empire had become as universal as any earthly empire ever was. When these kings are contesting with each other, and in all the struggles each of the contending parties hopes to find its own account, God will do his own work and fulfil his own counsels. These kings are all enemies to Christ's kingdom, and yet it shall be set up in defiance of them. (4.) It is a kingdom that knows no decay, is in no danger of destruction, and will not admit any succession or revolution.

It shall never be destroyed by any foreign force invading it, as many other kingdoms are; fire and sword cannot waste it; the combined powers of earth and hell cannot deprive either the subjects of their prince or the prince of his subjects; nor shall this kingdom be left to other people, as the kingdoms of the earth are. As Christ is a monarch that has no successor (for he himself shall reign for ever), so his kingdom is a monarchy that has no revolution. The kingdom of God was indeed taken from the Jews and given to the Gentiles (Matt. xxi. 43), but still it was Christianity that ruled, the kingdom of the Messiah. The Christian church is still the same; it is fixed on a rock, much fought against, but never to be prevailed against, by the gates of hell. (5.) It is a kingdom that shall be victorious over all opposition. It shall break in pieces and consume all those kingdoms, as the stone cut out of the mountain without hands broke in pieces the image, v. 44, 45. The kingdom of Christ shall wear out all other kingdoms, shall outlive them, and flourish when they are sunk with their own weight, and so wasted that their place knows them no more. All the kingdoms that appear against the kingdom of Christ shall be broken with a rod of iron, as a potter's vessel, Ps. ii. 9. And in the kingdoms that submit to the kingdom of Christ tyranny, and idolatry, and every thing that is their reproach, shall, as far as the gospel of Christ gets ground, be broken. The day is coming when Jesus Christ shall have put down all rule, principality, and power, and have made all his enemies his footstool; and then this prophecy will have its full accomplishment, and not till then, 1 Cor. xv. 24, 25. Our savior seems to refer to this (Matt. xxi. 44), when, speaking of himself as the stone set at nought by the Jewish builders, he says, On whomsoever this stone shall fall, it will grind him to powder. (6.) It shall be an everlasting kingdom. Those kingdoms of the earth that had broken in pieces all about them at length came, in their turn, to be in like manner broken; but the kingdom of Christ shall break other kingdoms in pieces and shall itself stand for ever. His throne shall be as the days of heaven, his seed, his subjects, as the stars of heaven, not only so innumerable, but so immutable. Of the increase of Christ's government and peace there shall be no end. The Lord shall reign for ever, not only to the end of time, but when time and days shall be no more, and God shall be all in all to eternity.

III. Daniel having thus interpreted the dream, to the satisfaction of Nebuchadnezzar, who gave him no interruption, so full was the interpretation that he had no question to ask, and so plain that he had no objection to make, he closes all with a solemn assertion, 1. Of the divine original of this dream: The great God (so he calls him, to express his own high thoughts of him, and to beget the like in the mind of this great king) has made known to the king what shall come to pass hereafter, which the gods of the magicians could not do. And thus a full confirmation was given to that great argument which Isaiah had long before urged against idolaters, and particularly the idolaters of Babylon, when he challenged the gods they worshipped to show things that are to come hereafter, that we may know that you are gods (Isa. xli. 23), and by this proved the God of Israel to be the true God, that he declares the end from the beginning, Isa. xlvi. 10. 2. Of the undoubted certainty of the things foretold by this dream. He who makes known these things is the same that has himself designed and determined them, and will by his providence effect them; and we are sure that his counsel shall stand, and cannot be altered, and therefore the dream is certain and the interpretation thereof sure. Note, Whatever God has made known we may depend upon.

Nebuchadnezzar's Honours Daniel. (b. c. 603.)

46 Then the king Nebuchadnezzar fell upon his face, and worshipped Daniel, and commanded that they should offer an oblation and sweet odours unto him. 47 The king answered unto Daniel, and said, Of a truth it is, that your God is a God of gods, and a Lord of kings, and a revealer of secrets, seeing thou couldest reveal this secret. 48 Then the king made Daniel a great man, and gave him many great gifts, and made him ruler over the whole province of Babylon, and chief of the governors over all the wise men of Babylon. 49 Then Daniel requested of the king, and he set Shadrach, Meshach, and Abednego, over the affairs of the province of Babylon: but Daniel sat in the gate of the king.

One might have expected that when Nebuchadnezzar was contriving to make his own kingdom everlasting he would be enraged at Daniel, who foretold the fall of it and that another kingdom of another nature should be the everlasting kingdom; but, instead of resenting it as an affront, he received it as an oracle, and here we are told what the expressions were of the impressions it made upon him. 1. He was ready to look upon Daniel as a little god. Though he saw him to be a man, yet from this wonderful discovery which he had made both of his secret thoughts, in telling him the dream, and of things to come, in telling him the interpretation of it, he concluded that he had certainly a divinity lodged in him, worthy his adoration; and therefore he fell upon his face and worshipped Daniel, v. 46. It was the custom of the country by prostration to give honour to kings, because they have something of a divine power in them (I have said, You are gods); and therefore this king, who had often received such veneration from others, now paid the like to Daniel, whom he supposed to have in him a divine knowledge, which he was so struck with an admiration of that he could not contain himself, but forgot both that Daniel was a man and that himself was a king. Thus did God magnify divine revelation and make it honourable, extorting from a proud potentate such a veneration but for one glimpse of it. He worshipped Daniel, and commanded that they should offer an oblation to him, and burn incense. Herein he cannot be justified, but may in some measure be excused, when Cornelius was thus ready to worship Peter, and John the angel, who both knew better. But, though it is not here mentioned, yet we have reason to think that Daniel refused these honours that he paid him, and said, as Peter to Cornelius, Stand up, I myself also am a man, or, as the angel to St. John, See thou do it not; for it is not said that the oblation was offered unto him, though the king commanded it, or rather said it, for so the word is. He said, in his haste, Let an oblation be offered to him. And that Daniel did say something to him which turned his eyes and thoughts another way is intimated in what follows (v. 47), The king answered Daniel. Note, It is possible for those to express a great honour for the ministers of God's word who yet have no true love for the word. Herod feared John, and heard him gladly, and yet went on in his sins, Mark vi. 20. 2. He readily acknowledged the God of Daniel to be the great God, the true God, the only living and true God. If Daniel will not suffer himself to be worshipped, he will (as Daniel, it is likely, directed him) worship God, by confessing (v. 47), Of a truth your God is a God of gods, such a God as there is no other, above all gods in dignity, over all gods in dominion. He is a Lord of kings, from whom they derive their power and to whom they are accountable; and he is both a discoverer and a revealer of secrets; what is most secret he sees and can reveal, and what he has revealed is what was secret and which none but himself could reveal, 1 Cor. ii. 10. 3. He preferred Daniel, made him a great man, v. 48. God made him a great man indeed when he took him into communion with himself, a greater man than Nebuchadnezzar could make him; but, because God had magnified him, therefore the king magnified him. Does wealth make men great? The king gave him many great gifts; and he had no reason to refuse them, when they all put him into so much the greater capacity of doing good to his brethren in captivity. These gifts were grateful returns for the good services he had done, and not aimed at, nor bargained for, by him, as the rewards of divination were by Balaam. Does power make a man great? He made him ruler over the whole province of Babylon, which no doubt had great influence upon the other provinces; he made him likewise chancellor of the university, chief of the governors over all the wise men of Babylon, to instruct those whom he had thus outdone; and, since they could not do what the king would have them do, they shall be obliged to do what Daniel would have them do. Thus it is fit that the fool should be servant to the wise in heart. Seeing Daniel could reveal this secret (v. 47), the king thus advanced him. Note, It is the wisdom of princes to advance and employ those who receive divine revelation, and are much conversant with it, who, as Daniel here, show themselves to be well acquainted with the kingdom of heaven. Joseph, like Daniel here, was advanced in the court of the king of Egypt for his interpreting his dreams; and he called him Zaphnath-paaneah—a revealer of secrets, as the king of Babylon here calls Daniel; so that the preambles to their patents of honour are the same— for, and in consideration of, their good services done to the crown in revealing secrets. 4. He preferred his companions for his sake, and upon his special instance and request, v. 49. Daniel himself sat in the gate of the king, as president of the council, chief-justice, or prime-minister of state, or perhaps chamberlain of the household; but he used his interest for his friends as became a good man, and procured places in the government for Shadrach,

Meshach, and Abednego. Those that helped him with their prayers shall share with him in his honours, such a grateful sense had he even of that service. The preferring of them would be a great stay and help to Daniel in his place and business. And these pious Jews, being thus preferred in Babylon, had great opportunity of serving their brethren in captivity, and of doing them many good offices, which no doubt they were ready to do. Thus, sometimes, before God brings his people into trouble, he prepares it, that it may be easy to them.

Chapter 3

In the close of the foregoing chapter we left Daniel's companions, Shadrach, Meshach, and Abednego, in honour and power, princes of the provinces, and preferred for their relation to the God of Israel and the interest they had in him. I know not whether I should say. It were well if this honour had all the saints. No, there are many whom it would not be good for; the saints' honour is reserved for another world. But here we have those same three men as much under the king's displeasure as when they were in his favour, and yet more truly, more highly, honoured by their God than there they were honoured by their prince, both by the grace wherewith he enabled them rather to suffer than to sin and by the miraculous and glorious deliverance which he wrought for them out of their sufferings. It is a very memorable story, a glorious instance of the power and goodness of God, and a great encouragement to the constancy of his people in trying times. The apostle refers to it when he mentions, among the believing heroes, those who by faith "quenched the violence of fire," Heb. xi. 34. We have here, I. Nebuchadnezzar's erecting and dedicating a golden image, and his requiring all his subjects, of what rank or degree soever, to fall down and worship it, and the general compliance of his people with that command, ver. 1-7. II. Information given against the Jewish princes for refusing to worship this golden image, ver. 8-12. III. Their constant persisting in that refusal, notwithstanding his rage and menaces, ver. 13-18. IV. The casting of them into the fiery furnace for their refusal, ver. 19-23. V. Their miraculous preservation in the fire by the power of God, and their invitation out of the fire by the favour of the king, who was by this miracle convinced of his error in casting them in, ver. 24-27. VI. The honour which the king gave to God hereupon, and the favour he showed to those faithful worthies, ver. 28-30.

1 Nebuchadnezzar the king made an image of gold, whose height was threescore cubits, and the breadth thereof six cubits: he set it up in the plain of Dura, in the province of Babylon. 2 Then Nebuchadnezzar the king sent to gather together the princes, the governors, and the captains, the judges, the treasurers, the counsellors, the sheriffs, and all the rulers of the provinces, to come to the dedication of the image which Nebuchadnezzar the king had set up. 3 Then the princes, the governors, and captains, the judges, the treasurers, the counsellors, the sheriffs, and all the rulers of the provinces, were gathered together unto the dedication of the image that Nebuchadnezzar the king had set up; and they stood before the image that Nebuchadnezzar had set up. 4 Then a herald cried aloud, To you it is commanded, O people, nations, and languages, 5 That at what time ye hear the sound of the cornet, flute, harp, sackbut, psaltery, dulcimer, and all kinds of music, ye fall down and worship the golden image that Nebuchadnezzar the king hath set up: 6 And whoso falleth not down and worshippeth shall the same hour be cast into the midst of a burning fiery furnace. 7 Therefore at that time, when all the people heard the sound of the cornet, flute, harp, sackbut, psaltery, and all kinds of music, all the people, the nations, and the languages, fell down and worshipped the golden image that Nebuchadnezzar the king had set up.

We have no certainty concerning the date of this story, only that if this image, which Nebuchadnezzar dedicated, had any relation to that which he dreamed of, it is probable that it happened not long after that; some reckon it to be about the seventh year of Nebuchadnezzar, a year before Jehoiachin's captivity, in which Ezekiel was carried away. Observe,

I. A golden image set up to be worshipped. Babylon was full of idols already, yet nothing will serve this imperious prince but they must have one more; for those who have forsaken the one only living God, and begin to set up many gods, will find the gods they set up so unsatisfying, and their desire after them so insatiable, that they will multiply them without measure, wander after them endlessly, and never know when they have sufficient. Idolaters are fond of novelty and variety. They choose new gods. Those that have many will wish to have more. Nebuchadnezzar the king, that he might exert the prerogative of his crown, to make what god he thought fit, set up this image, v. 1. Observe, 1. The valuableness of it; it was an image of gold, not all gold surely; rich as he was, it is probable that he could not afford that, but overlaid with gold. Note, The worshippers of false gods are not wont to mind charges in setting up images and worshipping them; they lavish gold out of the bag for that purpose (Isa. xlvi. 6), which shames our niggardliness in the worship of the true God. 2. The vastness of it; it was threescore cubits high and six cubits broad. It exceeded the ordinary stature of a man fifteen times (for that is reckoned but four cubits, or six feet), as if its being monstrous would make amends for its being lifeless. But why did Nebuchadnezzar set up this image? Some suggest that it was to clear himself from the imputation of having turned a Jew, because he had lately spoken with great honour of the God of Israel and had preferred some of his worshippers. Or perhaps he set it up as an image of himself, and designed to be himself worshipped in it. Proud princes affected to have divine honours paid them; Alexander did so, pretending himself to be the son of Jupiter Olympius. He was told that in the image he had seen in his dream he was represented by the head of gold, which was to be succeeded by kingdoms of baser metal; but here he sets up to be himself the whole image, for he makes it all of gold. See here, (1.) How the good impressions that were then made upon him were quite lost, and quickly. He then acknowledged that the God of Israel is of a truth a God of gods and a Lord of kings; and yet now, in defiance of the express law of that God, he sets up an image to be worshipped, not only continues in his former idolatries, but contrives new ones. Note, Strong convictions often come short of a sound conversion. Many a pang have owned the absurdity and dangerousness of sin, and yet have gone on in it. (2.) How that very dream and the interpretation of it, which then made such good impressions upon him, now had a quite contrary effect. Then it made him fall down as a humble worshipper of God; now it made him set up for a bold competitor with God. Then he thought it a great thing to be the golden head of the image, and owned himself obliged to God for it; but, his mind rising with his condition, now he thinks that too little, and, in contradiction to God himself and his oracle, he will be all in all.

II. A general convention of the states summoned to attend the solemnity of the dedication of this image, v. 2, 3. Messengers are despatched to all parts of the kingdom to gather together the princes, dukes, and lords, all the peers of the realm, with all officers civil and military, the captains and commanders of the forces, the judges, the treasurers or general receivers, the counsellors, and the sheriffs, and all the rulers of the provinces; they must all come to the dedication of this image upon pain and peril of what shall fall thereon. He summons the great men, for the great honour of his idol; it is therefore mentioned to the glory of Christ that kings shall bring presents unto him. If he can bring them to pay homage to his golden image, he doubts not but the inferior people will follow of course. In obedience to the king's summons all the magistrates and officers of that vast kingdom leave the services of their particular countries, and come to Babylon, to the dedication of this golden image; long journeys many of them took, and expensive ones, upon a very foolish errand; but, as the idols are senseless things, such are the worshippers.

III. A proclamation made, commanding all manner of persons present before the image, upon the signal given, to fall down prostrate, and worship the image, under the style and title of The golden image which Nebuchadnezzar the king has set up. A herald proclaims this aloud throughout this vast assembly of grandees, with their numerous train of servants and attendants, and a great crowd of people, no doubt, that were not sent for; let them all take notice, 1. That the king does strictly charge and command all manner of persons to fall down and worship the golden image; whatever other gods they worship at other times, now they must worship this. 2. That they must all do this just at the same time, in token of their communion with each other in this idolatrous service, and that, in order hereunto, notice shall be given by a concert of music, which would likewise serve to adorn the solemnity and to sweeten and soften the minds of those that were loth to yield and bring them to comply with the king's command. This mirth and gaiety in the worship would be very agreeable to carnal sensual minds, that are strangers to that spiritual worship which is due to God who is a spirit.

IV. The general compliance of the assembly with this command, v. 7. They heard the sound of the musical instruments, both wind-instruments and hand-instruments, the cornet and flute, with the harp, sackbut, psaltery, and dulcimer, the melody of which they thought was ravishing (and fit enough it was to excite such a devotion as they were then to pay), and immediately they all, as one man, as soldiers that are wont to be exercised by beat of drum, all the people, nations, and languages, fell down and worshipped the golden image. And no marvel when it was proclaimed, That whosoever would not worship this golden image should be immediately thrown into the midst of a burning fiery furnace, ready prepared for that purpose, v. 6. Here were the charms of music to allure them into a compliance and the terrors of the fiery furnace to frighten them into a compliance. Thus beset with temptation, they all yielded. Note, That way that sense directs the most will go; there is nothing so bad which the careless world will not be drawn to by a concert of music, or driven to by a fiery furnace. And by such methods as these false worship has been set up and maintained.

The Hebrew Princes Accused; Fortitude of the Jewish Princes. (b. c. 587.)

8 Wherefore at that time certain Chaldeans came near, and accused the Jews. 9 They spake and said to the king Nebuchadnezzar, O king, live for ever. 10 Thou, O king, hast made a decree, that every man that shall hear the sound of the cornet, flute, harp, sackbut, psaltery, and dulcimer, and all kinds of music, shall fall down and worship the golden image: 11 And whoso falleth not down and worshippeth, that he should be cast into the midst of a burning fiery furnace. 12 There are certain Jews whom thou hast set over the affairs of the province of Babylon, Shadrach, Meshach, and Abednego; these men, O king, have not regarded thee: they serve not thy gods, nor worship the golden image which thou hast set up. 13 Then Nebuchadnezzar in his rage and fury commanded to bring Shadrach, Meshach, and Abednego. Then they brought these men before the king. 14 Nebuchadnezzar spake and said unto them, Is it true, O Shadrach, Meshach, and Abednego, do not ye serve my gods, nor worship the golden image which I have set up? 15 Now if ye be ready that at what time ye hear the sound of the cornet, flute, harp, sackbut, psaltery, and dulcimer, and all kinds of music, ye fall down and worship the image which I have made; well: but if ye worship not, ye shall be cast the same hour into the midst of a burning fiery furnace; and who is that God that shall deliver you out of my hands? 16 Shadrach, Meshach, and Abednego, answered and said to the king, O Nebuchadnezzar, we are not careful to answer thee in this matter. 17 If it be so, our God whom we serve is able to deliver us from the burning fiery furnace, and he will deliver us out of thine hand, O king. 18 But if not, be it known unto thee, O king, that we will not serve thy gods, nor worship the golden image which thou hast set up.

It was strange that Shadrach, Meshach, and Abednego, would be present at this assembly, when, it is likely, they knew for what intent it was called together. Daniel, we may suppose, was absent, either his business calling him away or having leave from the king to withdraw, unless we suppose that he stood so high in the king's favour that none durst complain of him for his noncompliance. But why did not his companions keep out of the way? Surely because they would obey the king's orders as far as they could, and would be ready to bear a public testimony against this gross idolatry. They did not think it enough not to bow down to the image, but, being in office, thought themselves obliged to stand up against it, though it was the image which the king their master set up, and would be a golden image to those that worshipped it. Now,

I. Information is brought to the king by certain Chaldeans against these three gentlemen that they did not obey the king's edict, v. 8. Perhaps these Chaldeans that accused them were some of those magicians or astrologers that were particularly called Chaldeans (ch. ii. 2, 4) who bore a grudge to Daniel's companions for his sake, because he had eclipsed them, and so had these companions. They by their prayers had obtained the mercy which saved the lives of these Chaldeans, and, behold, how they requite them evil for good! for their love they are their adversaries. Thus Jeremiah stood before God, to speak good for those who afterwards dug a pit for his life, Jer. xviii. 20. We must not think it strange if we meet with such ungrateful men. Or perhaps they were such of the Chaldeans as expected the places to which they were advanced, and envied them their preferments; and who can stand before envy ? They appeal to the king himself concerning the edict, with all due respect to his majesty, and the usual compliment, O king! live forever (as if they aimed at nothing but his honour, and to serve his interest, when really they were putting him upon that which would endanger the ruin of him and his kingdom); they beg leave, 1. To put him in mind of the law he had lately made, That all manner of persons, without exception of nation or language, should fall down and worship this golden image; they put him in mind also of the penalty which by the law was to be inflicted upon recusants, that they were to be cast into the midst of the burning fiery furnace, v. 10, 11. It cannot be denied but that this was the law; whether a righteous law or no ought to be considered. 2. To inform him that these three men, Shadrach, Meshach, and Abednego, had not conformed to this edict, v. 12. It is probable that Nebuchadnezzar had no particular design to ensnare them in making the law, for then he would himself have had his eye upon them, and would not have needed this information; but their enemies, that sought an occasion against them, laid hold on this, and were forward to accuse them. To aggravate the matter, and incense the king the more against them, (1.) They put him in mind of the dignity to which the criminals had been preferred. Though they were Jews, foreigners, captives, men of a despised nation and religion, yet the king had set them over the affairs of the province of Babylon. It was therefore very ungrateful, and an insufferable piece of insolence, for them to disobey the king's command, when they had shared so much of the king's favour. And, besides, the high station they were in would make their refusal the more scandalous; it would be a bad example, and have a bad influence upon others; and therefore it was necessary that it should be severely animadverted upon. Thus princes that are incensed enough against innocent people commonly have but too many about them who do all they can to make them worse. (2.) They suggest that it was done maliciously, contumaciously, and in contempt of him and his authority: "They have set no regard upon thee; for they serve not the gods which thou servest, and which thou requirest them to serve, nor worship the golden image which thou hast set up."

II. These three pious Jews are immediately brought before the king, and arraigned and examined upon this information. Nebuchadnezzar fell into a great passion, and in his rage and fury commanded them to be seized, v. 13. How little was it the honour of this mighty prince that he had rule over so many nations when at the same time he had no rule over his own spirit, that there were so many who were subjects and captives to him when he was himself a perfect slave to his own brutish passions and led captive by them! How unfit was he to rule reasonable men who could not himself be ruled by reason! It needed not be a surprise to him to hear that these three men did not now serve his gods, for he knew very well they never had served them, and that their religion, which they had always adhered to, forbade them to do it. Nor had he any reason to think that they designed any contempt of his authority, for they had in all instances shown themselves respectful and dutiful to him as their prince. But it was especially unseasonable at this time, when he was in the midst of his devotions, dedicating his golden image, to be in such a rage and fury, and so much to discompose himself. The discretion of a man, one would think, should at least have deferred this anger. True devotion calms the spirit, quiets and meekens it; but superstition, and a devotion to false gods, inflame men's passions, inspire them with rage, and fury, and turn them into brutes. The wrath of a king is as the roaring of a lion; so was the wrath of this king; and yet, when he was in such a heat, these three men were brought before him, and appeared with an undaunted courage, and unshaken constancy.

III. The case is laid before them in short, and it is put to them whether they will comply or no. 1. The king asked them whether it was true that they had not worshipped the golden image when others did, v. 14. "Is it of purpose?" so some read it. "Was it designedly and deliberately done, or was it only through inadvertency, that you have not served my gods? What! you that I have nourished and brought up, that have been educated and maintained at my charge, that I have been so kind to and done so much for, you that have been in such reputation for wisdom, and therefore should better have known your duty to your prince; what! do not you serve my gods nor worship the golden image which I have set up?" Note, The faithfulness of God's servants to him has often been the wonder of their enemies and persecutors, who think it strange that they run not with them to the same excess of riot. 2. He was willing to admit them to a new trial; if they did on purpose not do it before, yet, it may be, upon second thoughts, they will change their minds; it is therefore repeated to them upon what terms they now stand, v. 15. (1.) The king is willing that music shall play again, only for their sakes, to soften them into a compliance; and if they will not, like the deaf adder, stop their ears, but will hearken to the voice of the charmers and will worship the golden image, well and good; their former omission shall be pardoned. But, (2.) The king is resolved, if they persist in their refusal, that they shall immediately be cast into the fiery furnace, and shall not have so much as an hour's reprieve. Thus does the matter lie in a little compass—Turn, or burn; and, because he knew they buoyed themselves up in their refusal with a confidence in their God, he insolently set him a defiance: "And who is that God that shall deliver you out of my hands? Let him, if he can." Now he forgot what he himself once owned, that their God was a God of gods and a Lord of kings, ch. ii. 47. Proud men are still ready to say, as Pharaoh, Who is the Lord that I should obey his voice? or, as Nebuchadnezzar, Who is the Lord, that I should fear his power?

IV. They give in their answer, which they all agree in, that they still adhere to their resolution not to worship the golden image, v. 16-18. We have here such an instance of fortitude and magnanimity as is scarcely to be paralleled. We call these the three children (and they were indeed young men), but we should rather call them the three champions, the first three of the worthies of God's kingdom among men. They did not break out into any intemperate heat or passion against those that did worship the golden image, did not insult or affront them; nor did they rashly thrust themselves upon the trial, or go out of their way to court martyrdom; but, when they were duly called to the fiery trial, they acquitted themselves bravely, with a conduct and courage that became sufferers for so good a cause. The king was not so daringly bad in making this idol, but they were as daringly good in witnessing against it. They keep their temper admirably well, do not call the king a tyrant or an idolater (the cause of God needs not the wrath of man), but, with an exemplary calmness and sedateness of mind, they deliberately give in their answer, which they resolve to abide by. Observe,

1. Their gracious and generous contempt of death, and the noble negligence with which they look upon the dilemma that they are put to: O Nebuchadnezzar! we are not careful to answer thee in this matter. They do not in sullenness deny him an answer, nor stand mute; but they tell him that they are in no care about it. There needs not an answer (so some read it); they are resolved not to comply, and the king is resolved they shall die if they do not; the matter therefore is determined, and why should it be disputed? But it is better read, "We want not an answer for thee, nor have it to seek, but come prepared." (1.) They needed no

time to deliberate concerning the matter of their answer; for they did not in the least hesitate whether they should comply or no. It was a matter of life and death, and one would think they might have considered awhile before they had resolved; life is desirable, and death is dreadful. But when the sin and duty that were in the case were immediately determined by the letter of the second commandment, and no room was left to question what was right, the life and death that were in the case were not to be considered. Note, Those that would avoid sin must not parley with temptation. When that which we are allured or affrighted to is manifestly evil the motion is rather to be rejected with indignation and abhorrence than reasoned with; stand not to pause about it, but say, as Christ has taught us, Get thee behind me, Satan. (2.) They needed no time to contrive how they should word it. While they were advocates for God, and were called out to witness in his cause, they doubted not but it should be given them in that same hour what they should speak, Matt. x. 19. They were not contriving an evasive answer, when a direct answer was expected from them; no, nor would they seem to court the king not to insist upon it. Here is nothing in their answer that looks like compliment; they begin not, as their accusers did, with, O king! live for ever, no artful insinuation, ad captandam benevolentiam—to put him into a good humour, but every thing that is plain and downright: O Nebuchadnezzar! we are not careful to answer thee. Note, Those that make their duty their main care need not be careful concerning the event.

2. Their believing confidence in God and their dependence upon him, v. 17. It was this that enabled them to look with so much contempt upon death, death in pomp, death in all its terrors: they trusted in the living God, and by that faith chose rather to suffer than to sin; they therefore feared not the wrath of the king, but endured, because by faith they had an eye to him that is invisible (Heb. xi. 25, 27): "If it be so, if we are brought to this strait, if we must be thrown into the fiery furnace unless we serve thy gods, know then," (1.) "That though we worship not thy gods yet we are not atheists; there is a God whom we can call ours, to whom we faithfully adhere." (2.) "That we serve this God; we have devoted ourselves to his honour; we employ ourselves in his work, and depend upon him to protect us, provide for us, and reward us." (3.) "That we are well assured that this God is able to deliver us from the burning fiery furnace; whether he will or no, we are sure that he can either prevent our being cast into the furnace or rescue us out of it." Note, The faithful servants of God will find him a Master able to bear them out in his service, and to control and overrule all the powers that are armed against them. Lord, if thou wilt, thou canst. (4.) "That we have reason to hope he will deliver us," partly because, in such a vast appearance of idolaters, it would be very much for the honour of his great name to deliver them, and partly because Nebuchadnezzar had defied him to do it—Who is that God that shall deliver you? God sometimes appears wonderfully for the silencing of the blasphemies of the enemy, as well as for the answering of the prayers of his people, Ps. lxxiv. 18-22; Deut. xxxii. 27. "But, if he do not deliver us from the fiery furnace, he will deliver us out of thy hand." Nebuchadnezzar can but torment and kill the body, and after that, there is no more that he can do; then they are got out of his reach, delivered out of his hand. Note, Good thoughts of God, and a full assurance that he is with us while we are with him, will help very much to carry us through sufferings; and, if he be for us, we need not fear what man can do unto us; let him do his worst. God will deliver us either from death or in death.

3. Their firm resolution to adhere to their principles, whatever might be the consequence (v. 18): "But, if not, though God should not think fit to deliver us from the fiery furnace (which yet we know he can do), if he should suffer us to fall into thy hand, and fall by thy hand, yet be it known unto thee, O king! we will not serve these gods, though they are thy gods, nor worship this golden image, though thou thyself hast set it up." They are neither ashamed nor afraid to own their religion, and tell the king to his face that they do not fear him, they will not yield to him; had they consulted with flesh and blood, much might have been said to bring them to a compliance, especially when there was no other way of avoiding death, so

great a death. (1.) They were not required to abjure their own God, or to renounce his worship, no, nor by any verbal profession or declaration to own this golden image to be a god, but only to bow down before it, which they might do with a secret reserve of their hearts for the God of Israel, inwardly detesting this idolatry, as Naaman bowed in the house of Rimmon. (2.) They were not to fall into a course of idolatry; it was but one single act that was required of them, which would be done in a minute, and the danger was over, and they might afterwards declare their sorrow for it. (3.) The king that commanded it had an absolute power; they were under it, not only as subjects, but as captives; and, if they did it, it was purely by coercion and duress, which would serve to excuse them. (4.) He had been their benefactor, had educated and preferred them, and in gratitude to him they ought to go as far as they could, though it were to strain a point, a point of conscience. (5.) They were now driven into a strange country, and to those that were so driven out it was, in effect, said, Go, and serve other gods, 1 Sam. xxvi. 19. It was taken for granted that in their disposition they would serve other gods, and it was made a part of the judgment, Deut. iv. 28. They might be excused if they should go down the stream, when it is so strong. (6.) Did not their kings, and their princes, and their fathers, yea, and their priests too, set up idols even in God's temple, and worship them there, and not only bow down to them, but erect altars, burn incense, and offer sacrifices, even their own children, to them? Did not all the ten tribes, for many ages, worship gods of gold at Dan and Bethel? And shall they be more precise than their fathers? Communis error facit jus—What all do must be right. (7.) If they should comply, they would save their lives and keep their places, and so be in a capacity to do a great deal of service to their brethren in Babylon, and to do it long; for they were young men, and rising men. But there is enough in that one word of God wherewith to answer and silence these and many more such like carnal reasonings: Thou shalt not bow down thyself to any images, nor worship them. They know they must obey God rather than man; they must rather suffer than sin, and must not do evil that good may come. And therefore none of these things move them; they are resolved rather to die in their integrity than live in their iniquity. While their brethren, who yet remained in their own land, were worshipping images by choice, they in Babylon would not be brought to it by constraint, but, as if they were good by antiperistasis, were most zealous against idolatry in an idolatrous country. And truly, all things considered, the saving of them from this sinful compliance was as great a miracle in the kingdom of grace as the saving of them out of the fiery furnace was in the kingdom of nature. These were those who formerly resolved not to defile themselves with the king's meat, and now they as bravely resolve not to defile themselves with his gods. Note, A stedfast self-denying adherence to God and duty in less instances will qualify and prepare us for the like in greater. And in this we must be resolute, never, under any pretence whatsoever, to worship images, or to say "A confederacy" with those that do so.

The Three Hebrews in the Furnace; Deliverance from the Furnace. (b. c. 587.)

19 Then was Nebuchadnezzar full of fury, and the form of his visage was changed against Shadrach, Meshach, and Abednego: therefore he spake, and commanded that they should heat the furnace one seven times more than it was wont to be heated.   20 And he commanded the most mighty men that were in his army to bind Shadrach, Meshach, and Abednego, and to cast them into the burning fiery furnace.   21 Then these men were bound in their coats, their hosen, and their hats, and their other garments, and were cast into the midst of the burning fiery furnace.   22 Therefore because the king's commandment was urgent, and the furnace exceeding hot, the flame of the fire slew those men that took up Shadrach, Meshach, and Abednego.   23 And these three men, Shadrach, Meshach, and Abednego, fell down bound into the midst of the burning fiery furnace.   24 Then Nebuchadnezzar the king was astonied, and rose up in haste, and spake, and said unto his counsellors, Did not we cast three men bound into the midst of the fire? They answered and said unto the king, True, O king.   25 He answered and said, Lo, I see four men loose, walking in the midst of the fire, and they have no hurt; and the form of the fourth is like the Son of God.   26 Then Nebuchadnezzar came near to the mouth of the burning fiery

furnace, and spake, and said, Shadrach, Meshach, and Abednego, ye servants of the most high God, come forth, and come hither. Then Shadrach, Meshach, and Abednego, came forth of the midst of the fire. 27 And the princes, governors, and captains, and the king's counsellors, being gathered together, saw these men, upon whose bodies the fire had no power, nor was a hair of their head singed, neither were their coats changed, nor the smell of fire had passed on them.

In these verses we have,

I. The casting of these three faithful servants of God into the fiery furnace. Nebuchadnezzar had himself known and owned so much of the true God that, one would have thought, though his pride and vanity induced him to make this golden image, and set it up to be worshipped, yet what these young men now said (whom he had formerly found to be wiser than all his wise men) would revive his convictions, and at least engage him to excuse them; but it proved quite otherwise. 1. Instead of being convinced by what they said, he was exasperated, and made more outrageous, v. 19. It made him full of fury, and the form of his visage was changed against these men. Note, Brutish passions the more they are indulged the more violent they grow, and even change the countenance, to the great reproach of the wisdom and reason of a man. Nebuchadnezzar, in this heat, exchanged the awful majesty of a prince upon his throne, or a judge upon the bench, for the frightful fury of a wild bull in a net. Would men in a passion but view their faces in a glass, they would blush at their own folly and turn all their displeasure against themselves. 2. Instead of mitigating their punishment, in consideration of their quality and the posts of honour they were in, he ordered it to be heightened, that they should heat the furnace seven times more than it was wont to be heated for other malefactors, that is, that they should put seven times more fuel to it, which, though it would not make their death more grievous, but rather dispatch them sooner, was designed to signify that the king looked upon their crime as seven times more heinous than the crimes of others, and so made their death more ignominious. But God brought glory to himself out of this foolish instance of the tyrant's rage; for, though it would not have made their death the more grievous, yet it did make their deliverance much the more illustrious. 3. He ordered them to be bound in their clothes, and cast into the midst of the burning fiery furnace, which was done accordingly, v. 20, 21. They were bound, that they might not struggle, or make any resistance, were bound in their clothes, for haste, or that they might be consumed the more slowly and gradually. But God's providence ordered it for the increase of the miracle, in that their clothes were not so much as singed. They were bound in their coats or mantles, their hosen or breeches, and their hats or turbans, as if, in detestation of their crime, they would have their clothes to be burnt with them. What a terrible death was this—to be cast bound into the midst of a burning fiery furnace! v. 23. It makes one's flesh tremble to think of it, and horror to take hold on one. It is amazing that the tyrant was so hard-hearted as to inflict such a punishment, and that the confessors were so stout-hearted as to submit to it rather than sin against God. But what is this to the second death, to that furnace into which the tares shall be cast in bundles, to that lake which burns eternally with fire and brimstone? Let Nebuchadnezzar heat his furnace as hot as he can, a few minutes will finish the torment of those who are cast into it; but hell-fire tortures and does not kill. The pain of damned sinners is more exquisite, and the smoke of their torment ascends for ever and ever, and those have no rest, no intermission, no cessation of their pains, who have worshipped the beast and his image (Rev. xiv. 10, 11), whereas their pain would be soon over that were cast into this furnace for not worshipping this Babylonian beast and his image.

4. It was a remarkable providence that the men, the mighty men, that bound them, and threw them into the furnace, were themselves consumed or suffocated by the flame, v. 22. The king's commandment was urgent, that they should dispatch them quickly, and be sure to

do it effectually; and therefore they resolved to go to the very mouth of the furnace, that they might throw them into the midst of it, but they were in such haste that they would not take time to arm themselves accordingly. The apocryphal additions to Daniel say that the flame ascended forty-nine cubits above the mouth of the furnace. Probably God ordered it so that the wind blew it directly upon them with such violence that it smothered them. God did thus immediately plead the cause of his injured servants, and take vengeance for them on their persecutors, whom he punished, not only in the very act of their sin, but by it. But these men were only the instruments of cruelty; he that bade them do it had the greater sin; yet they suffered justly for executing an unjust decree, and it is very probable that they did it with pleasure and were glad to be so employed. Nebuchadnezzar himself was reserved for a further reckoning. There is a day coming when proud tyrants will be punished, not only for the cruelties they have been guilty of, but for employing those about them in their cruelties, and so exposing them to the judgments of God.

II. The deliverance of these three faithful servants of God out of the furnace. When they were cast bound into the midst of that devouring fire we might well conclude that we should hear no more of them, that their very bones would be calcined; but, to our amazement, we here find that Shadrach, Meshach, and Abednego, are yet alive. 1. Nebuchadnezzar finds them walking in the fire. He was astonished, and rose up in haste, v. 24. Perhaps the slaying of the men that executed his sentence was that which astonished him, as well it might, for he had reason to think his own turn would be next; or it was some unaccountable impression upon his own mind that astonished him, and made him rise up in haste, and go to the furnace, to see what had become of those he had cast into it. Note, God can strike those with astonishment whose hearts are most hardened both against him and against his people. He that made the soul can make his sword to approach to it, even to that of the greatest tyrant. In his astonishment he calls his counsellors about him, and appeals to them.Did we not cast three men bound into the fire? It seems, it was done by order, not only of the king, but of the council. They durst not but concur with him, which he forced them to do, that they might share with him in the guilt and odium? "True, O king!" say they; "we did order such an execution to be done and it was done." "But now," says the king, "I have been looking into the furnace, and I see four men, loose, walking in the midst of the fire," v. 25. (1.) They were loosed from their bonds. The fire that did not so much as singe their clothes burnt the cords wherewith they were bound, and set them at liberty; thus God's people have their hearts enlarged, through the grace of God, by those very troubles with which their enemies designed to straiten and hamper them. (2.) They had no hurt, made no complaint, felt no pain or uneasiness in the least; the flame did not scorch them; the smoke did not stifle them; they were alive and as well as ever in the midst of the flames. See how God of nature can, when he pleases, control the powers of nature, to make them serve his purposes. Now was fulfilled in the letter gracious promise (Isa. xliii. 2),When thou walkest through the fire thou shalt not be burnt, neither shall the flame kindle upon thee. By faith they quench the violence of the fire, quench the fiery darts of the wicked. (3.) They walked in the midst of the fire. The furnace was large, so that they had room to walk; they were unhurt, so that they were able to walk; their minds were easy, so that they were disposed to walk, as in a paradise or garden of pleasure. Can a man walk upon hot coals and his feet not be burnt? Prov. vi. 28. Yes, they did it with as much pleasure as the king of Tyrus walked up and down in the midst of his stones of fire, his precious stones that sparkled as fire, Ezek. xxviii. 14. They were not striving to get out, finding themselves unhurt; but, leaving it to that God who preserved them in the fire to bring them out of it, they walked up and down in the midst of it unconcerned. One of the apocryphal writings relates at large the prayer which Azariah, one of the three, prayed in the fire (wherein he laments the calamities and iniquities of Israel, and entreats God's favour to his people), and the song of praise which they all three sang in the midst of the flames, in both which there are remarkable strains of devotion; but we have reason to think, with Grotius, that they were composed by some Jew of a later age, not as what were used, but only as what might have been used, on this occasion, and therefore we justly reject them as no part of holy writ. (4.) There was a fourth seen with them in the fire, whose form, in Nebuchadnezzar's judgment, was like the Son of God; he appeared as a divine person, a messenger from heaven, not as a servant, but as a son. Like an angel (so some); and angels are called sons of God, Job xxxviii. 7. In the apocryphal narrative of this story it is said, The angel of the Lord came down into the furnace; and Nebuchadnezzar here says (v. 28), God sent his angel and delivered them; and it was an angel that shut the lions' mouths when Daniel was in the den, ch. vi. 22. But some think it was the eternal Son of God, the angel of the covenant, and not a created angel. He appeared often in our nature before he assumed it in his incarnation, and never more seasonable, nor to give a more proper indication and presage of his great errand into the world in the fulness of time, than now, when, to deliver his chosen out of the fire, he came and walked with them in the fire. Note, Those that suffer for Christ have his gracious presence with them in their sufferings, even in the fiery furnace, even in the valley of the shadow of death, and therefore even there they need fear no evil. Hereby Christ showed that what is done against his people he takes as done against himself; whoever throws them into the furnace does, in effect, throw him in. I am Jesus, whom thou persecutest, Isa. lxiii. 9.

2. Nebuchadnezzar calls them out of the furnace (v. 26): He comes near to the mouth of the burning fiery furnace, and bids them come forth and come hither. Come forth, come (so some read it); he speaks with a great deal of tenderness and concern, and stands ready to lend them his hand and help them out. He is convinced by their miraculous preservation that he did evil in casting them into the furnace; and therefore he does not thrust them out privily; no verily, but he will come himself and fetch them out, Acts xvi. 37. Observe the respectful title that he gives them.

When he was in the heat of his fury and rage against them it is probable that he called them rebels, and traitors, and all the ill names he could invent; but now he owns them for the servants of the most high God, a God who now appears able to deliver them out of his hand. Note, Sooner or later, God will convince the proudest of men that he is the most high God, and above them, and too hard for them, even in those things wherein they deal proudly and presumptuously, Exod. xviii. 11. He will likewise let them know are who his servants, and that he owns them and will stand by them. Elijah prayed (1 Kings xviii. 36), Let it be known that thou art God and that I am thy servant. Nebuchadnezzar now embraces those whom he had abandoned, and is very officious about them, now that he perceives them to be the favourites of Heaven. Note, What persecutors have done against God's servants, when God opens their eyes, they must as far as they can undo again. How the fourth, whose form was like the Son of God, withdrew, and whether he vanished away or visibly ascended, we are not told, but of the other three we are informed, (1.) That they came forth out of the midst of the fire, as Abraham their father out of Ur (that is, the fire) of the Chaldees, into which, says this tradition of the Jews, he was cast, for refusing to worship idols, and out of which he was delivered, as those his three children were. When they had their discharge they did not tempt God by staying in any longer, but came forth as brands out of the burning. (2.) That it was made to appear, to the full satisfaction of all the amazed spectators, that they had not received the least damage by the fire, v. 27. All the great men came together to view them, and found that there was not so much as a hair of their head singed. Here that was true in the letter which our Saviour spoke figuratively, for an assurance to his suffering servants that they should sustain no real damage (Luke xxi. 18),There shall not a hair of your head perish. Their clothes did not so much as change colour, nor smell of fire, much less were their bodies in the least scorched or blistered; no, the fire had no power on them. The Chaldeans worshipped the fire, as a sort of image of the sun, so that, in restraining the fire now, God put contempt, not only upon their king, but upon their god too, and showed that his voice divides the flames of fire as well as the floods of water (Ps. xxix. 7), when he pleases to make a way for his people through the midst of it. It is our God only that is the consuming fire (Heb. xii. 29); other fire, if he but speak the word, shall not consume.

Nebuchadnezzar Gives Glory to God; Nebuchadnezzar Honours God. (b. c. 587.)

28 Then Nebuchadnezzar spake, and said, Blessed be the God of Shadrach, Meshach, and Abednego, who hath sent his angel, and delivered his servants that trusted in him, and have changed the king's word, and yielded their bodies, that they might not serve nor worship any god, except their own God.   29 Therefore I make a decree, That every people, nation, and language, which speak any thing amiss against the God of Shadrach, Meshach, and Abednego, shall be cut in pieces, and their houses shall be made a dunghill: because there is no other God that can deliver after this sort.   30 Then the king promoted Shadrach, Meshach, and Abednego, in the province of Babylon.

The strict observations that were made, super visum corporis—on inspecting their bodies, by the princes and governors, and all the great men who were present upon this public occasion, and who could not be supposed partial in favour of the confessors, contributed much to the clearing of this miracle and the magnifying of the power and grace of God in it. That indeed a notable miracle has been done is manifest, and we cannot deny it, Acts iv. 16. Let us now see what effect it had upon Nebuchadnezzar.

I. He gives glory to the God of Israel as a God able and ready to protect his worshippers (v. 28): "Blessed be the God of Shadrach, Meshach, and Abednego. Let him have the honour both of the faithful allegiance which his subjects bear to him and the powerful protection he grants to them, neither of which can be paralleled by any other nation and their gods." The king does himself acknowledge and adore him, and thinks it is fit that he should be acknowledged and adored by all. Blessed be thee God of Shadrach. Note, God can extort confessions of his blessedness even from those that have been ready to curse him to his face. 1. He gives him the glory of his power, that he was able to protect his worshippers against the most mighty and malign ant enemies: There is no other God that can deliver after this sort (v. 29), no, not this golden image which he had set up. For this reason there was no other god that obliged his worshippers to cleave to him only, and to suffer death rather than worship any other, as the God of Israel did, for they could not engage to bear them out in so doing, as he could. If God can work such deliverance as no other can, he may demand such obedience as no other may. 2. He gives him the glory of his goodness, that he was ready to do it (v. 28): He has sent his angel and delivered his servants. Bel could not save his worshippers from being burnt at the mouth of the furnace, but the God of Israel saved his from being burnt when they were cast into the midst of the furnace because they refused to worship any other god.
By this Nebuchadnezzar was plainly given to understand that all the great success which he had had, and should yet have, against the people of Israel, which he gloried in, as he had therein overpowered the God of Israel, was owing purely to their sin: if the body of that nation had faithfully adhered to their own God and the worship of him only, as these three men did, they would all have been delivered out of his hand as these three men were. And this was a necessary instruction for him at this time.

II. He applauds the constancy of these three men in their religion, and describes it to their honour, v. 28. Though he is not himself persuaded to own their God for his and to worship him, because, if he do so, he knows he must worship him only and renounce all others, and he calls him the God of Shadrach, not my God, yet he commends them for cleaving to him, and not serving nor worshipping any other God but their own. Note, There are many who are not religious themselves, and yet will own that those are clearly in the right that are religious and are stedfast in their religion. Though they are not themselves persuaded to close with it, they will commend those who, having closed with it, cleave to it. If men have given up their names to that God who will alone be served, let them keep to their principles, and serve him only, whatever it cost them. Such a constancy in the true religion will turn to men's praise, even among those that are without, when unsteadiness, treachery, and double dealing, are what all men will cry shame on. He commends them that they did this, 1. With a generous contempt of their lives, which they valued not, in comparison with the favour of God and the testimony of a good conscience. They yielded their own bodies to be cast into the fiery furnace rather than they would not only not forsake their God, but not affront him, by once paying that homage to any other which is due to him alone. Note, Those shall have their praise, if not of men, yet of God, who prefer their souls before their bodies, and will rather lose their lives than forsake their God. Those know not the worth and value of religion who do not think it worth suffering for. 2. They did it with a glorious contradiction to their prince: They changed the king's word, that is, they were contrary to it, and thereby put contempt upon both his precepts and threatenings, and made him repent and revoke both. Note, Even kings themselves must own that, when their commands are contrary to the commands of God, he is to be obeyed and not they. (3.) They did it with a gracious confidence in their God. They trusted in him that he would stand by them in what they did, that he would either bring them out of the fiery furnace back to their place on earth or lead them through the fiery furnace forward to their place in heaven; and in this confidence they became fearless of the king's wrath and regardless of their own lives. Note, A stedfast faith in God will produce a stedfast faithfulness to God. Now this honourable testimony, thus publicly borne by the king himself to these servants of God, we may well think, would have a good influence upon the rest of the Jews that were, or should be, captives in Babylon. Their neighbours could not with any confidence urge them to do that, nor could they for shame do that, which their brethren were so highly applauded by the king himself for not doing. Nay, and what God did for these his servants would help not only to keep the Jews close to their religion while they were in captivity, but to cure them of their inclination to idolatry, for which end they were sent into captivity; and, when it had had that blessed effect upon them, they might be assured that God would deliver them out of that furnace, as now he delivered their brethren out of this.

III. He issues a royal edict, strictly forbidding any to speak evil of the God of Israel, v. 29. We have reason to think that both the sins and the troubles of Israel had given great occasion, though no just occasion, to the Chaldeans to blaspheme the God of Israel, and, it is likely, Nebuchadnezzar himself had encouraged it; but now, though he is no true convert, nor is wrought upon to worship him, yet he resolves never to speak ill of him again, nor to suffer others to do so: "Whoever shall speak any thing amiss, any error (so some), or rather any reproach or blasphemy, whoever shall speak with contempt of the God of Shadrach, Meshach, and Abednego, they shall be counted the worst of malefactors, and dealt with accordingly, they shall be cut in pieces, as Agag was by the sword of Samuel, and their houses shall be demolished and made a dunghill." The miracle now wrought by the power of this God in defence of his worshippers, publicly in the sight of the thousands of Babylon, was a sufficient justification of this edict. And it would contribute much to the ease of the Jews in their captivity to be by this law screened from the fiery darts of reproach and blasphemy, with which otherwise they would have been continually annoyed. Note, It is a great mercy to the church, and a good point gained, when its enemies though they have not their hearts turned, yet have their mouths stopped and their tongues tied. If a heathen prince laid such a restraint upon the proud lips of blasphemers, much more should Christian princes do it; nay, in this thing, one would think that men should be a law to themselves, and that those who have so little love to God that they care not to speak well of him, yet could never find in their hearts, for we are sure they could never find cause, to speak any thing amiss of him.

IV. He not only reverses the attainder of these three men, but restores them to their places in the government (makes them to prosper, so the word is), and prefers them to greater and more advantageous trusts than they had been in before: He promoted them in the province of Babylon, which was much to their honour and the comfort of their brethren in captivity there. Note, It is the wisdom of princes to prefer and employ men of stedfastness in religion; for those are most likely to be faithful to them who are faithful to God, and it is likely to be well with them when God's favourites are made theirs.

Chapter 4

The penman of this chapter is Nebuchadnezzar himself: the story here recorded concerning him is given us in his own words, as he himself drew it up and published it; but Daniel, a prophet, by inspiration, inserts it in his history, and so it has become a part of sacred writ and a very memorable part. Nebuchadnezzar was as daring a rival with God Almighty for the sovereignty as perhaps any mortal man ever was; but here he fairly owns himself conquered, and gives it under his hand that the God of Israel is above him. Here is, I.

The preface to his narrative, wherein he acknowledges God's dominion over him, ver. 1-3. II. The narrative itself, wherein he relates, 1. His dream, which puzzled the magicians, ver. 1-18. 2. The interpretation of his dream by Daniel, who showed him that it was a prognostication of his own fall, advising him therefore to repent and reform, ver. 19-27. 3. The accomplishment of it in his running stark mad for seven years, and then recovering the use of his reason again, ver. 28-36. 4. The conclusion of the narrative, with a humble acknowledgment and adoration of God as Lord of all, ver. 37. This was extorted from him by the overruling power of that God who has all men's hearts in his hand, and stands upon record a lasting proof of God's supremacy, a monument of his glory, a trophy of his victory, and a warning to all not to think of prospering while they lift up or harden their hearts against God.

Nebuchadnezzar Magnifies God. (b. c. 570.)

1 Nebuchadnezzar the king, unto all people, nations, and languages, that dwell in all the earth; Peace be multiplied unto you. 2 I thought it good to show the signs and wonders that the high God hath wrought toward me. 3 How great are his signs! and how mighty are his wonders! his kingdom is an everlasting kingdom, and his dominion is from generation to generation.

Here is, I. Something of form, which was usual in writs, proclamations, or circular letters, issued by the king, v. 1. The royal style which Nebuchadnezzar makes use of has nothing in it of pomp or fancy, but is plain, short, and unaffected—Nebuchadnezzar the king. If at other times he made use of great swelling words of vanity in his title, how he laid them all aside; for he was old, he had lately recovered from a distraction which had humbled and mortified him, and was now in the actual contemplation of God's greatness and sovereignty. The declaration is directed not only to his own subjects, but to all to whom this present writing shall come—to all people, nations, and languages, that dwell in all the earth. He is not only willing that they should all hear of it, though it carry the account of his own infamy (which perhaps none durst have published if he had not done it himself, and therefore Daniel published the original paper), but he strictly charges and commands all manner of persons to take notice of it; for all are concerned, and it may be profitable to all. He salutes those to whom he writes, in the usual form, Peace be multiplied unto you. Note, It becomes kings with their commands to disperse their good wishes, and, as fathers of their country, to bless their subjects. So the common form with us. We send greeting, Omnibus quibus hae praesentes literae pervenerint, salutem—To all to whom these presents shall come, health; and sometimes Salutem sempiternam—Health and salvation everlasting.

II. Something of substance and matter. He writes this, 1. To acquaint others with the providences of God that had related to him (v. 2): I thought it good to show the signs and wonders that the high God (so he calls the true God) has wrought towards me. He thought it seemly (so the word is), that it was his duty, and did well become him, that it was a debt he owed to God and the world, now that he had recovered from his distraction, to relate to distant places, and record for future ages, how justly God had humbled him and how graciously he had at length restored him. All the nations, no doubt, had heard what befell Nebuchadnezzar, and rang of it; but he thought it fit that they should have a distinct account of it from himself, that they might know the hand of God in it, and what impressions were made upon his own spirit by it, and might speak of it not as a matter of news, but as a matter of religion. The events concerning him were not only wonders to be admired, but signs to be instructed by, signifying to the world that Jehovah is greater than all gods. Note, We ought to show to others God's dealings with us, both the rebukes we have been under and the favours we have received; and though the account hereof may reflect disgrace upon ourselves, as this did upon Nebuchadnezzar, yet we must not conceal it, as long as it may redound to the glory of God. Many will be forward to tell what God has done for their souls, because that turns to their own praise, who care not for telling what God has done against them, and how they deserved it; whereas we ought to give glory to God, not only by praising him for his mercies, but by confessing our sins, accepting the punishment of our iniquity, and in both taking shame to ourselves, as this mighty monarch here does. 2. To show how much he was himself affected with them and convinced by them, v. 3. We should always speak of the word and works of God with concern and seriousness and show ourselves affected with those great things of God which we desire others should take notice of. (1.) He admires God's doings.

He speaks of them as one amazed: How great are his signs, and how mighty are his wonders! Nebuchadnezzar was now old, had reigned above forty years, and had seen as much of the world and the revolutions of it as most men ever did; and yet never till now, when himself was nearly touched, was he brought to admire surprising events as God's signs and his wonders. Now, How great, how mighty, are they! Note, The more we see events to be the Lord's doing, and see in them the product of a divine power and the conduct of a divine wisdom, the more marvellous they will appear in our eyes, Ps. cxviii. 23; lxvi. 2. (2.) He thence infers God's dominion. This is that which he is at length brought to subscribe to: His kingdom is an everlasting kingdom; and not like his own kingdom, which he saw, and long since foresaw, in a dream, hastening towards a period. He now owns that there is a God that governs the world and has a universal, incontestable, absolute dominion in and over all the affairs of the children of men. And it is the glory of this kingdom that it is everlasting. Other reigns are confined to one generation, and other dynasties to a few generations, but God's dominion is from generation to generation. It should seem, Nebuchadnezzar here refers to what Daniel had foretold of a kingdom which the God of heaven would set up, that should never be destroyed (ch. ii. 44), which, though meant of the kingdom of the Messiah, he understood of the providential kingdom. Thus we may make a profitable practical use and application of those prophetical scriptures which yet we do not fully, and perhaps not rightly, comprehend the meaning of.

Nebuchadnezzar's Second Dream; Nebuchadnezzar Relates His Dream. (b. c. 570.)

4 I Nebuchadnezzar was at rest in mine house, and flourishing in my palace: 5 I saw a dream which made me afraid, and the thoughts upon my bed and the visions of my head troubled me. 6 Therefore made I a decree to bring in all the wise men of Babylon before me, that they might make known unto me the interpretation of the dream. 7 Then came in the magicians, the astrologers, the Chaldeans, and the soothsayers: and I told the dream before them; but they did not make known unto me the interpretation thereof. 8 But at the

last Daniel came in before me, whose name was Belteshazzar, according to the name of my god, and in whom is the spirit of the holy gods: and before him I told the dream, saying, 9 O Belteshazzar, master of the magicians, because I know that the spirit of the holy gods is in thee, and no secret troubleth thee, tell me the visions of my dream that I have seen, and the interpretation thereof. 10 Thus were the visions of mine head in my bed; I saw, and behold a tree in the midst of the earth, and the height thereof was great. 11 The tree grew, and was strong, and the height thereof reached unto heaven, and the sight thereof to the end of all the earth: 12 The leaves thereof were fair, and the fruit thereof much, and in it was meat for all: the beasts of the field had shadow under it, and the fowls of the heaven dwelt in the boughs thereof, and all flesh was fed of it. 13 I saw in the visions of my head upon my bed, and, behold, a watcher and a holy one came down from heaven; 14 He cried aloud, and said thus, Hew down the tree, and cut off his branches, shake off his leaves, and scatter his fruit: let the beasts get away from under it, and the fowls from his branches: 15 Nevertheless leave the stump of his roots in the earth, even with a band of iron and brass, in the tender grass of the field; and let it be wet with the dew of heaven, and let his portion be with the beasts in the grass of the earth: 16 Let his heart be changed from man's, and let a beast's heart be given unto him; and let seven times pass over him. 17 This matter is by the decree of the watchers, and the demand by the word of the holy ones: to the intent that the living may know that the most High ruleth in the kingdom of men, and giveth it to whomsoever he will, and setteth up over it the basest of men. 18 This dream I king Nebuchadnezzar have seen. Now thou, O Belteshazzar, declare the interpretation thereof, forasmuch as all the wise men of my kingdom are not able to make known unto me the interpretation: but thou artable; for the spirit of the holy gods is in thee.

Nebuchadnezzar, before he relates the judgments of God that had been wrought upon him for his pride, gives an account of the fair warning he had of them before they came, a due regard to which might have prevented them. But he was told of them, and of the issue of them, before they came to pass, that, when they did come to pass, by comparing them with the prediction of them, he might see, and say, that they were the Lord's doing, and might be brought to believe that there is a divine revelation in the world, as well as a divine Providence, and that the works of God agree with his word.

Now, in the account he here gives of his dream, by which he had notice of what was coming, we may observe,

I. The time when this alarm was given to him (v. 4); it was when he was at rest in his house, and flourishing in his palace. He had lately conquered Egypt, and with it completed his victories, and ended his wars, and made himself monarch of all those parts of the world, which was about the thirty-fourth or thirty-fifth year of his reign, Ezek. xxix. 17. Then he had this dream, which was accomplished about a year after. Seven years his distraction continued, upon his recovery from which he penned this declaration, lived about two years after, and died in his forty-fifth year. He had undergone a long fatigue in his wars, had made many a tedious and dangerous campaign in the field; but now at length he is at rest in his house, and there is no adversary, nor any evil occurrent. Note, God can reach the greatest of men with his terrors even when they are most secure, and think themselves at rest and flourishing.

II. The impression it made upon him (v. 5): I saw a dream which made me afraid. One would think no little thing would frighten him that had been a man of war from his youth, and used to look the perils of war in the face without change of countenance; yet, when God pleases, a dream strikes a terror upon him. His bed, no doubt, was soft, and easy, and well-guarded, and yet his own thoughts upon his bed made him uneasy, and the visions of his head, the creatures of his own imagination, troubled him. Note, God can make the greatest of men uneasy even when they say to their souls, Take your ease, eat, drink, and be merry; he can make those that have been the troublers of the world, and have tormented thousands, to be their own troublers, their own tormentors, and those that have been the terror of the mighty a terror to themselves. By the consternation which this dream put him into, and the impression it made upon him, he perceived it to be, not an ordinary dream, but sent of God on a special errand.

III. His consulting, in vain, with the magicians and astrologers concerning the meaning of it. He had not now forgotten the dream, as before, ch. ii. He had it ready enough, but he wanted to know the interpretation of it and what was prefigured by it, v. 6. Orders are immediately given to summon all the wise men of Babylon that were such fools as to pretend by magic, divination, inspecting the entrails of beasts, or observations of the stars, to predict things to come: they must all come together, to see if any, or all of them in consultation, could interpret the king's dream. It is probable that these people had sometimes, in a like case, given the king some sort of satisfaction, and by the rules of their art had answered the king's queries so as to please him, whether it were right or wrong, hit or missed; but now his expectation from them was disappointed: He told them the dream (v. 7), but they could not tell him the interpretation of it, though they had boasted, with great assurance (ch. ii. 4, 7), that, if they had but the dream told them, they would without fail interpret it. But the key of this dream was in a sacred prophecy (Ezek. xxxi. 3, &c.), where the Assyrian is compared, as Nebuchadnezzar here, to a tree cut down, for his pride; and that was a book they had not studied, nor acquainted themselves with, else they might have been let into the mystery of this dream. Providence ordered it so that they should be first puzzled with it, that Daniel's interpreting it afterwards might redound to the glory of the God of Daniel. Now was fulfilled what Isaiah foretold (ch. xlvii. 12, 13), that when the ruin of Babylon was drawing on her enchantments and sorceries, her astrologers and star-gazers, should not be able to do her any service.

IV. The court he made to Daniel, to engage him to expound his dream to him: At the last Daniel came in. v. 8. Either he declined associating with the rest because of their badness, or they declined his company because of his goodness; or perhaps the king would rather that his own magicians should have the honour of doing it if they could than that Daniel should have it; or Daniel, being governor of the wise men (ch. ii. 48), was, as is usual, last consulted. Many make God's word their last refuge, and never have recourse to it till they are driven off from all other succours. He compliments Daniel very highly, takes notice of the name which he had himself given him, in the choice of which he thinks he was very happy and that it was a good omen: "His name was Belteshazzar, from Bel, the name of my god." He applauds his rare endowments: He has the spirit of the holy gods, so he tells him to his face (v. 9), with which we may suppose that Daniel was so far from being puffed up that he was rather very much grieved to hear that which he had by gift from the God of Israel, the true and living God, ascribed to Nebuchadnezzar's god, a dunghill deity. Here is a strange medley in Nebuchadnezzar, but such as is commonly found in those that side with their corruptions against their convictions. 1. He retains the language and dialect of his idolatry, and therefore, it is to be feared, is no convert to the faith and worship of the living God. He is an idolater, and his speech betrayeth him. For he speaks of many gods, and is brought to acquiesce in one as sufficient, no, not in him who is all-sufficient. And some think, when he speaks of the spirit of the holy gods, that he supposes there are some evil malignant deities, whom men are concerned to worship, only to prevent their doing them a mischief, and some who are good beneficent deities, and that by the spirit of the latter Daniel was animated. He also owns that Bel was his god still, though he had once and again acknowledged the God of Israel to be Lord of all, ch. ii. 47; iii. 29.

He also applauds Daniel, not as a servant of God, but as master of the magicians (v. 9), supposing his knowledge to differ from theirs, not in kind, but only in degree; and he consulted him not as a prophet, but as a celebrated magician, so endeavouring to save the credit of the art when those blundered and were nonplussed who were masters of the art. See how close his idolatry sat to him. He has got a notion of many gods, and has chosen Bel for his god, and he cannot persuade himself to quit either his notion or his choice, though the absurdity of both had been evidenced to him, more than once, beyond contradiction. He, like other heathens, would not change his gods, though they were no gods, Jer. ii. 11. Many persist in a false way only because they think they cannot in honour leave it. See how loose his convictions sat, and how easily he had dropped them. He once called the God of Israel a God of gods, ch. ii. 47. Now he sets him upon a level with the rest of those whom he calls the holy gods. Note, If convictions be not speedily prosecuted, it is a thousand to one but in a little time they will be quite lost and forgotten. Nebuchadnezzar, not going forward with the acknowledgements he had been brought to make of the sovereignty of the true God, soon went backwards, and relapsed to the same veneration he had always had for his false gods. And yet, 2. He professes a great opinion of Daniel, whom he knows to be a servant of the true God, and of him only. He looked upon him as one that had such an insight, such a foresight, as none of his magicians had: I know that no secret troubles thee. Note, The spirit of prophecy quite outdoes the spirit of divination, even the enemies themselves being judges; for so it was adjudged here, upon a fair trial of skill.

V. The particular account he gives him of his dream.

1. He saw a stately flourishing tree, remarkable above all the trees of the wood. This tree was planted in the midst of the earth (v. 10), fitly representing him who reigned in Babylon, which was about the midst of the then known world. His dignity and eminency above all his neighbours were signified by the height of this tree, which was exceedingly great; it reached unto heaven. He over-topped those about him, and aimed to have divine honours given him; nay, he over-powered those about him, and the potent armies he had the command of, with which he carried all before him, are signified by the strength of this tree: it grew and was strong. And so much were Nebuchadnezzar and his growing greatness the talk of the nations, so much had they their eye upon him (some a jealous eye, all a wondering eye), that the sight of this tree is said to be to the end of all the earth. This tree had every thing in it that was pleasant to the eye and good for food (v. 12); The leaves thereof were fair, denoting the pomp and splendour of Nebuchadnezzar's court, which was the wonder of strangers and the glory of his own subjects. Nor was this tree for sight and state only, but for use. (1.) For protection; the boughs of it were for shelter both to the beasts and to the fowls. Princes should be a screen to their subjects from the heat and from the storm, should expose themselves to secure them, and study how to make them safe and easy. If the bramble be promoted over the trees, he invites them to come and trust in his shadow, such as it is, Judg. ix. 15. It is protection that draws allegiance. The kings of the earth are to their subjects but as the shadow of a great tree; but Christ is to his subjects as the shadow of a great rock, Isa. xxxii. 2. Nay, because that, though strong, may be cold, they are said to be hidden under the shadow of his wings (Ps. xvii. 8), where they are not only safe, but warm. (2.) For provision, The Assyrian was compared to a cedar (Ezek. xxxi. 6), which affords shadow only; but this tree here had much fruit—in it was meat for all and all flesh was fed of it. This mighty monarch, it should seem by this, not only was great, but did good; he did not impoverish, but enrich his country, and by his power and interest abroad brought wealth and trade to it. Those that exercise authority would be called benefactors (Luke xxii. 25), and the most effectual course they can take to support their authority is to be really benefactors. And see what is the best that great men, with their wealth and power can attain to, and that is to have the honour of having many to live upon them and to be maintained by them; for, as goods are increased, those are increased that eat them.

2. He heard the doom of this tree read, which he perfectly remembered, and related here,

perhaps word for word as he heard it. The sentence was passed upon it by an angel, whom he saw come down from heaven, and heard proclaim this sentence aloud. This angel is here called a watcher, or watchman, not only because angels by their nature are spirits, and therefore neither slumber nor sleep, but because by their office they are ministering spirits, and attend continually to their ministrations, watching all opportunities of serving their great Master. They, as watchers, encamp round those that fear God, to deliver them, and bear them up in their hands. This angel was a messenger, or ambassador (so some read it), and a holy one. Holiness becomes God's house; therefore angels that attend and are employed by him are holy ones; they preserve the purity and rectitude of their nature, and are in every thing conformable to the divine will. Let us review the doom passed upon the tree.

(1.) Orders are given that it be cut down (v. 14); now also the axe is laid to the root of this tree. Though it is ever so high, ever so strong, that cannot secure it when its day comes to fall; the beasts and fowls, that are sheltered in and under the boughs of it, are driven away and dispersed; the branches are cropped, the leaves shaken off, and the fruit scattered. Note, Worldly prosperity in its highest degree is a very uncertain thing; and it is no uncommon thing for those that have lived in the greatest pomp and power to be stripped of all that which they trusted to and gloried in. By the turns of providence, those who made a figure become captives, those who lived in plenty, and above what they had, are reduced to straits, and live far below what they had, and those perhaps are brought to be beholden to others who once had many depending upon them and making suit to them. But the trees of righteousness, that are planted in the house of the Lord and bring forth fruit to him, shall not be cut down, nor shall their leaf wither.

(2.) Care is taken that the root be preserved (v. 15); "Leave the stump of it in the earth, exposed to all weathers. There let it lie neglected and buried in the grass. Let the beasts that formerly sheltered themselves under the boughs now repose themselves upon the stump; but that it may not be raked to pieces, nor trodden to dirt, and to show that it is yet reserved for better days, let it be hooped round with a band of iron and brass, to keep it firm." Note, God in judgment remembers mercy; and may yet have good things in store for those whose condition seems most forlorn. There is hope of a tree, if it be cut down, that it will sprout again, that through the scent of water it will bud, Job xiv. 7-9.

(3.) The meaning of this is explained by the angel himself to Nebuchadnezzar, v. 16. Whoever is the person signified by this tree he is sentenced to be deposed from the honour, state, and dignity of a man, to be deprived of the use of his reason, and to be and live like a brute, till seven times pass over him. Let a beast's heart be given unto him. This is surely the saddest and sorest of all temporal judgments, worse a thousand times than death, and though, like it, least felt by those that lie under it, yet to be dreaded and deprecated more than any other. Nay, whatever outward affliction God is pleased to lay upon us, we have reason to bear it patiently, and to be thankful that he continues to us the use of our reason and the peace of our consciences. But those proud tyrants who set their heart as the heart of God (Ezek. xxvii. 2) may justly be deprived of the heart of man, and have a beast's heart given them.

(4.) The truth of it is confirmed (v. 17); This matter is by the decree of the watchers and the demand by the word of the holy ones. God has determined it, as a righteous Judge; he has signed this edict; pursuant to his eternal counsel, the decree has gone forth, And, [1.] The angels of heaven have subscribed to it, as attesting it, approving it, and applauding it. It is by the decree of the watchers; not that the great God needs the counsel or concurrence of the angels in any thing he determines or does, but, as he uses their ministration in executing his counsels, so he is sometimes represented, after the manner of men, as if he consulted them. Whom shall I send? Isa. vi. 8. Who shall persuade Ahab? 1 Kings xxii. 20. So it denotes the solemnity of this sentence. The king's breves, or short writs, pass, Teste me ipso—in my presence; but charters used to be signed, His testibus—In the presence of us whose names are under-written; such was Nebuchadnezzar's doom; it was by the decree of the watchers. [2.] The saints on earth petitioned for it, as well as the angels in heaven: The demand is by the word of the holy ones. God's suffering people, that had long groaned under the heavy yoke of Nebuchadnezzar's tyranny, cried to him for vengeance; they made the demand, and God gave this answer to it; for, when the oppressed cry to God, he will hear, Exod. xxii. 27. Sentence was passed, in Ahab's time, that there should be no more rain, at Elijah's word, when he made intercession against Israel, 1 Kings xvii. 1.

(5.) The design of it is declared. Orders are given for the cutting down of this tree, to the intent that the living may know that the Most High rules. This judgment must be executed, to convince the unthinking, unbelieving, world, that verily there is a God that judges in the earth, a God that governs the world, that not only has a kingdom of his own in it, and administers the affairs of that kingdom, but rules also in the kingdom of men, in the dominion that one man has over another, and gives that to whomsoever he will; from him promotion comes, Ps. lxxv. 6, 7. He advances men to power and dominion that little expected it, and crosses the projects of the ambitious and aspiring. Sometimes he sets up the basest of men, and serves his own purposes by them. He sets up mean men, as David from the sheepfold; he raises the poor out of the dust, to set them among princes, Ps. cxiii. 7, 8. Nay, sometimes he sets up bad men, to be a scourge to a provoking people. Thus he can do, thus he may do, thus he often does, and gives not account of any of his matters. By humbling Nebuchadnezzar it was designed that the living should be made to know this. The dead know it, that have gone to the world of spirits, the world of retribution; they know that the Most High rules; but the living must be made to know it and lay it to heart, that they may make their peace with God before it be too late.

Thus has Nebuchadnezzar fully and faithfully related his dream, what he saw and what he heard, and then demands of Daniel the interpretation of it (v. 18), for he found that no one else was able to interpret it, but was confident that he was: For the spirit of the holy gods is in thee, or of the Holy God, the proper title of the God of Israel. Much may be expected from those that have in them the Spirit of the Holy God. Whether Nebuchadnezzar had any jealousy that it was his own doom that was read by this dream does not appear; perhaps he was so vain and secure as to imagine that it was some other prince that was a rival with him, whose fall he had the pleasing prospect of given him in this dream; but, be it for him or against him, he is very solicitous to know the true meaning of it and depends upon Daniel to give it to him. Now, When God gives us general warnings of his judgments we should be desirous to understand his mind in them, to hear the Lord's voice crying in the city.

Nebuchadnezzar's Dream Interpreted. (b. c. 570.)

19 Then Daniel, whose name was Belteshazzar, was astonied for one hour, and his thoughts troubled him. The king spake, and said, Belteshazzar, let not the dream, or the interpretation thereof, trouble thee. Belteshazzar answered and said, My lord, the dream be to them that hate thee, and the interpretation thereof to thine enemies. 20 The tree that thou sawest, which grew, and was strong, whose height reached unto the heaven, and the sight thereof to all the earth; 21 Whose leaves were fair, and the fruit thereof much, and in it was meat for all; under which the beasts of the field dwelt, and upon whose branches the fowls of the heaven had their habitation: 22 It is thou, O king, that art grown and become strong: for thy greatness is grown, and reacheth unto heaven, and thy dominion to the end of the earth. 23 And whereas the king saw a watcher and a holy one coming down from heaven, and saying, Hew the tree down, and destroy it; yet leave the stump of the roots thereof in the earth, even with a band of iron and brass, in the tender grass of the field; and let it be wet with the dew of heaven, and let his portion be with the beasts of the field, till seven times

pass over him; 24 This is the interpretation, O king, and this is the decree of the most High, which is come upon my lord the king: 25 That they shall drive thee from men, and thy dwelling shall be with the beasts of the field, and they shall make thee to eat grass as oxen, and they shall wet thee with the dew of heaven, and seven times shall pass over thee, till thou know that the most High ruleth in the kingdom of men, and giveth it to whomsoever he will. 26 And whereas they commanded to leave the stump of the tree roots; thy kingdom shall be sure unto thee, after that thou shalt have known that the heavens do rule. 27 Wherefore, O king, let my counsel be acceptable unto thee, and break off thy sins by righteousness, and thine iniquities by showing mercy to the poor; if it may be a lengthening of thy tranquillity.

We have here the interpretation of Nebuchadnezzar's dream; and when once it is applied to himself, and it is declared that he is the tree in the dream (Mutato nomine de te fabula narratur—Change but the name, the fable speaks of thee), when once it is said, Thou art the man, there needs little more to be said for the explication of the dream. Out of his own mouth he is judged; so shall his doom be, he himself has decided it. The thing was so plain that Daniel, upon hearing the dream, was astonished for one hour, v. 19. He was struck with amazement and terror at so great a judgment coming upon so great a prince. His flesh trembled for fear of God. He was likewise struck with confusion when he found himself under a necessity of being the man that must bring to the king these heavy tidings, which, having received so many favours from the king, he had rather he should have heard from any one else; so far is he from desiring the woeful day that he dreads it, and the thoughts of it trouble him. Those that come after the ruined sinner are said to be astonished at his day, as those that went before, and saw it coming (as Daniel here), were affrighted, Job xviii. 20.

I. The preface to the interpretation is a civil compliment which, as a courtier, he passes upon the king. The king observed him to stand as one astonished, and, thinking he was loth to speak out for fear of offending him, he encouraged him to deal plainly and faithfully with him; Let not the dream, nor the interpretation thereof, trouble thee. This he speaks either, 1. As one that sincerely desired to know this truth. Note, Those that consult the oracles of God must be ready to receive them as they are, whether they be for them or against them, and must accordingly give their ministers leave to be free with them. Or, 2. As one that despised the truth, and set it at defiance. When we see how regardless he was of this warning afterwards we are tempted to think that this was his meaning; "Let it not trouble thee, for I am resolved it shall not trouble me; nor will I lay it to heart." But, whether he have any concern for himself or no, Daniel is concerned for him, and therefore wishes, "The dream be to those that hate thee. Let the ill it bodes light on the head of thy enemies, not on thy head." Though Nebuchadnezzar was an idolater, a persecutor, and an oppressor of the people of God, yet he was, at present, Daniel's prince; and therefore, though Daniel foresees, and is now going to foretell, ill concerning him, he dares not wish ill to him.
II. The interpretation itself is only a repetition of the dream, with application to the king. "As for the tree which thou sawest flourishing (v. 20, 21), it is thou, O king!" v. 22. And willing enough would the king be to hear this (as, before, to hear, Thou art the head of gold), but for that which follows. He shows the king his present prosperous state in the glass of his own dream; "Thy greatness has grown and reaches as near to heaven as human greatness can do, and thy dominion is to the end of the earth," ch. ii. 37, 38. "As for the doom passed upon the tree (v. 23), it is the decree of the Most High, which comes upon my lord the king," v. 24. He must not only be deposed from his throne, but driven from men, and being deprived of his reason, and having a beast's heart given him, his dwelling shall be with the beasts of the field, and with them he shall be a fellow-commoner: he shall eat grass as oxen, and, like them, lie out all weathers, and be wet with the dew of heaven, and this till seven times pass over him, that is, seven years; and then he shall know that the Most High rules, and when he is brought to know and own this he shall be restored to his dominion again (v.

26): "Thy kingdom shall be sure unto thee, shall remain as firm as the stump of the tree in the ground, and thou shalt have it, after thou shalt have known that the heavens do rule." God is here called the heavens, because it is in heaven that he has prepared his throne (Ps. ciii. 19), thence he beholds all the sons of men, Ps. xxxiii. 13. The heavens, even the heavens, are the Lord's; and the influence which the visible heavens have upon this earth is intended as a faint representation of the dominion the God of heaven has over this lower world; we are said to sin against heaven, Luke xv. 18. Note, Then only we may expect comfortably to enjoy our right in, and government of, both ourselves and others, when we dutifully acknowledge God's title to, and dominion over, us and all we have.

III. The close of the interpretation is the pious counsel which Daniel, as a prophet, gave the king, v. 27. Whether he appeared concerned or not at the interpretation of the dream, a word of advice would be very seasonable—if careless, to awaken him, if troubled, to comfort him; and it is not inconsistent with the dream and the interpretation of it, for Daniel knew not but it might be conditional, like the prediction of Nineveh's destruction. Observe, 1. How humbly he gives his advice, and with what tenderness and respect: "O king! let my counsel be acceptable unto thee; take it in good part, as coming from love, and well-meant, and let it not be misinterpreted." Note, Sinners need to be courted to their own good, and respectfully entreated to do well for themselves. The apostle beseeches men to suffer the word of exhortation, Heb. xiii. 22. We think it a good point gained if people will be persuaded to take good counsel kindly; nay, if they will take it patiently. 2. What his advice is. He does not counsel him to enter into a course of physic, for the preventing of the distemper in his head, but to break off a course of sin that he was in, to reform his life. He wronged his own subjects, and dealt unfairly with his allies; and he must break off this by righteousness, by rendering to all their due, making amends for wrong done, and not triumphing over right with might. He had been cruel to the poor, to God's poor, to the poor Jews; and he must break off this iniquity by showing mercy to those poor, pitying those oppressed ones, setting them at liberty or making their captivity easy to them. Note, It is necessary, in repentance, that we not only cease to do evil, but learn to do well, not only do no wrong to any, but do good to all. 3. What the motive is with which he backs this advice: If it may be a lengthening of thy tranquility. Though it should not wholly prevent the judgment, yet by this means a reprieve may be obtained, as by Ahab's humbling himself, 1 Kings xxi. 29. Either the trouble may be the longer before it comes or the shorter when it does come; yet he cannot assure him of this, but it may be, it may prove so. Note, The mere probability of preventing a temporal judgment is inducement enough to a work so good in itself as the leaving off of our sins and reforming of our lives, much more the certainty of preventing our eternal ruin. "That will be a healing of thy error" (so some read it); "thus the quarrel will be taken up, and all will be well again."

Nebuchadnezzar Driven among Beasts. (b. c. 569.)

28 All this came upon the king Nebuchadnezzar.   29 At the end of twelve months he walked in the palace of the kingdom of Babylon.   30 The king spake, and said, Is not this great Babylon, that I have built for the house of the kingdom by the might of my power, and for the honour of my majesty?   31 While the word was in the king's mouth, there fell a voice from heaven, saying, O king Nebuchadnezzar, to thee it is spoken; The kingdom is departed from thee.   32 And they shall drive thee from men, and thy dwelling shall be with the beasts of the field: they shall make thee to eat grass as oxen, and seven times shall pass over thee, until thou know that the most High ruleth in the kingdom of men, and giveth it to whomsoever he will.   33 The same hour was the thing fulfilled upon Nebuchadnezzar: and he was driven from men, and did eat grass as oxen, and his body was wet with the dew of heaven, till his hairs were grown like eagles' feathers, and his nails like birds' claws.

We have here Nebuchadnezzar's dream accomplished, and Daniel's application of it to him justified and confirmed. How he took it we are not told, whether he was pleased with Daniel or displeased; but here we have,

I. God's patience with him: All this came upon him, but not till twelve months after (v. 29), so long there was a lengthening of his tranquility, though it does not appear that he broke off his sins, or showed any mercy to the poor captives, for this was still God's quarrel with him, that he opened not the house of his prisoners, Isa. xiv. 17. Daniel having counselled him to repent, God so far confirmed his word that he gave him space to repent; he let him alone this year also, this one year more, before he brought this judgment upon him. Note, God is long-suffering with provoking sinners, because he is not willing that any should perish, but that all should come to repentance, 2 Pet. iii. 9.

II. His pride, and haughtiness, and abuse of that patience. He walked in the palace of the kingdom of Babylon, in pomp and pride, pleasing himself with the view of that vast city, which, with all the territories thereunto belonging, was under his command, and he said, either to himself or to those about him, perhaps some foreigners to whom he was showing his kingdom and the glory of it, Is not this great Babylon? Yes, it is great, of vast extent, no less that forty-five miles compass within the walls. It is full of inhabitants, and they are full of wealth. It is a golden city, and that is enough to proclaim it great, Isa. xiv. 4. See the grandeur of the houses, walls, towers, and public edifices. Every thing in Babylon he thinks looks great; "and this great Babylon I have built." Babylon was built many ages before he was born, but because he fortified and beautified it, and we may suppose much of it was rebuilt during his long and prosperous reign, he boasts that he has built it, as Augustus Caesar boasted concerning Rome, Lateritiam inveni, marmoream reliqui—I found it brick, but I left it marble. He boasts that he built it for the house of the kingdom, that is, the metropolis of his empire. This vast city, compared with the countries that belonged to his dominions, was but as one house. He built it with the assistance of his subjects, yet boasts that he did it by the might of his power; he built it for his security and convenience, yet, as if he had no occasion for it, boasts that he built it purely for the honour of his majesty. Note, Pride and self-conceitedness are sins that most easily beset great men, who have great things in the world. They are apt to take the glory to themselves which is due to God only.
III. His punishment for his pride. When he was thus strutting, and vaunting himself, and adoring his own shadow, while the proud word was in the king's mouth the powerful word came from heaven, by which he was immediately deprived, 1. Of his honour as a king: The kingdom has departed from thee. When he thought he had erected impregnable bulwarks for the preserving of his kingdom, now, in an instant, it has departed from him; when he thought it so well guarded that none could take it from him, behold, it departs of itself. As soon as he becomes utterly incapable to manage it, it is of course taken out of his hands. 2. He is deprived of his honour as a man. He loses his reason, and by that means loses his dominion: They shall drive thee from men, v. 32. And it was fulfilled (v. 33): he was driven from men the same hour. On a sudden he fell stark mad, distracted in the highest degree that ever any man was. His understanding and memory were gone, and all the faculties of a rational soul broken, so that he became a perfect brute in the shape of a man. He went naked, and on all four, like a brute, did himself shun the society of reasonable creatures and run wild into the fields and woods, and was driven out by his own servants, who, after some time of trial, despairing of his return to his right mind, abandoned him, and looked after him no more. He had not the spirit of a beast of prey (that of the royal lion), but of the abject and less honourable species, for he was made to eat grass as oxen; and, probably, he did not speak with human voice, but lowed like an ox. Some think that his body was all covered with hair; however, the hair of his head and beard, being never cut nor combed, grew like eagles feathers, and his nails like birds' claws. Let us pause a little, and view this miserable spectacle; and let us receive instruction from it. (1.) Let us see here what a mercy it is to have the use of our reason, how thankful we ought to be for it, and how careful we ought to be not to do

any thing which may either provoke God or may have a natural tendency to put us out of the possession of our own souls. Let us learn how to value our own reason, and to pity the case of those that are under the prevailing power of melancholy or distraction, or are delirious, and to be very tender in our censures of them and conduct towards them, for it is a trial common to men, and a case which, some time or other, may be our own. (2.) Let us see here the vanity of human glory and greatness. Is this Nebuchadnezzar the Great? What this despicable animal that is meaner than the poorest beggar? Is this he that looked so glorious on the throne, so formidable in the camp, that had politics enough to subdue and govern kingdoms, and now has not so much sense as to keep his own clothes on his back? Is this the man that made the earth to tremble, that did shake kingdoms? Isa. xiv. 16. Never let the wise man then glory in his wisdom, nor the mighty man in his strength. (3.) Let us see here how God resists the proud, and delights to abase them and put contempt upon them. Nebuchadnezzar would be more than a man, and therefore God justly makes him less than a man, and puts him upon a level with the beasts who set up for a rival with his Maker. See Job xl. 11-13.

Nebuchadnezzar Restored. (b. c. 562.)

34 And at the end of the days I Nebuchadnezzar lifted up mine eyes unto heaven, and mine understanding returned unto me, and I blessed the most High, and I praised and honoured him that liveth for ever, whose dominion is an everlasting dominion, and his kingdom is from generation to generation: 35 And all the inhabitants of the earth are reputed as nothing: and he doeth according to his will in the army of heaven, and among the inhabitants of the earth: and none can stay his hand, or say unto him, What doest thou? 36 At the same time my reason returned unto me; and for the glory of my kingdom, mine honour and brightness returned unto me; and my counsellors and my lords sought unto me; and I was established in my kingdom, and excellent majesty was added unto me. 37 Now I Nebuchadnezzar praise and extol and honour the King of heaven, all whose works are truth, and his ways judgment: and those that walk in pride he is able to abase.

We have here Nebuchadnezzar's recovery from his distraction, and his return to his right mind, at the end of the days prefixed, that is, of the seven years. So long he continued a monument of God's justice and a trophy of his victory over the children of pride, and he was made more so by being struck mad than if he had been in an instant struck dead with a thunderbolt; yet it was a mercy to him that he was kept alive, for while there is life there is hope that we may yet praise God, as he did here: At the end of the days (says he), I lifted up my eyes unto heaven (v. 34), looked no longer down towards the earth as a beast, but begun to look up as a man. Os homini sublime dedit—Heaven gave to man an erect countenance. But there was more in it than this; he looked up as a devout man, as a penitent, as a humble petitioner for mercy, being perhaps never till now made sensible of his own misery. And now,

I. He has the use of his reason so far restored to him that with it he glorifies God, and humbles himself under his mighty hand. He was told that he should continue in that forlorn case till he should know that the Most High rules, and here we have him brought to the knowledge of this: My understanding returned to me, and I blessed the Most High. Note, Those may justly be reckoned void of understanding that do not bless and praise God; nor do men ever rightly use their reason till they begin to be religious, nor live as men till they live to the glory of God. As reason is the substratum or subject of religion (so that creatures which have no reason are not capable of religion), so religion is the crown and glory of reason, and we have our reason in vain, and shall one day wish we had never had it, if we do not glorify God with it. This was the first act of Nebuchadnezzar's returning reason; and, when this became the employment of it, he was then, and not till then, qualified for all the other enjoyments of it. And till he was for a great while disabled to exercise it in other things he never was brought to apply it to this, which is the great end for which our reason is given us. His folly was the means whereby he became wise; he was not recovered by his dream of this judgment (that was soon forgotten like a dream), but he is made to feel it, and then his ear is opened to discipline. To bring him to himself, he must first be beside himself. And by this it appears that what good thoughts there were in his mind, and what good work was wrought there, were not of himself (for he was not his own man), but it was the gift of God. Let us see what Nebuchadnezzar is now at length effectually brought to the acknowledgment of; and we may learn from it what to believe concerning God. 1. That the most high God lives for ever, and his being knows neither change nor period, for he has it of himself. His flatterers often complimented him with, O king! live for ever. But he is now convinced that no king lives for ever, but the God of Israel only, who is still the same. 2. That his kingdom is like himself, everlasting, and his dominion from generation to generation; there is no succession, no revolution, in his kingdom. As he lives, so he reigns, for ever, and of his government there is no end. 3. That all nations before him are as nothing. He has no need of them; he makes no account of them. The greatest of men, in comparison with him, are less than nothing. Those that think highly of God think meanly of themselves. 4. That his kingdom is universal, and both the armies of heaven and the inhabitants of the earth are his subjects, and under his check and control. Both angels and men are employed by him, and are accountable to him; the highest angel is not above his command, nor the meanest of the children of men beneath his cognizance. The angels of heaven are his armies, the inhabitants of the earth his tenants. 5. That his power is irresistible, and his sovereignty uncontrollable, for he does according to his will, according to his design and purpose, according to his decree and counsel; whatever he pleases that he does; whatever he appoints that he performs; and none can resist his will, change his counsel, nor stay his hand, nor say unto him, What doest thou? None can arraign his proceedings, enquire into the meaning of them, nor demand a reason for them. Woe to him that strives with his Maker, that says to him, What doest thou? Or, Why doest thou so? 6. That every thing which God does is well done: His works are truth, for they all agree with his word. His ways are judgment, both wise and righteous, exactly consonant to the rules both of prudence and equity, and no fault is to be found with them. 7. That he has power to humble the haughtiest of his enemies that act in contradiction to him or competition with him: Those that walk in pride he is able to abuse (v. 37); he is able to deal with those that are most confident of their own sufficiency to contend with him.

II. He has the use of his reason so far restored to him as with it to re-enjoy himself, and the pleasures of his re-established prosperity (v. 36): At the same time my reason returned to me; he had said before (v. 34) that his understanding returned to him, and here he mentions it again, for the use of our reason is a mercy we can never be sufficiently thankful for. Now his lords sought to him; he did not need to seek to them, and they soon perceived, not only that he had recovered his reason and was fit to rule, but that he had recovered it with advantage, and was more fit to rule than ever. It is probable that the dream and the interpretation of it were well known, and much talked of, at court; and the former part of the prediction being fulfilled, that he should go distracted, they doubted not but that, according to the prediction, he should come to himself again at seven years' end, and, in confidence of that, when the time had expired they were ready to receive him; and then his honour and brightness returned to him, the same that he had before his madness seized him. He is now established in his kingdom as firmly as if there had been no interruption given him. He becomes a fool, that he may be wise, wiser than ever; and he that but the other day was in the depth of disgrace and ignominy has now excellent majesty added to him, beyond what he had when he went from kingdom to kingdom conquering and to conquer. Note, 1. When men are brought to honour God, particularly by a penitent confession of sin and a believing acknowledgment of his sovereignty, then, and not till then, they may expect that God will put honour upon them, will not only restore them to the dignity they lost by the sin of the first Adam, but add excellent majesty to them from the righteousness and grace of the second Adam. 2. Afflictions shall last no longer than till they have done the work for which they were sent. When this prince is brought to own God's dominion over himself. 3. All the accounts we take and give of God's dealing with us ought to conclude with praises to him. When Nebuchadnezzar is restored to his kingdom he praises, and extols, and honours the King of heaven (v. 37), before he applies himself to his secular business. Therefore we have our reason, that we may be in a capacity of praising him, and therefore our prosperity, that we may have cause to praise him.

It was not long after this that Nebuchadnezzar ended his life and reign. Abydenus, quoted by Eusebius (Praep. Evang. 1. 9), reports, from the tradition of the Chaldeans, that upon his death-bed he foretold the taking of Babylon by Cyrus. Whether he continued in the same good mind that here he seems to have been in we are not told, nor does any thing appear to the contrary but that he did: and, if so great a blasphemer and persecutor did find mercy, he was not the last. And, if our charity may reach so far as to hope he did, we must admire free grace, by which he lost his wits for a while that he might save his soul for ever.

Chapter 5

The destruction of the kingdom of Babylon had been long and often foretold when it was at a distance; in this chapter we have it accomplished, and a prediction of it the very same night that it was accomplished. Belshazzar now reigned in Babylon; some compute he had reigned seventeen years, others but three; we have here the story of his exit and the period of his kingdom. We must know that about two years before this Cyrus king of Persia, a growing monarch, came against Babylon with a great army; Belshazzar met him, fought him, and was routed by him in a pitched battle. He and his scattered forces retired into the city, where Cyrus besieged them. They were very secure, because the river Euphrates was their bulwark, and they had twenty years; provision in the city; but in the second year of the siege he took it, as is here related. We have in this chapter, I. The riotous, idolatrous, sacrilegious feast which Belshazzar made, in which he filled up the measure of his iniquity, ver. 1-4. II. The alarm given him in the midst of his jollity by a hand-writing on the wall, which none of his wise men could read or tell him the meaning of, ver. 5-9. III. The interpretation of the mystical characters by Daniel, who was at length brought in to him, and dealt plainly with him, and showed him his doom written, ver. 10-28. IV. The immediate accomplishment of the interpretation in the slaying of the king and seizing of the kingdom, ver. 30, 31.

Belshazzar's Feast; The Hand-writing on the Wall. (b. c. 538.)

1 Belshazzar the king made a great feast to a thousand of his lords, and drank wine before the thousand. 2 Belshazzar, whiles he tasted the wine, commanded to bring the golden and silver vessels which his father Nebuchadnezzar had taken out of the temple which was in Jerusalem; that the king, and his princes, his wives, and his concubines, might drink therein. 3 Then they brought the golden vessels that were taken out of the temple of the house of God which was at Jerusalem; and the king, and his princes, his wives, and his concubines, drank in them. 4 They drank wine, and praised the gods of gold, and of silver, of brass, of iron, of wood, and of stone. 5 In the same hour came forth fingers of a man's hand, and wrote over against the candlestick upon the plaster of the wall of the king's palace: and the king saw the part of the hand that wrote. 6 Then the king's countenance was changed, and his thoughts troubled him, so that the joints of his loins were loosed, and his knees smote one against another. 7 The king cried aloud to bring in the astrologers, the Chaldeans, and the soothsayers. And the king spake, and said to the wise men of Babylon, Whosoever shall read this writing, and show me the interpretation thereof, shall be clothed with scarlet, and

have a chain of gold about his neck, and shall be the third ruler in the kingdom. 8 Then came in all the king's wise men: but they could not read the writing, nor make known to the king the interpretation thereof. 9 Then was king Belshazzar greatly troubled, and his countenance was changed in him, and his lords were astonied.

We have here Belshazzar the king very gay, but all of a sudden very gloomy, and in straits in the fulness of his sufficiency. See how he affronts God, and God affrights him; and wait what will be the issue of this contest; and whether he that hardened his heart against God prospered.

I. See how the king affronted God, and put contempt upon him. He made a great feast, or banquet of wine; probably it was some anniversary solemnity, in honour off his birth-day or coronation-day, or in honour of some of their idols. Historians say that Cyrus, who was now with his army besieging Babylon, knew of this feast, and presuming that they then would be off their guard, somno vinoque sepulti—buried in sleep and wine, took that opportunity to attack the city, and so with the more ease made himself master of it. Belshazzar upon this occasion invited a thousand of his lords to come and drink with him. Perhaps they were such as had signalized themselves in defense of the city against the besiegers; or these were his great council of war, with whom, when they had well drunk, he would advise what was further to be done. And they were to look upon it as a great favour that he drank wine before them, for it was the pride of those eastern kings to be seldom seen. He drank wine before them, for he made this feast, as Ahasuerus did, to show the honour of his majesty. Now in this sumptuous feast, 1. He put an affront upon the providence of God and bade defiance to his judgments. His city was now besieged; a powerful enemy was at his gates; his life and kingdom lay at stake. In all this the hand of the Lord had gone out against him, and by it he called him to weeping, and mourning, and girding with sackcloth. God's voice cried in the city, as Jonah to Nineveh, Yet forty days, or fewer, and Babylon shall be destroyed. He should therefore, like the king of Nineveh, have proclaimed a fast; but, as one resolved to walk contrary to God, he proclaims a feast, and behold joy and gladness, slaying oxen, killing sheep, eating flesh, and drinking wine, as if he dared the Almighty to do his worst, Isa. xxii. 12, 13. To show how little fear he had of being forced to surrender, for want of provisions, he spent thus extravagantly. Note, Security and sensuality are sad presages of approaching ruin. Those that will not be warned by judgments of God may expect to be wounded by them. 2. He put an affront upon the temple of God, and bade defiance to his sanctuary, v. 2. While he tasted the wine, he commanded to bring the vessels of the temple, that they might drink in them. When he tasted how rich and fine the wine was, "O," said he, "it is a pity but we should have holy vessels to drink such delicious wine as this in," which was looked upon as a piece of wit, and, to carry on the humour, the vessels of the temple were immediately sent for. Nay, there seems to have been something more in it than a frolic, and that it was done in a malicious despite to the God of Israel. The heart of his people was very much upon these sacred vessels, as appears from Jer. xxvii. 16, 18. Their principal care, at their return, was about these, Ezra i. 7. Now, we may suppose, they had an expectation of their deliverance approaching, reckoning the seventy years of their captivity near a period; and some of them might perhaps have given out some words to that purport, that shortly they should have the vessels of the sanctuary restored to them, in defiance of which Belshazzar here proclaims them to be his own, will keep them in store no longer, but will make use of them among his own plate. Note, That mirth is sinful indeed, and fills the measure of men's iniquity apace, which profanes sacred things and jests with them. This ripened Babylon for ruin—that no songs would serve them but the songs of Zion (Ps. cxxxvii. 3), no vessels but the vessels of the sanctuary. Let those who thus sacrilegiously alienate what is dedicated to God and his honour know that he will not be mocked. 3. He put an affront upon God himself, and bade defiance to his deity; for they drank wine, and praised the gods of gold and silver, v. 4. They gave that glory to images, the work of their own hands and creatures of their own fancy, which is due to the true and living God only. They praised them either with sacrifices offered to them or with songs sung in honour of them. When their heads were giddy, and their hearts merry, with wine, they were in the fittest frame to praise the gods of gold and silver, wood and stone; for one would think that men in their senses, who had the command of a clear and sober thought, could not be guilty of so gross an absurdity; they must be intoxicated ere they could be so infatuated. Drunken worshippers, who are not men, but beasts, are the most proper for the service of dunghill deities, that are not gods, but devils. They have erred through wine, Isa. xxvii. 7. They drank wine, and praised their idol-gods, as if they had been the founders of their feast and the givers of all good things to them. Or, when they were drinking wine, they praised their gods by drinking healths to them; and the king drank wine before them (v. 1), that is, he began the health, first to this god, and then to the other, till they went through the bead-roll or farrago of them, those of wood and stone not excepted. Note, Immorality and impiety, vice and profaneness, strengthen the hands and advance the interests one of another. Drunken frolics were an introduction to idolatry, and then idolatrous healths were a shoeing-horn to further drunkenness.

II. See how God affrighted the king, and struck a terror upon him. Belshazzar and his lords are in the midst of their revels, the cups going round apace, and all upon the merry pin, drinking confusion, it may be, to Cyrus and his army, and roaring out huzzas, in confidence of the speedy raising of the siege; but the hour had come when that must be fulfilled which had been long ago said of the king of Babylon, when his city should be besieged by the Persians and Medes, Isa. xxi. 2-4. The night of my pleasures has he turned into fear to me. The mirth of this ball at court must be spoiled, and a damp cast upon their jollity, though the king himself be master of the revels; immediately, when God speaks the word, we have him and all his guests in the utmost confusion, and the end of their mirth is heaviness. 1. There appear the fingers of a man's hand writing on the plaster of the wall, before the king's face (v. 5), "the angel Gabriel," say the rabbin, "directing these fingers and writing by them." "That divine hand" (says a rabbi of our own, Dr. Lightfoot) "that had written the two tables for a law to his people now writes the doom of Babel and Belshazzar upon the wall." Here was nothing sent to frighten them which made a noise, or threatened their lives, no claps of thunder nor flashes of lightning, no destroying angel with his sword drawn in his hand, only a pen in the hand, writing upon the wall, over-against the candlestick, where they might all see it by the light of their own candle. Note, God's written word is sufficient to put the proudest boldest sinners into a fright, when he is pleased to give it the setting on. The king saw the part of the hand that wrote, but saw not the person whose hand it was, which made the thing more frightful. Note, What we see of God, the part of the hand that writes in the book of the creatures and the book of the scriptures (Lo, these are parts of his ways, Job xxvi. 14), may serve to possess us with awful thoughts concerning that of God which we do not see. If this be the finger of God, what is his arm made bare? And what is he? 2. The king is immediately seized with a panic fear (v. 6):His countenance was changed (his colour went and came); the joints of his loins were loosed, so that he had no strength in them, but was struck with a pain in his back, as is usual in a great fright; his knees smote one against another, so violently did he tremble like an aspen leaf. But what was the matter? Why is he in such a fright? He perceives not what is written, and how does he know but it may be some happy presage of deliverance to him and to his kingdom? But the business was his thoughts troubled him; his own guilty conscience flew in his face, and told him that he had no reason to expect any good news from Heaven, and that the hand of an angel could write nothing but terror to him. He that knew himself liable to the justice of God immediately concluded this to be an arrest in his name, a summons to appear before him.

Note, God can soon awaken the most secure and make the heart of the stoutest sinner to tremble; and there needs no more to do it than to let loose his own thoughts upon him; they will soon play the tyrant, and give him trouble enough. 3. The wise men of Babylon are immediately called in, to see what they can make of this writing upon the wall, v. 7. The king cried aloud, as one in haste, as one in earnest, to bring the whole college of magicians, to try if they can read this writing, and show the interpretation of it; for the king and all his lords cannot pretend to it, it is out of their sphere. The study of divine revelation (such as they had, or thought they had) and converse with the world of spirits were by the heathen confined to one profession, and no other meddled with it; but what is written to us by the finger of God is legible to all; whoever will may read the mind of God in the scriptures. To engage these wise men to exert the utmost of their skill in this matter, and provoke them to an emulation in the attempt, he promised that whoever would give him a satisfactory account of this writing should be dignified with the highest honours of the court. He knew what these pretenders to wisdom aimed at, and what would please them, and therefore promised them a scarlet robe and a gold chain, glorious things in the eyes of those that know no better. Nay, he should be primus par regni—chief minister of state, the third ruler in the kingdom, next to the king and his heir apparent. 4. The king is disappointed in his expectations from them; they can none of them read the writing, much less interpret it (v. 8), which increases the king's confusion, v. 9. He likes the thing yet worse and worse, and fears that mischief is towards him. His lords also, that had been partners with him in his jollity, are now sharers with him in his terrors; they also were astonished at their wits' end; and neither their numbers nor their refreshment by wine would serve to keep up their spirits. The reason why the wise men could not read the writing was not because it was written in any language or characters unknown to them, but God either cast a mist before their eyes or put such confusion upon their spirits that they could not read it, that the honour of expounding this mystical writing might be reserved for Daniel. Note, The terror of an awakened convinced conscience may justly be increased by the utter insufficiency of all creatures to give it ease or satisfaction.

Daniel Brought before Belshazzar. (b. c. 538.)

10 Now the queen, by reason of the words of the king and his lords, came into the banquet house: and the queen spake and said, O king, live for ever: let not thy thoughts trouble thee, nor let thy countenance be changed: 11 There is a man in thy kingdom, in whom is the spirit of the holy gods; and in the days of thy father light and understanding and wisdom, like the wisdom of the gods, was found in him; whom the king Nebuchadnezzar thy father, the king, I say, thy father, made master of the magicians, astrologers, Chaldeans, and soothsayers; 12 Forasmuch as an excellent spirit, and knowledge, and understanding, interpreting of dreams, and showing of hard sentences, and dissolving of doubts, were found in the same Daniel, whom the king named Belteshazzar: now let Daniel be called, and he will show the interpretation. 13 Then was Daniel brought in before the king. And the king spake and said unto Daniel, Art thou that Daniel, which art of the children of the captivity of Judah, whom the king my father brought out of Jewry? 14 I have even heard of thee, that the spirit of the gods is in thee, and that light and understanding and excellent wisdom is found in thee. 15 And now the wise men, the astrologers, have been brought in before me, that they should read this writing, and make known unto me the interpretation thereof: but they could not show the interpretation of the thing: 16 And I have heard of thee, that thou canst make interpretations, and dissolve doubts: now if thou canst read the writing, and make known to me the interpretation thereof, thou shalt be clothed with scarlet, and have a chain of gold about thy neck, and shalt be the third ruler in the kingdom. 17 Then Daniel answered and said before the king, Let thy gifts be to thyself, and give thy rewards to another; yet I will read the writing unto the king, and make known to him the interpretation. 18 O thou king, the most high God gave Nebuchadnezzar thy father a kingdom, and majesty, and glory, and honour: 19 And for the majesty that he gave him, all people, nations, and languages, trembled and feared before him: whom he would he slew; and whom he would he kept alive; and whom he would he set up; and whom he would he put down.

20 But when his heart was lifted up, and his mind hardened in pride, he was deposed from his kingly throne, and they took his glory from him: 21 And he was driven from the sons of men; and his heart was made like the beasts, and his dwelling was with the wild asses: they fed him with grass like oxen, and his body was wet with the dew of heaven; till he knew that the most high God ruled in the kingdom of men, and that he appointeth over it whomsoever he will. 22 And thou his son, O Belshazzar, hast not humbled thine heart, though thou knewest all this; 23 But hast lifted up thyself against the Lord of heaven; and they have brought the vessels of his house before thee, and thou, and thy lords, thy wives, and thy concubines, have drunk wine in them; and thou hast praised the gods of silver, and gold, of brass, iron, wood, and stone, which see not, nor hear, nor know: and the God in whose hand thy breath is, and whose are all thy ways, hast thou not glorified: 24 Then was the part of the hand sent from him; and this writing was written. 25 And this is the writing that was written, MENE, MENE, TEKEL, UPHARSIN. 26 This is the interpretation of the thing: MENE; God hath numbered thy kingdom, and finished it. 27 TEKEL; Thou art weighed in the balances, and art found wanting. 28 PERES; Thy kingdom is divided, and given to the Medes and Persians. 29 Then commanded Belshazzar, and they clothed Daniel with scarlet, and put a chain of gold about his neck, and made a proclamation concerning him, that he should be the third ruler in the kingdom.

Here is, I. The information given to the king, by the queen-mother, concerning Daniel, how fit he was to be consulted in this difficult case. It is supposed that this queen was the widow of Evil-Merodach, and was that famous Nitocris whom Herodotus mentions as a woman of extraordinary prudence. She was not present at the feast, as the king's wives and concubines were (v. 2); it was not agreeable to her age and gravity to keep a merry night. But, tidings of the fright which the king and his lords were put into being brought to her apartment, she came herself to the banqueting-house, to recommend to the king a physician for his melancholy. She entreated him not to be discouraged by the insufficiency of his wise men to solve this riddle, for that there was a man in his kingdom that had more than once helped his grandfather at such a dead lift, and, no doubt, could help him, v. 11, 12. She could not undertake to read the writing herself, but directed him to one that could; let Daniel be called now, who should have been called first. Now observe, 1. The high character she gives of Daniel: He is a man in whom is the spirit of the holy gods, who has something in him more than human, not only the spirit of a man, which, in all, is the candle of the Lord, but a divine spirit. According to the language of her country and religion, she could not give a higher encomium of any man; she speaks honourably of him as a man that had, (1.) An admirably good head: Light, and understanding, and wisdom, like the wisdom of the gods, were found in him. Such an insight had he into things secret, and such a foresight of things to come, that it was evident he was divinely inspired; he had knowledge and understanding beyond all the other wise men for interpreting dreams, explaining enigmas or hard sentences, untying knots, and resolving doubts. Solomon had a wonderful sagacity of this kind; but it should seem that in these things Daniel had more of an immediate divine direction. Behold, a greater than Solomon himself is here. Yet what was the wisdom of them both compared with the treasures of wisdom hidden in Christ? (2.) He had an admirably good heart. An excellent spirit was found in him, which was a great ornament to his wisdom and knowledge, and qualified him to receive that gift; for God gives to a man that is good in his sight wisdom, and knowledge, and joy. He was of a humble, holy, heavenly spirit, had a devout and gracious spirit, a spirit of zeal for the glory of God and the good of men. This was indeed an excellent spirit. 2. The account she gives of the respect that Nebuchadnezzar had for him; he was much in his favour, and was preferred by him: "The king thy father" (that is, thy grandfather, but even to many generations Nebuchadnezzar might well be called the father of that royal family, for he it was that raised it to such a pitch of grandeur), "the king, I say, thy father, made him master of the magicians." Perhaps Belshazzar had sometimes, in his pride, spoken slightly of Nebuchadnezzar, and his politics, and the methods of his government, and the ministers he employed, and thought himself wiser than he; and therefore his mother harps upon that. "The king, I say, thy father, to whose good management all thou hast owing, he pronounced him chief of, and gave him dominion over, all the wise men of Babylon, and named him Belteshazzar, according to the name of his god, thinking thereby to put honour upon him;" but Daniel, by constantly making use of his Jewish name himself (which he resolved to keep, in token of his faithful adherence to his religion), had worn out that name; only the queen-dowager remembered it, otherwise he was generally called Daniel. Note, It is a very good office to revive the remembrance of the good services of worthy men, who are themselves modest, and willing that they should be forgotten. 3. The motion she makes concerning him: Let Daniel be called, and he will show the interpretation. By this it appears that Daniel was now forgotten at court. Belshazzar was a stranger to him, knew not that he had such a jewel in his kingdom. With the new king there came in a new ministry, and the old one was laid aside. Note, There are a great many valuable men, and such as might be made very useful, that lie long buried in obscurity, and some that have done eminent services that live to be overlooked and taken no notice of; but, whatever men are, God is not unrighteous to forget the services done to his kingdom. Daniel, being turned out of his place, lived privately, and sought not any opportunity to come into notice again; yet he lived near the court and within call, though Babylon was now besieged, that he might be ready, if there were occasion, to do any good office, by what interest he had among the great ones, for the children of his people. But Providence so ordered it that now, just at the fall of that monarchy, he should by the queen's means be brought to court again, that he might lie there ready for preferment in the ensuing government. Thus do the righteous shine forth out of obscurity, and before honour is humility.

II. The introducing of Daniel to the king, and his request to him to read and expound the writing. Daniel was brought in before the king, v. 13. He was now nearly ninety years of age, so that his years, and honours, and former preferments, might have entitled him to a free admission into the king's presence; yet he was willing to be conducted in, as a stranger, by the master of the ceremonies. Note, 1. The king asks, with an air of haughtiness: Art thou that Daniel who art of the children of the captivity? Being a Jew, and a captive, he was loth to be beholden to him if he could help it. 2. He tells him what an encomium he had heard of him (v. 14), that the spirit of the gods was in him; and he had sent for him to try whether he deserved so high a character or no. 3. He acknowledges that all the wise men of Babylon were baffled; they could not read this writing, nor show the interpretation, v. 16. But, 4. He promises him the same rewards that he had promised them if he would do it, v. 16. It was strange that the magicians, when now, and in Nebuchadnezzar's time, once and again, they were nonplussed, did not attempt something to save their credit; if they had with a good assurance said, "This is the meaning of such a dream, such a writing," who could disprove them? But God so ordered it that they had nothing at all to say, as, when Christ was born, the heathen oracles were struck dumb.

III. The interpretation which Daniel gave of these mystic characters, which was so far from easing the king of his fears that we may suppose it increased them rather. Daniel was now in years, and Belshazzar was young; and therefore he seems to take a greater liberty of dealing plainly and roundly with him than he had done upon the like occasions with Nebuchadnezzar. In reproving any man, especially great men, there is need of wisdom to consider all circumstances; for they are the reproofs of instruction that are the way of life. In Daniel's discourse here,

1. He undertakes to read the writing which gave them this alarm, and to show them the interpretation of it, v. 17. He slights the offer he made him of rewards, is not pleased that it was mentioned, for he is not one of those that divine for money; what gratuities Nebuchadnezzar gave him afterwards he gladly accepted, but he scorned to bargain for them, or to read the writing to the king for and in consideration of such and such honours

promised him. No: "Let thy gifts be to thyself, for they will not be long thine, and give thy fee to another, to any of the wise men whom thou wouldst have most wished to earn it; I value it not." Daniel sees his kingdom now at its last gasp, and therefore looks with contempt upon his gifts and rewards. And thus should we despise all the gifts and rewards that this world can give did we see, as we may by faith, its final period hastening on. Let it give its perishing gifts to another; there are better gifts which we have our eyes and hearts upon; but let us do our duty in the world, do it all the real service we can, read God's writing to it in a profession of religion, and by an agreeable conversation make known the interpretation of it, and then trust God for his gifts, his rewards, in comparison with which all the world can give is mere trash and trifles.

2. He largely recounts to the king God's dealings with his father Nebuchadnezzar, which were intended for instruction and warning to him, v. 18, 21. This is not intended for a flourish or an amusement, but is a necessary preliminary to the interpretation of the writing. Note, That we may understand aright what God is doing with us, it is of use to us to review what he has done with others.

(1.) He describes the great dignity and power to which the divine Providence had advanced Nebuchadnezzar, v. 18, 19. He had a kingdom, and majesty, and glory, and honour, for aught we know, above what any heathen prince ever had before him; he thought that he got his glory by his own extraordinary conduct and courage, and ascribed his successes to a projecting active genius of his own; but Daniel tells him who now enjoyed what he had laboured for that it was the most high God, the God of gods and Lord of kings (as Nebuchadnezzar himself had called him), that gave him that kingdom, that vast dominion, that majesty wherewith he presided in the affairs of it, and that glory and honour which by his prosperous management he acquired. Note, Whatever degree of outward prosperity any arrive at, they must own that it is of God's giving, not their own getting. Let it never be said, My might, and the power of my hand, have gotten me this wealth, this preferment; but let it always be remembered that it is God that gives men power to get wealth, and gives success to their endeavours. Now the power which God gave to Nebuchadnezzar is here described to be very great in respect both of ability and of authority. [1.] His ability was so strong that it was irresistible; such was the majesty that God gave him, so numerous were the forces he had at command, and such an admirable dexterity he had at commanding them, that, which way soever his sword turned, it prospered. He could captivate and subdue nations by threatening them, without striking a stroke, for all people trembled and feared before him, and would compound with him for their lives upon any terms. See what force is, and what the fear of it does. It is that by which the brutal part of the world, even of the world of mankind, both governs and is governed. [2.] His authority was so absolute that it was uncontrollable. The power which was allowed him, which descended upon him, or which, at least, he assumed, was without contradiction, was absolute and despotic, none shared with him either in the legislative or in the executive part of it. In dispensing punishments he condemned or acquitted at pleasure: Whom he would he slew, and whom he would he saved alive, though both were equally innocent or equally guilty. The jus vitae et necis—the power of life and death was entirely in his hand. In dispensing rewards he granted or denied preferment at pleasure: Whom he would he set up, and whom he would he put down, merely for a humour, and without giving a reason so much as to himself; but it is all ex mero motu—of his own good pleasure, and stat pro ratione voluntas—his will stands for a reason. Such was the constitution of the eastern monarchies, such the manner of their kings.

(2.) He sets before him the sins which Nebuchadnezzar had been guilty of, whereby he had provoked God against him. [1.] He behaved insultingly towards those that were under him, and grew tyrannical and oppressive. The description given of his power intimates his abuse of his power, and that he was directed in what he did by humour and passion, not by reason and equity; so that he often condemned the innocent and acquitted the guilty, both which are an abomination to the Lord. He deposed men of merit and preferred unworthy men, to the great detriment of the public, and for this he was accountable to the most high God, that gave him his power. Note, It is a very hard and rare thing for men to have an absolute arbitrary power, and not to make an ill use of it. Camden has a distich of Giraldus, wherein he speaks of it as a rare instance, concerning our king Henry II of England, that never any man had so much power and did so little hurt with it.

Glorior hoc uno, quod nunquam vidimus unum,
Nec potuisse magis, nec nocuisse minus—
Of him I can say, exulting, that with the same power
to do harm no one was ever more inoffensive.

But that was not all. [2.] He behaved insolently towards the God above him, and grew proud and haughty (v. 20): His heart was lifted up,and there his sin and ruin began; his mind was hardened in pride, hardened against the commands of God and his judgments; he was willful and obstinate, and neither the word of God nor his rod made any lasting impression upon him. Note, Pride is a sin that hardens the heart in all other sins and renders the means of repentance and reformation ineffectual.

(3.) He reminds him of the judgments of God that were brought upon him for his pride and obstinacy, how he was deprived of his reason, and so deposed from his kingly throne (v. 20), driven from among men, to dwell with the wild asses, v. 21. He that would not govern his subjects by rules of reason had not reason sufficient for the government himself. Note, Justly does God deprive men of their reason when they become unreasonable and will not use it, and of their power when they become oppressive and use it ill. He continued like a brute till he knew and embraced that first principle of religion, That the most high God rules. And it is rather by religion than reason that man is distinguished from, and dignified above, the beasts; and it is more his honour to be a subject to the supreme Creator than to be lord of the inferior creatures. Note, Kings must know, or shall be made to know, that the most high God rules in their kingdoms (that is an imperium in imperio—an empire within an empire, not to be excepted against), and that he appoints over them whomsoever he will. As he makes heirs, so he makes princes.
3. In God's name, he exhibits articles of impeachment against Belshazzar. Before he reads him his doom, from the hand-writing on the wall, he shows him his crime, that God may be justified when he speaks, and clear when he judges. Now that which he lays to his charge is, (1.) That he had not taken warning by the judgments of God upon his father (v. 22): Thou his son, O Belshazzar! hast not humbled thy heart, though thou knewest all this. Note, It is a great offence to God if our hearts be not humbled before him to comply both with his precepts and with his providences, humbled by repentance, obedience, and patience; nay, he expects from the greatest of men that their hearts should be humbled before him, by an acknowledgment that, great as they are, to him they are accountable. And it is a great aggravation of the unhumbledness of our hearts when we know enough to humble them but do not consider and improve it, particularly when we know how others have been broken that would not bend, how others have fallen that would not stoop, and yet we continue stiff and inflexible. It makes the sin of children the more heinous if they tread in the steps of their parents' wickedness, though they have seen how dearly it has cost them, and how pernicious the consequences of it have been. Do we know this, do we know all this, and yet are we not humbled? (2.) That he had affronted God more impudently than Nebuchadnezzar himself had done, witness the revels of this very night, in the midst of which he was seized with this horror (v. 23): "Thou hast lifted up thyself against the Lord of heaven, hast swelled with rage against him, and taken up arms against his crown and dignity, in this particular instance, that thou hast profaned the vessels of his house, and made the utensils of his sanctuary instruments of thy iniquity, and, in an actual designed contempt of him, hast praised the

gods of silver and gold, which see not, nor hear, nor know anything, as if they were to be preferred before the God that sees, and hears, and knows every thing." Sinners that are resolved to go on in sin are well enough pleased with gods that neither see, nor hear, nor know, for then they may sin securely; but they will find, to their confusion, that though those are the gods they choose those are not the gods they must be judged by, but one to whom all things are naked and open. (3.) That he had not answered the end of his creation and maintenance: The God in whose hand thy breath is, and whose are all thy ways, hast thou not glorified. This is a general charge, which stands good against us all; let us consider how we shall answer it.

Observe, [1.] Our dependence upon God as our creator, preserver, benefactor, owner, and ruler; not only from his hand our breath was at first, but in his hand our breath is still; it is he that holds our souls in life, and, if he take away our breath, we die. Our times being in his hand, so is our breath, by which our times are measured. In him we live, and move, and have our being; we live by him, live upon him, and cannot live without him. The way of man is not in himself, not at his own command, at his own disposal, but his are all our ways; for our hearts are in his hand, and so are the hearts of all men, even of kings, who seem to act most as free-agents. [2.] Our duty to God, in consideration of this dependence; we ought to glorify him, to devote ourselves to his honour and employ ourselves in his service, to make it our care to please him and our business to praise him. [3.] Our default in this duty, notwithstanding that dependence; we have not done it; for we have all sinned, and come short of the glory of God. This is the indictment against Belshazzar; there needs no proof, it is made good by the notorious evidence of the fact, and his own conscience cannot but plead guilty to it. And therefore,

4. He now proceeds to read the sentence, as he found it written upon the wall: "Then" (says Daniel) "when thou hast come to such a height of impiety as thus to trample upon the most sacred things, then when thou wast in the midst of thy sacrilegious idolatrous feast, then was the part of the hand, the writing fingers, sent from him, from that God whom thou didst so daringly affront, and who had borne so long with thee, but would bear no longer; he sent them, and this writing, thou now seest, was written, v. 24. It is he that now writes bitter things against thee, and makes thee to possess thy iniquities," Job xiii. 26. Note, As the sin of sinners is written in the book of God's omniscience, so the doom of sinners is written in the book of God's law; and the day is coming when those books shall be opened, and they shall be judged by them. Now the writing was, Mene, Mene, Tekel, Upharsin, v. 25. It is well that we have an authentic exposition of these words annexed, else we could make little of them, so concise are they; the signification of them is, He has numbered, he has weighed, and they divide. The Chaldean wise men, because they knew not that there is but one God only, could not understand who this He should be, and for that reason (some think) the writing puzzled them. (1.) Mene; that is repeated, for the thing is certain—Mene, mene; that signifies, both in Hebrew and Chaldee, He has numbered and finished, which Daniel explains thus (v. 26): "God has numbered thy kingdom, the years and days of the continuance of it; these were numbered in the counsel of God, and now they are finished; the term has expired for and during which thou wast to hold it, and now it must be surrendered. Here is an end of thy kingdom." (2.) Tekel; that signifies, in Chaldee, Thou art weighed, and, in Hebrew, Thou art too light. So Dr. Lightfoot. For this king and his actions are weighed in the just and unerring balances of divine equity. God does as perfectly know his true character as the goldsmith knows the weight of that which he has weighed in the nicest scales. God does not give judgment against him till he has first pondered his actions, and considered the merits of his case. "But thou art found wanting, unworthy to have such a trust lodged in thee, a vain, light, empty man, a man of no weight or consideration." (3.) Upharsin, which should be rendered, and Pharsin, or Peres. Parsin, in Hebrew, signifies the Persians; Paresin, in Chaldee, signifies dividing; Daniel puts both together (v. 28): "Thy kingdom is divided, is rent from thee, and

given to the Medes and Persians, as a prey to be divided among them." Now this may, without any force, be applied to the doom of sinners. Mene, Tekel, Peres, may easily be made to signify death, judgment, and hell. At death, the sinner's days are numbered and finished; after death the judgment, when he will be weighed in the balance and found wanting; and after judgment the sinner will be cut asunder, and given as a prey to the devil and his angels. Daniel does not here give Belshazzar such advice and encouragement to repent as he had given Nebuchadnezzar, because he saw the decree had gone forth and he would not be allowed any space to repent.

One would have thought that Belshazzar would be exasperated against Daniel, and, seeing his own case desperate, would be in a rage against him. But he was so far convicted by his own conscience of the reasonableness of all he said that he objected nothing against it; but, on the contrary, gave Daniel the reward he promised him, put on him the scarlet gown and the gold chain, and proclaimed him the third ruler in the kingdom (v. 29), because he would be as good as his word, and because it was not Daniel's fault if the exposition of the hand-writing was not such as he desired. Note, Many show great respect to God's prophets who yet have no regard to his word. Daniel did not value these titles and ensigns of honour, yet would not refuse them, because they were tokens of his prince's good-will: but we have reason to think that he received them with a smile, foreseeing how soon they would all wither with him that bestowed them. They were like Jonah's gourd, which came up in a night and perished in a night, and therefore it was folly for him to be exceedingly glad of them.

Daniel Deals Plainly with Belshazzar; Interpreting of the Writing on the Wall. (b. c. 538.)
30 In that night was Belshazzar the king of the Chaldeans slain.   31 And Darius the Median took the kingdom, being about threescore and two years old.

Here is, 1. The death of the king. Reason enough he had to tremble, for he was just falling into the hands of the king of terrors, v. 30. In that night, when his heart was merry with wine, the besiegers broke into the city, aimed at the palace; there they found the king, and gave him his death's wound. He could not find any place so secret as to conceal him, or so strong as to protect him. Heathen writers speak of Cyrus's taking Babylon by surprise, with the assistance of two deserters that showed him the best way into the city. And it was foretold what a consternation it would be to the court, Jer. li. 11, 39. Note, Death comes as a snare upon those whose hearts are overcharged with surfeiting and drunkenness. 2. The transferring of the kingdom into other hands. From the head of gold we now descend to the breast and arms of silver. Darius the Mede took the kingdom in partnership with, and by the consent of, Cyrus, who had conquered it, v. 31. They were partners in war and conquest, and so they were in dominion, ch. vi. 28. Notice is taken of his age, that he was now sixty-two years old, for which reason Cyrus, who was his nephew, gave him the precedency. Some observe that being now sixty-two years old, in the last year of the captivity, he was born in the eighth year of it, and that was the year when Jeconiah was carried captive and all the nobles, &c. See 2 Kings xxiv. 13-15. Just at that time when the most fatal stroke was given was a prince born that in process of time should avenge Jerusalem upon Babylon, and heal the wound that was now given. Thus deep are the counsels of God concerning his people, thus kind are his designs towards them.

Chapter 6

Daniel does not give a continued history of the reigns in which he lived, nor of the state-affairs of the kingdoms of Chaldea and Persia, though he was himself a great man in those affairs; for what are those to us? But he selects such particular passages of story as serve for the confirming of our faith in God and the encouraging of our obedience to him, for the things written aforetime were written for our learning. It is a very observable improvable story that we have in this chapter, how Daniel by faith "stopped the mouths of lions," and so "obtained a good report," Heb. xi. 33. The three children were cast into the fiery furnace for not committing a known sin, Daniel was cast into the lions' den for not omitting a known duty, and God's miraculously delivering both them and him is left upon record for the encouragement of his servants in all ages to be resolute and constant both in their abhorrence of that which is evil and in their adherence to that which is good, whatever it cost them. In this chapter we have, I. Daniel's preferment in the court of Darius, ver. 1-3. II. The envy and malice of his enemies against him, ver. 4, 5. III. The decree they obtained against prayer for thirty days, ver. 6-9. IV. Daniel's continuance and constancy in prayer, notwithstanding that decree, ver. 10. V. Information given against him for it, and the casting of him into the den of lions, ver. 11-17. VI. His miraculous preservation in the lions' den, and deliverance out of it, ver. 18-23. VII. The casting of his accusers into the den, and their destruction there, ver. 24. VIII. The decree which Darius made upon this occasion, in honour of the God of Daniel, and the prosperity of Daniel afterwards, ver. 25-28. And this God is our God for ever and ever.

Daniel Preferred by Darius. (b. c. 537.)

1 It pleased Darius to set over the kingdom a hundred and twenty princes, which should be over the whole kingdom;   2 And over these three presidents; of whom Daniel was first: that the princes might give accounts unto them, and the king should have no damage.   3 Then this Daniel was preferred above the presidents and princes, because an excellent spirit was in him; and the king thought to set him over the whole realm.   4 Then the presidents and princes sought to find occasion against Daniel concerning the kingdom; but they could find none occasion nor fault; forasmuch as he was faithful, neither was there any error or fault found in him.   5 Then said these men, We shall not find any occasion against this Daniel, except we find it against him concerning the law of his God.

We are told concerning Daniel,

I. What a great man he was. When Darius, upon his accession to the crown of Babylon by conquest, new-modelled the government, he made Daniel prime-minister of state, set him at the helm, and made him first commissioner both of the treasury and of the great seal. Darius's dominion was very large; all he got by his conquests and acquests was that he had so many more countries to take care of; no more can be expected from himself than what one man can do, and therefore others must be employed under him. He set over the kingdom 120 princes (v. 1), and appointed them their districts, in which they were to administer justice, preserve the public peace, and levy the king's revenue. Note, Inferior magistrates are ministers of God to us for good as well as the sovereign; and therefore we must submit ourselves both to the king as supreme and to the governors that are constituted and commissioned by him, 1 Pet. ii. 13, 14. Over these princes there was a triumvirate, or three presidents, who were to take and state the public accounts, to receive appeals from the princes, or complaints against them in case of mal-administration, that the king should have no damage (v. 2), that he should not sustain loss in his revenue and that the power he delegated to the princes might not be abused to the oppression of the subject, for by that the king (whether he thinks so or no) receives real damage, both as it alienates the affections of his people from him and as it provokes the displeasure of his God against him. Of these three Daniel was chief, because he was found to go beyond them all in all manner of princely qualifications. He was preferred above the presidents and princes (v. 3), and so wonderfully well pleased the king was with his management that he thought to set him over the whole realm, and let him place and displace at his pleasure. Now, 1. We must take notice of it to the praise of Darius that he would prefer a man thus purely for his personal merit, and his fitness for business; and those sovereigns that would be well served must go by that rule.

Daniel had been a great man in the kingdom that was conquered, and for that reason, one would think, should have been looked upon as an enemy, and as such imprisoned or banished. He was a native of a foreign kingdom, and a ruined one, and upon that account might have been despised as a stranger and captive. But, Darius, it seems, was very quick-sighted in judging of men's capacities, and was soon aware that this Daniel had something extraordinary in him, and therefore, though no doubt he had creatures of his own, not a few, that expected preferment in this newly-conquered kingdom, and were gaping for it, and those that had been long his confidants would depend upon it that they should be now his presidents, yet so well did he consult the public welfare that, finding Daniel to excel them all in prudence and virtue, and probably having heard of his being divinely inspired, he made him his right hand. 2. We must take notice of it, to the glory of God, that, though Daniel was now very old (it was above seventy years since he was brought a captive to Babylon), yet he was as able as ever for business both in body and mind, and that he who had continued faithful to his religion through all the temptations of the foregoing reigns in a new government was as much respected as ever. He kept in by being an oak, not by being a willow, by a constancy in virtue, not by a pliableness to vice. Such honesty is the best policy, for it secures a reputation; and those who thus honour God he will honour.

II. What a good man he was: An excellent spirit was in him, v. 3. And he was faithful to every trust, dealt fairly between the sovereign and the subject, and took care that neither should be wronged, so that there was no error, or fault, to be found in him, v. 4. He was not only not chargeable with any treachery or dishonesty, but not even with any mistake or indiscretion. He never made any blunder, nor had any occasion to plead inadvertency or forgetfulness for his excuse. This is recorded for an example to all that are in places of public trust to approve themselves both careful and conscientious, that they may be free, not only from fault, but from error, not only from crime, but from mistake.

III. What ill-will was borne him, both for his greatness and for his goodness. The presidents and princes envied him because he was advanced above them, and probably hated him because he had a watchful eye upon them and took care they should not wrong the government to enrich themselves. See here, 1. The cause of envy, and that is every thing that is good. Solomon complains of it as a vexation that for every right work a man is envied of his neighbour (Eccl. iv. 4), that the better a man is the worse he is thought of by his rivals. Daniel is envied because he has a more excellent spirit than his neighbours. 2. The effect of envy, and that is every thing that is bad. Those that envied Daniel sought no less than his ruin. His disgrace would not serve them; it was his death that they desired. Wrath is cruel, and anger is outrageous, but who can stand before envy? Prov. xxvii. 4. Daniel's enemies set spies upon him, to observe him in the management of his place; they sought to find occasion against him, something on which to ground an accusation concerning the kingdom, some instance of neglect or partiality, some hasty word spoken, some person borne hard upon, or some necessary business overlooked. And if they could but have found the mote, the mole-hill, of a mistake, it would have been soon improved to the beam, to the mountain, of an unpardonable misdemeanour. But they could find no occasion against him; they owned that they could not. Daniel always acted honestly, and now the more warily, and stood the more upon his guard, because of his observers, Ps. xxvii. 11. Note, We have all need to walk circumspectly, because we have many eyes upon us, and some that watch for our halting. Those especially have need to carry their cup even that have it full. They concluded, at length, that they should not find any occasion against him except concerning the law of his God v. 5. It seems then that Daniel kept up the profession of his religion, and held it fast without wavering or shrinking, and yet that was no bar to his preferment; there was no law that required him to be of the king's religion, or incapacitated him to bear office in the state unless he were. It was all one to the king what God he prayed to, so long as he did the business of his place faithfully and well. He was at the king's service usque ad aras—as far as the altars; but there he left him. In this matter therefore his enemies hoped to ensnare him. Quaerendum est crimen laesae religionis ubi majestatis deficit—When treason could not be charged upon him he was accused of impiety. Grotius. Note, It is an excellent thing, and much for the glory of God, when those who profess religion conduct themselves so inoffensively in their whole conversation that their most watchful spiteful enemies may find no occasion of blaming them, save only in the matters of their God, in which they walk according to their consciences. It is observable that, when Daniel's enemies could find no occasion against him concerning the kingdom, they had so much sense of justice left that they did not suborn witnesses against him to accuse him of crimes he was innocent of, and to swear treason upon him, wherein they shame many that were called Jews and are called Christians.

A Plot against Daniel. (b. c. 537.)

6 Then these presidents and princes assembled together to the king, and said thus unto him, King Darius, live for ever. 7 All the presidents of the kingdom, the governors, and the princes, the counsellors, and the captains, have consulted together to establish a royal statute, and to make a firm decree, that whosoever shall ask a petition of any God or man for thirty days, save of thee, O king, he shall be cast into the den of lions. 8 Now, O king, establish the decree, and sign the writing, that it be not changed, according to the law of the Medes and Persians, which altereth not. 9 Wherefore king Darius signed the writing and the decree. 10 Now when Daniel knew that the writing was signed, he went into his house; and his windows being open in his chamber toward Jerusalem, he kneeled upon his knees three times a day, and prayed, and gave thanks before his God, as he did aforetime.

Daniel's adversaries could have no advantage against him from any law now in being; they therefore contrive a new law, by which they hope to ensnare him, and in a matter in which they knew they should be sure of him; and such was his fidelity to his God that they gained their point. Here is,

I. Darius's impious law. I call it Darius's, because he gave the royal assent to it, and otherwise it would not have been of force; but it was not properly his: he contrived it not, and was perfectly wheedled to consent to it. The presidents and princes framed the edict, brought in the bill, and by their management it was agreed to by the convention of the states, who perhaps were met at this time upon some public occasion. It is pretended that this bill which they would have to pass into a law was the result of mature deliberation, that all the presidents of the kingdom, the governors, princes, counsellors, and captains, had consulted together about it, and that they not only agreed to it, but advised it, for divers good causes and considerations, that they had done what they could to establish it for a firm decree; nay, they intimate to the king that it was carried nemine contradicente—unanimously: "All the presidents are of this mind;" and yet we are sure that Daniel, the chief of the three presidents, did not agree to it, and have reason to think that many more of the princes excepted against it as absurd and unreasonable. Note, It is no new thing for that to be represented, and with great assurance too, as the sense of the nation, which is far from being so; and that which few approve of is sometimes confidently said to be that which all agree to. But, O the infelicity of kings, who, being under a necessity of seeing and hearing with other people's eyes and ears, are often wretchedly imposed upon! These designing men, under colour of doing honour to the king, but really intending the ruin of his favourite, press him to pass this into a law, and make it a royal statute, that whosoever shall ask a petition of any god or man for thirty days, save of the king, shall be put to death after the most barbarous manner, shall be cast into the den of lions, v. 7. This is the bill they have been hatching, and they lay it before the king to be signed and passed into a law. Now, 1. There is nothing in it that has the least appearance of good, but that it magnifies the king, and makes him seem both very great and very kind to his subjects, which, they suggest, will be of good service to him now that he has newly come to his throne, and will confirm his interests.

All men must be made to believe that the king is so rich, and withal so ready to all petitioners, that none in any want or distress need to apply either to God or man for relief, but to him only. And for thirty days together he will be ready to give audience to all that have any petition to present to him. It is indeed much for the honour of kings to be benefactors to their subjects and to have their ears open to their complaints and requests; but if they pretend to be their sole benefactors, and undertake to be to them instead of God, and challenge that respect from them which is due to God only, it is their disgrace, and not their honour. But, 2. There is a great deal in it that is apparently evil. It is bad enough to forbid asking a petition of any man. Must not a beggar ask an alms, or one neighbour beg a kindness of another? If the child want bread, must he not ask it of his parents, or be cast into the den of lions if he do? Nay, those that have business with the king, may they not petition those about him to introduce them? But it was much worse, and an impudent affront to all religion, to forbid asking a petition of any god. It is by prayer that we give glory to God, fetch in mercy from God; and so keep up our communion with God; and to interdict prayer for thirty days is for so long to rob God of all the tribute he has from man and to rob man of all the comfort he has in God. When the light of nature teaches us that the providence of God has the ordering and disposing of all our affairs does not the law of nature oblige us by prayer to acknowledge God and seek to him? Does not every man's heart direct him, when he is in want or distress, to call upon God, and must this be made high treason? We could not live a day without God; and can men live thirty days without prayer? Will the king himself be tied up for so long from praying to God; or, if it be allowed him, will he undertake to do it for all his subjects? Did ever any nation thus slight their gods? But see what absurdities malice will drive men to. Rather than not bring Daniel into trouble for praying to his God, they will deny themselves and all their friends the satisfaction of praying to theirs. Had they proposed only to prohibit the Jews from praying to their God, Daniel would have been as effectually ensnared; but they knew the king would not pass such a law, and therefore made it thus general. And the king, puffed up with a fancy that this would set him up as a little god, was fond of the feather in his cap (for so it was, and not a flower in his crown) and signed the writing and the decree (v. 9), which, being once done, according to the constitution of the united kingdom of the Medes and Persians, was not upon any pretence whatsoever to be altered or dispensed with, or the breach of it pardoned.

II. Daniel's pious disobedience to this law, v. 10. He did not retire into the country, nor abscond for some time, though he knew the law was levelled against him; but, because he knew it was so, therefore he stood his ground, knowing that he had now a fair opportunity of honouring God before men, and showing that he preferred his favour, and his duty to him, before life itself. When Daniel knew that the writing was signed he might have gone to the king, and expostulated with him about it; nay, he might have remonstrated against it, as grounded upon a misinformation that all the presidents had consented to it, whereas he that was chief of them had never been consulted about it; but he went to his house, and applied himself to his duty, cheerfully trusting God with the event. Now observe,

1. Daniel's constant practice, which we were not informed of before this occasion, but which we have reason to think was the general practice of the pious Jews. (1.) He prayed in his house, sometimes alone and sometimes with his family about him, and made a solemn business of it. Cornelius was a man that prayed in his house, Acts x. 30. Note, Every house not only may be, but ought to be, a house of prayer; where we have a tent God must have an alter, and on it we must offer spiritual sacrifices. (2.) In every prayer he gave thanks. When we pray to God for the mercies we want we must praise him for those we have received. Thanksgiving must be a part of every prayer. (3.) In his prayer and thanksgiving he had an eye to God as his God, his in covenant, and set himself as in his presence. He did this before

his God, and with a regard to him. (4.) When he prayed and gave thanks he kneeled upon his knees, which is the most proper gesture in prayer, and most expressive of humility, and reverence, and submission to God. Kneeling is a begging posture, and we come to God as beggars, beggars for our lives, whom it concerns to be importunate. (5.) He opened the windows of his chamber, that the sight of the visible heavens might affect his heart with an awe of that God who dwells above the heavens; but that was not all: he opened them towards Jerusalem, the holy city, though now in ruins, to signify the affection he had for its very stones and dust (Ps. cii. 14) and the remembrance he had of its concerns daily in his prayers. Thus, though he himself lived great in Babylon, yet he testified his concurrence with the meanest of his brethren the captives, in remembering Jerusalem and preferring it before his chief joy, Ps. cxxxvii. 5, 6. Jerusalem was the place which God had chosen to put his name there; and, when the temple was dedicated, Solomon's prayer to God was that if his people should in the land of their enemies pray unto him with their eye towards the land which he gave them, and the city he had chosen, and the house which was built to his name, then he would hear and maintain their cause (1 Kings viii. 48, 49), to which prayer Daniel had reference in this circumstance of his devotions. (6.) He did this three times a day, three times every day according to the example of David (Ps. lv. 17), Morning, evening, and at noon, I will pray. It is good to have our hours of prayer, not to bind, but to remind conscience; and, if we think our bodies require refreshment by food thrice a day, can we think seldomer will serve our souls? This is surely as little as may be to answer the command of praying always. (7.) He did this so openly and avowedly that all who knew him knew it to be his practice; and he thus showed it, not because he was proud of it (in the place where he was there was no room for that temptation, for it was not reputation, but reproach, that attended it), but because he was not ashamed of it. Though Daniel was a great man, he did not think it below him to be thrice a day upon his knees before his Maker and to be his own chaplain; though he was an old man, he did not think himself past it; nor, though it had been his practice from his youth up, was he weary of this well doing. Though he was a man of business, vast business, for the service of the public, he did not think that would excuse him from the daily exercises of devotion. How inexcusable then are those who have but little to do in the world, and yet will not do thus much for God and their souls! Daniel was a man famous for prayer, and for success in it (Ezek. xiv. 14), and he came to be so by thus making a conscience of prayer and making a business of it daily; and in thus doing God blessed him wonderfully.

2. Daniel's constant adherence to this practice, even when it was made by the law a capital crime. When he knew that the writing was signed he continued to do as he did aforetime, and altered not one circumstance of the performance. Many a man, yea, and many a good man, would have thought it prudence to omit it for these thirty days, when he could not do it without hazard of his life; he might have prayed so much oftener when those days had expired and the danger was over, or he might have performed the duty at another time, and in another place, so secretly that it should not be possible for his enemies to discover it; and so he might both satisfy his conscience and keep up his communion with God, and yet avoid the law, and continue in his usefulness. But, if he had done so, it would have been thought, both by his friends and by his enemies, that he had thrown up the duty for this time, through cowardice and base fear, which would have tended very much to the dishonour of God and the discouragement of his friends. Others who moved in a lower sphere might well enough act with caution; but Daniel, who had so many eyes upon him, must act with courage; and the rather because he knew that the law, when it was made, was particularly levelled against him. Note, We must not omit duty for fear of suffering, no, nor so much as seems to come short of it. In trying times great stress is laid upon our confessing Christ before men (Matt. x. 32), and we must take heed lest, under pretence of discretion, we be found guilty of cowardice in the cause of God. If we do not think that this example of Daniel obliges us to do likewise, yet I am sure it forbids us to censure those that do, for God owned him in it. By

his constancy to his duty it now appears that he had never been used to admit any excuse for the omission of it; for, if ever any excuse would serve to put it by, this would have served now, (1.) That it was forbidden by the king his master, and in honour of the king too; but it is an undoubted maxim, in answer to that, We are to obey God rather than men. (2.) That it would be the loss of his life, but it is an undoubted maxim, in answer to that, Those who throw away their souls (as those certainly do that live without prayer) to save their lives make but a bad bargain for themselves; and though herein they make themselves, like the king of Tyre, wiser than Daniel, at their end they will be fools.

Daniel in the Den of Lions. (b. c. 537.)

11 Then these men assembled, and found Daniel praying and making supplication before his God. 12 Then they came near, and spake before the king concerning the king's decree; Hast thou not signed a decree, that every man that shall ask a petition of any God or man within thirty days, save of thee, O king, shall be cast into the den of lions? The king answered and said, The thing is true, according to the law of the Medes and Persians, which altereth not. 13 Then answered they and said before the king, That Daniel, which is of the children of the captivity of Judah, regardeth not thee, O king, nor the decree that thou hast signed, but maketh his petition three times a day. 14 Then the king, when he heard these words, was sore displeased with himself, and set his heart on Daniel to deliver him: and he laboured till the going down of the sun to deliver him. 15 Then these men assembled unto the king, and said unto the king, Know, O king, that the law of the Medes and Persians is, That no decree nor statute which the king establisheth may be changed. 16 Then the king commanded, and they brought Daniel, and cast him into the den of lions. Now the king spake and said unto Daniel, Thy God whom thou servest continually, he will deliver thee. 17 And a stone was brought, and laid upon the mouth of the den; and the king sealed it with his own signet, and with the signet of his lords; that the purpose might not be changed concerning Daniel.

Here is 1. Proof made of Daniel's praying to his God, notwithstanding the late edict to the contrary (v. 11): These men assembled, then came tumultuously together, so the word is, the same that was used v. 6, borrowed from Ps. ii. 1, Why do the heathen rage? They came together to visit Daniel, perhaps under pretence of business, at that time which they knew to be his usual hour of devotion; and, if they had not found him so engaged, they would have upbraided him with his faint-heartedness and distrust of his God, but (which they rather wished to do) they found him on his knees praying and making supplication before his God. For his love they are his adversaries; but, like his father David, he gives himself unto prayer, Ps. cix. 4. 2. Complaint made of it to the king. When they had found occasion against Daniel concerning the law of his God they lost no time, but applied to the king (v. 12), and having appealed to his whether there was not such a law made, and gained from him a recognition of it, and that it was so ratified that it might not be altered, they proceeded to accuse Daniel, v. 13. They so describe him, in the information they give, as to exasperate the king and incense him the more against him: "He is of the children of the captivity of Judah; he is of Judah, that despicable people, and now a captive in a despicable state, that can call nothing his own but what he has by the king's favour, and yet he regards not thee, O king! nor the decree that thou hast signed." Note, It is no new thing for that which is done faithfully, in the conscience towards God, to be misrepresented as done obstinately and in contempt of the civil powers, that is, for the best saints to be reproached as the worst men. Daniel regarded God, and therefore prayed, and we have reason to think prayed for the king and his government, yet this is construed as not regarding the king. That excellent spirit which Daniel was endued with, and that established reputation which he had gained, could not protect him from these poisonous darts. They do not say, He makes his petition to his God, lest Darius should take notice of that to his praise, but only, He makes his petition, which is the thing the law forbids. 3. The great concern the king was in hereupon. He now perceived that, whatever they pretended, it was not to honour him, but in spite to Daniel, that they had proposed that law, and now he is sorely displeased with himself for gratifying them in it, v. 14. Note, When men indulge a proud vain-glorious humour, and please themselves with that which feeds it, they know not what vexations they are preparing for themselves; their flatterers may prove their tormentors, and are but spreading a net for their feet. Now, the king sets his heart to deliver Daniel; both by argument and by authority he labours till the going down of the sun to deliver him, that is, to persuade his accusers not to insist upon his prosecution. Note, We often do that, through inconsideration, which afterwards we see cause a thousand times to wish undone again, which is a good reason why we should ponder the path of our feet, for then all our ways will be established. 4. The violence with which the prosecutors demanded judgment, v. 15. We are not told what Daniel said; the king himself is his advocate, he needs not plead his own cause, but silently commits himself and it to him that judges righteously. But the prosecutors insist upon it that the law must have its course; it is a fundamental maxim in the constitution of the government of the Medes and Persians, which had now become the universal monarchy, that no decree or statute which the king establishes may be changed. The same we find Esth. i. 19; viii. 8. The Chaldeans magnified the will of their king, by giving him a power to make and unmake laws at his pleasure, to slay and keep alive whom he would. The Persians magnified the wisdom of their king, by supposing that whatever law he solemnly ratified it was so well made that there could be no occasion to alter it, or dispense with it, as if any human foresight could, in framing a law, guard against all inconveniences. But, if this maxim be duly applied to Daniel's case (as I am apt to think it is not, but perverted), while it honours the king's legislative power it hampers his executive power, and incapacitates him to show that mercy which upholds the throne, and to pass acts of indemnity, which are the glories of a reign. Those who allow not the sovereign's power to dispense with a disabling statute, yet never question his power to pardon an offence against a penal statute. But Darius is denied this power. See what need we have to pray for princes that God would give them wisdom, for they are often embarrassed with great difficulties, even the wisest and best are. 5. The executing of the law upon Daniel. The king himself, with the utmost reluctance, and against his conscience, signs the warrant for his execution; and Daniel, that venerable grave man, who carried such a mixture of majesty and sweetness in his countenance, who had so often looked great upon the bench, and at the council-board, and greater upon his knees, who had power with God and man, and had prevailed, is brought, purely for worshipping his God, as if he had been one of the vilest of malefactors, and thrown into the den of lions, to be devoured by them, v. 16. One cannot think of it without the utmost compassion to the gracious sufferer and the utmost indignation at the malicious prosecutors. To make sure work, the stone laid upon the mouth of the den is sealed, and the king (an over-easy man) is persuaded to seal it with his own signet (v. 17), that unhappy signet with which he had confirmed the law that Daniel falls by. But his lords cannot trust him, unless they add their signets too. Thus, when Christ was buried, his adversaries sealed the stone that was rolled to the door of his sepulchre. 6. The encouragement which Darius gave to Daniel to trust in God: Thy God whom thou servest continually, he will deliver thee, v. 16. Here (1.) He justifies Daniel from guilt, owning all his crime to be serving his God continually, and continuing to do so even when it was made a crime. (2.) He leaves it to God to free him from punishment, since he could not prevail to do it: He will deliver thee. He is sure that his God can deliver him, for he believes him to be an almighty God, and he has reason to think he will do it, having heard of his delivering Daniel's companions in a like case from the fiery furnace, and concluding him to be always faithful to those who approve themselves faithful to him. Note, Those who serve God continually he will continually preserve, and will bear them out in his service.

Daniel's Preservation and Deliverance. (b. c. 537.)

18 Then the king went to his palace, and passed the night fasting: neither were instruments

of music brought before him: and his sleep went from him.   19 Then the king arose very early in the morning, and went in haste unto the den of lions.   20 And when he came to the den, he cried with a lamentable voice unto Daniel: and the king spake and said to Daniel, O Daniel, servant of the living God, is thy God, whom thou servest continually, able to deliver thee from the lions?   21 Then said Daniel unto the king, O king, live for ever.   22 My God hath sent his angel, and hath shut the lions' mouths, that they have not hurt me: forasmuch as before him innocency was found in me; and also before thee, O king, have I done no hurt.   23 Then was the king exceeding glad for him, and commanded that they should take Daniel up out of the den. So Daniel was taken up out of the den, and no manner of hurt was found upon him, because he believed in his God.   24 And the king commanded, and they brought those men which had accused Daniel, and they cast them into the den of lions, them, their children, and their wives; and the lions had the mastery of them, and brake all their bones in pieces or ever they came at the bottom of the den.

Here is, I. The melancholy night which the king had, upon Daniel's account, v. 18. He had said, indeed, that God would deliver him out of the danger, but at the same time he could not forgive himself for throwing him into the danger; and justly might God deprive him of a friend whom he had himself used so barbarously. He went to his palace, vexed at himself for what he had done, and calling himself unwise and unjust for not adhering to the law of God and nature with a non obstante—a negative to the law of the Medes and Persians. He ate no supper, but passed the night fasting; his heart was already full of grief and fear. He forbade the music; nothing is more unpleasing that songs sung to a heavy heart. He went to bed, but got no sleep, was full of tossings to and fro till the dawning of the day. Note, the best way to have a good night is to keep a good conscience, then we may lie down in peace.

II. The solicitous enquiry he made concerning Daniel the next morning, v. 19, 20. He was up early, very early; for how could he lie in bed when he could not sleep for dreaming of Daniel, nor lie awake quietly for thinking of him? And he was no sooner up than he went in haste to the den of lions, for he could not satisfy himself to send a servant (that would not sufficiently testify his affection for Daniel), nor had he patience to stay so long as till a servant would return. When he comes to the den, not without some hopes that God had graciously undone what he had wickedly done, he cries, with a lamentable voice, as one full of concern and trouble, O Daniel! art thou alive? He longs to know, yet trembles to ask the question, fearing to be answered with the roaring of the lions after more prey: O Daniel! servant of the living God, has thy God whom thou servest made it to appear that he is able to deliver thee from the lions? If he rightly understood himself when he called him the living God, he could not doubt of his ability to keep Daniel alive, for he that has life in himself quickens whom he will; but has he thought fit in this case to exert his power? What he doubted of we are sure of, that the servants of the living God have a Master who is well able to protect them and bear them out in his service.

III. The joyful news he meets with-that Daniel is alive, is safe, and well, and unhurt in the lions' den, v. 21, 22. Daniel knew the king's voice, though it was now a lamentable voice, and spoke to him with all the deference and respect that were due to him: O king! live for ever. He does not reproach him for his unkindness to him, and his easiness in yielding to the malice of his persecutors; but, to show that he has heartily forgiven him, he meets him with his good wishes. Note, We should not upbraid those with the diskindnesses they have done us who, we know, did them with reluctance, and are very ready to upbraid themselves with them. The account Daniel gives the king is very pleasant; it is triumphant. 1. God has preserved his life by a miracle. Darius had called him Daniel's god (thy God whom thou servest), to which Daniel does as it were echo back, Yea, he is my God, whom I own, and who owns me, for he has sent his angel. The same bright and glorious being that was seen in the form of the Son of God with the three children in the fiery furnace had visited Daniel, and, it is likely, in a visible appearance had enlightened the dark den, and kept Daniel company all night, and had shut the lions' mouths, that they had not in the least hurt him. The angel's presence made even the lions' den his strong-hold, his palace, his paradise; he had never had a better night in his life. See the power of God over the fiercest creatures, and believe his power to restrain the roaring lion that goes about continually seeking to devour from hurting those that are his. See the care God takes of his faithful worshippers, especially when he calls them out to suffer for him. If he keeps their souls from sin, comforts their souls with his peace, and receives their souls to himself, he does in effect stop the lions' mouths, that they cannot hurt them. See how ready the angels are to minister for the good of God's people, for they own themselves their fellow servants. 2. God has therein pleaded his cause. He was represented to the king as disaffected to him and his government. We do not find that he said any thing in his own vindication, but left it to God to clear up his integrity as the light; and he did it effectually, by working a miracle for his preservation. Daniel, in what he had done, had not offended either God or the king: Before him whom I prayed to innocency was found in me. He pretends not to a meritorious excellence, but the testimony of his conscience concerning his sincerity is his comfort—As also that before thee, O king! I have done no hurt, nor designed thee any affront.

IV. The discharge of Daniel from his confinement. His prosecutors cannot but own that the law is satisfied, though they are not, or, if it be altered, it is by a power superior to that of the Medes and Persians; and therefore no cause can be shown why Daniel should not be fetched out of the den (v. 23): The king was exceedingly glad to find him alive, and gave orders immediately that they should take him out of the den, as Jeremiah out of the dungeon; and, when they searched, no manner of hurt was found upon him; he was nowhere crushed nor scarred, but was kept perfectly well, because he believed in his God. Note, Those who boldly and cheerfully trust in God to protect them in the way of their duty shall never be made ashamed of their confidence in him, but shall always find him a present help.

V. The committing of his prosecutors to the same prison, or place of execution rather, v. 24. Darius is animated by this miracle wrought for Daniel, and now begins to take courage and act like himself. Those that would not suffer him to show mercy to Daniel shall, now that God has done it for him, be made to feel his resentments; and he will do justice for God who had shown mercy for him. Daniel's accusers, now that his innocency is cleared, and Heaven itself has become his compurgator, have the same punishment inflicted upon them which they designed against him, according to the law of retaliation made against false accusers, Deut. xix. 18, 19. Such they were to be reckoned now that Daniel was proved innocent; for, though the fact was true, yet it was not a fault. They were cast into the den of lions, which perhaps was a punishment newly invented by themselves; however, it was what they maliciously designed for Daniel. Nec lex est justior ulla quàm necis artifices arte perire suâ—No law can be more just than that which adjudges the devisers of barbarity to perish by it, Ps. vii. 15, 16; ix. 15, 16. And now Solomon's observation is verified (Prov. xi. 8), The righteous is delivered out of trouble, and the wicked cometh in his stead. In this execution we may observe, 1. The king's severity, in ordering their wives and children to be thrown to the lions with them. How righteous are God's statutes above those of the nations! for God commanded that the children should not die for the fathers' crimes, Deut. xxiv. 16. Yet they were put to death in extraordinary cases, as those of Achan, and Saul, and Haman. 2. The lion's fierceness. They had the mastery of them immediately, and tore them to pieces before they came to the bottom of the den. This verified and magnified the miracle of their sparing Daniel; for hereby it appeared that it was not because they had not appetite, but because they had not leave. Mastiffs that are kept muzzled are the more fierce when the muzzle is taken off; so were these lions. And the Lord is known by those judgments which he executes.

The Decree of Darius. (b. c. 537.)

25 Then king Darius wrote unto all people, nations, and languages, that dwell in all the earth; Peace be multiplied unto you. 26 I make a decree, That in every dominion of my kingdom men tremble and fear before the God of Daniel: for he is the living God, and stedfast for ever, and his kingdom that which shall not be destroyed, and his dominion shall be even unto the end. 27 He delivereth and rescueth, and he worketh signs and wonders in heaven and in earth, who hath delivered Daniel from the power of the lions. 28 So this Daniel prospered in the reign of Darius, and in the reign of Cyrus the Persian.

Darius here studies to make some amends for the dishonour he had done both to God and Daniel, in casting Daniel into the lions' den, by doing honour to both.

I. He gives honour to God by a decree published to all nations, by which they are required to fear before him. And this is a decree which is indeed fit to be made unalterable, according to the laws of the Medes and Persians, for it is the everlasting gospel, preached to those that dwell on the earth, Rev. xiv. 7. Fear God, and give glory to him. Observe, 1. To whom he sends this decree—to all people, nations and languages, that dwell in all the earth, v. 25. These are great words, and it is true that all the inhabitants of the earth are obliged to that which is here decreed; but here they mean no more than every dominion of his kingdom, which, though it contained many nations, did not contain all nations; but so it is, those that have much are ready to think they have all. 2. What the matter of the decree is—that men tremble and fear before the God of Daniel. This goes further than Nebuchadnezzar's decree upon a similar occasion, for that only restrained people from speaking amiss of this God, but this requires them to fear before him, to keep up and express awful reverent thoughts of him. And well might this decree he prefaced, as it is, with Peace be multiplied unto you, for the only foundation of true and abundant peace is laid in the fear of God, for that is true wisdom. If we live in the fear of God, and walk according to that rule, peace shall be upon us, peace shall be multiplied to us. But, though this decree goes far, it does not go far enough; had he done right, and come up to his present convictions, he would have commanded all men not only to tremble and fear before this God, but to love him and trust in him, to forsake the service of their idols, and to worship him only, and call upon him as Daniel did. But idolatry had been so long and so deeply rooted that it was not to be extirpated by the edicts of princes, nor by any power less than that which went along with the glorious gospel of Christ. 3. What are the causes and considerations moving him to make this decree. They are sufficient to have justified a decree for the total suppression of idolatry, much more will they serve to support this. There is good reason why all men should fear before this God, for, (1.) His being is transcendent. "He is the living God, lives as a God, whereas the gods we worship are dead things, have not so much as an animal life." (2.) His government is incontestable. He has a kingdom, and a dominion; he not only lives, but reigns as an absolute sovereign. (3.) Both his being and his government are unchangeable. He is himself stedfast for ever, and with him is no shadow of turning. And his kingdom too is that which shall not be destroyed by any external force, nor has his dominion any thing in itself that threatens a decay or tends towards it, and therefore it shall be even to the end. (4.) He has an ability sufficient to support such an authority, v. 27. He delivers his faithful servants from trouble and rescues them out of trouble; he works signs and wonders, quite above the utmost power of nature to effect, both in heaven and on earth, by which it appears that he is sovereign Lord of both. (5.) He has given a fresh proof of all this in delivering his servant Daniel from the power of the lions. This miracle, and that of the delivering of the three children, were wrought in the eyes of the world, were seen, published, and attested by two of the greatest monarchs that ever were, and were illustrious confirmations of the first principles of religion, abstracted from the narrow scheme of Judaism, effectual confutations of all the errors of heathenism, and very proper preparations for pure catholic Christianity.

II. He puts honour upon Daniel (v. 28): So this Daniel prospered. See how God brought to him good out of evil. This bold stroke which his enemies made at his life was a happy occasion of taking them off, and their children too, who otherwise would still have stood in the way of his preferment, and have been upon all occasions vexatious to him; and now he prospered more than ever, was more in favour with his prince and in reputation with the people, which gave him a great opportunity of doing good to his brethren. Thus out of the eater(and that was a lion too) comes forth meat, and out of the strong sweetness.

Chapter 7

The six former chapters of this book were historical; we now enter with fear and trembling upon the six latter, which are prophetical, wherein are many things dark and hard to be understood, which we dare not positively determine the sense of, and yet many things plain and profitable, which I trust God will enable us to make a good use of. In this chapter we have, I. Daniel's vision of the four beasts, ver. 1-8. II. His vision of God's throne of government and judgment, ver. 9-14. III. The interpretation of these visions, given him by an angel that stood by, ver. 15-28. Whether those visions look as far forward as the end of time, or whether they were to have a speedy accomplishment, is hard to say, nor are the most judicious interpreters agreed concerning it.

The Vision of the Four Beasts. (b. c. 555.)

1 In the first year of Belshazzar king of Babylon Daniel had a dream and visions of his head upon his bed: then he wrote the dream, and told the sum of the matters.   2 Daniel spake and said, I saw in my vision by night, and, behold, the four winds of the heaven strove upon the great sea.   3 And four great beasts came up from the sea, diverse one from another.   4 The first was like a lion, and had eagle's wings: I beheld till the wings thereof were plucked, and it was lifted up from the earth, and made stand upon the feet as a man, and a man's heart was given to it.   5 And behold another beast, a second, like to a bear, and it raised up itself on one side, and it had three ribs in the mouth of it between the teeth of it: and they said thus unto it, Arise, devour much flesh.   6 After this I beheld, and lo another, like a leopard, which had upon the back of it four wings of a fowl; the beast had also four heads; and dominion was given to it.   7 After this I saw in the night visions, and behold a fourth beast, dreadful and terrible, and strong exceedingly; and it had great iron teeth: it devoured and brake in pieces, and stamped the residue with the feet of it: and it was diverse from all the beasts that were before it; and it had ten horns.   8 I considered the horns, and, behold, there came up among them another little horn, before whom there were three of the first horns plucked up by the roots: and, behold, in this horn were eyes like the eyes of man, and a mouth speaking great things.

The date of this chapter places it before ch. v., which was in the last year of Belshazzar, and ch. iv., which was in the first of Darius; for Daniel had those visions in the first year of Belshazzar, when the captivity of the Jews in Babylon was drawing near a period. Belshazzar's name here is, in the original, spelt differently from what it used to be; before it was Bel-she-azar—Bel is he that treasures up riches. But this is Bel-eshe-zar—Bel is on fire by the enemy. Bel was the god of the Chaldeans; he had prospered, but is now to be consumed.

We have, in these verses, Daniel's vision of the four monarchies that were oppressive to the Jews. Observe,

I. The circumstances of this vision. Daniel had interpreted Nebuchadnezzar's dream, and now he is himself honoured with similar divine discoveries (v. 1): He had visions of his head upon his bed, when he was asleep; so God sometimes revealed himself and his mind to the children of men, when deep sleep fell upon them (Job xxxiii. 15); for when we are most retired from the world, and taken off from the things of sense, we are most fit for communion with God. But when he was awake he wrote the dream for his own use, lest he should forget it as a dream which passes away; and he told the sum of the matters to his brethren the Jews for their use, and gave it to them in writing, that it might be communicated to those at a distance and preserved for their children after them, who shall see these things accomplished. The Jews, misunderstanding some of the prophecies of Jeremiah and Ezekiel, flattered themselves with hopes that, after their return to their own land, they should enjoy a complete and uninterrupted tranquility; but that they might not so deceive themselves, and their calamities be made doubly grievous by the disappointment, God by this prophet lets them know that they shall have tribulation: those promises of their prosperity were to be accomplished in the spiritual blessings of the kingdom of grace; as Christ has told his disciples they must expect persecution, and the promises they depend upon will be accomplished in the eternal blessings of the kingdom of glory. Daniel both wrote these things and spoke them, to intimate that the church should be taught both by the scriptures and by ministers' preaching, both by the written word and by word of mouth; and ministers in their preaching are to tell the sum of the matters that are written.

II. The vision itself, which foretels the revolutions of government in those nations which the church of the Jews, for the following ages, was to be under the influence of. 1. He observed the four winds to strive upon the great sea, v. 2. They strove which should blow strongest, and, at length, blow alone. This represents the contests among princes for empire, and the shakings of the nations by these contests, to which those mighty monarchies, which he was now to have a prospect of, owed their rise. One wind from any point of the compass, if it blow hard, will cause a great commotion in the sea; but what a tumult must needs be raised when the four winds strive for mastery! This is it which the kings of the nations are contending for in their wars, which are as noisy and violent as the battle of the winds; but how is the poor sea tossed and torn, how terrible are its concussions, and how violent its convulsions, while the winds are at strife which shall have the sole power of troubling it! Note, This world is like a stormy tempestuous sea; thanks to the proud ambitious winds that vex it. 2. He saw four great beasts come up from the sea, from the troubled waters, in which aspiring minds love to fish. The monarchs and monarchies are represented by beasts, because too often it is by brutish rage and tyranny that they are raised and supported. These beasts were diverse one from another (v. 3), of different shapes, to denote the different genius and complexion of the nations in whose hands they were lodged. (1.) The first beast was like a lion, v. 4. This was the Chaldean monarchy, that was fierce and strong, and made the kings absolute. This lion had eagle's wings, with which to fly upon the prey, denoting the wonderful speed that Nebuchadnezzar made in his conquest of kingdoms. But Daniel soon sees the wings plucked, a full stop put to the career of their victorious arms. Divers countries that had been tributaries to them revolt from them, and make head against them; so that this monstrous animal, this winged lion, is made to stand upon the feet as a man, and a man's heart is given to it. It has lost the heart of a lion, which it had been famous for (one of our English kings was called Coeur de Lion—Lion-heart), has lost its courage and become feeble and faint, dreading every thing and daring nothing; they are put in fear, and made to know themselves to be but men. Sometimes the valour of a nation strangely sinks, and it becomes cowardly and effeminate, so that what was the head of the nations in an age or two becomes the tail. (2.) The second beast was like a bear, v. 5. This was the Persian monarchy, less strong and generous than the former, but no less ravenous. This bear raised up itself on one side against the lion, and soon mastered it. It raised up one dominion; so some read it. Persia and Media, which in Nebuchadnezzar's image were the two arms in one breast, now set up a joint government. This bear had three ribs in the mouth of it between the teeth, the remains of those nations it had devoured, which were the marks of its voraciousness, and yet an indication that though it had devoured much it could not devour all; some ribs still stuck in the teeth of it, which it could not conquer. Whereupon it was said to it, "Arise, devour much flesh; let alone the bones, the ribs, that cannot be conquered, and set upon that which will be an easier prey." The princes will stir up both the kings and the people to push on their conquests, and let nothing stand before them. Note, Conquests, unjustly made, are but like those of the beasts of prey, and in this much worse, that the beasts prey not upon those of their own kind, as wicked and unreasonable men do. (3.) The third beast was like a leopard, v. 6. This was the Grecian monarchy, founded by Alexander the Great, active, crafty, and cruel, like a leopard. He had four wings of a fowl; the lion seems to have had but two wings; but the leopard had four, for though Nebuchadnezzar made great despatch in his conquests Alexander made much greater. In six years' time he gained the whole empire of Persia, a great part besides of Asia, made himself master of Syria, Egypt, India, and other nations. This beast had four heads; upon Alexander's death his conquests were divided among his four chief captains; Seleucus Nicanor had Asia the Great; Perdiccas, and after him Antigonus, had Asia the Less; Cassander had Macedonia; and Ptolemeus had Egypt.

Dominion was given to this beast; it was given of God, from whom alone promotion comes. (4.) The fourth beast was more fierce, and formidable, and mischievous, than any of them, unlike any of the other, nor is there any among the beasts of prey to which it might be compared, v. 7. The learned are not agreed concerning this anonymous beast; some make it to be the Roman empire, which, when it was in its glory, comprehended ten kingdoms, Italy, France, Spain, Germany, Britain, Sarmatia, Pannonia, Asia, Greece, and Egypt; and then the little horn which rose by the fall of three of the other horns (v. 8) they make to be the Turkish empire, which rose in the room of Asia, Greece, and Egypt. Others make this fourth beast to be the kingdom of Syria, the family of the Seleucidae, which was very cruel and oppressive to the people of the Jews, as we find in Josephus and the history of the Maccabees. And herein that empire was diverse from those which went before, that none of the preceding powers compelled the Jews to renounce their religion, but the kings of Syria did, and used them barbarously. Their armies and commanders were the great iron teeth with which they devoured and broke in pieces the people of God, and they trampled upon the residue of them. The ten horns are then supposed to be ten kings that reigned successively in Syria; and then the little horn is Antiochus Epiphanes, the last of the ten, who by one means or other undermined three of the kings, and got the government. He was a man of great ingenuity, and therefore is said to have eyes like the eyes of a man; and he was very bold and daring, had a mouth speaking great things. We shall meet with him again in these prophecies.

The Vision of the Four Beasts. (b. c. 555.)

9 I beheld till the thrones were cast down, and the Ancient of days did sit, whose garment was white as snow, and the hair of his head like the pure wool: his throne was like the fiery flame, and his wheels as burning fire. 10 A fiery stream issued and came forth from before him: thousand thousands ministered unto him, and ten thousand times ten thousand stood before him: the judgment was set, and the books were opened. 11 I beheld then because of the voice of the great words which the horn spake: I beheld even till the beast was slain, and his body destroyed, and given to the burning flame. 12 As concerning the rest of the beasts, they had their dominion taken away: yet their lives were prolonged for a season and time. 13 I saw in the night visions, and, behold, one like the Son of man came with the clouds of heaven, and came to the Ancient of days, and they brought him near before him. 14 And there was given him dominion, and glory, and a kingdom, that all people, nations, and languages, should serve him: his dominion is an everlasting dominion, which shall not pass away, and his kingdom that which shall not be destroyed.

Whether we understand the fourth beast to signify the Syrian empire, or the Roman, or the former as the figure of the latter, it is plain that these verses are intended for the comfort and support of the people of God in reference to the persecutions they were likely to sustain both from the one and from the other, and from all their proud enemies in every age; for it is written for their learning on whom the ends of the world have come, that they also, through patience and comfort of this scripture, might have hope. Three things are here discovered that are very encouraging:—

I. That there is a judgment to come, and God is the Judge. Now men have their day, and every pretender thinks he should have his day, and struggles for it. But he that sits in heaven laughs at them, for he sees that his day is coming, Ps. xxxvii. 13. I beheld (v. 9) till the thrones were cast down, not only the thrones of these beasts, but all rule, authority, power, that are set up in opposition to the kingdom of God among men (1 Cor. xv. 24): such are the thrones of the kingdoms of the world, in comparison with God's kingdom; those that see them set up need but wait awhile, and they will see them cast down. I beheld till thrones were set up (so it may as well be read), Christ's throne and the throne of his Father. One of the rabbin confesses that these thrones are set up, one for God, another for the Son of David. It is the judgment that is here set, v. 10. Now, 1. This is intended to proclaim God's wise and righteous government of the world by his providence; and an unspeakable satisfaction it gives to all good men, in the midst of the convulsions and revolutions of states and kingdoms, that the Lord has prepared his throne in the heavens and his kingdom rules over all (Ps. ciii. 19), that verily there is a God that judges in the earth, Ps. lviii. 11. 2. Perhaps it points at the destruction brought by the providence of God upon the empire of Syria, or that of Rome, for their tyrannizing over the people of God. But, 3. It seems principally designed to describe the last judgment, for though it follow not immediately upon the dominion of the fourth beast, nay, though it be yet to come, perhaps many ages to come, yet it was intended that in every age the people of God should encourage themselves, under their troubles, with the belief and prospect of it. Enoch, the seventh from Adam, prophesied of it, Jude 14. Does the mouth of the enemy speak great things, v. 8. Here are far greater things which the mouth of the Lord has spoken. Many of the New-Testament predictions of the judgment to come have a plain allusion to this vision, especially St John's vision of it, Rev. xx. 11, 12. (1.) The Judge is the Ancient of days himself, God the Father, the glory of whose presence is here described. He is called the Ancient of days, because he is God from everlasting to everlasting. Among men we reckon that with the ancient is wisdom, and days shall speak; shall not all flesh then be silent before him who is the Ancient of days? The glory of the Judge is here set forth by his garment, which was white as snow, denoting his splendour and purity in all the administrations of his justice; and the hair of his head clean and white, as the pure wool, that, as the white and hoary head, he may appear venerable. (2.) The throne is very formidable. It is like the fiery flame, dreadful to the wicked that shall be summoned before it. And the throne being movable upon wheels, or at least the chariot in which he rode the circuit, the wheels thereof are as burning fire, to devour the adversaries; for our God is a consuming fire, and with him are everlasting burnings, Isa. xxxiii. 14. This is enlarged upon, v. 10. As to all his faithful friends there proceeds out of the throne of God and the Lamb a pure river of water of life (Rev. xxii. 1), so to all his implacable enemies there issues and comes forth from his throne a fiery stream, a stream of brimstone (Isa. xxx. 33), a fire that shall devour before him. He is a swift witness, and his word a word upon the wheels. (3.) The attendants are numerous and very splendid. The Shechinah is always attended with angels; it is so here (v. 10): Thousand thousands minister to him, and ten thousand times ten thousand stand before him. It is his glory that he has such attendants, but much more his glory that he neither needs them nor can be benefited by them. See how numerous the heavenly hosts are (there are thousands of angels), and how obsequious they are—they stand before God, ready to go on his errands and to take the first intimation of his will and pleasure. They will particularly be employed as ministers of his justice in the last judgment day, when the Son of man shall come, and all the holy angels with him. Enoch prophesied that the Lord should come with his holy myriads. (4.) The process is fair and unexceptionable: The judgment is set, publicly and openly, that all may have recourse to it; and the books are opened. As in courts of judgment among men the proceedings are in writing and upon record, which is laid open when the cause comes to a hearing, the examination of witnesses is produced, and affidavits are read, to clear the matter of fact, and the statute and common-law books are consulted to find out what is the law, so, in the judgment of the great day, the equity of the sentence will be as incontestably evident as if there were books opened to justify it.

II. That the proud and cruel enemies of the church of God will certainly be reckoned with and brought down in due time, v. 11, 12. This is here represented to us, 1. In the destroying of the fourth beast. God's quarrel with this beast is because of the voice of the great words which the horn spoke, bidding defiance to Heaven, and triumphing over all that is sacred; this provokes God more than any thing, for the enemy to behave himself proudly, Deut. xxxii. 27.

Therefore Pharaoh must be humbled, because he has said, Who is the Lord? and has said, I will pursue, I will overtake. Enoch foretold that therefore the Lord would come to judge the world, that he might convince all that are ungodly of their hard speeches, Jude 15. Note, Great words are but idle words, for which men must give account in the great day. And see what becomes of this beast that talks so big: He is slain, and his body destroyed and given to the burning flame. The Syrian empire, after Antiochus, was destroyed. He himself died of a miserable disease, his family was rooted out, the kingdom wasted by the Parthians and Armenians, and at length made a province of the Roman empire by Pompey. And the Roman empire itself (if we take that for the fourth beast), after it began to persecute Christianity, declined and wasted away, and the body of it was destroyed. So shall all thy enemies perish, O Lord! and be slain before thee. 2. In the diminishing and weakening of the other three beasts (v. 12): They had their dominion taken away, and so were disabled from doing the mischiefs they had done to the church and people of God; but a prolonging in life was given them, for a time and a season, a set time, the bounds of which they could not pass. The power of the foregoing kingdoms was quite broken, but the people of them still remained in a mean, weak, and low condition. We may allude to this in describing the remainders of sin in the hearts of good people; they have corruptions in them, the lives of which are prolonged, so that they are not perfectly free from sin, but the dominion of them is taken away, so that sin does not reign in their mortal bodies. And thus God deals with his church's enemies; sometimes he breaks the teeth of them (Ps. iii. 7), when he does not break the neck of them, crushes the persecution, but reprieves the persecutors, that they may have space to repent. And it is fit that God, in doing his own work, should take his own time and way.

III. That the kingdom of the Messiah shall be set up, and kept up, in the world, in spite of all the opposition of the powers of darkness. Let the heathen rage and fret as long as they please, God will set his King upon his holy hill of Zion. Daniel sees this in vision, and comforts himself and his friends with the prospect of it. This is the same with Nebuchadnezzar's foresight of the stone cut out of the mountain without hands, which broke in pieces the image; but in this vision there is much more of pure gospel than in that. 1. The Messiah is here called the Son of man—one like unto the Son of man; for he was made in the likeness of sinful flesh, was found in fashion as a man. I saw one like unto the Son of man, one exactly agreeing with the idea formed in the divine counsels of him that in the fulness of time was to be the Mediator between God and man. He is like unto the son of man, but is indeed the Son of God. Our Savior seems plainly to refer to this vision when he says (John v. 27) that the Father has therefore given him authority to execute judgment because he is the Son of man, and because he is the person whom Daniel saw in vision, to whom a kingdom and dominion were to be given. 2. He is said to come with the clouds of heaven. Some refer this to his incarnation; he descended in the clouds of heaven, came into the world unseen, as the glory of the Lord took possession of the temple in a cloud. The empires of the world were beasts that rose out of the sea; but Christ's kingdom is from above: he is the Lord from heaven. I think it is rather to be referred to his ascension; when he returned to the Father the eye of his disciples followed him, till a cloud received him out of their sight, Acts i. 9. He made that cloud his chariot, wherein he rode triumphantly to the upper world. He comes swiftly, irresistibly, and comes in state, for he comes with the clouds of heaven. 3. He is here represented as having a mighty interest in Heaven. When the cloud received him out of the sight of his disciples, it is worth while to enquire (as the sons of the prophets concerning Elijah in a like case) whither it carried him, where it lodged him; and here we are told, abundantly to our satisfaction, that he came to the Ancient of days; for he ascended to his Father and our Father, to his God and our God (John xx. 17); from him he came forth, and to him he returns, to be glorified with him, and to sit down at his right hand. It was with a great deal of pleasure that he said, Now I go to him that sent me. But was he welcome? Yes, not doubt, he was, for they brought him near before him; he was introduced into his Father's presence, with the attendance and adorations of all the angels of God, Heb. i. 6. God caused him to draw near and approach to him, as an advocate and undertaker for us (Jer. xxx. 21), that we through him might be made nigh. By this solemn near approach which he made to the Ancient of days it appears that the Father accepted the sacrifice he offered, and the satisfaction he made, and was entirely well pleased with all he had done. He was brought near, as our high priest, who for us enters within the veil, and as our forerunner, 4. He is here represented as having a mighty influence upon this earth, v. 14. When he went to be glorified with his Father he had a power given him over all flesh, John xvii. 2, 5. With the prospect of this Daniel and his friends are here comforted, that not only the dominion of the church's enemies shall be taken away (v. 12), but the church's head and best friend shall have the dominion given him; to him every knee shall bow and every tongue confess. Phil. ii. 9, 10. To him are given glory and a kingdom, and they are given by him who has an unquestionable right to give them, which, some think with an eye to these words, our Savior teaches us to acknowledge in the close of the Lord's prayer, For thine is the kingdom, the power, and the glory. It is here foretold that the kingdom of the exalted Redeemer shall be, (1.) A universal kingdom, the only universal monarchy, whatever others have pretended to, or aimed at: All people, nations, and languages, shall fear him, and be under his jurisdiction, either as his willing subjects or as his conquered captives, to be either ruled or overruled by him. One way or other, the kingdoms of the world shall all become his kingdoms. (2.) An everlasting kingdom. His dominion shall not pass away to any successor, much less to any invader, and his kingdom is that which shall not be destroyed. Even the gates of hell, or the infernal powers and policies, shall not prevail against it. The church shall continue militant to the end of time, and triumphant to the endless ages of eternity.

The Vision of the Four Beasts. (b. c. 555.)

15 I Daniel was grieved in my spirit in the midst of my body, and the visions of my head troubled me. 16 I came near unto one of them that stood by, and asked him the truth of all this. So he told me, and made me know the interpretation of the things. 17 These great beasts, which are four, are four kings, which shall arise out of the earth. 18 But the saints of the most High shall take the kingdom, and possess the kingdom for ever, even for ever and ever. 19 Then I would know the truth of the fourth beast, which was diverse from all the others, exceeding dreadful, whose teeth were of iron, and his nails of brass; which devoured, brake in pieces, and stamped the residue with his feet; 20 And of the ten horns that were in his head, and of the other which came up, and before whom three fell; even of that horn that had eyes, and a mouth that spake very great things, whose look was more stout than his fellows. 21 I beheld, and the same horn made war with the saints, and prevailed against them; 22 Until the Ancient of days came, and judgment was given to the saints of the most

High; and the time came that the saints possessed the kingdom. 23 Thus he said, The fourth beast shall be the fourth kingdom upon earth, which shall be diverse from all kingdoms, and shall devour the whole earth, and shall tread it down, and break it in pieces. 24 And the ten horns out of this kingdom are ten kings that shall arise: and another shall rise after them; and he shall be diverse from the first, and he shall subdue three kings. 25 And he shall speak great words against the most High, and shall wear out the saints of the most High, and think to change times and laws: and they shall be given into his hand until a time and times and the dividing of time. 26 But the judgment shall sit, and they shall take away his dominion, to consume and to destroy it unto the end. 27 And the kingdom and dominion, and the greatness of the kingdom under the whole heaven, shall be given to the people of the saints of the most High, whose kingdom is an everlasting kingdom, and all dominions shall serve and obey him. 28 Hitherto is the end of the matter. As for me Daniel, my cogitations much troubled me, and my countenance changed in me: but I kept the matter in my heart.

Here we have, I. The deep impressions which these visions made upon the prophet. God in them put honour upon him, and gave him satisfaction, yet not without a great allay of pain and perplexity (v. 15): I Daniel was grieved in my spirit, in the midst of my body. The word here used for the body properly signifies a sheath or scabbard, for the body is no more to the soul; that is the weapon; it is that which we are principally to take care of. The visions of my head troubled me, an again (v. 28), my cogitations much troubled me. The manner in which these things were discovered to him quite overwhelmed him, and put his thoughts so much to the stretch that his spirits failed him, and the trance he was in tired him and made him faint. The things themselves that were discovered amazed and astonished him, and put him into a confusion, till by degrees he recollected and conquered himself, and set the comforts of the vision over against the terrors of it.

II. His earnest desire to understand the meaning of them (v. 16): I came near to one of those that stood by, to one of the angels that appeared attending the Son of man in his glory, and asked him the truth (the true intent and meaning) of all this. Note, It is a very desirable thing to take the right and full sense of what we see and hear from God; and those that would know must ask by faithful and fervent prayer and by accomplishing a diligent search.

III. The key that was given him, to let him into the understanding of this vision. The angel told him, and told him so plainly that he made him know the interpretation of the thing, and so made him somewhat more easy.

1. The great beasts are great kings and their kingdoms, great monarchs and their monarchies, which shall arise out of the earth, as those beasts did out of the sea, v. 17. They are but terraefilii—from beneath; they savour of the earth, and their foundation is in the dust; they are of the earth earthy, and they are written in the dust, and to the dust they shall return.

2. Daniel pretty well understands the first three beasts, but concerning the fourth he desires to be better informed, because it differed so much from the rest, and was exceedingly dreadful, and not only so, but very mischievous, or it devoured and broke in pieces, v. 19. Perhaps it was this that put Daniel into such a fright, and this part of the visions of his head troubled him more than any of the rest. But especially he desired to know what the little horn was, that had eyes, and a mouth that spoke very great things, and whose countenance was more fearless and formidable than that of any of his fellows, v. 20. And this he was most inquisitive about because it was this horn that made war with the saints, and prevailed against them, v. 21. While no more is intimated than that the children of men make war with one another, and prevail against one another, the prophet does not show himself so much concerned (let the potsherds strive with the potsherds of the earth, and be dashed in pieces one against another); but when they make war with the saints, when the precious sons of Zion, comparable to fine gold, are broken as earthen pitchers, it is time to ask, "What is the meaning of this? Will the Lord cast off his people? Will he suffer their enemies to trample

upon them and triumph over them? What is this same horn that shall prevail so far against the saints?" To this his interpreter answers (v. 23-25) that this fourth beast is a fourth kingdom, that shall devour the whole earth, or (as it may be read) the whole land. That the ten horns are ten kings, and the little horn is another king that shall subdue three kings, and shall be very abusive to God and his people, shall act, (1.) Very impiously towards God. He shall speak great words against the Most High, setting him, and his authority and justice, at defiance. (2.) Very imperiously towards the people of God. He shall wear out the saints of the Most High; he will not cut them off at once, but wear them out by long oppressions and a constant course of hardships put upon them, ruining their estates and weakening their families. The design of Satan has been to wear out the saints of the Most High, that they may be no more in remembrance; but the attempt is vain, for while the world stands God will have a church in it. He shall think to change times and laws, to abolish all the ordinances and institutions of religion, and to bring every body to say and do just as he would have them. He shall trample upon laws and customs, human and divine.

Diruit, aedificut, mutat quadrata rotundis—He pulls down, he builds, he changes square into round, as if he meant to alter even the ordinances of heaven themselves. And in these daring attempts he shall for a time prosper and have success; they shall be given into his hand until time, times, and half a time (that is, for three years and a half), that famous prophetical measure of time which we meet with in the Revelation, which is sometimes called forty-two months, sometimes 1260 days, which come all to one. But at the end of that time the judgment shall sit and take away his dominion (v. 26), which he expounds (v. 11) of the beast being slain and his body destroyed. And (as Mr. Mede reads v. 12) as to the rest of the beast, the ten horns, especially the little ruffling horn (as he calls it), they had their dominion taken away. Now the question is, Who is this enemy, whose rise, reign, and ruin, are foretold? Interpreters are not agreed. Some will have the fourth kingdom to be that of the Seleucidae, and the little horn to be Antiochus, and show the accomplishment of all this in the history of the Maccabees; so Junius, Piscator, Polanus, Broughton, and many others: but others will have the fourth kingdom to be that of the Romans, and the little horn to be Julius Caesar, and the succeeding emperors (says Calvin), the antichrist, the papal kingdom (says Mr. Joseph Mede), that wicked one, which, as this little horn, is to be consumed by the brightness of Christ's second coming. The pope assumes a power to change times and laws, potestas autokratorike—an absolute and despotic power, as he calls it. Others make the little horn to be the Turkish empire; so Luther, Vatablus, and others. Now I cannot prove either side to be wrong; and therefore, since prophecies sometimes have many fulfillings, and we ought to give scripture its full latitude (in this as in many other controversies), I am willing to allow that they are both in the right, and that this prophecy has primary reference to the Syrian empire, and was intended for the encouragement of the Jews who suffered under Antiochus, that they might see even these melancholy times foretold, but might foresee a glorious issue of them at last, and the final overthrow of their proud oppressors; and, which is best of all, might foresee, not long after, the setting up of the kingdom of the Messiah in the world, with the hopes of which it was usual with the former prophets to comfort the people of God in their distresses. But yet it has a further reference, and foretels the like persecuting power and rage in Rome heathen, and no less in Rome papal, against the Christian religion, that was in Antiochus against the pious Jews and their religion. And St. John, in his visions and prophecies, which point primarily at Rome, has plain reference, in many particulars, to these visions of Daniel.

3. He has a joyful prospect given him of the prevalency of God's kingdom among men, and its victory over all opposition at last. And it is very observable that in the midst of the predictions of the force and fury of the enemies this is brought in abruptly (v. 18 and again v. 22), before it comes, in the course of the vision, to be interpreted, v. 26, 27. And this also refers, (1.) To the prosperous days of the Jewish church, after it had weathered the storm

under Antiochus, and the power which the Maccabees obtained over their enemies. (2.) To the setting up of the kingdom of the Messiah in the world by the preaching of his gospel. For judgment Christ comes into this world, to rule by his Spirit, and to make all his saints kings and priests to their God. (3.) To the second coming of Jesus Christ, when the saints shall judge the world, shall sit down with him on his throne and triumph in the complete downfall of the devil's kingdom. Let us see what is here foretold. [1.] The Ancient of days shall come, v. 22. God shall judge the world by his Son, to whom he has committed all judgment, and, as an earnest of that, he comes for the deliverance of his oppressed people, comes for the setting up of his kingdom in the world. [2.] The judgment shall sit, v. 26. God will make it appear that he judges in the earth, and will, both in wisdom and in equity, plead his people's righteous cause. At the great day he will judge the world in righteousness by that man whom he has ordained. [3.] The dominion of the enemy shall be taken away, v. 26. All Christ's enemies shall be made his footstool, and shall be consumed and destroyed to the end: these were the apostle uses concerning the man of sin, 2 Thess. ii. 8. He shall be consumed with the spirit of Christ's mouth and destroyed with the brightness of his coming. [4.] Judgment is given to the saints of the Most High. The apostles are entrusted with the preaching of a gospel by which the world shall be judged. All the saints by their faith and obedience condemn an unbelieving disobedient world; in Christ their head they shall judge the world, shall judge the twelve tribes of Israel, Matt. xix. 28. See what reason we have to honour those that fear the Lord; how mean and despicable soever the saints now appear in the eye of the world, and how much contempt soever is poured upon them; they are the saints of the Most High; they are near and dear to God, and he owns them for his, and judgment is given to them. [5.] That which is most insisted upon is that the saints of the Most High shall take the kingdom, and possess the kingdom for ever, v. 18. And again (v. 22), The time came that the saints possessed the kingdom. And again (v. 27), The kingdom and dominion, and the greatness of the kingdom under the whole heavens, shall be given to the people of the saints of the Most High. Far be it from us to infer hence that dominion is founded on grace, or that this will warrant any, under pretence of saintship, to usurp kingship. No; Christ's kingdom is not of this world; but this intimates the spiritual dominion of the saints over their own lusts and corruptions, their victories over Satan and his temptations, and the triumphs of the martyrs over death and its terrors. It likewise promises that the gospel kingdom shall be set up, a kingdom of grace, the privileges and comforts of which now, under the heavens, shall be the earnest and first-fruits of the kingdom of glory in the heavens. When the empire became Christian, and princes used their power for the defence and advancement of Christianity, then the saints possessed the kingdom. The saints rule by the Spirit's ruling in them (and this is the victory overcoming the world, even their faith) and by making the kingdoms of this world to become Christ's kingdom.

But the full accomplishment of this will be in the everlasting happiness of the saints, the kingdom that cannot be moved, which we, according to his promise, look for (that is the greatness of the kingdom), the crown of glory that fades not away—that is the everlasting kingdom. See what an emphasis is laid upon this (v. 18): The saints shall possess the kingdom for ever, even for ever and ever; and the reason is because he whose saints they are is the Most High and his kingdom is an everlasting kingdom, v. 27. He is so, and therefore theirs shall be so. Because I live, you shall live also, John xiv. 19. His kingdom is theirs; they reckon themselves exalted in his exaltation, and desire no greater honour and satisfaction to themselves than that all dominions should serve and obey him, as they shall do, v. 27. They shall either be brought into subjection to his golden sceptre or brought to destruction by his iron rod.
Daniel, in the close, when he ends that matter, tells us what impressions this vision made upon him; it overwhelmed his spirits to such a degree that his countenance was changed, and it made him look pale; but he kept the matter in his heart. Note, The heart must be the treasury and store-house of divine things; there we must hide God's word, as the Virgin

Mary kept the sayings of Christ, Luke ii. 51. Daniel kept the matter in his heart, with a design, not to keep it from the church, but to keep it for the church, that what he had received from the Lord he might fully and faithfully deliver to the people. Note, It concerns God's prophets and ministers to treasure up the things of God in their minds, and there to digest them well. If we would have God's word ready in our mouths when we have occasion for it, we must keep it in our hearts at all times.

Chapter 8

The visions and prophecies of this chapter look only and entirely at the events that were then shortly to come to pass in the monarchies of Persia and Greece, and seem not to have any further reference at all. Nothing is here said of the Chaldean monarchy, for that was now just at its period; and therefore this chapter is written not in Chaldee, as the six foregoing chapters were, for the benefit of the Chaldeans, but in Hebrew, and so are the rest of the chapters to the end of the book, for the service of the Jews, that they might know what troubles were before them and what the issue of them would be, and might provide accordingly. In this chapter we have, I. The vision itself of the ram, and the he-goat, and the little horn that should fight and prevail against the people of God, for a certain limited time, ver. 1-14. II. The interpretation of this vision by an angel, showing that the ram signified the Persian empire, the he-goat the Grecian, and the little horn a king of the Grecian monarchy, that should set himself against the Jews and religion, which was Antiochus Epiphanes, ver. 15-27. The Jewish church, from its beginning, had been all along, more or less, blessed with prophets, men divinely inspired to explain God's mind to them in his providences and give them some prospect of what was coming upon them; but, soon after Ezra's time, divine inspiration ceased, and there was no more any prophet till the gospel day dawned. And therefore the events of that time were here foretold by Daniel, and left upon record, that even then God might not leave himself without witness, nor them without a guide.

The Vision of the Ram and Goat. (b. c. 553.)

1 In the third year of the reign of king Belshazzar a vision appeared unto me, even unto me Daniel, after that which appeared unto me at the first. 2 And I saw in a vision; and it came to pass, when I saw, that I was at Shushan in the palace, which is in the province of Elam; and I saw in a vision, and I was by the river of Ulai. 3 Then I lifted up mine eyes, and saw, and, behold, there stood before the river a ram which had two horns: and the two horns were high; but one was higher than the other, and the higher came up last. 4 I saw the ram pushing westward, and northward, and southward; so that no beasts might stand before him, neither was there any that could deliver out of his hand; but he did according to his will, and became great. 5 And as I was considering, behold, a he goat came from the west on the face of the whole earth, and touched not the ground: and the goat had a notable horn between his eyes. 6 And he came to the ram that had two horns, which I had seen standing before the river, and ran unto him in the fury of his power. 7 And I saw him come close unto the ram, and he was moved with choler against him, and smote the ram, and brake his two horns: and there was no power in the ram to stand before him, but he cast him down to the ground, and stamped upon him: and there was none that could deliver the ram out of his hand. 8 Therefore the he goat waxed very great: and when he was strong, the great horn was broken; and for it came up four notable ones toward the four winds of heaven. 9 And out of one of them came forth a little horn, which waxed exceeding great, toward the south, and toward the east, and toward the pleasant land. 10 And it waxed great, even to the host of heaven; and it cast downsome of the host and of the stars to the ground, and stamped upon them. 11 Yea, he magnified himself even to the prince of the host, and by him the daily sacrifice was taken away, and the place of his sanctuary was cast down. 12 And a host was given him against the daily sacrifice by reason of transgression, and it cast down the

truth to the ground; and it practised, and prospered. 13 Then I heard one saint speaking, and another saint said unto that certain saint which spake, How long shall be the vision concerning the daily sacrifice, and the transgression of desolation, to give both the sanctuary and the host to be trodden under foot? 14 And he said unto me, Unto two thousand and three hundred days; then shall the sanctuary be cleansed.

Here is, I. The date of this vision, v. 1. It was in the third year of the reign of Belshazzar, which proved to be his last year, as many reckon; so that this chapter also should be, in order of time, before the fifth. That Daniel might not be surprised at the destruction of Babylon, now at hand, God gives him a foresight of the destruction of other kingdoms hereafter, which in their day had been as potent as that of Babylon. Could we foresee the changes that shall be hereafter, when we are gone, we should the less admire, and be less affected with, the changes in our own day; for that which is done is that which shall be done, Eccl. i. 9. Then it was that a vision appeared to me, even to me, Daniel. Here he solemnly attests the truth of it: it was to him, even to him, that the vision was shown; he was the eye-witness of it. And this vision puts him in mind of a former vision which appeared to him at the first, in the first year of this reign, which he makes mention of because this vision was an explication and confirmation of that, and points at many of the same events. That seems to have been a dream, a vision in his sleep; this seems to have been when he was awake.

II. The scene of this vision. The place where that was laid was in Shushan the palace, one of the royal seats of the kings of Persia, situated on the banks of the river Ulai, which surrounded the city; it was in the province of Elam, that part of Persia which lay next to Babylon. Daniel was not there in person, for he was now in Babylon, a captive, in some employment under Belshazzar, and might not go to such a distant country, especially being now an enemy's country. But he was there in vision; as Ezekiel, when a captive in Babylon, was often brought, in the spirit, to the land of Israel. Note, The soul may be a liberty when the body is in captivity; for, when we are bound, the Spirit of the Lord is not bound. The vision related to that country, and therefore there he was made to fancy himself to be as strongly affected as if he had really been there.

III. The vision itself and the process of it.

1. He saw a ram with two horns, v. 3. This was the second monarchy, of which the kingdoms of Media and Persia were the two horns. The horns were very high; but that which came up last was the higher, and got the start of the former. So the last shall be first, and the first last. The kingdom of Persia, which rose last, in Cyrus, became more eminent than that of the Medes.
2. He saw this ram pushing all about him with his horns (v. 4), westward (towards Babylon, Syria, Greece, and Asia the less), northward(towards the Lydians, Armenians, and Scythians), and southward (towards Arabia, Ethiopia, and Egypt), for all these nations did the Persian empire, one time or other, make attempts upon for the enlarging of their dominion. And at last he became so powerful that no beasts might stand before him. This ram, though of a species of animal often preyed upon, became formidable even to the beasts of prey themselves, so that there was no standing before him, no escaping him, none that could deliver out of his hand, but all must yield to him: the kings of Persia did according to their will, prospered in all their ways abroad, had an uncontrollable power at home, and became great. He thought himself great because he did what he would; but to do good is that which makes men truly great.

3. He saw this ram overcome by a he-goat. He was considering the ram (wondering that so weak an animal should come to be so prevalent) and thinking what would be the issue; and, behold, a he-goat came, v. 5. This was Alexander the Great, the son of Philip king of

Macedonia. He came from the west, from Greece, which lay west from Persia. He fetched a great compass with his army: he came upon the face of the whole earth; he did in effect conquer the world, and then sat down and wept because there was not another world to be conquered. Unus Pellaeo juveni non sufficit orbis—One world was too little for the youth of Pellae. This he-goat (a creature famed for comeliness in going, Prov. xxx. 31) went on with incredible swiftness, so that he touched not the ground, so lightly did he move; he rather seemed to fly above the ground than to go upon the ground; or none touched him in the earth, that is, he met with little or no opposition. This he-goat, or buck, had a notable horn between his eyes, like a unicorn. He had strength, and knew his own strength; he saw himself a match for all his neighbours. Alexander pushed his conquests on so fast, and with so much fury, that none of the kingdoms he attacked had courage to make a stand, or give check to the progress of his victorious arms. In six years he made himself master of the greatest part of the then known world. Well might he be called a notable horn, for his name still lives in history as the name of one of the most celebrated commanders in war that ever the world knew. Alexander's victories and achievements are still the entertainment of the ingenious. This he-goat came to the ram that had two horns, v. 6. Alexander with his victorious army attacked the kingdom of Persia, an army consisting of no more than 30,000 foot and 5000 horse. He ran unto him, to surprise him ere he could get intelligence of his motions, in the fury of his power. He came close to the ram. Alexander with his army came up with Darius Codomannus, then emperor of Persia, being moved with choler against him, v. 7. It was with the greatest violence that Alexander pushed on his war against Darius, who, though he brought vast numbers into the field, yet, for want of skill, was an unequal match for him, so that Alexander was too hard for him whenever he engaged him, smote him, cast him down to the ground, and stamped upon him, which three expressions, some think, refer to the three famous victories that Alexander obtained over Darius, at Granicus, at Issus, and at Arbela, by which he was at length totally routed, having, in the last battle, had 600,000 men killed, so that Alexander became absolute master of all the Persian empire, broke his two horns, the kingdoms of Media and Persia.

The ram that had destroyed all before him (v. 4) now is himself destroyed; Darius has no power to stand before Alexander, not has he any friends or allies to help to deliver him out of his hand. Note, Those kingdoms which, when they had power, abused it, and, because none could oppose them, withheld not themselves from the doing of any wrong, may expect to have their power at length taken from them, and to be served in their own kind, Isa. xxxiii. 1.

4. He saw the he-goat made hereby very considerable; but the great horn, that had done all this execution, was broken, v. 8. Alexander was about twenty years old when he began his wars. When he was about twenty-six he conquered Darius, and became master of the whole Persian empire; but when he was about thirty-two or thirty-three years of age, when he was strong, in his full strength, he was broken. He was not killed in war, in the bed of honour, but died of a drunken surfeit, or, as some suspect, by poison and left no child living behind him to enjoy that which he had endlessly laboured for, but left a lasting monument of the vanity of worldly pomp and power, and their insufficiency to make a man happy.

5. He saw this kingdom divided into four parts, and that instead of that one great horn there came up four notable ones, Alexander's four captains, to whom he bequeathed his conquests; and he had so much that, when it was divided among four, they had each of them enough for any one man. These four notable horns were towards the four winds of heaven, the same with the four heads of the leopard (ch. vii. 6), the kingdoms of Syria and Egypt, Asia and Greece-Syria lying to the east, Greece to the west, Asia Minor to the north, and Egypt to the south. Note, Those that heap up riches know not who shall gather them, nor whose all those things shall be which they have provided.

6. He saw a little horn which became a great persecutor of the church and people of God; and this was the principal thing that was intended to be shown to him in this vision, as afterwards, ch. xi. 30, &c. All agree that this was Antiochus Epiphanes (so he called himself)—the illustrious, but others called him Antiochus Epimanes—Antiochus the furious. He is called here (as before, ch. vii. 8), a little horn, because he was in his original contemptible; there were others between him and the kingdom, and he was of a base servile disposition, had nothing in him of princely qualities, and had been for some time a hostage and prisoner at Rome, whence he made his escape, and, though, the youngest brother, and his elder living, got the kingdom. He waxed exceedingly great towards the south, for he seized upon Egypt, and towards the east, for he invaded Persia and Armenia. But that which is here especially taken notice of is the mischief that he did to the people of the Jews. They are not expressly named, or prophecies must not be too plain; but they are here so described that it would be easy for those who understood scripture-language to know who were meant; and the Jews, having notice of this before, might be awakened to prepare themselves and their children beforehand for these suffering trying times. (1.) He set himself against the pleasant land, the land of Israel, so called because it was the glory of all lands, for fruitfulness and all the delights of human life, but especially for the tokens of God's presence in it, and its being blessed with divine revelations and institutions; it was Mount Zion that was beautiful for situation, the joy of the whole earth, Ps. xlviii. 2. The pleasantness of that land was that there the Messiah was to be born, who would be both the consolation and the glory of his people Israel. Note, We have reason to reckon that a pleasant place which is a holy place, in which God dwells, and where we may have opportunity of communing with him. Surely, It is good to be here.(2.) He fought against the host of heaven, that is, the people of God, the church, which is the kingdom of heaven, the church-militant here on earth. The saints, being born from above, and citizens of heaven, and doing the will of God, by his grace, in some measure, as the angels of heaven do it, may be well called a heavenly host. Or the priests and Levites, who were employed in the service of the tabernacle, and there warred a good warfare, were this host of heaven. These Antiochus set himself against; he waxed great to the host of heaven, in opposition to them and in defiance of them. (3.) He cast down some of the host (that is, of the stars, for they are called the host of heaven) to the ground, and stamped upon them. Some of those that were most eminent both in church and state, that were burning and shining lights in their generation, he either forced to comply with his idolatries or put them to death; he got them into his hands, and then trampled upon them and triumphed over them; as good old Eleazar, and the seven brethren, whom he put to death with cruel tortures, because they would not eat swine's flesh, 2 Mac. vi. 7. He gloried in it that herein he insulted Heaven itself and exalted his throne above the stars of God, Isa. xiv. 13. (4.) He magnified himself even to the prince of the host. He set himself against the high priest, Onias, whom he deprived of his dignity, or rather against God himself, who was Israel's King of old, who reigns for ever Zion's King, who himself heads his own host that fight his battles. Against him Antiochus magnified himself; as Pharaoh, when he said, Who is the Lord? Note, Those who persecute the people of God persecute God himself. (5.) He took away the daily sacrifice. The morning and evening lamb, which God appointed to be offered every day upon his altar to his honour, Antiochus forbade and restrained the offering of. No doubt he took away all other sacrifices, but only the daily sacrifice is mentioned, because that was the greatest loss of all, for in that they kept up their constant communion with God, which they preferred before that which is only occasional. God's people reckon their daily sacrifices, their morning and evening exercises of devotion, the most needful of their daily business and the most delightful of their daily comforts, and would not for all the world part with them. (6.) He cast down the place of his sanctuary. He did not burn and demolish the temple, but he cast it down, when he profaned it, made it the temple of Jupiter Olympius, and set up his image in it. He also cast down the truth to the ground, trampled upon the book of the law, that word of truth, tore it, and burnt it, and did what he could to destroy it quite, that it might be lost and forgotten for ever. These were the

projects of that wicked prince. In these he practised. And (would you think it?) in these he prospered. He carried the matter very far, seemed to have gained his point, and went near to extirpate that holy religion which God's right hand had planted. But lest he or any other should triumph, as if herein he had prevailed against God himself and been too hard for him, the matter is here explained and set in a true light. [1.] He could not have done this if God had not permitted him to do it, could have had no power against Israel unless it had been given him from above. God put this power into his hand, and gave him a host against the daily sacrifice. God's providence put that sword into his hand by which he was enabled thus to bear down all before him. Note, We ought to eye and own the hand of God in all the enterprises and all the successes of the church's enemies against the church. They are but the rod in God's hand. [2.] God would not have permitted it if his people had not provoked him to do so. It is by reason of transgression, the transgression of Israel, to correct them for that, that Antiochus is employed to give them all this trouble. Note, When the pleasant land and all its pleasant things are laid waste, it must be acknowledged that sin is the procuring cause of all the desolation. Who gave Jacob to the spoil? Did not the Lord, he against whom we have sinned? Isa. xlii. 24. The great transgression of the Jews after the captivity (when they were cured of idolatry) was a contempt and profanation of the holy things, snuffing at the service of God, bringing the torn and the lame for sacrifice, as if the table of the Lord were a contemptible thing (so we find Mal. i. 7, 8, &c., and that the priests were guilty of this Mal. ii. 1, 8), and therefore God sent Antiochus to take away the daily sacrifice and cast down the place of his sanctuary. Note, It is just with God to deprive those of the privileges of his house who despise and profane them, and to make those know the worth of ordinances by the want of them who would not know it by the enjoyment of them.

7. He heard the time of this calamity limited and determined, not the time when it should come (that is not here fixed, because God would have his people always prepared for it), but how long it should last, that, when they had no more any prophets to tell them how long (Ps. lxxiv. 9, which psalm seems to have been calculated for this dark and doleful day), they might have this prophecy to give them a prospect of deliverance in due time. Now concerning this we have here,
(1.) The question asked concerning it, v. 13. Observe [1.] By whom the question was put: I heard one saint speaking to this purport, and then another saint seconded him. "O that we knew how long this trouble will last!" The angels here are called saints, for they are holy ones (ch. iv. 13), the holy myriads, Jude 14. The angels concern themselves in the affairs of the church, and enquire concerning them, if, as here, concerning its temporal salvations, much more do they desire to look into the great salvation, 1 Pet. i. 12. One saint spoke of the thing, and another enquired concerning it. Thus John, who lay in Christ's bosom, was beckoned to by Peter to ask Christ a question, John xiii. 23, 24. [2.] To whom the question was put. He said unto Palmoni that spoke. Some make this certain saint to be a superior angel who understood more than the rest, to whom therefore they came with their enquiries. Others make it to be the eternal Word, the Son of God. He is the unknown One. Palmoni seems to be compounded of Peloni Almoni, which is used (Ruth iv. 1) for Ho, such a one, and (2 Kings vi. 8) for such a place. Christ was yet the nameless One. Wherefore asked thou after my name, seeing it is secret? Judg. xiii. 18. He is the numberer of secrets (as some translate it), for from him there is nothing hidden—the wonderful numberer, so others; his name is called Wonderful. Note, If we would know the mind of God, we must apply to Jesus Christ, who lay in the bosom of the Father, and in whom are hidden all the treasures of wisdom and knowledge, not hidden from us, but hidden for us. [3.] The question itself that was asked: "How long shall be the vision concerning the daily sacrifice? How long shall the prohibition of it continue? How long shall the pleasant land be made unpleasant by that severe interdict? How long shall the transgression of desolation(the image of Jupiter), that great transgression which makes all our sacred things desolate, how long shall that stand in the temple? How long shall the sanctuary and the host, the holy place and the holy persons

that minister in it, be trodden under foot by the oppressor?" Note, Angels are concerned for the prosperity of the church on earth and desirous to see an end of its desolations. The angels asked, for the satisfaction of Daniel, not doubting but he was desirous to know, how long these calamities should last? The question takes it for granted that they should not last always. The rod of the wicked shall not rest upon the lot of the righteous, though it may come upon their lot. Christ comforted himself in his sufferings with this, The things concerning me have an end (Luke xxii. 37), and so may the church in hers. But it is desirable to know how long they shall last, that we may provide accordingly.

(2.) The answer given to this question, v. 14. Christ gives instruction to the holy angels, for they are our fellow-servants; but here the answer was given to Daniel, because for his sake the question was asked: He said unto me. God sometimes gives in great favours to his people, in answer to the enquiries and requests of their friends for them. Now, [1.] Christ assures him that the trouble shall end; it shall continue 2300 days and no longer, so many evenings and mornings (so the word is), so many nychthemerai, so many natural days, reckoned, as in the beginning of Genesis, by the evenings and mornings, because it was the evening and the morning sacrifice that they most lamented the loss of, and thought the time passed very slowly while they were deprived of them. Some make the morning and the evening, in this number, to stand for two, and then 2300 evenings and as many mornings will make but 1150 days; and about so many days it was that the daily sacrifice was interrupted: and this comes nearer to the computation (ch. vii. 25) of a time, times, and the dividing of a time. But it is less forced to understand them of so many natural days; 2300 days make six years and three months, and about eighteen days; and just so long they reckon from the defection of the people, procured by Menelaus the high priest in the 142nd year of the kingdom of the Seleucidae, the sixth month of that year, and the 6th day of the month (so Josephus dates it), to the cleansing of the sanctuary, and the reestablishment of religion among them, which was in the 148th year, the 9th month, and the 25th day of the month, 1 Mac. iv. 52. God reckons the time of his people's afflictions he is afflicted. Rev. ii. 10, Thou shalt have tribulation ten days. [2.] He assures him that they shall see better days afterwards: Then shall the sanctuary be cleansed. Note, The cleansing of the sanctuary is a happy token for good to any people; when they begin to be reformed they will soon be relieved. Though the righteous God may, for the correction of his people, suffer his sanctuary to be profaned for a while, yet the jealous God will, for his own glory, see to the cleansing of it in due time. Christ died to cleanse his church, and he will so cleanse it as at length to present it blameless to himself.

The Vision of the Ram and Goat. (b. c. 553.)

15 And it came to pass, when I, even I Daniel, had seen the vision, and sought for the meaning, then, behold, there stood before me as the appearance of a man. 16 And I heard a man's voice between the banks of Ulai, which called, and said, Gabriel, make this man to understand the vision. 17 So he came near where I stood: and when he came, I was afraid, and fell upon my face: but he said unto me, Understand, O son of man: for at the time of the end shall be the vision. 18 Now as he was speaking with me, I was in a deep sleep on my face toward the ground: but he touched me, and set me upright. 19 And he said, Behold, I will make thee know what shall be in the last end of the indignation: for at the time appointed the end shall be. 20 The ram which thou sawest having two horns are the kings of Media and Persia. 21 And the rough goat is the king of Grecia: and the great horn that is between his eyes is the first king. 22 Now that being broken, whereas four stood up for it, four kingdoms shall stand up out of the nation, but not in his power. 23 And in the latter time of their kingdom, when the transgressors are come to the full, a king of fierce countenance, and understanding dark sentences, shall stand up. 24 And his power shall be mighty, but not by his own power: and he shall destroy wonderfully, and shall prosper, and practise, and shall destroy the mighty and the holy people. 25 And through his policy also

he shall cause craft to prosper in his hand; and he shall magnify himself in his heart, and by peace shall destroy many: he shall also stand up against the Prince of princes; but he shall be broken without hand.   26 And the vision of the evening and the morning which was told is true: wherefore shut thou up the vision; for it shall be for many days.   27 And I Daniel fainted, and was sick certain days; afterward I rose up, and did the king's business; and I was astonished at the vision, but none understood it.

Here we have,

I. Daniel's earnest desire to have this vision explained to him (v. 15): I sought the meaning. Note, Those that rightly know the things of God cannot but desire to know more and more of them, and to be led further into the mystery of them; and those that would find the meaning of what they have seen or heard from God must seek it, and seek it diligently. Seek and you shall find. Daniel considered the thing, compared it with the former discoveries, to try if he could understand it; but especially he sought by prayer (as he had done ch. ii. 18), and he did not seek in vain.

II. Orders given to the angel Gabriel to inform him concerning this vision. One in the appearance of a man (who, some think, was Christ himself, for who besides could command angels?) orders Gabriel to make Daniel understand this vision. Sometimes God is pleased to make use of the ministration of angels, not only to protect his children, but to instruct them, to serve the kind intentions, not only of his providence, but of his grace.

III. The consternation that Daniel was in upon the approach of his instructor (v. 17): When he came near I was afraid. Though Daniel was a man of great prudence and courage, and had been conversant with the visions of the Almighty, yet the approach of an extraordinary messenger from heaven put him into this fright. He fell upon his face, not to worship the angel, but because he could no longer bear the dazzling lustre of his glory. Nay, being prostrate upon the ground, he fell into a deep sleep, (v. 18), which came not from any neglect of the vision, or indifference towards it, but was an effect of his faintness and the oppression of spirit he was under, through the abundance of revelations. The disciples in the garden slept for sorrow; and, as there, so here, the spirit was willing, but the flesh was weak. Daniel would have kept awake, and could not.

IV. The relief which the angel gave to Daniel, with great encouragement to him to expect a satisfactory discovery of the meaning of this vision. 1. He touched him, and set him upon his feet, v. 18. Thus when John, in a similar case, was in similar consternation, Christ laid his right hand upon him, Rev. i. 17. It was a gentle touch that the angel here gave to Daniel, to show that he came not to hurt him, not to plead against him with his great power, or with a hand heavy upon him, but to help him, to put strength into him (Job xxiii. 6), which God can do with a touch. When we are slumbering and grovelling on this earth we are very unfit to hear from God, and to converse with him. But, if God design instruction for us, he will be his grace awaken us out of our slumber, raise us from things below, and set us upright. 2. He promised to inform him: "Understand, O son of man! v. 17. Thou shalt understand, if thou wilt but apply thy mind to understand." He calls him son of man to intimate that he would consider his frame, and would deal tenderly with him, accommodating himself to his capacity as a man. Or thus he preaches humility to him; though he be admitted to converse with angels, he must not be puffed up with it, but must remember that he is a son of man. Or perhaps this title puts honour upon him: the Messiah was lately called the Son of man (ch. vii. 13), and Daniel is akin to him, and is a figure of him as a prophet and one greatly beloved. He assures him that he shall be made to know what shall be in the last end of the indignation, v. 19. Let it be laid up for a comfort to those who shall live to see these calamitous times that there shall be an end of them; the indignation shall cease (Isa. x. 25); it shall be overpast, Isa. xxvi. 20. It may intermit and return again, but the last end shall be glorious; good will follow it, nay, and good will be brought out of it. He tells him (v. 17), "At the time of the end shall be the vision; when the last end of the indignation comes, when the course of this providence is completed, then the vision shall be made plain and intelligible by the event, as the event shall be made plain and intelligible by the vision." Or, "At the time of the end of the Jewish church, in the latter days of it, shall this vision be accomplished, 300 or 400 years hence; understand it therefore, that thou mayest leave it on record for the generations to come." But is he ask more particularly, "When is the time of the end? And how long will it be before it arrive?" let this answer suffice (v. 19): At the time appointed the end shall be; it is fixed in the divine counsel, which cannot be altered and which must not be pried into.

V. The exposition which he gave him of the vision.

1. Concerning the two monarchies of Persia and Greece, v. 20-22. The ram signified the succession of the kings of Media and Persia; the rough goat signified the kings of Greece; the great horn was Alexander; the four horns that rose in his room were the four kingdoms into which his conquests were cantoned, of which before, v. 8. They are said to stand up out of the nations, but not in his power; none of them ever made the figure that Alexander did. Josephus relates that when Alexander had taken Tyre, and subdued Palestine, and was upon his march to Jerusalem, Jaddas, who was them high priest (Nehemiah mentions one of his name, ch. xii. 11), fearing his rage, had recourse to God by prayer and sacrifice for the common safety, and was by him warned in a dream that upon Alexander's approach he should throw open the gates of the city, and that he and the rest of the priests should go forth to meet him in their habits, and all the people in white. Alexander, seeing this company at a distance, went himself alone to the high priest, and, having prostrated himself before that God whose name was engraven in the golden plate of his mitre, he first saluted him; and, being asked by one of his own captains why he did so, he said that while he was yet in Macedon, musing on the conquest of Asia, there appeared to him a man like unto this, and thus attired, who invited him into Asia, and assured him of success in the conquest of it. The priests led him to the temple, where he offered sacrifice to the God of Israel as they directed him; and there they showed him this book of the prophet Daniel, that it was there foretold that a Grecian should come and destroy the Persians, which animated him very much in the expedition he was now meditating against Darius. Hereupon he took the Jews and their religion under his protection, promised to be kind to those of their religion in Babylon and Media, whither he was now marching, and in honour of him all the priests that had sons born that year called them Alexander. Joseph. lib. 11.

2. Concerning Antiochus, and his oppression of the Jews. This is said to be in the latter time of the kingdom of the Greeks, when the transgressors are come to the full (v. 23); that is, when the degenerate Jews have filled up the measure of their iniquity, and are ripe for this destruction, so that God cannot in honour bear with them any longer then shall stand up this king, to be flagellum Dei—the rod in God's hand for the chastising of the Jews. Now observe here, (1.) His character: He shall be a king of fierce countenance, insolent and furious, neither fearing God nor regarding man, understanding dark sentences, or (rather) versed in dark practices, the hidden things of dishonesty; he was master of all the arts of dissimulation and deceit, and knew the depths of Satan as well as any man. He was wise to do evil. (2.) His success. He shall make dreadful havoc of the nations about him: His power shall be mighty, bear down all before it, but not by his own power (v. 24), but partly by the assistance of his allies, Eumenes and Attalus, partly by the baseness and treachery of many of the Jews, even of the priests that came into his interests, and especially by the divine permission. it was not by his own power, but by a power given him from above, that he destroyed wonderfully, and thought he made himself a great man by being a great destroyer. He destroys wonderfully indeed, for he destroys, [1.] The mighty people, and they cannot

resist him by their power. The princes of Egypt cannot stand before him with all their forces, but he practises against them and prospers. Note, The mighty ones of the earth commonly meet with those at length that are too hard for them, that are more mighty than they. Let not the strong man then glory in his strength, be it ever so great, unless he could be sure that there were none stronger than he. [2.] He destroys the holy people, or the people of the holy ones; and their sacred character does neither deter him from destroying them nor defend them from being destroyed. All things come alike to all, and there is one event to the mighty and to the holy in this world. [3.] The methods by which he will gain this success, not by true courage, wisdom, or justice, but by his policy and craft (v. 25), by fraud and deceit, and serpentine subtlety: He shall cause craft to prosper; so cunningly shall he carry on his projects that he shall gain his point by the art of wheedling. By peace he shall destroy many, as others do by war; under the pretence of treaties, leagues, and alliances, with them, he shall encroach on their rights, and trick them into a subjection to him. Thus sometimes what a nation truly brave has gained in a righteous war a nation truly base has regained in a treacherous peace, and craft has been caused to prosper. [4.] The mischief that he shall do to religion: He shall magnify himself in his heart, and think himself fit to prescribe and give law to every body, so that he shall stand up against the Prince of princes, that is, against God himself. He will profane his temple and altar, prohibit his worship, and persecute his worshippers. See what a height of impudence some men's impiety brings them to; they openly bid defiance to God himself though he is the Kings of kings. [5.] The ruin that he shall be brought to at last: He shall be broken without hand, that is, without the hand of man. He shall not be slain in war, nor shall he be assassinated, as tyrants commonly were, but he shall fall into the hand of the living God and die by an immediate stroke of his vengeance. He, hearing that the Jews had cast the image of Jupiter Olympius out of the temple, where he had placed it, was so enraged at the Jews that he vowed he would make Jerusalem a common burial-place, and determined to march thither immediately; but no sooner had he spoken these proud words than he was struck with an incurable plague in his bowels; worms bred so fast in his body that whole flakes of flesh sometimes dropped from him; his torments were violent, and the stench of his disease such that none could endure to come near him.

He continued in this misery very long. At first he persisted in his menaces against the Jews; but at length, despairing of his recovery, he called his friends together, and acknowledged all those miseries to have fallen upon him for the injuries he had done to the Jews and his profaning the temple at Jerusalem. Then he wrote courteous letters to the Jews, and vowed that if he recovered he would let them have the free exercise of their religion. But, finding his disease grow upon him, when he could no longer endure his own smell, he said, It is meet to submit to God, and for man who is mortal not to set himself in competition with God, and so died miserably in a strange land, on the mountains of Pacata near Babylon: so Ussher's Annals, A.M. 3840, about 160 years before the birth of Christ.

3. As to the time fixed for the continuance of the cessation of the daily sacrifice, it is not explained here, but only confirmed (v. 26). That vision of the evening and morning is true, in the proper sense of the words, and needs no explication. How unlikely soever it might be that God should suffer his own sanctuary to be thus profaned, yet it is true, it is too true, so it shall be.
VI. Here is the conclusion of this vision, and here, 1. The charge given to Daniel to keep it private for the present: Shut thou up the vision; let it not be publicly know among the Chaldeans, lest the Persians, who were now shortly to possess the kingdom, should be incensed against the Jews by it, because the downfall of their kingdom was foretold by it, which would be unseasonable now that the edict for their release was expected from the king of Persia. Shut it up, for it shall be for many days. It was about 300 years from the time of this vision to the time of the accomplishment of it; therefore he must shut it up for the

present, even from the people of the Jews, lest it should amaze and perplex them, but let it be kept safely for the generations to come, that should live about the time of the accomplishment of it, for to them it would be both most intelligible and most serviceable. Note, What we know of the things of God should be carefully laid up, that hereafter, when there is occasion, it may be faithfully laid out; and what we have not now any use for, yet we may have another time. Divine truths should be sealed up among our treasures, that we may find them again after many days. 2. The care he took to keep it private, having received such a charge, v. 27. He fainted, and was sick, with the multitude of his thoughts within him occasioned by this vision, which oppressed and overwhelmed him the more because he was forbidden to publish what he had seen, so that his belly was as wine which has no vent, he was ready to burst like new bottles, Job xxxii. 19. However, he kept it to himself, stifled and smothered the concern he was in; so that those he conversed with could not perceive it, but he did the king's business according to the duty of his place, whatever it was. Note, As long as we live in this world we must have something to do in it; and even those whom God has most dignified with his favours must not think themselves above their business; nor must the pleasure of communion with God take us off from the duties of our particular callings, but still we must in them abide with God. Those especially that are entrusted with public business must see to it that they conscientiously discharge their trust.

Chapter 9

In this chapter we have, I. Daniel's prayer for the restoration of the Jews who were in captivity, in which he confesses sin, and acknowledges the justice of God in their calamities, but pleads God's promises of mercy which he had yet in store for them, ver. 1-19. II. An immediate answer sent him by an angel to his prayer, in which, 1. He is assured of the speedy release of the Jews out of their captivity, ver. 20-23. And, 2. He is informed concerning the redemption of the world by Jesus Christ (of which that was a type), what should be the nature of it and when it should be accomplished, ver. 24-27. And it is the clearest, brightest, prophecy of the Messiah, in all the Old Testament.

Daniel's Confession and Prayer. (b. c. 538.)

1 In the first year of Darius the son of Ahasuerus, of the seed of the Medes, which was made king over the realm of the Chaldeans; 2 In the first year of his reign I Daniel understood by books the number of the years, whereof the word of the Lord came to Jeremiah the prophet, that he would accomplish seventy years in the desolations of Jerusalem. 3 And I set my face unto the Lord God, to seek by prayer and supplications, with fasting, and sackcloth, and ashes:
We left Daniel, in the close of the foregoing chapter, employed in the king's business; but here we have him employed in better business than any king had for him, speaking to God and hearing from him, not for himself only, but for the church, whose mouth he was to God, and for whose use the oracles of God were committed to him, relating to the days of the Messiah. Observe, 1. When it was that Daniel had this communion with God (v. 1), in the first year of Darius the Mede, who was newly made king of the Chaldeans, Babylon being conquered by him and his nephew, or grandson, Cyrus. In this year the seventy years of the Jews' captivity ended, but the decree for their release was not yet issued out; so that this address of Daniel's to God seems to have been ready in that year, and, probably, before he was cast into the lions' den. And one powerful inducement, perhaps, it was to him then to keep so close to the duty of prayer, though it cost him his life, that he had so lately experienced the benefit and comfort of it. 2. What occasioned his address to God by prayer (v. 2): He understood by books that seventy years was the time fixed for the continuance of the desolations of Jerusalem. v. 2. The book by which he understood this was the book of the prophecies of Jeremiah, in which he found it expressly foretold (Jer. xxix. 10), After

seventy years be accomplished in Babylon (and therefore they must be reckoned from the first captivity, in the third year of Jehoiakim, which Daniel had reason to remember by a good token, for it was in that captivity that he was carried away himself, ch. i. 1),I will visit you, and perform my good word towards you. It was likewise said (Jer. xxv. 11), This whole land shall be seventy years a desolation (chorbath), the same word that Daniel here uses for the desolations of Jerusalem, which shows that he had that prophecy before him when he wrote this. Though Daniel was himself a great prophet, and one that was well acquainted with the visions of God, yet he was a diligent student in the scripture, and thought it no disparagement to him to consult Jeremiah's prophecies. He was a great politician, and prime-minister of state to one of the greatest monarchs upon earth, and yet could find both heart and time to converse with the word of God. The greatest and best men in the world must not think themselves above their Bibles. 3. How serious and solemn his address to God was when he understood that the seventy years were just upon expiring (for it appears, by Ezekiel's dating of his prophecies, that they exactly computed the years of their captivity), then he set his face to seek God by prayer. Note, God's promises are intended, not to supersede, but to excite and encourage, our prayers; and, when we see the day of the performance of them approaching, we should the more earnestly plead them with God and put them in suit. So Daniel did here; he prayed three times a day, and, no doubt, in every prayer made mention of the desolations of Jerusalem; yet he did not think that enough, but even in the midst of his business set time apart for an extraordinary application to Heaven on Jerusalem's behalf. God had said to Ezekiel that though Daniel, among others, stood before him, his intercession should not prevail to prevent the judgment (Ezek. xiv. 14), yet he hopes, now that the warfare is accomplished (Isa. xl. 2), his prayer may be heard for the removing of the judgment.

When the day of deliverance dawns it is time for God's praying people to bestir themselves; something extraordinary is then expected and required from them, besides their daily sacrifice. Now Daniel sought by prayer and supplications, for fear lest the sins of the people should provoke him to defer their deliverance longer than was intended, or rather that the people might be prepared by the grace of God for the deliverance now that the providence of God was about to work it out for them. Now observe, (1.) The intenseness of his mind in this prayer; I set my face unto the Lord God to seek him, which denotes the fixedness of his thoughts, the firmness of his faith, and the fervour of his devout affections, in the duty. We must, in prayer, set God before us, an set ourselves as in his presence; to him we must direct our prayer and must look up. Probably, in token of his setting his face towards God, he did, as usual, set his face towards Jerusalem, to affect his own heart the more with the desolations of it. (2.) The mortification of his body in this prayer. In token of his deep humiliation before God for his own sins, and the sins of his people, and the sense he had of his unworthiness, when he prayed he fasted, put on sackcloth, and lay in as he's, the more to affect himself with the desolations of Jerusalem, which he was praying for the repair of, and to make himself sensible that he was now about an extraordinary work.

Daniel's Confession and Prayer; Daniel's Prayer for His People. (b. c. 538.)

4 And I prayed unto the Lord my God, and made my confession, and said, O Lord, the great and dreadful God, keeping the covenant and mercy to them that love him, and to them that keep his commandments; 5 We have sinned, and have committed iniquity, and have done wickedly, and have rebelled, even by departing from thy precepts and from thy judgments: 6 Neither have we hearkened unto thy servants the prophets, which spake in thy name to our kings, our princes, and our fathers, and to all the people of the land. 7 O Lord, righteousness belongeth unto thee, but unto us confusion of faces, as at this day; to the men of Judah, and to the inhabitants of Jerusalem, and unto all Israel, that are near, and that are far off, through all the countries whither thou hast driven them, because of their trespass

that they have trespassed against thee. 8 O Lord, to us belongeth confusion of face, to our kings, to our princes, and to our fathers, because we have sinned against thee. 9 To the Lord our God belong mercies and forgivenesses, though we have rebelled against him; 10 Neither have we obeyed the voice of the Lord our God, to walk in his laws, which he set before us by his servants the prophets 11 Yea, all Israel have transgressed thy law, even by departing, that they might not obey thy voice; therefore the curse is poured upon us, and the oath that is written in the law of Moses the servant of God, because we have sinned against him. 12 And he hath confirmed his words, which he spake against us, and against our judges that judged us, by bringing upon us a great evil: for under the whole heaven hath not been done as hath been done upon Jerusalem. 13 As it is written in the law of Moses, all this evil is come upon us: yet made we not our prayer before the Lord our God, that we might turn from our iniquities, and understand thy truth. 14 Therefore hath the Lord watched upon the evil, and brought it upon us: for the Lord our God is righteous in all his works which he doeth: for we obeyed not his voice. 15 And now, O Lord our God, that hast brought thy people forth out of the land of Egypt with a mighty hand, and hast gotten thee renown, as at this day; we have sinned, we have done wickedly. 16 O Lord, according to all thy righteousness, I beseech thee, let thine anger and thy fury be turned away from thy city Jerusalem, thy holy mountain: because for our sins, and for the iniquities of our fathers, Jerusalem and thy people are become a reproach to all that are about us. 17 Now therefore, O our God, hear the prayer of thy servant, and his supplications, and cause thy face to shine upon thy sanctuary that is desolate, for the Lord's sake. 18 O my God, incline thine ear, and hear; open thine eyes, and behold our desolations, and the city which is called by thy name: for we do not present our supplications before thee for our righteousnesses, but for thy great mercies. 19 O Lord, hear; O Lord, forgive; O Lord, hearken and do; defer not, for thine own sake, O my God: for thy city and thy people are called by thy name.

We have here Daniel's prayer to God as his God, and the confession which he joined with that prayer: I prayed, and made my confession. Note, In every prayer we must make confession, not only of the sins we have been guilty of (which we commonly call confession), but of our faith in God and dependence upon him, our sorrow for sin and our resolutions against it. It must be our confession, must be the language of our own convictions and that which we ourselves do heartily subscribe to.

Let us go over the several parts of this prayer, which we have reason to think that he offered up much more largely than is here recorded, these being only the heads of it.
I. Here is his humble, serious, reverent address to God, 1. As a God to be feared, and whom it is our duty always to stand in awe of: "O Lord! the great and dreadful God, that art able to deal with the greatest and most terrible of the church's enemies." 2. As a God to be trusted, and whom it is our duty to depend upon and put a confidence in: Keeping the covenant and mercy to those that love him, and, as a proof of their love to him, keep his commandments. If we fulfil our part of the bargain, he will not fail to fulfil his. He will be to his people as good as his word, for he keeps covenant with them, and not one iota of his promise shall fall to the ground; nay, he will be better than his word, for he keeps mercy to them, something more than was in the covenant. It was proper for Daniel to have his eye upon God's mercy now that he was to lay before him the miseries of his people, and upon God's covenant now that he was to sue for the performance of a promise. Note, We should, in prayer, look both at God's greatness and his goodness, his majesty and mercy in conjunction.

II. Here is a penitent confession of sin, the procuring cause of all the calamities which his people had for so many years been groaning under, v. 5, 6. When we seek to God for national mercies we ought to humble ourselves before him for national sins. These are the sins Daniel here laments; and we may here observe the variety of words he makes use of to set forth the greatness of their provocations (for it becomes penitents to lay load upon themselves): We have sinned in many particular instances, nay, we have committed iniquity, we have driven a trade of sin, we have done wickedly with a hard heart and a stiff neck, and herein we have rebelled, have taken up arms against the King of kings, his crown and dignity. Two things aggravated their sins:—1. That they had violated the express laws God had given them by Moses: "We have departed from thy precepts and from thy judgments, and have not conformed to them. And (v. 10) we have not obeyed the voice of the Lord our God." That which speaks the nature of sin, that it is the transgression of the law, does sufficiently speak the malignity of it; if sin be made to appear sin, it cannot be made to appear worse; its sinfulness is its greatest hatefulness, Rom. vii. 13. God has set his laws before us plainly and fully, as the copy we should write after, yet we have not walked in them, but turned aside, or turned back. 2. That they had slighted the fair warnings God had given them by the prophets, which in every age he had sent to them, rising up betimes and sending them (v. 6): "We have not hearkened to thy servants the prophets, who have put us in mind of thy laws, and of the sanctions of them; though they spoke in thy name, we have not regarded them; though they delivered their message faithfully, with a universal respect to all orders and degrees of men, to our kings and princes, whom they had the courage and confidence to speak to, to our fathers, and to all the people of the land, whom they had the condescension and compassion to speak to, yet we have not hearkened to them, nor heard them, or not heeded them, or not complied with them." Mocking God's messengers, and despising his words, were Jerusalem's measure-filling sins, 2 Chron. xxxvi. 16. This confession of sin is repeated here, and much insisted on; penitents should again and again accuse and reproach themselves till they find their hearts thoroughly broken. All Israel have transgressed thy law, v. 11. It is Israel, God's professing people, who have known better, and from whom better is expected—Israel, God's peculiar people, whom he has surrounded with his favours; not here and there one, but it is all Israel, the generality of them, the body of the people, that have transgressed by departing and getting out of the way, that they might not hear, and so might not obey, thy voice. This disobedience is that which all true penitents do most sensibly charge upon themselves (v. 14): We obeyed not his voice, and (v. 15) we have sinned, we have done wickedly. Those that would find mercy must thus confess their sins.

III. Here is a self-abasing acknowledgment of the righteousness of God in all the judgments that were brought upon them; and it is evermore the way of true penitents thus to justify God, that he may be clear when he judges, and the sinner may bear all the blame. 1. He acknowledges that it was sin that plunged them in all these troubles. Israel is dispersed through all the countries about, and so weakened, impoverished, and exposed. God's hand has driven them hither and thither, some near, where they are known and therefore the more ashamed, others afar off, where they are not known and therefore the more abandoned, and it is because of their trespass that they have trespassed (v. 7); they mingled themselves with the nations that they might be debauched by them, and now God mingles them with the nations that they might be stripped by them. 2. He owns the righteousness of God in it, that he had done them no wrong in all he had brought upon them, but had dealt with them as they deserved (v. 7): "O Lord! righteousness belongs to thee; we have no fault to find with thy providence, no exceptions to make against thy judgments, for (v. 14) the Lord our God is righteous in all his works which he does, even in the sore calamities we are now under, for we obeyed not the words of his mouth, and therefore justly feel the weight of his hand." This seems to be borrowed from Lam. i. 18. 3. He takes notice of the fulfilling of the scripture in what was brought upon them. In very faithfulness he afflicted them; for it was according to the word which he had spoken. The curse is poured upon us and the oath, that is, the curse that was ratified by an oath in the law of Moses, v. 11. This further justifies God in their troubles, that he did but inflict the penalty of the law, which he had given them fair notice of. It was necessary for the preserving of the honour of God's veracity, and saving his government from contempt, that the threatenings of his word should be accomplished, otherwise they look but as bugbears, nay, they seem not at all frightful. Therefore he has confirmed his words which spoke against us because we broke his laws, and against our judges that judged us because they did not according to the duty of their place punish the breach of God's laws. He told them many a time that if they did not execute justice, as terrors to evil-workers, he must and would take the work into his own hands; and now he has confirmed what he said by bringing upon us a great evil, in which the princes and judges themselves deeply shared. Note, It contributes very much to our profiting by the judgments of God's hand to observe how exactly they agree with the judgments of his mouth. 4. He aggravates the calamities they were in, lest they should seem, having been long used to them, to make light of them, and so to lose the benefit of the chastening of the Lord by despising it. "It is not some of the common troubles of life that we are complaining of, but that which has in it some special marks of divine displeasure; for under the whole heaven has not been done as has been done upon Jerusalem," v. 12. It is Jeremiah's lamentation in the name of the church, Was ever sorrow like unto my sorrow? which must suppose another similar question, Was ever sin like unto my sin? 5. He puts shame upon the whole nation, from the highest to the lowest; and if they will say Amen to his prayer, as it was fit they should if they would come in for a share in the benefit of it, they must all put their hand upon their mouth, and their mouth in the dust: "To us belongs confusion of faces as at this day (v. 7); we lie under the shame of the punishment of our iniquity, for shame is our due." If Israel had retained their character, and had continued a holy people, they would have been high above all nations in praise, and name, and honour (Deut. xxvi. 19); but now that they have sinned and done wickedly confusion and disgrace belong to them, to the men of Judah and the inhabitants of Jerusalem, the inhabitants both of the country and of the city, for they have been all alike guilty before God; it belongs to all Israel, both to the two tribes, that are near, by the rivers of Babylon, and to the ten tribes, that are afar off, in the land of Assyria. "Confusion belongs not only to the common people of our land, but to our kings, our princes, and our fathers (v. 8), who should have set a better example, and have used their authority and influence for the checking of the threatening torrent of vice profaneness." 6. He imputes the continuance of the judgment to their incorrigibleness under it (v. 13, 14): "All this evil has come upon us, and has lain long upon us, yet made we not our prayer before the Lord our God, not in a right manner, as we should have made it, with a humble, lowly, penitent, and obedient heart. We have been smitten, but have not returned to him that smote us.

We have not entreated the face of the Lord our God" (so the word is); "we have taken no care to make our peace with God and reconcile ourselves to him." Daniel set his brethren a good example of praying continually, but he was sorry to see how few there were that followed his example; in their affliction it was expected that they would seek God early, but they sought him not, that they might turn from their iniquities and understand his truth. The errand upon which afflictions are sent is to bring men to turn from their iniquities and to understand God's truth; so Elihu had explained them, Job xxxvi. 10. God by them opens men's ears to discipline and commands that they return from iniquity. And if men were brought rightly to understand God's truth, and to submit to the power and authority of it, they would turn from the error of their ways. Now the first step towards this is to make our prayer before the Lord our God, that the affliction may be sanctified before it is removed, and that the grace of God may go along with the providence of God, to make it answer the end. Those who in their affliction make not their prayer to God, who cry not when he binds them, are not likely to turn from iniquity or to understand his truth. "Therefore, because we have not improved the affliction, the Lord has watched upon the evil, as the judge takes care that execution be done according to the sentence. Because we have not been melted, he has kept us still in the furnace, and watched over it, to make the heat yet more intense;" for when God judges he will overcome, and will be justified in all his proceedings.

IV. Here is a believing appeal to the mercy of God, and to the ancient tokens of his favour to Israel, and the concern of his own glory in their interests. 1. It is some comfort to them (and not a little) that God has been always ready to pardon sin (v. 9): To the Lord our God belong mercies and forgiveness; this refers to that proclamation of his name, Exod. xxxiv. 6, 7, The Lord God, gracious and merciful, forgiving iniquity. Note, It is very encouraging to poor sinners to recollect that mercies belong to God, as it is convincing and humbling to them to recollect that righteousness belongs to him; and those who give him the glory of his righteousness may take to themselves the comfort of his mercies, Ps. lxii. 12. There are abundant mercies in God, and not only forgiveness but forgivenesses; he is a God of pardons (Neh. ix. 17, marg.); he multiplies to pardon, Isa. lv. 7. Though we have rebelled against him, yet with him there is mercy, pardoning mercy, even for the rebellious. 2. It is likewise a support to them to think that God had formerly glorified himself by delivering them out of Egypt; so far he looks back for the encouragement of his faith (v. 15): "Thou hast formerly brought thy people out of Egypt with a mighty hand, and wilt thou not now with the same mighty hand bring them out of Babylon? Were they then formed into a people, and shall they not now be reformed and new-formed? Are they now sinful and unworthy, and were they not so then? Are their oppressors now mighty and haughty, and were they not so then? And has not God said that their deliverance out of Babylon shall outshine even that out of Egypt?" Jer. xvi. 14, 15. The force of this plea lies in that, "Thou hast gotten thyself renown, hast made thyself a name" (so the word is) "as at this day, even to this day, by bringing us out of Egypt; and wilt thou lose the credit of that by letting us perish in Babylon? Didst thou get a renown by that deliverance which we have so often commemorated, and wilt thou not now get thyself a renown by this which we have so often prayed for, and so long waited for?"

V. Here is a pathetic complaint of the reproach that God's people lay under, and the ruins that God's sanctuary lay in, both which redounded very much to the dishonour of God and the diminution of that name and renown which God had gained by bringing them out of Egypt. 1. God's holy people were despised. By their sins and the iniquities of their fathers they had profaned their crown and made themselves despicable, and then though they are, in name and profession, God's people, and upon that account truly great and honourable, yet they become a reproach to all that are round about them. Their neighbours laugh them to scorn, and triumph in their disgrace. Note, Sin is a reproach to any people, but especially to God's people, that have more eyes upon them and have more honour to lose than other people. 2. God's holy place was desolate. Jerusalem, the holy city, was a reproach (v. 16) when it lay in ruins; it was an astonishment and a hissing to all that passed by. The sanctuary, the holy house, was desolate (v. 17), the altars were demolished, and all the buildings laid in ashes. Note, The desolations of the sanctuary are the grief of all the saints, who reckon all their comforts in this world buried in the ruins of the sanctuary.

VI. Here is an importunate request to God for the restoring of the poor captive Jews to their former enjoyments again. The petition is very pressing, for God gives us leave in prayer to wrestle with him: "O Lord! I beseech thee, v. 16. If ever thou wilt do any thing for me, do this; it is my heart's desire and prayer. Now therefore, O our God! hear the prayer of thy servant and his supplication (v. 17), and grant an answer of peace." Now what are his petitions? What are his requests? 1. That God would turn away his wrath from them; that is it which all the saints dread and deprecate more than any thing: O let thy anger be turned away from thy Jerusalem, thy holy mountain! v. 16. He does not pray for the turning again of their captivity (let the Lord do with them as seems good in his eyes), but he prays first for the turning away of God's wrath. Take away the cause, and the effect will cease. 2. That he would lift up the light of his countenance upon them (v. 17): "Cause thy face to shine upon thy sanctuary that is desolate; return in thy mercy to us, and show that thou art reconciled to us, and then all shall be well." Note, The shining of God's face upon the desolations of the sanctuary is all in all towards the repair of it; and upon that foundation it must be rebuilt. If therefore its friends would begin their work at the right end, they must first be earnest with

God in prayer for his favour, and recommend his desolate sanctuary to his smiles. Cause thy face to shine and then we shall be saved, Ps. lxxx. 3. 3. That he would forgive their sins, and then hasten their deliverance (v. 19): O Lord! hear; O Lord! forgive. "That the mercy prayed for may be granted in mercy, let the sin that threatens to come between us and it be removed: O Lord! hearken and do, not hearken and speak only, but hearken and do; do that for us which none else can, and that speedily—defer not, O my God!" Now that he saw the appointed day approaching he could in faith pray that God would make haste to them and not defer. David often prays, Make haste, O God! to help me.

VII. Here are several pleas and arguments to enforce the petitions. God gives us leave not only to pray, but to plead with him, which is not to move him (he himself knows what he will do), but to move ourselves, to excite our fervency and encourage our faith. 1. They disdain a dependence upon any righteousness of their own; they pretend not to merit any thing at God's hand but wrath and the curse (v. 18): "We do not present our supplications before thee with hope to speed for our righteousness, as if we were worthy to receive thy favour for any good in us, or done by us, or could demand any thing as a debt; we cannot insist upon our own justification, no, though we were more righteous than we are; nay, though we knew nothing amiss of ourselves, yet are we not thereby justified, nor would we answer, but we would make supplication to our Judge." Moses had told Israel long before that, whatever God did for them, it was not for their righteousness, Deut. ix. 4, 5. And Ezekiel had of late told them that their return out of Babylon would be not for their sakes, Ezek. xxxvi. 22, 32. Note, Whenever we come to God for mercy we must lay aside all conceit of, and confidence in, our own righteousness. 2. They take their encouragement in prayer from God only, as knowing that his reasons of mercy are fetched from within himself, and therefore from him we must borrow all our pleas for mercy, and so give honour to him when we are suing for grace and mercy from him. (1.) "Do it for thy own sake (v. 19), for the accomplishment of thy own counsel, the performance of thy own promise, and the manifestation of thy own glory." Note, God will do his own work, not only in his own way and time, but for his own sake, and so we must take it. (2.) "Do it for the Lord's sake, that is, for the Lord Christ's sake," for the sake of the Messiah promised, who is the Lord (so the most and best of our Christian interpreters understand it), for the sake of Adonai, so David called the Messiah (Ps. cx. 1), and mercy is prayed for for the church for the sake of the Son of man (Ps. lxxx. 17), and for thy Word's sake, he is Lord of all. It is for his sake that God causes his face to shine upon sinners when they repent and turn to him, because of the satisfaction he has made. In all our prayers that therefore must be our plea; we must make mention of his righteousness, even of his only, Ps. lxxi. 16. Look upon the face of the anointed. He has himself directed us to ask in his name. (3.) "Do it according to all thy righteousness (v. 16), that is, plead for us against our persecutors and oppressors according to thy righteousness. Though we are ourselves unrighteous before God, yet with reference to them we have a righteous cause, which we leave it with the righteous God to appear in the defence of." Or, rather, by the righteousness of God here is meant his faithfulness to his promise. God had, according to his righteousness, executed the threatening, v. 11. "Now, Lord, wilt thou not do according to all thy righteousness? Wilt thou not be as true to thy promises as thou hast been to thy threatenings and accomplish them also?" (4.) "Do it for thy great mercies (v. 18), to make it to appear that thou art a merciful God." The good things we ask of God we call mercies, because we expect them purely from God's mercy. And, because misery is the proper object of mercy, the prophet here spreads the deplorable condition of the church before God, as it were to move his compassion: "Open thy eyes and behold our desolations, especially the desolations of the sanctuary. O look with pity upon a pitiable case!" Note, The desolations of the church must in prayer be laid before God and then left with him. (5.) "Do it for the sake of the relation we stand in to thee. The sanctuary that is desolate is thy sanctuary (v. 17), dedicated to thy honour, employed in thy service, and the place of thy residence. Jerusalem is thy city and thy holy mountain (v. 16); it is the city which is called by thy name," v. 18. It was the city which God had chosen out of all the tribes of Israel, to put his name there. "The people that have become a reproach are thy people, and thy name suffers in the reproach cast upon them (v. 16); they are called by thy name, v. 19. Lord, thou hast a property in them, and therefore art interested in their interests; wilt thou not provide for thy own, for those of thy own house? They are thine, save them," Ps. cxix. 94.

Daniel's Prayer Answered; The Answer to Daniel's Prayer; The Coming of the Messiah; Destruction of Jerusalem Foretold. (b. c. 538.)

20 And whiles I was speaking, and praying, and confessing my sin and the sin of my people Israel, and presenting my supplication before the Lord my God for the holy mountain of my God; 21 Yea, whiles I was speaking in prayer, even the man Gabriel, whom I had seen in the vision at the beginning, being caused to fly swiftly, touched me about the time of the evening oblation. 22 And he informed me, and talked with me, and said, O Daniel, I am now come forth to give thee skill and understanding. 23 At the beginning of thy supplications the commandment came forth, and I am come to show thee; for thou art greatly beloved: therefore understand the matter, and consider the vision. 24 Seventy weeks are determined upon thy people and upon thy holy city, to finish the transgression, and to make an end of sins, and to make reconciliation for iniquity, and to bring in everlasting righteousness, and to seal up the vision and prophecy, and to anoint the most Holy. 25 Know therefore and understand, that from the going forth of the commandment to restore and to build Jerusalem unto the Messiah the Prince shall be seven weeks, and threescore and two weeks: the street shall be built again, and the wall, even in troublous times. 26 And after threescore and two weeks shall Messiah be cut off, but not for himself: and the people of the prince that shall come shall destroy the city and the sanctuary; and the end thereof shall be with a flood, and unto the end of the war desolations are determined. 27 And he shall confirm the covenant with many for one week: and in the midst of the week he shall cause the sacrifice and the oblation to cease, and for the overspreading of abominations he shall make it desolate, even until the consummation, and that determined shall be poured upon the desolate.

We have here the answer that was immediately sent to Daniel's prayer, and it is a very memorable one, as it contains the most illustrious prediction of Christ and gospel-grace that is extant in all the Old Testament. If John Baptist was the morning-star, this was the day-break to the Sun of righteousness, the day-spring from on high. Here is,

I. The time when this answer was given.

1. It was while Daniel was at prayer. This he observed and laid a strong emphasis upon: While I was speaking (v. 20), yea, while I was speaking in prayer (v. 21), before he rose from his knees, and while there was yet more which he intended to say.

(1.) He mentions the two heads he chiefly insisted upon in prayer, and which perhaps he designed yet further to enlarge upon. [1.] He was confessing sin and lamenting that—"both my sin and the sin of my people Israel." Daniel was a very great and good man, and yet he finds sin of his own to confess before God and is ready to confess it; for there is not a just man upon earth that does good and sins not, nor that sins and repents not. St. John puts himself into the number of those who deceive themselves if they say that they have no sin, and who therefore confess their sins, 1 John i. 8. Good men find it an ease to their consciences to pour out their complaints before the Lord against themselves; and that is confessing sin. He also confessed the sin of his people, and bewailed that. Those who are heartily concerned for the glory of God, the welfare of the church, and the souls of men, will mourn for the sins of others as well as for their own. [2.] He was making supplication before the Lord his God, and presenting it to him as an intercessor for Israel; and in this prayer his concern was for the holy mountain of his God, Mount Zion. The desolations of the sanctuary lay nearer his heart than those of the city and the land; and the repair of that, and the setting up of the public worship of God of Israel again, were the things he had in view, in the deliverance he was preparing for, more than re-establishment of their civil interests. Now,

(2.) While Daniel was thus employed, [1.] He had a grant made him of the mercy he prayed for. Note, God is very ready to hear prayer and to give an answer of peace. Now was fulfilled what God had spoken Isa. lxv. 24, While they are yet speaking, I will hear. Daniel grew very fervent in prayer, and his affections were very strong, v. 18, 19. And, while he was speaking with such fervour and ardency, the angel came to him with a gracious answer. God is well pleased with lively devotions. We cannot now expect that God should send us answers to our prayer by angels, but, if we pray with fervency for that which God has promised, we may by faith take the promise as an immediate answer to the prayer; for he is faithful that has promised. [2.] He had a discovery made to him of a far greater and more glorious redemption which God would work out for his church in the latter days. Note, Those that would be brought acquainted with Christ and his grace must be much in prayer.

2. It was about the time of the evening oblation, v. 21. The altar was in ruins, and there was no oblation offered upon it, but, it should seem, the pious Jews in their captivity were daily thoughtful of the time when it should have been offered, and at that hour were ready to weep at the remembrance of it, and desired and hoped that their prayer should be set forth before God as incense, and the lifting up of their hands, and their hearts with their hands, should be acceptable in his sight as the evening-sacrifice, Ps. cxli. 2. The evening oblation was a type of the great sacrifice which Christ was to offer in the evening of the world, and it was in the virtue of that sacrifice that Daniel's prayer was accepted when he prayed for the Lord's sake; and for the sake of that this glorious discovery of redeeming love was made to him. The Lamb opened the seals in the virtue of his own blood.

II. The messenger by whom this answer was sent. It was not given him in a dream, nor by a voice from heaven, but, for the greater certainty and solemnity of it, an angel was sent on purpose, appearing in a human shape, to give this answer to Daniel. Observe,

1. Who this angel, or messenger, was; it was the man Gabriel. If Michael the archangel be, as many suppose, no other than Jesus Christ, this Gabriel is the only created angel that is named in scripture. Gabriel signifies the mighty one of God; for the angels are great in power and might, 2 Pet. ii. 11. It was he whom I had seen in the vision at the beginning. Daniel heard him called by his name, and thence learned it (Dan. viii. 16); and, though then he trembled at his approach, yet he observed him so carefully that now he knew him again, knew him to be the same that he had seen at the beginning, and, being somewhat better acquainted with him, was not now so terrified at the sight of him as he had been at first. When this angel said to Zacharias, I am Gabriel (Luke i. 19), he intended thereby to put him in mind of this notice which he had given to Daniel of the Messiah's coming when it was at a distance, for the confirming of his faith in the notice he was then about to give of it as at the door.

2. The instructions which this messenger received from the Father of lights to whom Daniel prayed (v. 23): At the beginning of thy supplications the word, the commandment, came forth from God. Notice was given to the angels in heaven of this counsel of God, which they were desirous to look into; and orders were given to Gabriel to go immediately and bring the notice of it to Daniel. By this it appears that it was not any thing which Daniel said that moved God, for the answer was given as he began to pray; but God was well pleased

with his serious solemn address to the duty, and, in token of that, sent him this gracious message. Or perhaps it was at the beginning of Daniel's supplications that Cyrus's word, or commandment, went forth to restore and to build Jerusalem, that going forth spoken of v. 25. "The thing was done this very day; the proclamation of liberty to the Jews was signed this morning, just when thou wast praying for it;" and now, at the close of this fast-day, Daniel had notice of it, as, at the close of the day of atonement, the jubilee-trumpet sounded to proclaim liberty.

3. The haste he made to deliver his message: He was caused to fly swiftly, v. 21. Angels are winged messengers, quick in their motions, and delay not to execute the orders they receive; they run and return like a flash of lightning, Ezek. i. 14. But, it should seem, sometimes they are more expeditious than at other times, and make a quicker despatch, as here the angel was caused to fly swiftly; that is, he was ordered and he was enabled to fly swiftly. Angels do their work in obedience to divine command and in dependence upon divine strength. Though they excel in wisdom, they fly swifter or slower as God directs; and, though they excel in power, they fly but as God causes them to fly. Angels themselves are to us what he makes them to be; they are his ministers, and do his pleasure, Ps. ciii. 21.

4. The prefaces or introductions to his message. (1.) He touched him (v. 21), as before (ch. viii. 18), not to awaken him out of sleep as then, but to give him a hint to break off his prayer and to attend to that which he has to say in answer to it. Note, In order to the keeping up of our communion with God we must not only be forward to speak to God, but as forward to hear what he has to say to us; when we have prayed we must look up, must look after our prayers, must set ourselves upon our watch-tower. (2.) He talked with him (v. 22), talked familiarly with him, as one friend talks with another, that his terror might not make him afraid. He informed him on what errand he came, that he was sent from heaven on purpose with a kind message to him: "I have come to show thee (v. 23), to tell thee that which thou didst not know before." He had shown him the troubles of the church under Antiochus, and the period of those troubles (ch. viii. 19); but now he has greater things to show him, for he that is faithful in a little shall be entrusted with more. "Nay, I have now come forth to give thee skill and understanding (v. 22), not only to show thee these things, but to make thee understand them." (3.) He assured him that he was a favourite of Heaven, else he would not have had this intelligence sent him, and he must take it for a favour: "I have come to show thee, for thou art greatly beloved. Thou art a man of desires, acceptable to God, and whom he has a favour for." Note, Though God loves all his children, yet there are some that are more than the rest greatly beloved. Christ had one disciple that lay in his bosom; and that beloved disciple was he that was entrusted with the prophetical visions of the New Testament, as Daniel was with those of the Old. For what greater token can there be of God's favour to any man than for the secrets of the Lord to be with him? Abraham is the friend of God; and therefore Shall I hide from Abraham that thing which I do? Gen. xviii. 17. Note, Those may reckon themselves greatly beloved of God to whom, and in whom, he reveals his Son. Some observe that the title which this angel Gabriel gives to the Virgin Mary is much the same with this which he here gives to Daniel, as if he designed to put her in mind of it—Thou that art highly favoured; as Daniel, greatly beloved. (4.) He demands his serious attention to the discovery he was now about to make to him: Therefore understand the matter, and consider the vision, v. 23. This intimates that it was a thing well worthy of his regard, above any of the visions he had been before favoured with. Note, Those who would understand the things of God must consider them, must apply their minds to them, ponder upon them, and compare spiritual things with spiritual. The reason why we are so much in the dark concerning the revealed will of God, and mistake concerning it, is want of consideration. This vision both requires and deserves consideration.

III. The message itself. It was delivered with great solemnity, received no doubt with great attention, and recorded with great exactness; but in it, as is usual in prophecies, there are things dark and hard to be understood. Daniel, who understood by the book of the prophet Jeremiah the expiration of the seventy years of the captivity, is now honourably employed to make known to the church another more glorious release, which that was but a shadow of, at the end of another seventy, not years, but weeks of years. He prayed over that prophecy, and received this in answer to that prayer. He had prayed for his people and the holy city— that they might be released, that it might be rebuilt; but God answers him above what he was able to ask or think. God not only grants, but outdoes, the desires of those that fear him, Ps. xxi. 4.

1. The times here determined are somewhat hard to be understood. In general, it is seventy weeks, that is, seventy times seven years, which makes just 490 years. The great affairs that are yet to come concerning the people of Israel, and the city of Jerusalem, will lie within the compass of these years.

(1.) These years are thus described by weeks, |1.| In conformity to the prophetic style, which is, for the most part, abstruse, and out of the common road of speaking, that the things foretold might not lie too obvious. |2.| To put an honour upon the division of time into weeks, which is made purely by the sabbath day, and to signify that that should be perpetual. |3.| With reference to the seventy years of the captivity; as they had been so long kept out of the possession of their own land, so, being now restored to it they should seven times as long be kept in the possession of it. So much more does God delight in showing mercy than in punishing. The land had enjoyed its sabbaths, in a melancholy sense, seventy years, Lev. xxvi. 34. But now the people of the Lord shall, in a comfortable sense, enjoy their sabbaths seven times seventy years, and in them seventy sabbatical years, which makes ten jubilees. Such proportions are there in the disposals of Providence, that we might see and admire the wisdom of him who has determined the times before appointed.

(2.) The difficulties that arise about these seventy weeks are, |1.| Concerning the time when they commence and whence they are to be reckoned. They are here dated from the going forth of the commandments to restore and to build Jerusalem, v. 25. I should most incline to understand this of the edict of Cyrus mentioned Ezra i. 1, for by it the people were restored; and, though express mention be not made there of the building of Jerusalem, yet that is supposed in the building of the temple, and was foretold to be done by Cyrus, Isa. xliv. 28. He shall say to Jerusalem, Thou shalt be built. That was, both in prophecy and in history, the most famous decree for the building of Jerusalem; nay, it should seem, this going forth of the commandment (which may as well be meant of God's command concerning it as of Cyrus's) is the same with that going forth of the commandment mentioned v. 23, which was at the beginning of Daniel's supplications. And it looks very graceful that the seventy weeks should begin immediately upon the expiration of the seventy years. And there is nothing to be objected against this but that by this reckoning the Persian monarchy, from the taking of Babylon by Cyrus to Alexander's conquest of Darius, lasted but 130 years; whereas, by the particular account given of the reigns of the Persian emperors, it is computed that it continued 230 years. So Thucydides, Xenophon, and others reckon. Those who fix it to that first edict set aside these computations of the heathen historians as uncertain and not to be relied upon. But others, willing to reconcile them, begin the 490 years, not at the edict of Cyrus (Ezra i. 1), but at the second edict for the building of Jerusalem, issued out by Darius Nothus above 100 years after, mentioned Ezra vi. Others fix on the seventh year of Artaxerxes Mnemon, who sent Ezra with a commission, Ezra vii. 8-12. The learned Mr. Poole, in his Latin Synopsis, has a vast and most elaborate collection of what has been said, pro and con, concerning the different beginnings of these weeks, with which the learned may entertain themselves. |2.| Concerning the termination of them; and here likewise interpreters are not agreed. Some make them to end at the death of Christ, and think the express words of this famous prophecy will warrant us to conclude that from this very hour when Gabriel spoke to Daniel, at the time of the evening oblation, to the hour when Christ died, which was towards evening too, it was exactly 490 years; and I am willing enough to be of that opinion. But others think, because it is said that in the midst of the weeks (that is, the last of the seventy weeks) he shall cause the sacrifice and the oblation to cease, they end three years and a half after the death of Christ, when the Jews having rejected the gospel, the apostles turned to the Gentiles. But those who make them to end precisely at the death of Christ read it thus, "He shall make strong the testament to the many; the last seven, or the last week, yea, half that seven, or half that week (namely, the latter half, the three years and a half which Christ spent in his public ministry), shall bring to an end sacrifice and oblation." Others make these 490 years to end with the destruction of Jerusalem, about thirty-seven years after the death of Christ, because these seventy weeks are said to be determined upon the people of the Jews and the holy city; and much is said here concerning the destruction of the city and the sanctuary. [3.] Concerning the division of them into seven weeks, and sixty-two weeks, and one week; and the reason of this is as hard to account for as any thing else. In the first seven weeks, or forty-nine years, the temple and city were built; and in the last single week Christ preached his gospel, by which the Jewish economy was taken down, and the foundations were laid of the gospel city and temple, which were to be built upon the ruins of the former.

(3.) But, whatever uncertainty we may labour under concerning the exact fixing of these times, there is enough clear and certain to answer the two great ends of determining them. [1.] It did serve them to raise and support the expectations of believers. There were general promises of the coming of the Messiah made to the patriarchs; the preceding prophets had often spoken of him as one that should come, but never was the time fixed for his coming until now. And, though there might be so much doubt concerning the date of this reckoning that they could not ascertain the time just to a year, yet by the light of this prophecy they were directed about what time to expect him. And we find, accordingly, that when Christ came he was generally looked for as the consolation of Israel, and redemption in Jerusalem by him, Luke ii. 25, 38. There were those that for this reason thought the kingdom of God should immediately appear (Luke xix. 11), and some think it was this that brought a more than ordinary concourse of people to Jerusalem, Acts ii. 5. [2.] It does serve still to refute and silence the expectations of unbelievers, who will not own that Jesus is he who should come, but still look for another. This prediction should silence them, and will condemn them; for, reckon these seventy weeks from which of the commandments to build Jerusalem we please, it is certain that they have expired above 1500 years ago; so that the Jews are for ever without excuse, who will not own that the Messiah has come when they have gone so far beyond their utmost reckoning for his coming. But by this we are confirmed in our belief of the Messiah's being come, and that our Jesus is he, that he came just at the time prefixed, a time worthy to be had in everlasting remembrance.

2. The events here foretold are more plain and easy to be understood, at least to us now. Observe what is here foretold,

(1.) Concerning the return of the Jews now speedily to their own land, and their settlement again there, which was the thing that Daniel now principally prayed for; and yet it is but briefly touched upon here in the answer to his prayer. Let this be a comfort to the pious Jews, that a commandment shall go forth to restore and to build Jerusalem, v. 25. And the commandment shall not be in vain; for though the times will be very troublous, and this good work will meet with great opposition, yet it shall be carried on, and brought to perfection at last. The street shall be built again, as spacious and splendid as ever it was.

Note, as long as we are here in this world we must expect troublous times, upon some account or other. Even when we have joyous times we must rejoice with trembling; it is but a gleam, it is but a lucid interval of peace and prosperity; the clouds will return after the rain. When the Jews are restored in triumph to their own land, yet there they must expect troublous times, and prepare for them. But this is our comfort, that God will carry on his own work, will build up his Jerusalem, will beautify it, will fortify it, even in troublous times; nay, the troublousness of the times may by the grace of God contribute to the advancement of the church. The more it is afflicted the more it multiplies.

(2.) Concerning the Messiah and his undertaking. The carnal Jews looked for a Messiah that could deliver them from the Roman yoke and give them temporal power and wealth, whereas they were here told that the Messiah should come upon another errand, purely spiritual, and upon the account of which he should be the more welcome.

[1.] Christ came to take away sin, and to abolish that. Sin had made a quarrel between God and man, had alienated men from God and provoked God against man; it was this that put dishonour upon God and brought misery upon mankind; this was the great mischief-maker. He that would do God a real service, and man a real kindness, must be the destruction of this. Christ undertakes to be so, and for this purpose he is manifested, to destroy the works of the devil. He does not say to finish your transgressions and your sins, but transgression and sin in general, for he is the propitiation not only for our sins, that are Jews, but for the sins of the whole world. He came, First, To finish transgression, to restrain it (so some), to break the power of it, to bruise the head of that serpent that had done so much mischief, to take away the usurped dominion of that tyrant, and to set up a kingdom of holiness and love in the hearts of men, upon the ruins of Satan's kingdom there, that, where sin and death had reigned, righteousness and life through grace might reign. When he died he said, It is finished; sin has now had its death-wound given it, like Samson's, Let me die with the Philistines. Animamque in vulnere ponit—He inflicts the wound and dies. Secondly, To make an end of sin, to abolish it, that it may not rise up in judgment against us, to obtain the pardon of it, that it may not be our ruin, to seal up sins (so the margin reads it), that they may not appear or break out against us, to accuse and condemn us, as, when Christ cast the devil into the bottomless pit, he set a seal upon him, Rev. xx. 3. When sin is pardoned it is sought for and not found, as that which is sealed up. Thirdly, To make reconciliation for iniquity, as by a sacrifice, to satisfy the justice of God and so to make peace and bring God and man together, not only as an arbitrator, or referee, who only brings the contending parties to a good understanding one of another, but as a surety, or undertaker, for us. He is not only the peace-maker, but the peace. He is the atonement.

[2.] He came to bring in an everlasting righteousness. God might justly have made an end of the sin by making an end of the sinner; but Christ found out another way, and so made an end of sin as to save the sinner from it, by providing a righteousness for him. We are all guilty before God, and shall be condemned as guilty, if we have not a righteousness wherein to appear before him. Had we stood, our innocency would have been our righteousness, but, having fallen, we must have something else to plead; and Christ has provided us a plea. The merit of his sacrifice is our righteousness; with this we answer all the demands of the law; Christ has died, yea, rather, has risen again. Thus Christ is the Lord our righteousness, for he is made of God to us righteousness, that we might be made the righteousness of God in him. By faith we apply this to ourselves and plead it with God, and our faith is imputed to us for righteousness, Rom. iv. 3, 5. This is an everlasting righteousness, for Christ, who is our righteousness, and the prince of our peace, is the everlasting Father. It was from everlasting in the counsels of it and will be to everlasting in the consequences of it. The application of it was from the beginning, for Christ was the Lamb slain from the foundation of the world; and it will be to the end, for he is able to save to the uttermost. It is of everlasting virtue (Heb. x. 12); it is the rock that follows us to Canaan. [3.] He came to seal up the vision and prophecy, all the prophetical visions of the Old Testament, which had reference to the Messiah. He sealed them up, that is, he accomplished them, answered to them to a tittle; all things that were written in the law, the prophets, and the psalms, concerning the Messiah, were fulfilled in him. Thus he confirmed the truth of them as well as his own mission. He sealed them up, that is, he put an end to that method of God's discovering his mind and will, and took another course by completing the scripture-canon in the New Testament, which is the more sure word of prophecy than that by vision, 2 Pet. i. 19; Heb. i. 1. [4.] He came to anoint the most holy, that is, himself, the Holy One, who was anointed (that is, appointed to his work and qualified for it) by the Holy Ghost, that oil of gladness which he received without measure, above his fellows; or to anoint the gospel-church, his spiritual temple, or holy place, to sanctify and cleanse it, and appropriate it to himself (Eph. v. 26), or to consecrate for us a new and living way into the holiest, by his own blood (Heb. x. 20), as the sanctuary was anointed, Exod. xxx. 25, &c. He is called Messiah (v. 25, 26), which signifies Christ-Anointed (John i. 41), because he received the unction both for himself and for all that are his.

[5.] In order to all this the Messiah must be cut off, must die a violent death, and so be cut off from the land of the living, as was foretold, Isa. liii. 8. Hence, when Paul preaches the death of Christ, he says that he preached nothing but what the prophet said should come, Acts xxvi. 22, 23. And thus it behoved Christ to suffer. He must be cut off, but not for himself—not for any sin of his own, but, as Caiaphas prophesied, he must die for the people, in our stead and for our good,—not for any advantage of his own (the glory he purchased for himself was no more than the glory he had before, John xvii. 4, 5); no; it was to atone for our sins, and to purchase life for us, that he was cut off. [6.] He must confirm the covenant with many. He shall introduce a new covenant between God and man, a covenant of grace, since it had become impossible for us to be saved by a covenant of innocence. This covenant he shall confirm by his doctrine and miracles, by his death and resurrection, by the ordinances of baptism and the Lord's supper, which are the seals of the New Testament, assuring us that God is willing to accept us upon gospel-terms. His death made his testament of force, and enabled us to claim what is bequeathed by it. He confirmed it to the many, to the common people; the poor were evangelized, when the rulers and Pharisees believed not on him. Or, he confirmed it with many, with the Gentile world. The New Testament was not (like the Old) confined to the Jewish church, but was committed to all nations. Christ gave his life a ransom for many. [7.] He must cause the sacrifice and oblation to cease. By offering himself a sacrifice once for all he shall put an end to all the Levitical sacrifices, shall supersede them and set them aside; when the substance comes the shadows shall be done away. He causes all the peace-offerings to cease when he has made peace by the blood of his cross, and by it confirmed the covenant of peace and reconciliation. By the preaching of his gospel to the world, with which the apostles were entrusted, he took men off from expecting remission by the blood of bulls and goats, and so caused the sacrifice and oblation to cease. The apostle in his epistle to the Hebrews shows what a better priesthood, altar, and sacrifice, we have now than they had under the law, as a reason why we should hold fast our profession.

(3.) Concerning the final destruction of Jerusalem, and of the Jewish church and nation; and this follows immediately upon the cutting off of the Messiah, not only because it was the just punishment of those that put him to death, which was the sin that filled up the measure of their iniquity and brought ruin upon them, but because, as things were, it was necessary to the perfecting of one of the great intentions of his death. He died to take away the ceremonial law, quite to abolish that law of commandments, and to vacate the obligation of it. But the Jews would not be persuaded to quit it; still they kept it up with more zeal than ever; they would hear no talk of parting with it; they stoned Stephen (the first Christian martyr) for saying that Jesus should change the customs which Moses delivered them (Acts

vi. 14); so that there was no way to abolish the Mosaic economy but by destroying the temple, and the holy city, and the Levitical priesthood, and that whole nation which so incurably doted on them. This was effectually done in less than forty years after the death of Christ, and it was a desolation that could never be repaired to this day. And this is it which is here largely foretold, that the Jews who returned out of captivity might not be overmuch lifted up with the rebuilding of their city and temple, because in process of time they would be finally destroyed, and not as now for seventy years only, but might rather rejoice in hope of the coming of the Messiah, and the setting up of his spiritual kingdom in the world, which should never be destroyed. Now, |1.| It is here foretold that the people of the prince that shall come shall be the instruments of this destruction, that is, the Roman armies, belonging to a monarchy yet to come (Christ is the prince that shall come, and they are employed by him in this service; they are his armies, Matt. xxii. 7), or the Gentiles (who, though now strangers, shall become the people of the Messiah) shall destroy the Jews. |2.| That the destruction shall be by war, and the end of that war shall be this desolation determined. The wars of the Jews with the Romans were by their own obstinacy made very long and very bloody, and they issued at length in the utter extirpation of that people. |3.| That the city and sanctuary shall in a particular manner be destroyed and laid quite waste. Titus the Roman general would fain have saved the temple, but his soldiers were so enraged against the Jews that he could not restrain them from burning it to the ground, that this prophecy might be fulfilled. |4.| That all the resistance that shall be made to this destruction shall be in vain: The end of it shall be with a flood. It shall be a deluge of destruction, like that which swept away the old world, and which there will be no making head against. |5.| That hereby the sacrifice and oblation shall be made to cease. And it must needs cease when the family of the priests was so extirpated, and the genealogies of it were so confounded, that (they say) there is no man in the world that can prove himself of the seed of Aaron. |6.| that there shall be an overspreading of abominations, a general corruption of the Jewish nation and an abounding of iniquity among them, for which it shall be made desolate, 1 Thess. ii. 16. Or it is rather to be understood of the armies of the Romans, which were abominable to the Jews (they could not endure them), which overspread the nation, and by which it was made desolate; for these are the words which Christ refers to, Matt. xxiv. 15, When you shall see the abomination of desolation, spoken of by Daniel, stand in the holy place, then let those who shall be in Judea flee, which is explained Luke xxi. 20, When you shall see Jerusalem encompassed with armies then flee. |7.| That the desolation shall be total and final: He shall make it desolate, even until the consummation, that is, he shall make it completely desolate. It is a desolation determined, and it will be accomplished to the utmost. And when it is made desolate, it should seem, there is something more determined that is to be poured upon the desolate (v. 27), and what should that be but the spirit of slumber (Rom. xi. 8, 25), that blindness which has happened to Israel until the fulness of the Gentiles shall come in? And then all Israel shall be saved.

Chapter 10

This chapter and the two next (which conclude this book) make up one entire vision and prophecy, which was communicated to Daniel for the use of the church, not by signs and figures, as before (ch. vii. and viii.), but by express words; and this was about two years after the vision in the foregoing chapter. Daniel prayed daily, but had a vision only now and then. In this chapter we have some things introductory to the prophecy, in the eleventh chapter the particular predictions, and ch. xii. the conclusion of it. This chapter shows us, I. Daniel's solemn fasting and humiliation, before he had this vision, ver. 1-3. II. A glorious appearance of the Son of God to him, and the deep impression it made upon him, ver. 4-9. III. The encouragement that was given him to expect such a discovery of future events as should be satisfactory and useful both to others and to himself, and that he should be enabled both to understand the meaning of this discovery, though difficult, and to bear up under the lustre of it, though dazzling and dreadful, ver. 10-21.

Vision near the River Hiddekel. (b. c. 534.)

1 In the third year of Cyrus king of Persia a thing was revealed unto Daniel, whose name was called Belteshazzar; and the thing was true, but the time appointed was long: and he understood the thing, and had understanding of the vision. 2 In those days I Daniel was mourning three full weeks. 3 I ate no pleasant bread, neither came flesh nor wine in my mouth, neither did I anoint myself at all, till three whole weeks were fulfilled. 4 And in the four and twentieth day of the first month, as I was by the side of the great river, which is Hiddekel; 5 Then I lifted up mine eyes, and looked, and behold a certain man clothed in linen, whose loins were girded with fine gold of Uphaz: 6 His body also was like the beryl, and his face as the appearance of lightning, and his eyes as lamps of fire, and his arms and his feet like in colour to polished brass, and the voice of his words like the voice of a multitude. 7 And I Daniel alone saw the vision: for the men that were with me saw not the vision; but a great quaking fell upon them, so that they fled to hide themselves. 8 Therefore I was left alone, and saw this great vision, and there remained no strength in me: for my comeliness was turned in me into corruption, and I retained no strength. 9 Yet heard I the voice of his words: and when I heard the voice of his words, then was I in a deep sleep on my face, and my face toward the ground.

This vision is dated in the third year of Cyrus, that is, of his reign after the conquest of Babylon, his third year since Daniel became acquainted with him and a subject to him. Here is,

I. A general idea of this prophecy (v. 1): The thing was true; every word of God is so; it was true that Daniel had such a vision, and that such and such things were said. This he solemnly attests upon the word of a prophet. Et hoc paratus est verificare—He was prepared to verify it; and, if it was a word spoken from heaven, no doubt it is stedfast and may be depended upon. But the time appointed was long, as long as to the end of the reign of Antiochus, which was 300 years, a long time indeed when it is looked upon as to come. Nay, and because it is usual with the prophets to glance at things spiritual and eternal, there is that in this prophecy which looks in type as far forward as to the end of the world and the resurrection of the dead; and then he might well say, The time appointed was long. It was, however, made as plain to him as if it had been a history rather than a prophecy; he understood the thing; so distinctly was it delivered to him, and received by him, that he could say he had understanding of the vision. It did not so much operate upon his fancy as upon his understanding.

II. An account of Daniel's mortification of himself before he had this vision, not in expectation of it, nor, when he prayed that solemn prayer ch. ix., does it appear that he had any expectation of the vision in answer to it, but purely from a principle of devotion and pious sympathy with the afflicted people of God. He was mourning full three weeks (v. 2), for his own sins and the sins of his people, and their sorrows. Some think that the particular occasion of his mourning was slothfulness and indifference of many of the Jews, who, though they had liberty to return to their own land, continued still in the land of their captivity, not knowing how to value the privileges offered them; and perhaps it troubled him the more because those that did so justified themselves by the example of Daniel, though they had not that reason to stay behind which he had. Others think that it was because he heard of the obstruction given to the building of the temple by the enemies of the Jews, who hired counsellors against them, to frustrate their purpose (Ezra iv. 4, 5), all the days of Cyrus, and gained their point from his son Cambyses, or Artaxerxes, who governed while Cyrus was absent in the Scythian war. Note, Good men cannot but mourn to see how slowly the work of God goes on in the world and what opposition it meets with, how weak its friends are and how active its enemies. During the days of Daniel's mourning he ate no pleasant bread; he could not live without meat, but he ate little, and very sparingly, and mortified himself in the quality as well as the quantity of what he ate, which may truly be reckoned fasting, and a token of humiliation and sorrow. He did not eat the pleasant bread he used to eat, but that which was course and unpalatable, which he would not be tempted to eat any more of than was just necessary to support nature. As ornaments, so delicacies, are very disagreeable to a day of humiliation. Daniel ate no flesh, drank no wine, nor anointed himself, for those three week's time, v. 3. Though he was now a very old man, and might plead that the decay of his nature required what was nourishing, though he was a very great man, and might plead that, being used to dainty meats, he could not do without them, it would prejudice his health if he were, yet, when it was both to testify and to assist his devotion, he could thus deny himself; let this be noted to the shame of many young people in the common ranks of life who cannot persuade themselves thus to deny themselves.

III. A description of that glorious person whom Daniel saw in vision, which, it is generally agreed, could be no other that Christ himself, the eternal Word. He was by the side of the river Hiddekel (v. 4), probably walking there, not for diversion, but devotion and contemplation, as Isaac walked in the field, to meditate; and, being a person of distinction, he had his servants attending him at some distance. There he looked up, and saw one man Christ Jesus. It must be he, for he appears in the same resemblance wherein he appeared to St. John in the isle of Patmos, Rev. i. 13-15. His dress was priestly, for he is the high priest of our profession, clothed in linen, as the high priest himself was on the day of atonement, that great day; his loins were girded (in St. John's vision his paps were girded) with a golden girdle of the finest gold, that of Uphaz, for every thing about Christ is the best in its kind. The girding of the loins denotes his ready and diligent application to his work, as his Father's servant, in the business of our redemption. His shape was amiable, his body like the beryl, a precious stone of a sky-colour. His countenance was awful, and enough to strike a terror on the beholders, for his face was as the appearance of lightning, which dazzles the eyes, both brightens and threatens. His eyes were bright and sparkling, as lamps of fire. His arms and feet shone like polished brass, v. 6. His voice was loud, and strong, and very piercing, like the voice of a multitude. The vox Dei—voice of God can overpower the vox populi—voice of the people. Thus glorious did Christ appear, and it should engage us, 1. To think highly and honourably of him. Now consider how great this man is, and in all things let him have the pre-eminence. 2. To admire his condescension for us and our salvation. Over all this splendour he drew a veil when he took upon him the form of a servant, and emptied himself.

IV. The wonderful influence that this appearance had upon Daniel and his attendants, and the terror that it struck upon him and them.

1. His attendants saw not the vision; it was not fit that they should be honoured with the sight of it. There is a divine revelation vouchsafed to all, from converse with which none are excluded who do not exclude themselves; but such a vision must be peculiar to Daniel, who was a favourite. Paul's companions were aware of the light, but saw no man, Acts ix. 7; xxii. 9. Note, It is the honour of those who are beloved of God that, what is hidden from others, is known to them. Christ manifests himself to them, but not to the world, John xiv. 22. But, though they saw not the vision, they were seized with an unaccountable trembling; either from the voice they heard, or from some strange concussion or vibration of the air they felt, so it was that a great quaking fell upon them, so that they fled to hide themselves, probably among the willows that grew by the river's side. Note, Many have a spirit of bondage to fear who never receive a spirit of adoption, to whom Christ has been, and will be, never otherwise than a terror. Now the fright that Daniel's attendants were in is a confirmation of the truth of the vision; it could not be Daniel's fancy, or the product of a heated imagination of his own, for it had a real, powerful, and strange effect upon those about him.

2. He himself saw it, and saw it alone, but he was not able to bear the sight of it. It not only dazzled his eyes, but overwhelmed his spirit, so that there remained no strength in him, v. 8. He said, as Moses himself, I exceedingly fear and quake. His spirits were all so employed, either in an intense speculation of the glory of this vision or in the fortifying of his heart against the terror of it, that his body was left in a manner lifeless and spiritless. He had no vigour in him, and was but one remove from a dead carcase; he looked as pale as death, his colour was gone, his comeliness in him was turned into corruption, and he retained no strength. Note, the greatest and best of men cannot bear the immediate discoveries of the divine glory; no man can see it and live; it is next to death to see a glimpse of it, as Daniel here; but glorified saints see Christ as he is and can bear the sight. But, though Daniel was thus dispirited with the vision of Christ, yet he heard the voice of his words and knew what he said. Note, We must take heed lest our reverence of God's glory, by which we should be awakened to hear his voice both in his word and in his providence, should degenerate into such a dread of him as will disable or indispose us to hear it. It should seem that when the vision of Christ terrified Daniel the voice of his words soon pacified and composed him, silenced his fear, and laid him to sleep in a holy security and serenity of mind: When I heard the voice of his words I fell into a slumber, a sweet slumber, on my face, and my face towards the ground. When he saw the vision he threw himself prostrate, into a posture of the most humble adoration, and dropped asleep, not as careless of what he heard and saw, but charmed with it. Note, How dreadful soever Christ may appear to those who are under convictions of sin, and in terror by reason of it, there is enough in his word to quiet their spirits and make them easy, if they will but attend to it and apply it.

Daniel Alarmed and Comforted. (b. c. 534.)

10 And, behold, a hand touched me, which set me upon my knees and upon the palms of my hands. 11 And he said unto me, O Daniel, a man greatly beloved, understand the words that I speak unto thee, and stand upright: for unto thee am I now sent. And when he had spoken this word unto me, I stood trembling. 12 Then said he unto me, Fear not, Daniel: for from the first day that thou didst set thine heart to understand, and to chasten thyself before thy God, thy words were heard, and I am come for thy words. 13 But the prince of the kingdom of Persia withstood me one and twenty days: but, lo, Michael, one of the chief princes, came to help me; and I remained there with the kings of Persia. 14 Now I am come to make thee understand what shall befall thy people in the latter days: for yet the vision is for many days. 15 And when he had spoken such words unto me, I set my face toward the ground, and I became dumb. 16 And, behold, one like the similitude of the sons of men touched my lips: then I opened my mouth, and spake, and said unto him that stood before me, O my lord, by the vision my sorrows are turned upon me, and I have retained no strength. 17 For how can the servant of this my lord talk with this my lord? for as for me, straightway there remained no strength in me, neither is there breath left in me. 18 Then there came again and touched me one like the appearance of a man, and he strengthened me, 19 And said, O man greatly beloved, fear not: peace be unto thee, be strong, yea, be strong. And when he had spoken unto me, I was strengthened, and said, Let my lord speak; for thou hast strengthened me. 20 Then said he, Knowest thou wherefore I come unto thee? and now will I return to fight with the prince of Persia: and when I am gone forth, lo, the prince of Grecia shall come. 21 But I will show thee that which is noted in the scripture of truth: and there is none that holdeth with me in these things, but Michael your prince.

Much ado here is to bring Daniel to be able to bear what Christ has to say to him. Still we have him in a fright, hardly and very slowly recovering himself; but he is still answered and supported with good words and comfortable words. Let us see how Daniel is by degrees brought to himself, and gather up the several passages that are to the same purport.

I. Daniel is in a great consternation and finds it very difficult to get clear of it. The hand that touched him set him at first upon his knees and the palms of his hands, v. 10. Note, Strength and comfort commonly come by degrees to those that have been long cast down and disquieted; they are first helped up a little, and then more. After two days he will revive us, and then the third day he will raise us up. And we must not despise the day of small things, but be thankful for the beginnings of mercy. Afterwards he is helped up, but he stands trembling (v. 11), for fear lest he fall again. Note, Before God gives strength and power unto his people he makes them sensible of their own weakness. I trembled in myself, that I might rest in the day of trouble, Hab. iii. 16. But when, afterwards, Daniel recovered so much strength in his limbs that he could stand steadily, yet he tells us (v. 15) that he set his face towards the ground and became dumb; he was as a man astonished, who knew not what to say, struck dumb with admiration and fear, and was loth to enter into discourse with one so far above him; he kept silence, yea, even from good, till he had recollected himself a little. Well, at length he recovered, not only the use of his feet, but the use of his tongue; and, when he opened his mouth (v. 16), that which he had to say was to excuse his having been so long silent, for really he durst not speak, he could not speak: "O my lord" (so, in great humility, this prophet calls the angel, though the angels, in great humility, called themselves fellow-servants to the prophets, Rev. xxii. 9), "by the vision my sorrows are turned upon me; they break in up on me with violence; the sense of my sinful sorrowful state turns upon me when I see thy purity and brightness." Note, Man, who has lost his integrity, has reason to blush, and be ashamed of himself, when he sees or considers the glory of the blessed angels that keep their integrity. "My sorrows are turned upon me, and I have retained no strength to resist them or bear up a head against them." And again (v. 17), like one half dead with the fright, he complains, "As for me, straightway there remained no strength in me to receive these displays of the divine glory and these discoveries of the divine will; nay, there is no breath left in me." Such a deliquium did he suffer that he could not draw one breath after another, but panted and languished, and was in a manner breathless. See how well it is for us that the treasure of divine revelation is put into earthen vessels, that God speaks to us by men like ourselves and not by angels. Whatever we may wish, in a peevish dislike of the method God takes in dealing with us, it is certain that if we were tried we should all be of Israel's mind at Mt. Sinai, when they said to Moses, Speak thou to us, and we will hear, but let not God speak to us lest we die, Exod. xx. 19. If Daniel could not bear it, how could we? Now this he insists upon as an excuse for his irreverent silence, which otherwise would have been blame-worthy: How can the servant of this my lord talk with this my lord? v. 17. Note, Whenever we enter into communion with God it becomes us to have a due sense of the vast distance and disproportion that there are between us and the holy angels, and of the infinite distance, and no proportion at all, between us and the holy God, and to acknowledge that we cannot order our speech by reason of darkness. How shall we that are dust and ashes speak to the Lord of glory?

II. The blessed angel that was employed by Christ to converse with him gave him all the encouragement and comfort that could be. It should seem, it was not he whose glory he saw in vision (v. 5, 6) that here touched him, and talked with him; that was Christ, but this seems to have been the angel Gabriel, whom Christ had once before ordered to instruct Daniel, ch. viii. 16. That glorious appearance (as that of the God of glory to Abraham, Acts vii. 2) was to give authority and to gain attention to what the angel should say. Christ himself comforted John when he in a like case fell at his feet as dead (Rev. i. 17); but here he did it by the angel, whom Daniel saw in a glory much inferior to that of the vision in the verses before; for he was like the similitude of the sons of men (v. 16), one like the appearance of a man, v. 18. When he only appeared, as he had done before (ch. ix. 21), we do not find that Daniel was put into any disorder by it, as he was by this vision; and therefore he is here employed a third time with Daniel.

1. He lent him his hand to help him, touched him, and set him upon his hands and knees (v. 10), else he would still have lain grovelling, touched his lips (v. 16), else he would have been still dumb; again he touched him (v. 18), and put strength into him, else he would still have been staggering and trembling. Note, The hand of God's power going along with the word of his grace is alone effectual to redress all our grievances, and to rectify whatever is amiss in us. One touch from heaven brings us to our knees, sets us on our feet, opens our lips, and strengthens us; for it is God that works on us, and works in us, both to will and to do that which is good.

2. He assured him of the great favour that God had for him: Thou art a man greatly beloved (v. 11); and again (v. 19), O man greatly beloved! Note, Nothing is more likely, nothing more effectual, to revive the drooping spirits of the saints than to be assured of God's love to them. Those are greatly beloved indeed whom God loves; and it is comfort enough to know it.

3. He silenced his fears, and encouraged his hopes, with good words and comfortable words. He said unto him, Fear not, Daniel (v. 12); and again (v. 19), O man greatly beloved! fear not; peace be unto thee; be strong, yea, be strong. Never did any tender mother quiet her child, when any thing had grieved or frightened it, with more compassion and affection than the angel here quieted Daniel. Those that are beloved of God have no reason to be afraid of any evil; peace is to them; God himself speaks peace to them; and they ought, upon the warrant of that, to speak peace to themselves; and that peace, that joy of the Lord, will be their strength. Will God plead against us with his great power? will he take advantage against us of our being overcome by his terror? No, but he will put strength into us, Job xxiii. 6. So he did into Daniel here, when, by reason of the lustre of the vision, no strength of his own remained in him; and he acknowledges it (v. 19): When he had spoken to me I was strengthened.

Note, God by his word puts life, and strength, and spirit into his people; for if he says, Be strong, power goes along with the word. And, now that Daniel has experienced the efficacy of God's strengthening word and grace, he is ready for any thing: "Now, Let my lord speak, and I can hear it, I can bear it, and am ready to do according to it, for thou hast strengthened me." Note, To those that (like Daniel here) have no might God increases strength, Isa. xl. 29. And we cannot keep up our communion with God but by strength derived from him; but, when he is pleased to put strength into us, we must make a good use of it, and say, Speak, Lord, for thy servant hears. Let God enable us to comply with his will, and then, whatever it is, we will stand complete in it. Da quod jubes, et jube quod vis—Give what thou commandest, and then command what thou wilt.

4. He assured him that his fastings and prayers had come up for a memorial before God, as the angel told Cornelius (Acts x. 4): Fear not, Daniel, v. 12. It is natural to fallen man to be afraid of an extraordinary messenger from heaven, as dreading to hear evil tidings thence; but Daniel need not fear, for he has by his three weeks' humiliation and supplication sent extraordinary messengers to heaven, which he may expect to return with an olive-branch of peace: "From the first day that thou didst set thy heart to understand the word of God, which is to be the rule of thy prayers, and to chasten thyself before thy God, that thou mightest put an edge upon thy prayers, thy words were heard," as, before, at the beginning of thy supplication, ch. ix. 23. Note, As the entrance of God's word is enlightening to the upright, so the entrance of their prayers is pleasing to God, Ps. cxix. 130. From the first day that we begin to look towards God in a way of duty he is ready to meet us in a way of mercy. Thus ready is God to hear prayer. I said, I will confess, and thou forgavest.

5. He informed him that he was sent to him on purpose to bring him a prediction of the future state of the church, as a token of God's accepting his prayers for the church:

"Knowest thou wherefore I come unto thee? If thou knewest on what errand I come, thou wouldst not be put into such a consternation by it." Note, If we rightly understood the meaning of God's dealings with us, and the methods of his providence and grace concerning us, we should be better reconciled to them. "I have come for thy words (v. 12), to bring thee a gracious answer to thy prayers." Thus, when God's praying people call to him, he says, Here I am (Isa. lviii. 9); what would you have with me? See the power of prayer, what glorious things it has, in its time, fetched from heaven, what strange discoveries! On what errand did this angel come to Daniel? He tells him (v. 14): I have come to make thee understand what shall befal thy people in the latter days. Daniel was a curious inquisitive man, that had all his days been searching into secret things, and it would be a great gratification to him to be let into the knowledge of things to come. Daniel had always been concerned for the church; its interests lay much upon his heart, and it would be a particular satisfaction to him to know what its state should be, and he would know the better what to pray for as long as he lived. He was now lamenting the difficulties which his people met with in the present day; but, that he might not be offended in those, the angel must tell him what greater difficulties are yet before them; and, if they be wearied now that they only run with the footmen, how will they contend with horses? Note, It would abate our resentment of present troubles to consider that we know not but much greater are before us, which we are concerned to provide for. Daniel must be made to know what shall befal his people in the latter days of the church, after the cessation of prophecy, and when the time drew nigh for the Messiah to appear, for yet the vision is for many days; the principal things that this vision was intended to give the church the foresight of would come to pass in the days of Antiochus, nearly 300 years after this. Now that which the angel is entrusted to communicate to Daniel, and which Daniel is encouraged to expect from him, is not any curious speculations, moral prognostications, nor rational prospects of his own, though he is an angel, but what he has received from the Lord. It was the revelation of Jesus Christ that the angel gave to St. John to be delivered to the churches, Rev. i. 1. So here (v. 21): I will show thee what is written in the scriptures of truth, that is, what is fixed in the determinate counsel and foreknowledge of God. The decree of God is a thing written, it is a scripture which remains and cannot be altered. What I have written I have written. As there are scriptures for the revealed will of God, the letters-patent, which are published to the world, so there are scriptures for the secret will of God, the close rolls, which are sealed among his treasures, the book of his decrees. Both are scriptures of truth; nothing shall be added to nor taken from either of them. The secret things belong not to us, only now and then some few paragraphs have been copied out from the book of God's counsels, and delivered to the prophets for the use of the church, as here to Daniel; but they are the things revealed, even the words of this law, which belong to us and to our children; and we are concerned to study what is written in these scriptures of truth, for they are things which belong to our everlasting peace.

6. He gave him a general account of the adversaries of the church's cause, from whom it might be expected that troubles would arise, and of its patrons, under whose protection it might be assured of safety and victory at last. (1.) The kings of the earth are and will be its adversaries; for they set themselves against the Lord, and against his Anointed, Ps. ii. 2. The angel told Daniel that he was to have come to him with a gracious answer to his prayers, but that the prince of the kingdom of Persia withstood him one and twenty days, just the three weeks that Daniel had been fasting and praying. Cambyses king of Persia had been very busy to embarrass the affairs of the Jews, and to do them all the mischief he could, and the angel had been all that time employed to counter-work him; so that he had been constrained to defer his visit to Daniel till now, for angels can be but in one place at a time. Or, as Dr. Lightfoot says, This new king of Persia, by hindering the temple, had hindered those good tidings which otherwise he should have brought him. The kings and kingdoms of the world were indeed sometimes helpful to the church, but more often they were injurious to it. "When I have gone forth from the kings of Persia, when their monarchy is brought down

for their unkindness to the Jews, then the prince of Grecia shall come," v. 20. The Grecian monarchy, though favourable to the Jews at first, as the Persian was, will yet come to be vexatious to them. Such is the state of the church-militant; when it has got clear of one enemy it has another to encounter: and such a hydra's head is that of the old serpent; when one storm has blown over it is not long before another rises. (2.) The God of heaven is, and will be, its protector, and, under him, the angels of heaven are its patrons and guardians. [1.] Here is the angel Gabriel busy in the service of the church, making his part good in defence of it twenty-one days, against the prince of Persia, and remaining there with the kings of Persia, as consul, or liege-ambassador, to take care of the affairs of the Jews in that court, and to do them service, v. 13. And, though much was done against them by the kings of Persia (God permitting it), it is probably that much more mischief would have been done them, and they would have been quite ruined (witness Haman's plot) if God had not prevented it by the ministration of angels. Gabriel resolves, when he has despatched this errand to Daniel, that he will return to fight with the prince of Persia, will continue to oppose him, and will at length humble and bring down that proud monarchy (v. 20), though he knows that another as mischievous, even that of Grecia, will rise instead of it. [2.] Here is Michael our prince, the great protector of the church, and the patron of its just but injured cause: The first of the chief princes, v. 13. Some understand it not of a created angel, but an archangel of the highest order, 1 Thess. iv. 16; Jude 9. Others think that Michael the archangel is no other than Christ himself, the angel of the covenant, and the Lord of the angels, he whom Daniel saw in vision, v. 5. He came to help me (v. 13); and there is none but he that holds with me in these things, v. 21. Christ is the church's prince; angels are not, Heb. ii. 5. He presides in the affairs of the church and effectually provides for its good. He is said to hold with the angels, for it is he that makes them serviceable to the heirs of salvation; and, if he were not on the church's side, its case were bad. But, says David, and so says the church, The Lord takes my part with those that help me, Ps. cxviii. 7. The Lord is with those that uphold my soul, Ps. liv. 4.

Chapter 11

This chapter and the two next (which conclude this book) make up one entire vision and prophecy, which was communicated to Daniel for the use of the church, not by signs and figures, as before (ch. vii. and viii.), but by express words; and this was about two years after the vision in the foregoing chapter. Daniel prayed daily, but had a vision only now and then. In this chapter we have some things introductory to the prophecy, in the eleventh chapter the particular predictions, and ch. xii. the conclusion of it. This chapter shows us, I. Daniel's solemn fasting and humiliation, before he had this vision, ver. 1-3. II. A glorious appearance of the Son of God to him, and the deep impression it made upon him, ver. 4-9. III. The encouragement that was given him to expect such a discovery of future events as should be satisfactory and useful both to others and to himself, and that he should be enabled both to understand the meaning of this discovery, though difficult, and to bear up under the lustre of it, though dazzling and dreadful, ver. 10-21.

Vision near the River Hiddekel. (b. c. 534.)

1 In the third year of Cyrus king of Persia a thing was revealed unto Daniel, whose name was called Belteshazzar; and the thing was true, but the time appointed was long: and he understood the thing, and had understanding of the vision.   2 In those days I Daniel was mourning three full weeks.   3 I ate no pleasant bread, neither came flesh nor wine in my mouth, neither did I anoint myself at all, till three whole weeks were fulfilled.   4 And in the four and twentieth day of the first month, as I was by the side of the great river, which is Hiddekel;   5 Then I lifted up mine eyes, and looked, and behold a certain man clothed in linen, whose loins were girded with fine gold of Uphaz: 6 His body also was like the beryl,

and his face as the appearance of lightning, and his eyes as lamps of fire, and his arms and his feet like in colour to polished brass, and the voice of his words like the voice of a multitude. 7 And I Daniel alone saw the vision: for the men that were with me saw not the vision; but a great quaking fell upon them, so that they fled to hide themselves. 8 Therefore I was left alone, and saw this great vision, and there remained no strength in me: for my comeliness was turned in me into corruption, and I retained no strength. 9 Yet heard I the voice of his words: and when I heard the voice of his words, then was I in a deep sleep on my face, and my face toward the ground.

This vision is dated in the third year of Cyrus, that is, of his reign after the conquest of Babylon, his third year since Daniel became acquainted with him and a subject to him. Here is,

I. A general idea of this prophecy (v. 1): The thing was true; every word of God is so; it was true that Daniel had such a vision, and that such and such things were said. This he solemnly attests upon the word of a prophet. Et hoc paratus est verificare—He was prepared to verify it; and, if it was a word spoken from heaven, no doubt it is stedfast and may be depended upon. But the time appointed was long, as long as to the end of the reign of Antiochus, which was 300 years, a long time indeed when it is looked upon as to come. Nay, and because it is usual with the prophets to glance at things spiritual and eternal, there is that in this prophecy which looks in type as far forward as to the end of the world and the resurrection of the dead; and then he might well say, The time appointed was long. It was, however, made as plain to him as if it had been a history rather than a prophecy; he understood the thing; so distinctly was it delivered to him, and received by him, that he could say he had understanding of the vision. It did not so much operate upon his fancy as upon his understanding.

II. An account of Daniel's mortification of himself before he had this vision, not in expectation of it, nor, when he prayed that solemn prayer ch. ix., does it appear that he had any expectation of the vision in answer to it, but purely from a principle of devotion and pious sympathy with the afflicted people of God. He was mourning full three weeks (v. 2), for his own sins and the sins of his people, and their sorrows. Some think that the particular occasion of his mourning was slothfulness and indifference of many of the Jews, who, though they had liberty to return to their own land, continued still in the land of their captivity, not knowing how to value the privileges offered them; and perhaps it troubled him the more because those that did so justified themselves by the example of Daniel, though they had not that reason to stay behind which he had. Others think that it was because he heard of the obstruction given to the building of the temple by the enemies of the Jews, who hired counsellors against them, to frustrate their purpose (Ezra iv. 4, 5), all the days of Cyrus, and gained their point from his son Cambyses, or Artaxerxes, who governed while Cyrus was absent in the Scythian war. Note, Good men cannot but mourn to see how slowly the work of God goes on in the world and what opposition it meets with, how weak its friends are and how active its enemies. During the days of Daniel's mourning he ate no pleasant bread; he could not live without meat, but he ate little, and very sparingly, and mortified himself in the quality as well as the quantity of what he ate, which may truly be reckoned fasting, and a token of humiliation and sorrow. He did not eat the pleasant bread he used to eat, but that which was course and unpalatable, which he would not be tempted to eat any more of than was just necessary to support nature. As ornaments, so delicacies, are very disagreeable to a day of humiliation. Daniel ate no flesh, drank no wine, nor anointed himself, for those three week's time, v. 3. Though he was now a very old man, and might plead that the decay of his nature required what was nourishing, though he was a very great man, and might plead that, being used to dainty meats, he could not do without them, it would prejudice his health if he were, yet, when it was both to testify and to assist his devotion, he could thus deny himself; let this be noted to the shame of many young people in the common ranks of life who cannot persuade themselves thus to deny themselves.

III. A description of that glorious person whom Daniel saw in vision, which, it is generally agreed, could be no other that Christ himself, the eternal Word. He was by the side of the river Hiddekel (v. 4), probably walking there, not for diversion, but devotion and contemplation, as Isaac walked in the field, to meditate; and, being a person of distinction, he had his servants attending him at some distance. There he looked up, and saw one man Christ Jesus. It must be he, for he appears in the same resemblance wherein he appeared to St. John in the isle of Patmos, Rev. i. 13-15. His dress was priestly, for he is the high priest of our profession, clothed in linen, as the high priest himself was on the day of atonement, that great day; his loins were girded (in St. John's vision his paps were girded) with a golden girdle of the finest gold, that of Uphaz, for every thing about Christ is the best in its kind. The girding of the loins denotes his ready and diligent application to his work, as his Father's servant, in the business of our redemption. His shape was amiable, his body like the beryl, a precious stone of a sky-colour. His countenance was awful, and enough to strike a terror on the beholders, for his face was as the appearance of lightning, which dazzles the eyes, both brightens and threatens. His eyes were bright and sparkling, as lamps of fire. His arms and feet shone like polished brass, v. 6. His voice was loud, and strong, and very piercing, like the voice of a multitude. The vox Dei—voice of God can overpower the vox populi—voice of the people. Thus glorious did Christ appear, and it should engage us, 1. To think highly and honourably of him. Now consider how great this man is, and in all things let him have the pre-eminence. 2. To admire his condescension for us and our salvation. Over all this splendour he drew a veil when he took upon him the form of a servant, and emptied himself.

IV. The wonderful influence that this appearance had upon Daniel and his attendants, and the terror that it struck upon him and them.

1. His attendants saw not the vision; it was not fit that they should be honoured with the sight of it. There is a divine revelation vouchsafed to all, from converse with which none are excluded who do not exclude themselves; but such a vision must be peculiar to Daniel, who was a favourite. Paul's companions were aware of the light, but saw no man, Acts ix. 7; xxii. 9. Note, It is the honour of those who are beloved of God that, what is hidden from others, is known to them. Christ manifests himself to them, but not to the world, John xiv. 22. But, though they saw not the vision, they were seized with an unaccountable trembling; either from the voice they heard, or from some strange concussion or vibration of the air they felt, so it was that a great quaking fell upon them, so that they fled to hide themselves, probably among the willows that grew by the river's side. Note, Many have a spirit of bondage to fear who never receive a spirit of adoption, to whom Christ has been, and will be, never otherwise than a terror. Now the fright that Daniel's attendants were in is a confirmation of the truth of the vision; it could not be Daniel's fancy, or the product of a heated imagination of his own, for it had a real, powerful, and strange effect upon those about him.

2. He himself saw it, and saw it alone, but he was not able to bear the sight of it. It not only dazzled his eyes, but overwhelmed his spirit, so that there remained no strength in him, v. 8. He said, as Moses himself, I exceedingly fear and quake. His spirits were all so employed, either in an intense speculation of the glory of this vision or in the fortifying of his heart against the terror of it, that his body was left in a manner lifeless and spiritless. He had no vigour in him, and was but one remove from a dead carcase; he looked as pale as death, his colour was gone, his comeliness in him was turned into corruption, and he retained no strength. Note, the greatest and best of men cannot bear the immediate discoveries of the divine glory; no man can see it and live; it is next to death to see a glimpse of it, as Daniel here; but glorified saints see Christ as he is and can bear the sight. But, though Daniel was

thus dispirited with the vision of Christ, yet he heard the voice of his words and knew what he said. Note, We must take heed lest our reverence of God's glory, by which we should be awakened to hear his voice both in his word and in his providence, should degenerate into such a dread of him as will disable or indispose us to hear it. It should seem that when the vision of Christ terrified Daniel the voice of his words soon pacified and composed him, silenced his fear, and laid him to sleep in a holy security and serenity of mind: When I heard the voice of his words I fell into a slumber, a sweet slumber, on my face, and my face towards the ground. When he saw the vision he threw himself prostrate, into a posture of the most humble adoration, and dropped asleep, not as careless of what he heard and saw, but charmed with it. Note, How dreadful soever Christ may appear to those who are under convictions of sin, and in terror by reason of it, there is enough in his word to quiet their spirits and make them easy, if they will but attend to it and apply it.
Daniel Alarmed and Comforted. (b. c. 534.)

10 And, behold, a hand touched me, which set me upon my knees and upon the palms of my hands. 11 And he said unto me, O Daniel, a man greatly beloved, understand the words that I speak unto thee, and stand upright: for unto thee am I now sent. And when he had spoken this word unto me, I stood trembling. 12 Then said he unto me, Fear not, Daniel: for from the first day that thou didst set thine heart to understand, and to chasten thyself before thy God, thy words were heard, and I am come for thy words. 13 But the prince of the kingdom of Persia withstood me one and twenty days: but, lo, Michael, one of the chief princes, came to help me; and I remained there with the kings of Persia. 14 Now I am come to make thee understand what shall befall thy people in the latter days: for yet the vision is for many days. 15 And when he had spoken such words unto me, I set my face toward the ground, and I became dumb. 16 And, behold, one like the similitude of the sons of men touched my lips: then I opened my mouth, and spake, and said unto him that stood before me, O my lord, by the vision my sorrows are turned upon me, and I have retained no strength. 17 For how can the servant of this my lord talk with this my lord? for as for me, straightway there remained no strength in me, neither is there breath left in me. 18 Then there came again and touched me one like the appearance of a man, and he strengthened me, 19 And said, O man greatly beloved, fear not: peace be unto thee, be strong, yea, be strong. And when he had spoken unto me, I was strengthened, and said, Let my lord speak; for thou hast strengthened me. 20 Then said he, Knowest thou wherefore I come unto thee? and now will I return to fight with the prince of Persia: and when I am gone forth, lo, the prince of Grecia shall come. 21 But I will show thee that which is noted in the scripture of truth: and there is none that holdeth with me in these things, but Michael your prince.

Much ado here is to bring Daniel to be able to bear what Christ has to say to him. Still we have him in a fright, hardly and very slowly recovering himself; but he is still answered and supported with good words and comfortable words. Let us see how Daniel is by degrees brought to himself, and gather up the several passages that are to the same purport.
I. Daniel is in a great consternation and finds it very difficult to get clear of it. The hand that touched him set him at first upon his knees and the palms of his hands, v. 10. Note, Strength and comfort commonly come by degrees to those that have been long cast down and disquieted; they are first helped up a little, and then more. After two days he will revive us, and then the third day he will raise us up. And we must not despise the day of small things, but be thankful for the beginnings of mercy. Afterwards he is helped up, but he stands trembling (v. 11), for fear lest he fall again. Note, Before God gives strength and power unto his people he makes them sensible of their own weakness. I trembled in myself, that I might rest in the day of trouble, Hab. iii. 16. But when, afterwards, Daniel recovered so much strength in his limbs that he could stand steadily, yet he tells us (v. 15) that he set his face towards the ground and became dumb; he was as a man astonished, who knew not what to

say, struck dumb with admiration and fear, and was loth to enter into discourse with one so far above him; he kept silence, yea, even from good, till he had recollected himself a little. Well, at length he recovered, not only the use of his feet, but the use of his tongue; and, when he opened his mouth (v. 16), that which he had to say was to excuse his having been so long silent, for really he durst not speak, he could not speak: "O my lord" (so, in great humility, this prophet calls the angel, though the angels, in great humility, called themselves fellow-servants to the prophets, Rev. xxii. 9), "by the vision my sorrows are turned upon me; they break in up on me with violence; the sense of my sinful sorrowful state turns upon me when I see thy purity and brightness." Note, Man, who has lost his integrity, has reason to blush, and be ashamed of himself, when he sees or considers the glory of the blessed angels that keep their integrity. "My sorrows are turned upon me, and I have retained no strength to resist them or bear up a head against them." And again (v. 17), like one half dead with the fright, he complains, "As for me, straightway there remained no strength in me to receive these displays of the divine glory and these discoveries of the divine will; nay, there is no breath left in me." Such a deliquium did he suffer that he could not draw one breath after another, but panted and languished, and was in a manner breathless. See how well it is for us that the treasure of divine revelation is put into earthen vessels, that God speaks to us by men like ourselves and not by angels. Whatever we may wish, in a peevish dislike of the method God takes in dealing with us, it is certain that if we were tried we should all be of Israel's mind at Mt. Sinai, when they said to Moses, Speak thou to us, and we will hear, but let not God speak to us lest we die, Exod. xx. 19. If Daniel could not bear it, how could we? Now this he insists upon as an excuse for his irreverent silence, which otherwise would have been blame-worthy: How can the servant of this my lord talk with this my lord? v. 17. Note, Whenever we enter into communion with God it becomes us to have a due sense of the vast distance and disproportion that there are between us and the holy angels, and of the infinite distance, and no proportion at all, between us and the holy God, and to acknowledge that we cannot order our speech by reason of darkness. How shall we that are dust and ashes speak to the Lord of glory?

II. The blessed angel that was employed by Christ to converse with him gave him all the encouragement and comfort that could be. It should seem, it was not he whose glory he saw in vision (v. 5, 6) that here touched him, and talked with him; that was Christ, but this seems to have been the angel Gabriel, whom Christ had once before ordered to instruct Daniel, ch. viii. 16. That glorious appearance (as that of the God of glory to Abraham, Acts vii. 2) was to give authority and to gain attention to what the angel should say. Christ himself comforted John when he in a like case fell at his feet as dead (Rev. i. 17); but here he did it by the angel, whom Daniel saw in a glory much inferior to that of the vision in the verses before; for he was like the similitude of the sons of men (v. 16), one like the appearance of a man, v. 18. When he only appeared, as he had done before (ch. ix. 21), we do not find that Daniel was put into any disorder by it, as he was by this vision; and therefore he is here employed a third time with Daniel.

1. He lent him his hand to help him, touched him, and set him upon his hands and knees (v. 10), else he would still have lain grovelling, touched his lips (v. 16), else he would have been still dumb; again he touched him (v. 18), and put strength into him, else he would still have been staggering and trembling. Note, The hand of God's power going along with the word of his grace is alone effectual to redress all our grievances, and to rectify whatever is amiss in us. One touch from heaven brings us to our knees, sets us on our feet, opens our lips, and strengthens us; for it is God that works on us, and works in us, both to will and to do that which is good.
2. He assured him of the great favour that God had for him: Thou art a man greatly beloved (v. 11); and again (v. 19), O man greatly beloved! Note, Nothing is more likely, nothing more effectual, to revive the drooping spirits of the saints than to be assured of God's love to

them. Those are greatly beloved indeed whom God loves; and it is comfort enough to know it.

3. He silenced his fears, and encouraged his hopes, with good words and comfortable words. He said unto him, Fear not, Daniel (v. 12); and again (v. 19), O man greatly beloved! fear not; peace be unto thee; be strong, yea, be strong. Never did any tender mother quiet her child, when any thing had grieved or frightened it, with more compassion and affection than the angel here quieted Daniel. Those that are beloved of God have no reason to be afraid of any evil; peace is to them; God himself speaks peace to them; and they ought, upon the warrant of that, to speak peace to themselves; and that peace, that joy of the Lord, will be their strength. Will God plead against us with his great power? will he take advantage against us of our being overcome by his terror? No, but he will put strength into us, Job xxiii. 6. So he did into Daniel here, when, by reason of the lustre of the vision, no strength of his own remained in him; and he acknowledges it (v. 19): When he had spoken to me I was strengthened.

Note, God by his word puts life, and strength, and spirit into his people; for if he says, Be strong, power goes along with the word. And, now that Daniel has experienced the efficacy of God's strengthening word and grace, he is ready for any thing: "Now, Let my lord speak, and I can hear it, I can bear it, and am ready to do according to it, for thou hast strengthened me." Note, To those that (like Daniel here) have no might God increases strength, Isa. xl. 29. And we cannot keep up our communion with God but by strength derived from him; but, when he is pleased to put strength into us, we must make a good use of it, and say, Speak, Lord, for thy servant hears. Let God enable us to comply with his will, and then, whatever it is, we will stand complete in it. Da quod jubes, et jube quod vis—Give what thou commandest, and then command what thou wilt.

4. He assured him that his fastings and prayers had come up for a memorial before God, as the angel told Cornelius (Acts x. 4): Fear not, Daniel, v. 12. It is natural to fallen man to be afraid of an extraordinary messenger from heaven, as dreading to hear evil tidings thence; but Daniel need not fear, for he has by his three weeks' humiliation and supplication sent extraordinary messengers to heaven, which he may expect to return with an olive-branch of peace: "From the first day that thou didst set thy heart to understand the word of God, which is to be the rule of thy prayers, and to chasten thyself before thy God, that thou mightest put an edge upon thy prayers, thy words were heard," as, before, at the beginning of thy supplication, ch. ix. 23. Note, As the entrance of God's word is enlightening to the upright, so the entrance of their prayers is pleasing to God, Ps. cxix. 130. From the first day that we begin to look towards God in a way of duty he is ready to meet us in a way of mercy. Thus ready is God to hear prayer. I said, I will confess, and thou forgavest.

5. He informed him that he was sent to him on purpose to bring him a prediction of the future state of the church, as a token of God's accepting his prayers for the church: "Knowest thou wherefore I come unto thee? If thou knewest on what errand I come, thou wouldst not be put into such a consternation by it." Note, If we rightly understood the meaning of God's dealings with us, and the methods of his providence and grace concerning us, we should be better reconciled to them. "I have come for thy words (v. 12), to bring thee a gracious answer to thy prayers." Thus, when God's praying people call to him, he says, Here I am (Isa. lviii. 9); what would you have with me? See the power of prayer, what glorious things it has, in its time, fetched from heaven, what strange discoveries! On what errand did this angel come to Daniel? He tells him (v. 14): I have come to make thee understand what shall befal thy people in the latter days. Daniel was a curious inquisitive man, that had all his days been searching into secret things, and it would be a great gratification to him to be let into the knowledge of things to come. Daniel had always been concerned for the church; its interests lay much upon his heart, and it would be a particular

satisfaction to him to know what its state should be, and he would know the better what to pray for as long as he lived. He was now lamenting the difficulties which his people met with in the present day; but, that he might not be offended in those, the angel must tell him what greater difficulties are yet before them; and, if they be wearied now that they only run with the footmen, how will they contend with horses? Note, It would abate our resentment of present troubles to consider that we know not but much greater are before us, which we are concerned to provide for. Daniel must be made to know what shall befal his people in the latter days of the church, after the cessation of prophecy, and when the time drew nigh for the Messiah to appear, for yet the vision is for many days; the principal things that this vision was intended to give the church the foresight of would come to pass in the days of Antiochus, nearly 300 years after this. Now that which the angel is entrusted to communicate to Daniel, and which Daniel is encouraged to expect from him, is not any curious speculations, moral prognostications, nor rational prospects of his own, though he is an angel, but what he has received from the Lord. It was the revelation of Jesus Christ that the angel gave to St. John to be delivered to the churches, Rev. i. 1. So here (v. 21): I will show thee what is written in the scriptures of truth, that is, what is fixed in the determinate counsel and foreknowledge of God. The decree of God is a thing written, it is a scripture which remains and cannot be altered. What I have written I have written. As there are scriptures for the revealed will of God, the letters-patent, which are published to the world, so there are scriptures for the secret will of God, the close rolls, which are sealed among his treasures, the book of his decrees. Both are scriptures of truth; nothing shall be added to nor taken from either of them. The secret things belong not to us, only now and then some few paragraphs have been copied out from the book of God's counsels, and delivered to the prophets for the use of the church, as here to Daniel; but they are the things revealed, even the words of this law, which belong to us and to our children; and we are concerned to study what is written in these scriptures of truth, for they are things which belong to our everlasting peace.

6. He gave him a general account of the adversaries of the church's cause, from whom it might be expected that troubles would arise, and of its patrons, under whose protection it might be assured of safety and victory at last. (1.) The kings of the earth are and will be its adversaries; for they set themselves against the Lord, and against his Anointed, Ps. ii. 2. The angel told Daniel that he was to have come to him with a gracious answer to his prayers, but that the prince of the kingdom of Persia withstood him one and twenty days, just the three weeks that Daniel had been fasting and praying. Cambyses king of Persia had been very busy to embarrass the affairs of the Jews, and to do them all the mischief he could, and the angel had been all that time employed to counter-work him; so that he had been constrained to defer his visit to Daniel till now, for angels can be but in one place at a time. Or, as Dr. Lightfoot says, This new king of Persia, by hindering the temple, had hindered those good tidings which otherwise he should have brought him. The kings and kingdoms of the world were indeed sometimes helpful to the church, but more often they were injurious to it. "When I have gone forth from the kings of Persia, when their monarchy is brought down for their unkindness to the Jews, then the prince of Grecia shall come," v. 20. The Grecian monarchy, though favourable to the Jews at first, as the Persian was, will yet come to be vexatious to them. Such is the state of the church-militant; when it has got clear of one enemy it has another to encounter: and such a hydra's head is that of the old serpent; when one storm has blown over it is not long before another rises. (2.) The God of heaven is, and will be, its protector, and, under him, the angels of heaven are its patrons and guardians. [1.] Here is the angel Gabriel busy in the service of the church, making his part good in defence of it twenty-one days, against the prince of Persia, and remaining there with the kings of Persia, as consul, or liege-ambassador, to take care of the affairs of the Jews in that court, and to do them service, v. 13. And, though much was done against them by the kings of Persia (God permitting it), it is probably that much more mischief would have been done them, and they would have been quite ruined (witness Haman's plot) if God had not

prevented it by the ministration of angels. Gabriel resolves, when he has despatched this errand to Daniel, that he will return to fight with the prince of Persia, will continue to oppose him, and will at length humble and bring down that proud monarchy (v. 20), though he knows that another as mischievous, even that of Grecia, will rise instead of it. [2.] Here is Michael our prince, the great protector of the church, and the patron of its just but injured cause: The first of the chief princes, v. 13. Some understand it not of a created angel, but an archangel of the highest order, 1 Thess. iv. 16; Jude 9. Others think that Michael the archangel is no other than Christ himself, the angel of the covenant, and the Lord of the angels, he whom Daniel saw in vision, v. 5. He came to help me (v. 13); and there is none but he that holds with me in these things, v. 21. Christ is the church's prince; angels are not, Heb. ii. 5. He presides in the affairs of the church and effectually provides for its good. He is said to hold with the angels, for it is he that makes them serviceable to the heirs of salvation; and, if he were not on the church's side, its case were bad. But, says David, and so says the church, The Lord takes my part with those that help me, Ps. cxviii. 7. The Lord is with those that uphold my soul, Ps. liv. 4.

Chapter 12

The angel Gabriel, in this chapter, performs his promise made to Daniel in the foregoing chapter, that he would "show him what should befal his people in the latter days," according to that which was "written in the scriptures of truth:" very particularly does he here foretel the succession of the kings of Persia and Grecia, and the affairs of their kingdoms, especially the mischief which Antiochus Epiphanes did in his time to the church, which was foretold before (ch. viii. 11-12). Here is, I. A brief prediction of the setting up of the Grecian monarchy upon the ruins of the Persian monarchy, which was now newly begun, ver. 1-4. II. A prediction of the affairs of the two kingdoms of Egypt and Syria, with reference to each other, ver. 5-20. III. Of the rise of Antiochus Epiphanes, and his actions and successes, ver. 21-29. IV. Of the great mischief that he should do to the Jewish nation and religion, and his contempt of all religion, ver. 30-39. V. Of his fall and ruin at last, when he is in the heat of his pursuit, ver. 40-45.

Ruin of the Persian Monarchy. (b. c. 534.)

1 Also I in the first year of Darius the Mede, even I, stood to confirm and to strengthen him. 2 And now will I show thee the truth. Behold, there shall stand up yet three kings in Persia; and the fourth shall be far richer than they all: and by his strength through his riches he shall stir up all against the realm of Grecia. 3 And a mighty king shall stand up, that shall rule with great dominion, and do according to his will. 4 And when he shall stand up, his kingdom shall be broken, and shall be divided toward the four winds of heaven; and not to his posterity, nor according to his dominion which he ruled: for his kingdom shall be plucked up, even for others beside those.

Here, 1. The angel Gabriel lets Daniel know the good service he has done to the Jewish nation (v. 1): "In the first year of Darius the Mede, who destroyed Babylon and released the Jews out of that house of bondage, I stood a strength and fortress to him, that is, I was instrumental to protect him, and give him success in his ward, and, after he had conquered Babylon, to confirm him in his resolution to release the Jews," which, it is likely, met with much opposition. Thus by the angel, and at the request of the watcher, the golden head was broken, and the axe laid to the root of the tree. Note, We must acknowledge the hand of God in the strengthening of those that are friends to the church for the service they are to do it, and confirming them in their good resolutions; herein he uses the ministry of angels more than we are aware of. And the many instances we have known of God's care of his church formerly encourage us to depend upon him in further straits and difficulties. 2. He foretels the reign of four Persian kings (v. 2): Now I will tell thee the truth, that is, the true meaning of the visions of the great image, and of the four beasts, and expound in plain terms what was before represented by dark types. (1.) There shall stand up three kings in

Persia, besides Darius, in whose reign this prophecy is dated, ch. ix. 1. Mr. Broughton makes these three to be Cyrus, Artaxasta or Artaxerxes, called by the Greeks Cambyses, and Ahasuerus that married Esther, called Darius son of Hystaspes. To these three the Persians gave these attributes—Cyrus was a father, Cambyses a master, and Darius a hoarder up. So Herodotus. (2.) There shall be a fourth, far richer than they all, that is, Xerxes, of whose wealth the Greek authors take notice. By his strength (his vast army, consisting of 800,000 men at least) and his riches, with which he maintained and paid that vast army, he stirred up all against the realm of Greece. Xerxes's expedition against Greece is famous in history, and the shameful defeat that he met with. He who when he went out was the terror of Greece, in his return was the scorn of Greece. Daniel needed not to be told what disappointment he would meet with, for he was a hinderer of the building of the temple; but soon after, about thirty years after the first return from captivity, Darius, a young king, revived the building of the temple, owning the hand of God against his predecessors for hindering it, Ezra vi. 7. 3. He foretels Alexander's conquests and the partition of his kingdom, v. 3. He is that mighty king that shall stand up against the kings of Persia, and he shall rule with great dominion, over many kingdoms, and with a despotic power, for he shall do according to his will, and undo likewise, which, by the law of the Medes and Persians, their kings could not. When Alexander, after he had conquered Asia, would be worshipped as a god, then this was fulfilled, that he shall do according to his will. That is God's prerogative, but was his pretension. But (v. 4) his kingdom shall soon be broken, and divided into four parts, but not to his posterity, nor shall any of his successors reign according to his dominion; none of them shall have such large territories nor such an absolute power. His kingdom was plucked up for others besides those of his own family. Arideus, his brother, was made king in Macedonia; Olympias, Alexander's mother, killed him, and poisoned Alexander's two sons, Hercules and Alexander. Thus was his family rooted out by its own hands. See what decaying perishing things worldly pomp and possessions are, and the powers by which they are got. Never was the vanity of the world and its greatest things shown more evidently than in the story of Alexander. All is vanity and vexation of spirit.

The Affairs of Egypt and Syria; The Reign of Antiochus Magnus; The Fall of Antiochus Magnus. (b. c. 534.)

5 And the king of the south shall be strong, and one of his princes; and he shall be strong above him, and have dominion; his dominion shall be a great dominion. 6 And in the end of years they shall join themselves together; for the king's daughter of the south shall come to the king of the north to make an agreement: but she shall not retain the power of the arm; neither shall he stand, nor his arm: but she shall be given up, and they that brought her, and he that begat her, and he that strengthened her in these times. 7 But out of a branch of her roots shall one stand up in his estate, which shall come with an army, and shall enter into the fortress of the king of the north, and shall deal against them, and shall prevail: 8 And shall also carry captives into Egypt their gods, with their princes, and with their precious vessels of silver and of gold; and he shall continue more years than the king of the north. 9 So the king of the south shall come into his kingdom, and shall return into his own land. 10 But his sons shall be stirred up, and shall assemble a multitude of great forces: and one shall certainly come, and overflow, and pass through: then shall he return, and be stirred up, even to his fortress. 11 And the king of the south shall be moved with choler, and shall come forth and fight with him, even with the king of the north: and he shall set forth a great multitude; but the multitude shall be given into his hand. 12 And when he hath taken away the multitude, his heart shall be lifted up; and he shall cast down many ten thousands: but he shall not be strengthened by it. 13 For the king of the north shall return, and shall set forth a multitude greater than the former, and shall certainly come after certain years with a great army and with much riches. 14 And in those times there shall many stand up against the king of the south: also the robbers of thy people shall exalt themselves to establish the

vision; but they shall fall.   15 So the king of the north shall come, and cast up a mount, and take the most fenced cities: and the arms of the south shall not withstand, neither his chosen people, neither shall there be any strength to withstand.   16 But he that cometh against him shall do according to his own will, and none shall stand before him: and he shall stand in the glorious land, which by his hand shall be consumed.   17 He shall also set his face to enter with the strength of his whole kingdom, and upright ones with him; thus shall he do: and he shall give him the daughter of women, corrupting her: but she shall not stand on his side, neither be for him.   18 After this shall he turn his face unto the isles, and shall take many: but a prince for his own behalf shall cause the reproach offered by him to cease; without his own reproach he shall cause it to turn upon him.   19 Then he shall turn his face toward the fort of his own land: but he shall stumble and fall, and not be found.   20 Then shall stand up in his estate a raiser of taxes in the glory of the kingdom: but within few days he shall be destroyed, neither in anger, nor in battle.

Here are foretold,

I. The rise and power of two great kingdoms out of the remains of Alexander's conquests, v. 5. 1. The kingdom of Egypt, which was made considerable by Ptolemaeus Lagus, one of Alexander's captains, whose successors were, from him, called the Lagidae. He is called the king of the south, that is, Egypt, named here, v. 8, 42, 43. The countries that at first belonged to Ptolemy are reckoned to be Egypt, Phoenicia, Arabia, Libya, Ethiopia, &c. Theocr. Idyl. 17. 2. The kingdom of Syria, which was set up by Seleucus Nicanor, or the conqueror; he was one of Alexander's princes, and became stronger than the other, and had the greatest dominion of all, was the most powerful of all Alexander's successors. It was said that he had no fewer than seven-two kingdoms under him. Both these were strong against Judah (the affairs of which are particularly eyed in this prediction); Ptolemy, soon after he gained Egypt, invaded Judea, and took Jerusalem on a sabbath, pretending a friendly visit. Seleucus also gave disturbance to Judea.

II. The fruitless attempt to unite these two kingdoms as iron and clay in Nebuchadnezzar's image (v. 6): "At the end of certain years, about seventy after Alexander's death, the Lagidae and the Seleucidae shall associate, but not in sincerity. Ptolemy Philadelphus, king of Egypt, shall marry his daughter Berenice to Antiochus Theos, king of Syria," who had already a wife called Laodice. "Berenice shall come to the king of the north, to make an agreement, but it shall not hold: She shall not retain the power of the arm; neither she nor her posterity shall establish themselves in the kingdom of the north, neither shall Ptolemy her father, nor Antiochus her husband (between whom there was to be a great alliance), stand, nor their arm, but she shall be given up and those that brought her," all that projected that unhappy marriage between her and Antiochus, which occasioned so much mischief, instead of producing a coalition between the northern and southern crowns, as was hoped. Antiochus divorced Berenice, took his former wife Laodice again, who soon after poisoned him, procured Berenice and her son to be murdered, and set up her own son by Antiochus to be king, who was called Seleucus Callinicus.

III. A war between the two kingdoms, v. 7, 8. A branch from the same root with Berenice shall stand up in his estate. Ptolemaeus Euergetes, the son and successor of Ptolemaeus Philadelphus, shall come with an army against Seleucus Callinicus, king of Syria, to avenge his sister's quarrel, and shall prevail; and he shall carry away a rich booty both of persons and goods into Egypt, and shall continue more years than the king of the north. This Ptolemy reigned forty-six years; and Justin says that if his own affairs had not called him home he would, in this war, have made himself master of the whole kingdom of Syria. But (v. 9) he shall be forced to come into his kingdom and return into his own land, to keep peace there, so that he can no longer carry on the war abroad. Note, It is very common for a treacherous peace to end in a bloody war.

IV. The long and busy reign of Antiochus the Great, king of Syria. Seleucus Callinicus, that king of the north that was overcome (v. 7) and died miserably, left two sons, Seleucus and Antiochus; these are his sons, the sons of the king of the north, that shall be stirred up, and shall assemble a multitude of great forces, to recover what their father had lost, v. 10. But Seleucus the elder, being weak, and unable to rule his army, was poisoned by his friends, and reigned only two years; and his brother Antiochus succeeded him, who reigned thirty-seven years, and was called the Great. And therefore the angel, though he speaks of sons at first, goes on with the account of one only, who was but fifteen years old when he began to reign, and he shall certainly come, and overflow, and over-run, and shall be restored at length to what his father lost. 1. The king of the south, in this war, shall at first have very great success. Ptolemaeus Philopater, moved with indignation at the indignities done by Antiochus the Great, shall (though otherwise a slothful prince) come forth, and fight with him, and shall bring a vast army into the field of 70,000 foot, and 5000 horse, and seventy-three elephants. And the other multitude (the army of Antiochus, consisting of 62,000 foot, and 6000 horse, and 102 elephants) shall be given into his hand. Polybius, who lived with Scipio, has given a particular account of this battle of Raphia. Ptolemaeus Philopater, having gained this victory, grew very insolent; his heart was lifted up; then he went into the temple of God at Jerusalem, and, in defiance of the law, entered the most holy place, for which God has a controversy with him, so that, though he shall cast down many myriads, yet he shall not be strengthened by it, so as to secure his interest. For, 2. The king of the north, Antiochus the Great, shall return with a greater army than the former; and, at the end of times (that is, years) he shall come with a mighty army, and great riches, against the king of the south, that is, Ptolemaeus Epiphanes, who succeeded Ptolemaeus Philopater his father, when he was a child, which gave advantage to Antiochus the Great. In this expedition he had some powerful allies (v. 14): Many shall stand up against the king of the south. Philip of Macedon was confederate with Antiochus against the king of Egypt, and Scopas his general, whom he sent into Syria; Antiochus routed him, destroyed a great part of his army; whereupon the Jews willingly yielded to Antiochus, joined with him, helped him to besiege Ptolemaeus's garrisons. They the robbers of thy people shall exalt themselves to establish the vision, to help forward the accomplishment of this prophecy; but they shall fall, and shall come to nothing, v. 14. Hereupon (v. 15) the king of the north, this same Antiochus Magnus, shall carry on his design against the king of the south another way. (1.) He shall surprise his strong-holds; all that he has got in Syria and Samaria, and the arms of the south, all the power of the king of Egypt, shall not be able to withstand him. See how dubious and variable the turns of the scale of war are; like buying and selling, it is winning and losing; sometimes one side gets the better and sometimes the other; yet neither by chance; it is not, as they call it, the fortune of war, but according to the will and counsel of God, who brings some low and raises others up. (2.) He shall make himself master of the land of Judea (v. 16): He that comes against him (that is, the king of the north) shall carry all before him and do what he pleases, and he shall stand and get footing in the glorious land; so the land of Israel was, and by his hand it was wasted and consumed, for with the spoil of that good land he victualled his vast army. The land of Judea lay between these two potent kingdoms of Egypt and Syria, so that in all the struggles between them that was sure to suffer, for to it they both bore ill will. Yet some read this, By his hand it shall be perfected; as if it intimated that the land of Judea, being taken under the protection of this Antiochus, shall flourish, and be in better condition than it had been. (3.) He shall still push on his war against the king of Egypt, and set his face to enter with the strength of his whole kingdom, taking advantage of the infancy of Ptolemy Epiphanes, and the upright ones, many of the pious Israelites, siding with him, v. 17. In prosecution of his design, he shall give him his daughter Cleopatra to wife, designing, as Saul in giving his daughter Cleopatra to David, that she should be a snare to him, and do him a mischief; but she shall not stand on her father's side, nor be for him, but for her husband, and so that plot failed him. (4.) His war with the Romans is here foretold (v. 18): He shall turn his face to the isles (v. 18), the isles of the Gentiles (Gen. x. 5), Greece and Italy. He took many of the isles about the Hellespont-Rhodes, Samos, Delos, &c., which by war or treaty he made himself master of; but a prince, or state (so some), even the Roman senate, or a leader, even the Roman general, shall return his reproach with which he abused the Romans upon himself, or shall make his shame rest on himself, and without his own shame, or any disgrace to himself, shall pay him again. This was fulfilled when the two Scipios were sent with an army against Antiochus. Hannibal was then with him, and advised him to invade Italy and waste it as he had done; but he did not take his advice; and Scipio joined battle with him, and gave him a total defeat, though Antiochus had 70,000 men and the Romans but 30,000. Thus he caused the reproach offered by him to cease. (5.) His fall. When he was totally routed by the Romans, and was forced to abandon to them all he had in Europe, and had a very heavy tribute exacted from him, he turned to his own land, and, not knowing which way to raise money to pay his tribute, he plundered a temple of Jupiter, which so incensed his own subjects against him that they set upon him, and killed him; so he was overthrown, and fell, and was no more found, v. 19. (6.) His next successor, v. 20. There rose up one in his place, a raiser of taxes, a sender forth of the extortioner, or extorter. This character was remarkably answered in Seleucus Philopater, the elder son of Antiochus the Great, who was a great oppressor of his own subjects, and exacted abundance of money from them; and, when he was told he would thereby lose his friends, he said he knew no better friend he had then money. He likewise attempted to rob the temple at Jerusalem, which this seems especially to refer to. But within a few days he shall be destroyed, neither in anger nor in battle, but poisoned by Heliodorus, one of his own servants, when he had reigned but twelve years, and done nothing remarkable.

V. From all this let us learn, 1. That God in his providence sets up one, and pulls down another, as he pleases, advances some from low beginnings and depresses others that were very high. Some have called great men the foot-balls of fortune; or, rather, they are the tools of Providence. 2. This world is full of wars and fightings, which come from men's lusts, and make it a theatre of sin and misery. 3. All the changes and revolutions of states and kingdoms, and every event, even the most minute and contingent, were plainly and perfectly foreseen by the God of heaven, and to him nothing is new. 4. No word of God shall fall to the ground; but what he has designed, what he has declared, shall infallibly come to pass; and even the sins of men shall be made to serve his purpose, and contribute to the b ringing of his counsels to birth in their season; and yet God is not the author of sin. 5. That, for the right understanding of some parts of scripture, it is necessary that heathen authors be consulted, which give light to the scripture, and show the accomplishment of what is there foretold; we have therefore reason to bless God for the human learning with which many have done great service to divine truths.

The Reign of Antiochus Epiphanes; Cruelty and Impiety of Antiochus; The Death of Antiochus. (b. c. 534.)

21 And in his estate shall stand up a vile person, to whom they shall not give the honour of the kingdom: but he shall come in peaceably, and obtain the kingdom by flatteries. 22 And with the arms of a flood shall they be overflown from before him, and shall be broken; yea, also the prince of the covenant. 23 And after the league made with him he shall work deceitfully: for he shall come up, and shall become strong with a small people. 24 He shall enter peaceably even upon the fattest places of the province; and he shall do that which his fathers have not done, nor his fathers' fathers; he shall scatter among them the prey, and spoil, and riches: yea, and he shall forecast his devices against the strong holds, even for a time. 25 And he shall stir up his power and his courage against the king of the south with a great army; and the king of the south shall be stirred up to battle with a very great and mighty army; but he shall not stand: for they shall forecast devices against him. 26 Yea, they

that feed of the portion of his meat shall destroy him, and his army shall overflow: and many shall fall down slain. 27 And both these kings' hearts shall be to do mischief, and they shall speak lies at one table; but it shall not prosper: for yet the end shall be at the time appointed. 28 Then shall he return into his land with great riches; and his heart shall be against the holy covenant; and he shall do exploits, and return to his own land. 29 At the time appointed he shall return, and come toward the south; but it shall not be as the former, or as the latter. 30 For the ships of Chittim shall come against him: therefore he shall be grieved, and return, and have indignation against the holy covenant: so shall he do; he shall even return, and have intelligence with them that forsake the holy covenant. 31 And arms shall stand on his part, and they shall pollute the sanctuary of strength, and shall take away the daily sacrifice, and they shall place the abomination that maketh desolate. 32 And such as do wickedly against the covenant shall he corrupt by flatteries: but the people that do know their God shall be strong, and do exploits. 33 And they that understand among the people shall instruct many: yet they shall fall by the sword, and by flame, by captivity, and by spoil, many days. 34 Now when they shall fall, they shall be holpen with a little help: but many shall cleave to them with flatteries. 35 And some of them of understanding shall fall, to try them, and to purge, and to make them white, even to the time of the end: because it is yet for a time appointed. 36 And the king shall do according to his will; and he shall exalt himself, and magnify himself above every god, and shall speak marvellous things against the God of gods, and shall prosper till the indignation be accomplished: for that that is determined shall be done. 37 Neither shall he regard the God of his fathers, nor the desire of women, nor regard any god: for he shall magnify himself above all. 38 But in his estate shall he honour the God of forces: and a god whom his fathers knew not shall he honour with gold, and silver, and with precious stones, and pleasant things. 39 Thus shall he do in the most strong holds with a strange god, whom he shall acknowledge and increase with glory: and he shall cause them to rule over many, and shall divide the land for gain. 40 And at the time of the end shall the king of the south push at him: and the king of the north shall come against him like a whirlwind, with chariots, and with horsemen, and with many ships; and he shall enter into the countries, and shall overflow and pass over. 41 He shall enter also into the glorious land, and many countries shall be overthrown: but these shall escape out of his hand, even Edom, and Moab, and the chief of the children of Ammon. 42 He shall stretch forth his hand also upon the countries: and the land of Egypt shall not escape. 43 But he shall have power over the treasures of gold and of silver, and over all the precious things of Egypt: and the Libyans and the Ethiopians shall be at his steps. 44 But tidings out of the east and out of the north shall trouble him: therefore he shall go forth with great fury to destroy, and utterly to make away many. 45 And he shall plant the tabernacles of his palace between the seas in the glorious holy mountain; yet he shall come to his end, and none shall help him.

All this is a prophecy of the reign of Antiochus Epiphanes, the little horn spoken of before (ch. viii. 9) a sworn enemy to the Jewish religion, and a bitter persecutor of those that adhered to it. What troubles the Jews met with in the reigns of the Persian kings were not so particularly foretold to Daniel as these, because then they had living prophets with them, Haggai and Zechariah, to encourage them; but these troubles in the days of Antiochus were foretold, because, before that time, prophecy would cease, and they would find it necessary to have recourse to the written word. Some things in this prediction concerning Antiochus are alluded to in the New-Testament predictions of the antichrist, especially v. 36, 37. And as it is usual with the prophets, when they foretel the prosperity of the Jewish church, to make use of such expressions as were applicable to the kingdom of Christ, and insensibly to slide into a prophecy of that, so, when they foretel the troubles of the church, they make use of such expressions as have a further reference to the kingdom of the antichrist, the rise and ruin of that. Now concerning Antiochus, the angel foretels here,

I. His character: He shall be a vile person. He called himself Epiphanes—the illustrious, but his character was the reverse of his surname. The heathen writers describe him to be an odd-humoured man, rude and boisterous, base and sordid. He would sometimes steal out of the court into the city, and herd with any infamous company incognito—in disguise he made himself a companion of the common sort, and of the basest strangers that came to town. He had the most unaccountable whims, so that some took him to be silly, others to be mad. Hence he was called Epimanes—the madman. He is called a vile person, for he had been a long time a hostage at Rome for the fidelity of his father when the Romans had subdued him; and it was agreed that, when the other hostages were exchanged, he should continue a prisoner at large.

II. His accession to the crown. By a trick he got his elder brother's son, Demetrius, to be sent a hostage to Rome, in exchange for him, contrary to the cartel; and, his elder brother being made away with by Heliodorus (v. 20), he took the kingdom. The states of Syria did not give it to him (v. 21), because they knew it belonged to his elder brother's son, nor did he get it by the sword, but came in peaceably, pretending to reign for his brother's son, Demetrius, then a hostage at Rome. But with the help of Eumenes and Attalus, neighbouring princes, he gained an interest in the people, and by flatteries obtained the kingdom, established himself in it, and crushed Heliodorus, who made head against him with the arms of a flood; those that opposed him were overflown and broken before him, even the prince of the covenant, his nephew, the rightful heir, whom he pretended to covenant with that he would resign to him whenever he should return, v. 22. But (v. 23) after the league made with him he shall work deceitfully, as one whose avowed maxim it is that princes ought not to be bound by their word any longer than it is for their interest. And with a small people, that at first cleave to him, he shall become strong, and (v. 24) he shall enter peaceably upon the fattest places of the kingdom of Syria, and, very unlike his predecessors, shall scatter among the people the prey, and the spoil, and riches, to insinuate himself into their affections; but, at the same time, he shall forecast his devices against the strong-holds, to make himself master of them, so that his generosity shall last but for a time; when he has got the garrisons into his hands he will scatter his spoil no more, but rule by force, as those commonly do that come in by fraud. He that comes in like a fox reigns like a lion. Some understand these verses of his first expedition into Egypt, when he came not as an enemy, but as a friend and guardian to the young king Ptolemaeus Philometer, and therefore brought with him but few followers, yet those stout men, and faithful to his interest, whom he placed in divers of the strong-holds in Egypt, thereby making himself master of them.

III. His war with Egypt, which was his second expedition thither. This is described, v. 25, 27. Antiochus shall stir up his power and courage against Ptolemaeus Philometer king of Egypt. Ptolemy, thereupon, shall be stirred up to battle against him, shall come against him with a very great and mighty army; but Ptolemy, though he has such a vast army, shall not be able to stand before him; for Antiochus's army shall overthrow his, and overpower it, and great multitudes of the Egyptian army shall fall down slain. And no marvel, for the king of Egypt shall be betrayed by his own counsellors; those that feed of the portion of his meat, that eat of his bread and live upon him, being bribed by Antiochus, shall forecast devices against him, and even they shall destroy him; and what fence is there against such treachery? After the battle, a treaty of peace shall be set on foot, and these two kings shall meet at one council-board, to adjust the articles of peace between them; but they shall neither of them be sincere in it, for they shall, in their pretences and promises of amity and friendship, lie to one another, for their hearts shall be at the same time to do one another all the mischief they can. And then no marvel that it shall not prosper. The peace shall not last; but the end of it shall be at the time appointed in the divine Providence, and then the war shall break out again, as a sore that is only skinned over.

IV. Another expedition against Egypt. From the former he returned with great riches (v. 28), and therefore took the first occasion to invade Egypt again, at the time appointed by the divine Providence, two years after, in the eighth year of his reign, v. 29. He shall come towards the south. But this attempt shall not succeed, as the two former did, nor shall he gain his point, as he had done before once and again; for (v. 30) the ships of Chittim shall come against him, that is, the navy of the Romans, or only ambassadors from the Roman senate, who came in ships. Ptolemaeus Philometer, king of Egypt, being now in a strict alliance with the Romans, craved their aid against Antiochus, who had besieged him and his mother Cleopatra in the city of Alexandria. The Roman senate thereupon sent an embassy to Antiochus, to command him to raise the siege, and, when he desired some time to consider of it and consult with his friends about it, Popilius, one of the ambassadors, with his staff drew a circle about him, and told him, as one having authority, he should give a positive answer before he came out of that circle; whereupon, fearing the Roman power, he was forced immediately to give orders for the raising of the siege and the retreat of his army out of Egypt. So Livy and others relate the story which this prophecy refers to. He shall be grieved, and return; for it was a great vexation to him to be forced to yield thus.

V. His rage and cruel practices against the Jews. This is that part of his government, or mis-government rather, which is most enlarged upon in this prediction. In his return from his expedition into Egypt (which is prophesied of, v. 28) he did exploits against the Jews, in the sixth year of his reign; then he spoiled the city and temple. But the most terrible storm was in his return from Egypt, two years after, prophesied of v. 30. Then he took Judea in his way home; and, because he could not gain his point in Egypt by reason of the Romans interposing, he wreaked his revenge upon the poor Jews, who gave him no provocation, but had greatly provoked God to permit him to do it, Dan. viii. 23.

1. He had a rooted antipathy to the Jews' religion: His heart was against the holy covenant, v. 28. And (v. 30) he had indignation against the holy covenant, that covenant of peculiarity by which the Jews were incorporated a people distinct from all other nations, and dignified above them. He hated the law of Moses and the worship of the true God, and was vexed at the privileges of the Jewish nation and the promises made to them. Note, That which is the hope and joy of the people of God is the envy of their neighbours, and that is the holy covenant. Esau hated Jacob because he had got the blessing. Those that are strangers to the covenant are often enemies to it.
2. He carried on his malicious designs against the Jews by the assistance of some perfidious apostate Jews. He kept up intelligence with those that forsook the holy covenant (v. 30), some of the Jews that were false to their religion, and introduced the customs of the heathen, with whom they made a covenant. See the fulfilling of this, 1 Mac. i. 11-15, where it is expressly said, concerning those renegado Jews, that they made themselves uncircumcised and forsook the holy covenant. We read (2 Mac. iv. 9) of Jason, the brother of Onias the high priest, who by the appointment of Antiochus set up a school at Jerusalem, for the training up of youth in the fashions of the heathen; and (2 Mac. iv. 23, &c.) of Menelaus, who fell in with the interests of Antiochus, and was the man that helped him into Jerusalem, now in his last return from Egypt. We read much in the book of the Maccabees of the mischief done to the Jews by these treacherous men of their own nation, Jason and Menelaus, and their party. These upon all occasions he made use of. "Such as do wickedly against the covenant, such as throw up their religion, and comply with the heathen, he shall corrupt with flatteries, to harden them in their apostasy, and to make use of them as decoys to draw in others," v. 32. Note, It is not strange if those who do not live up to their religion, but in their conversations do wickedly against the covenant, are easily corrupted by flatteries to quit their religion. Those that make shipwreck of a good conscience will soon make shipwreck of the faith.

3. He profaned the temple. Arms stand on his part (v. 31), not only his own army which he now brought from Egypt, but a great party of deserters from the Jewish religion that joined with them; and they polluted the sanctuary of strength, not only the holy city, but the

temple. The story of this we have, 1 Mac. i. 21, &c. He entered proudly into the sanctuary, took away the golden altar, and the candlestick, &c. And therefore (v. 25) there was a great mourning in Israel; the princes and elders mourned, &c. And (2 Mac. v. 15, &c.) Antiochus went into the most holy temple, Menelaus, that traitor to the laws and to his own country, being his guide. Antiochus, having resolved to bring all about him to be of his religion, took away the daily sacrifice, v. 31. Some observe that the word Tammidh, which signifies no more than daily, is only here, and in the parallel place, used for the daily sacrifice, as if there were a designed liberty left to supply it either with sacrifice, which was suppressed by Antiochus, or with gospel-worship, which was suppressed by the Antichrist. Then he set up the abomination of desolation upon the altar (1 Mac. i. 54), even an idol altar (v. 59), and called the temple the temple of Jupiter Olympius, 2 Mac. vi.

2.

4. He persecuted those who retained their integrity. Though there are many who forsake the covenant and do wickedly against it, yet there is a people who do know their God and retain the knowledge of him, and they shall be strong and do exploits, v. 32. When others yield to the tyrant's demands, and surrender their consciences to his impositions, they bravely keep their ground, resist the temptation, and make the tyrant himself ashamed of his attempt upon them. Good old Eleazar, one of the principal scribes, when he had swine's flesh thrust into his mouth, did bravely spit it out again, though he knew he must be tormented to death for so doing, and was so, 2 Mac. vi. 19. The mother and her seven sons were put to death for adhering to their religion, 2 Mac. vii. This might well be called doing exploits; for to choose suffering rather than sin is a great exploit. And it was by faith, by being strong in faith, that they did those exploits, that they were tortured, not accepting deliverance, as the apostle speaks, probably with reference to that story, Heb. xi. 35. Or it may refer to the military courage and achievements of Judas Maccabaeus and others in opposition to Antiochus. Note, The right knowledge of God is, and will be, the strength of the soul, and, in the strength of that, gracious souls do exploits. Those that know his name will put their trust in him, and by that trust will do great things. Now, concerning this people that knew their God, we are here told, (1.) That they shall instruct many, v. 33. They shall make it their business to show others what they have learned themselves of the difference between truth and falsehood, good and evil. Note, Those that have the knowledge of God themselves should communicate their knowledge to those about them, and this spiritual charity must be extensive: they must instruct many. Some understand this of a society newly erected for the propagating of divine knowledge, called Assideans, godly men, pietists (so the name signifies), that were both knowing and zealous in the law; these instructed many. Note, In times of persecution and apostasy, which are trying times, those that have knowledge ought to make use of it for the strengthening and establishing of others. Those that understand aright themselves ought to do what they can to bring others to understand; for knowledge is a talent that must be traded with. Or, They shall instruct many by their perseverance in their duty and their patient suffering for it. Good examples instruct many, and with many are the most powerful instructions. (2.) They shall fall by the cruelty of Antiochus, shall be put to the torture, and put to death, by his rage. Though they are so excellent and intelligent themselves, and so useful and serviceable to others, yet Antiochus shall show them no mercy, but they shall fall for some days; so it may be read, Rev. ii. 10, Thou shalt have tribulation ten days. We read much, in the books of the Maccabees, of Antiochus's barbarous usage of the pious Jews, how many he slew in wars and how many he murdered in cold blood. Women were put to death for having their children circumcised, and their infants were hanged about their necks, 1 Mac. i. 60, 61. But why did God suffer this? How can this be reconciled with the justice and goodness of God? I answer, Very well, if we consider what it was that God aimed at in this (v. 35): Some of those of understanding shall fall, but it shall be for the good of the church and for their own spiritual benefit. It shall be

to try them, and to purge, and to make them white. They needed these afflictions themselves. The best have their spots, which must be washed off, their dross, which must be purged out; and their troubles, particularly their share in the public troubles, help to do this; being sanctified to them by the grace of God, they are means of mortifying their corruptions, weaning them from the world, and awakening them to greater seriousness and diligence in religion. They try them, as silver in the furnace is refined from its dross; they purge them, as wheat in the barn is winnowed from the chaff; and they make them white, as cloth by the fuller is cleared from its spots. See 1 Pet. i. 7. Their sufferings for righteousness' sake would try and purge the nation of the Jews, would convince them of the truth, excellency, and power of that holy religion which these understanding men died for their adherence to. The blood of the martyrs is the seed of the church; it is precious blood, and not a drop of it should be shed but upon such a valuable consideration. (3.) The cause of religion, though it be thus run upon, shall not be run down. When they shall fall they shall not be utterly cast down, but they shall be holpen with a little help, v. 34. Judas Maccabaeus, and his brethren, and a few with them, shall make head against the tyrant, and assert the injured cause of their religion; they pulled down the idolatrous altars, circumcised the children that they found uncircumcised, recovered the law out of the hand of the Gentiles, and the work prospered in their hands, 1 Mac. ii. 45, &c. Note, Those that stand by the cause of religion when it is threatened and struck at, though they may not immediately be delivered and made victorious, shall yet have present help. And a little help must not be despised; but, when times are very bad, we must be thankful forsome reviving. It is likewise foretold that many shall cleave to them with flatteries; when they see the Maccabees prosper some Jews shall join with them that are no true friends to religion, but will only pretend friendship either with design to betray them or in hope to rise with them; but the fiery trial (v. 35) will separate between the precious and the vile, and by it those that are perfect will be made manifest and those that are not. (4.) Though these troubles may continue long, yet they will have an end. They are for a time appointed, a limited time, fixed in the divine counsels. This warfare shall be accomplished. Hitherto the power of the enemy shall come, and no further; here shall its proud waves be stayed.

5. He grew very proud, insolent, and profane, and, being puffed up with his conquests, bade defiance to Heaven, and trampled upon every thing that was sacred, v. 36, &c. And here some think begins a prophecy of the antichrist, the papal kingdom. It is plain that St. Paul, in his prophecy of the rise and reign of the man of sin, alludes to this (2 Thess. ii. 4), which shows that Antiochus was a type and figure of that enemy, as Babylon also was; but, this being joined in a continued discourse with the foregoing prophecies concerning Antiochus, to me it seems probably that it principally refers to him, and in him had its primary accomplishment, and has reference to the other only by way of accommodation. (1.) He shall impiously dishonour the God of Israel, the only living and true God, called here the God of gods. He shall, in defiance of him and his authority, do according to his will against his people and his holy religion; he shall exalt himself above him, as Sennacherib did, and shall speak marvellous things against him and against his laws and institutions. This was fulfilled when Antiochus forbade sacrifices to be offered in God's temple, and ordered the sabbaths to be profaned, the sanctuary and the holy people to be polluted, &c., to the end that they might forget the law and change all the ordinances, and this upon pain of death, 1 Mac. i. 45. (2.) He shall proudly put contempt upon all other gods, shall magnify himself above every god, even the gods of the nations. Antiochus wrote to his own kingdom that every one should leave the gods he had worshipped, and worship such as he ordered, contrary to the practice of all the conquerors that went before him, 1 Mac. i. 41, 42. And all the heathen agreed according to the commandment of the king; fond as they were of their gods, they did not think them worth suffering for, but, their gods being idols, it was all alike to them what gods they worshipped. Antiochus did not regard any god, but magnified himself above all, v. 37. He was so proud that he thought himself above the condition of a

mortal man, that he could command the waves of the sea, and reach to the stars of heaven, as his insolence and haughtiness are expressed, 2 Mac. ix. 8, 10. Thus he carried all before him, till the indignation was accomplished (v. 36), till he had run his length, and filled up the measure of his iniquity; for that which is determined shall be done, and nothing more, nothing short. (3.) He shall, contrary to the way of the heathen, disregard the god of his fathers, v. 37. Though an affection to the religion of their ancestors was, among the heathen, almost as natural to them as the desire of women (for, if you search through the isles of Chittim, you will not find an instance of a nation that has changed its gods, Jer. ii. 10, 11), yet Antiochus shall not regard the god of his fathers; he made laws to abolish the religion of his country, and to bring in the idols of the Greeks. And though his predecessors had honoured the God of Israel, and given great gifts to the temple at Jerusalem (2 Mac. iii. 2, 3), he offered the greatest indignities to God and his temple. His not regarding the desire of women may denote his barbarous cruelty (he shall spare no age or sex, no, not the tender ones) or his unnatural lusts, or, in general, his contempt of every thing which men of honour have a concern for, or it might be accomplished in something we meet not with in history. Its being joined to his not regarding the god of his fathers intimates that the idolatries of his country had in them more of the gratifications of the flesh than those of other countries (Lucian has written of the Syrian goddesses), and yet that would not prevail to keep him to them. (4.) He shall set up an unknown god, a new god, v. 38. In his estate, in the room of the god of his fathers (Apollo and Diana, deities of pleasure), he shall honour the god of forces, a supposed deity of power, a god whom his fathers knew not, nor worshipped; because he will be thought in wisdom and strength to excel his fathers, he shall honour this god with gold, and silver, and precious stones, thinking nothing too good for the god he has taken a fancy to. This seems to be Jupiter Olympius, known among the Phoenicians by the name of Baal-Semen, the lord of heaven, but never introduced among the Syrians till Antiochus introduced it. Thus shall he do in the most strong holds, in the temple of Jerusalem, which is called the sanctuary of strength (v. 31), and here the fortresses of munitions; there he shall set up the image of this strange god. Some read it, He shall commit the munitions of strength, or of the most strong God (that is, the city Jerusalem), to a strange god; he put it under the protection and government of Jupiter Olympius. This god he shall not only acknowledge, but shall increase with glory, by setting his image even upon God's altar. And he shall cause those that minister to this idol to rule over many, shall put them into places of power and trust, and they shall divide the land for gain, shall be maintained richly out of the profits of the country. Some by the Mahuzzim, or god of forces, that Antiochus shall worship, understand money, which is said to answer all things, and which is the great idol of worldly people.

Now here is very much that is applicable to the man of sin; he exalts himself above all that is called god or that is worshipped; magnifies himself above all; his flatterers call him our lord god the pope. By forbidding marriage, and magnifying the single life, he pretends not to regard the desire of women; and honours the god of forces, the god Mahuzzim, or strong holds, saints and angels, whom his followers take for their protectors, as the heathen did of old their demons; these they make presidents of several countries, &c. These they honour with vast treasures dedicated to them, and therein the learned Mr. Mede thinks that this prophecy was fulfilled, and that it is referred to 1 Tim. iv. 1, 2.

VI. Here seems to be another expedition into Egypt, or, at least, a struggle with Egypt. The Romans had tied him up from invading Ptolemy, but now that king of the south pushes at him (v. 40), makes an attempt upon some of his territories, where upon Antiochus, the king of the north, comes against him like a whirlwind, with incredible swiftness and fury, with chariots, and horses, and many ships, a great force. He shall come trough countries, and shall overflow and pass over. In this flying march many countries shall be overthrown by him; and he shall enter into the glorious land, the land of Israel; it is the same word that is translated the pleasant land, ch. viii. 9. He shall make dreadful work among the nations thereabout; yet some shall escape his fury, particularly Edom and Moab, and the chief of the children of Ammon, v. 41. He did not put these countries under contribution, because they had joined with him against the Jews. But especially the land of Egypt shall not escape, but he will quite beggar that, so bare will he strip it. This some reckon his fourth and last expedition against Egypt, in the tenth or eleventh year of his reign, under pretence of assisting the younger brother of Ptolemaeus Philometer against him. We read not of any great slaughter made in this expedition, but great plunder; for, it should seem, that was what he came for: He shall have power over the treasures of gold and silver, and all the precious things of Egypt, v. 43. Polybius, in Athenaeus, relates that Antiochus, having got together abundance of wealth, by spoiling young Philometer, and breaking league with him, and by the contributions of his friends, bestowed a vast deal upon a triumph, in imitation of Paulus Æmilius, and describes the extravagance of it; here we are told how he got that money which he spent so profusely. Notice is here taken likewise of the use he made of the Lybians and Ethiopians, who bordered upon Egypt; they were at his steps; he had them at his foot, had them at his beck, and they made inroads upon Egypt to serve him.

VII. Here is a prediction of the fall and ruin of Antiochus, as before (ch. viii. 25), when he is in the height of his honour, flushed with victory, and laden with spoils, tidings out of the east and out of the north (out of the north-east) shall trouble him, v. 44. Or, He shall have intelligence, both from the eastern and northern parts, that the king of Parthia is invading his kingdom. This obliged him to drop the enterprises he had in hand, and to go against the Persians and Parthians that were revolting from him; and this vexed him, for now he thought utterly to ruin and extirpate the Jewish nation, when that expedition called him off, in which he perished. This is explained by a passage in Tacitus (though an impious one) where he commends Antiochus for his attempt to take away the superstition of the Jews, and bring in the manners of the Greeks, among them (ut teterrimam gentem in melius mutaret—to meliorate an odious nation), and laments that he was hindered from accomplishing it by the Parthian war. Now here is, 1. The last effort of his rage against the Jews. When he finds himself perplexed and embarrassed in his affairs he shall go forth with great fury to destroy and utterly to make away many, v. 44. The story of this we have 1 Mac. iii. 27, &c., what a rage Antiochus was in when he heard of the successes of Judas Maccabaeus, and the orders he gave to Lysias to destroy Jerusalem. Then he planted the tabernacles of his palace, or tents of his court, between the seas, between the Great Sea and the Dead Sea. He set up his royal pavilion at Emmaus near Jerusalem, in token that, though he could not be present himself, yet he gave full power to his captains to prosecute the war against the Jews with the utmost rigour. He placed his tent there, as if he had taken possession of the glorious holy mountain and called it his own.

Note, When impiety grows very impudent we may see its ruin near. 2. His exit: He shall come to his end and none shall help him; God shall cut him off in the midst of his days and none shall be able to prevent his fall. This is the same with that which was foretold ch. viii. 25 (He shall be broken without hand), where we took a view of his miserable end. Note, When God's time shall come to bring proud oppressors to their end none shall be able to help them, nor perhaps inclined to help them; for those that covet to be feared by all when they are in their grandeur, when they come to be in distress will find themselves loved by none; none will lend them so much as a hand or a prayer to help them; and, if the Lord do not help, who shall?

Of the kings that came after Antiochus nothing is here prophesied, for that was the most malicious mischievous enemy to the church, that was a type of the son of perdition, whom the Lord shall consume with the breath of his mouth and destroy with the brightness of his coming, and none shall help him.

Made in the USA
San Bernardino, CA
29 July 2016